The Romance of
COUNTRY INNS

*May your home
always be filled
with the innkeeping spirit—
laughter, good friends,
bountiful feasts, and
heirloom memories.*

GAIL GRECO

The Romance of
COUNTRY INNS

A Decorating Book for Your Home

Rooms ◆ Gardens ◆ Crafts ◆ Recipes ◆ Restoration

❖ ❖ ❖

GAIL GRECO

Photographs by Tom Bagley

RUTLEDGE HILL PRESS

Nashville, Tennessee

Published in Nashville, Tennessee by Rutledge Hill Press, Inc. 211 Seventh Avenue North, Nashville, TN 37219. Distributed in Canada by H.B. Fenn & Company, Ltd., 1090 Lorimar Drive, Mississauga, Ontario L5S 1R7.

All photographs were taken on location specifically for this book.

All patterns and projects submitted for this book were presented as original or original adaptations, lacking any previous active copyright.

The Resource Guide is a service to the reader. No fee was accepted for inclusion.

Photo art direction and styling by Gail Greco.

Textile project consultant and editor: Dorothy Greco

Patterns and projects artist: Kathy Whyte

Hand-stitchery projects consultant: Patricia Moore

Stagecoach valance designer: Lois Arey

Carpentry consultant: Keith Millison

Bread in photo on page 224 courtesy of Breads and Spreads

Cookware in photo on page 228 courtesy of DuPont "No-Stick Systems" and Steelon by LeCooks Ware.

Jacket and text design by Bruce Gore, Gore Studio, Inc.

Typography by ProtoType Graphics, Nashville, Tennessee

Color Separations by Capitol Engraving, Nashville, Tennessee

Printed in the United States of America by R.R. Donnelley & Sons

Library of Congress Cataloging-in-Publication Data

Greco, Gail.
     The romance of country inns : a decorating book for your home :
  rooms, gardens, crafts, recipes, restoration / Gail Greco :
  photographs by Tom Bagley.
         p.   cm.
     Includes bibliographical references and index.
     ISBN 1-55853-175-0
     1. Decoration and ornament, Rustic—United States.   2. Interior
  decoration—United States—History—20th century—Themes, motives.
  3. Hotels—United States—Decoration—Influence.   I. Title.
  NK2004.G75   1993
  747.213—dc20   93–11708
                                                                   CIP

1 2 3 4 5 6 7 8 9 — 99 98 97 96 95 94 93

DEDICATION

*To my sister and partner
in decorating crime.*

Dot, thanks for cheerleading
even my earliest madcap decorating schemes
back when we shared the same room.
You never protested.
You just believed in me
and went along with the adventure.
Today, even though we live in separate worlds,
you continue to applaud my ideas.
Only now, I get involved in your
fanciful decorating plots as well!
What fun!

*. . . And to the innkeepers,
who never cease to inspire me.*

Other Books by Gail Greco

Bridal Shower Handbook

A Country Inn Breakfast

Great Cooking with Country Inn Chefs

Secrets of Entertaining from America's Best Innkeepers

Tea-Time at the Inn

World Class Cuisine

❖ ❖ ❖

CONTENTS

A LIGHT AT THE INN
The Way to Find Romance at Home

11

Early American

**Period Indulgences from an Old
Shipbuilder's Home**
THE CAPTAIN LORD MANSION

Kennebunkport, Maine

19

Making a Federal Case Out of It
CLIFTON INN

Charlottesville, Virginia

25

**Wildflower Jewels Paint
the Landscape**
GARDENS OF EDEN

Lancaster, Pennsylvania

33

American Country

**Enchanted Cottages Through
the Looking Glass**
MAPLE LEAF COTTAGE INN

Elsah, Illinois

41

Contents

❖ ❖ ❖

**Vignettes of Affection from a
House of Collections**

RIVERWIND

Deep River, Connecticut

47

Portrait of an Innkeeper's Art

THE SOUTHERN HOTEL

Ste. Genevieve, Missouri

55

Farmhouse

A Cameo of Preservation Comes Full Circle

THE INN AT THE ROUND BARN FARM

Waitsfield, Vermont

65

**A Fantasia of Leaf and Bud
Plays a Posy Rhapsody**

BLUE LAKE RANCH

Hesperus, Colorado

71

**Spinning Yarns and Drying Flowers
While the Sheep Play**

SWEET BASIL HILL FARM

Gurnee, Illinois

77

Victorian

New Impressions from a Bygone Era

THE CHICAGO PIKE INN

Coldwater, Michigan

85

Oh, How Their Garden Grows

TWIN GATES

Lutherville, Maryland

91

Rooms that Bloom with "Hart" and Soul

WALNUT STREET INN

Springfield, Missouri

97

Contents

❖ ❖ ❖

The Curtain Rises on Today's Victorian
ARSENIC & OLD LACE
Eureka Springs, Arkansas
103

Main Street Revival

A Steeple in the Marshes Rises Again
CHRISTMAS FARM
Wittman, Maryland
109

**At the Head of the Class with
Scholarly Composition**
THE SCHOOL HOUSE BED & BREAKFAST
Rocheport, Missouri
115

Innkeepers' Passions Awaken an Old Hotel
CORNER GEORGE INN
Maeystown, Illinois
123

**Beauty Behind the Bars:
An Innmate's Escape**
THE JAILER'S INN
Bardstown, Kentucky
131

Decorating from the Other Side of the Track
TROUT CITY BERTH & BREAKFAST
Buena Vista, Colorado
137

Regional

Blue Skies, Red Peppers, and the Good Life
CASA BENAVIDES
Taos, New Mexico
143

Romancing the Stones
CANYON VILLA
Sedona, Arizona
149

'Arts and Crafts' at an Inn with a Mission
THE PEBBLE HOUSE
Lakeside, Michigan
155

Contents

❖ ❖ ❖

Cherished Longings for the Log Look
LOG CABIN GUEST HOUSE
Galena, Illinois
159

Country European

In Every Room a Flower Blooms
THE INN ON SUMMER HILL
Summerland, California
165

**An Inn of Many Lands
Embraces a Traveler's Interlude**
HILLBROOK INN
Charles Town, West Virginia
171

**The Fresh Feel and Tender Touch
of Gemütlich**
SWISS WOODS
Lititz, Pennsylvania
177

Old World Presence Spins New Ideas
ANTRIM 1844
Taneytown, Maryland
183

Take-Home Tips from the Innkeepers

More Innterior Decorating
193
Quick Decorating Tips
The Innkeepers' Ten Keys to Successful Decorating

Inn the Garden
203
Sharing Your Garden
Garden Variety of Tips
Ten Secrets to Starting and Maintaining a Garden
Perennial Garden Plot
Herb Garden Plot

Country Inn Recipes
211

Bringing It All Home with the Author
223

Contents

❖ ❖ ❖

Inn the Workshop

Restoration and Renovation
231
The Ten Commandments of Restoration
On Moving a Building
How to Build a New/Old Addition
Quick Restoration/Renovation Tips
How to Convert a Double Bed to a Queen Size
Blueprint for a Brick Kitchen Alcove

Decorating Techniques
241
Room Designing Planner
The Art of Stenciling
Sponge Painting
Decorating Walls Elegantly with Brown Paper
How to Cover Interior Walls with Fabric

Sewing Projects
253
Home-Sweet-Home Cross-Stitch Sampler
Padded Hangers
Tea Cozy
Yo-Yo Quilt Placemats
Picture Frame Bow Hanger
The Best-Ever, Easy-to-Remove Dust Ruffle
Sleeping Beauty Canopy
A Crowning Bed Chamber
Good Morning Awning Headboard

Curtains
264
Shady Lacy
Tab Tops Turn a New Angle
Scalloped Swag
Stagecoach Valance
Angel-Wing Swag
Breath of Spring Lace Cornice
Crunch 'n' Pouf Curtain

Craft Projects
271
Fee Fi Faux Pies
Half-Moon Branch Swag
Napkin Rings
Topiary Doors
Hazelnut Pomander
Apple Wreath

COUNTRY INN RESOURCE GUIDE   277

INN DIRECTORY   280

INDEX   283

A LIGHT AT THE INN
The Way to Find Romance at Home

I WAS 15 when I knew I wanted to be an interior decorator. Every time I walked into a room—even at school—I was rearranging the furniture in my head; changing colors, adding fabrics and accent pieces; deleting clutter, and complementing the room's architecture. I was so excited about decorating that I appreciated every style from Colonial to Contemporary and everything in between when it was done well. I didn't know which style I would embrace in my own home someday.

During those years, I decorated the only thing that was partially my domain—the bedroom I shared with my younger sister. While saving for college, about all I could afford was paint, so that was somewhat limiting. Finally, after I had covered two of our four walls with canary yellow and two in bright orange, my mother suggested: "You might want to pursue writing. You are very good at it."

Today, I receive many compliments on my own home decor and many say I should have been an interior designer. But actually, Mom pointed me in the right direction and I never regretted my career choice. I have met and continue to enjoy tackling numerous decorating challenges in my own homes over the years. Being a designer would have kept me from being a writer, while being a writer has not kept me from being a designer—of sorts. Perhaps that is why I thoroughly relished putting this book together—a project that combined both yearnings into one.

This most recent book showcases the keepers of small

◀ *Author Gail Greco sorts through fabrics for a new project in her office at home. To see how she brought some of the innkeepers' ideas home, see page 223. The mural in her dining room (above, right) is one such idea she learned from an innkeeper.*

inns as today's experts in creating romance and the role models to help us bring that same feeling into our own homes. From decorating and gardening, to cooking and entertaining, and the love of bringing an old building back to life—it all spells romance. Everything an innkeeper does at the inn is meant to suggest something soothing, something pampering, something adventurous and exciting. Whether it be a sumptuous candlelit breakfast or a note by the bed that says, "May angels guard you through the night" (à la **Richmond Hill Inn,** an inn I visited for my last book), all amenities lead to romantic visions, romantic thoughts, and romantic exchanges from the private ones to the public. Inns show us how to bring poetry into our lives.

They provide an atmosphere for living in a dream world for a few days. Bed-and-breakfast and country inns are

❖ ❖ ❖

▲ *Gingerbread men dance above the hearth at **Riverwind**.*

escapes from the rigors of daily life and help their visitors put things into perspective again. Staying at an inn is the ultimate in romance both of the poetic kind and the boy-meets-girl variety.

Innkeepers: They Bring Good Things to Life

When an inn's light shines brightly from the roadway, beckoning travelers to its comforting doorstep, it is inviting more than just an overnight stay. A light at the inn signals there is romance inside and an opportunity to make your life a little bit better. The visit to an inn can be a lasting

one, filled with impressions you want to integrate into your own environment.

Let's face it. We cannot all be innkeepers. Many of us think we might like to be, but we may be confusing the role of the innkeeper with that of the guest. They are two different experiences altogether. We live in a fantasy world for a few days and think the innkeepers do, too. But they are always busy behind the scenes, creating that atmosphere we cherish so much. Innkeeping is hard work. The alternative? We can have the best of both worlds when we take a hint of the inn's spirit home.

The more inns I see, the more I want to see. Inns are designer playgrounds that stimulate and perk up the senses in every way. Even their brochures are winsome and inviting. Take this description of the Red Oak Room at **The Maples Inn:** "Nestle under the covers of this quaint country room, which features two wing-backed chairs and comfortable double bed. Open the paned glass windows to enjoy the fresh sea breeze." Or, there is the explanation of the Weeping Willow Room: "A bay window and authentic cast iron queen-size bed characterize this delightfully sunny room. Sit back in an old-fashioned rocker and enjoy a captivating book from the inn's library."

That inns even name their rooms is romance personified. Why give a beautifully created space a number, when it deserves a name? As you will see in my section, "Bringing It All Home . . ." I like to name my rooms, too.

Since no two inns are alike, there is a plethora of patterns and shapes to study all across America. There are artful scenes and vignettes everywhere you turn at an inn. Thus inns provide all of us with the opportunity to experience home design firsthand.

You may not be able to visit the inns as frequently as I do, so I've brought the inns to you. Now, you can be inspired by this country's greatest home-decorating resource—bed-and-breakfast and country inns.

Innkeepers: America's Newest Preservationists

Innkeepers are responsible for saving more old houses in America than any one group. And saving an old home

❖ ❖ ❖

is a labor of love, and hard work, yet ironically romantic in and of itself. When you see that gaoler's lantern alive with light at an inn, it is symbolic. If it were not for the many couples with vision and courage to buy and fix up some real wrecks in the early 1980s, a big chunk of America's architecture would not have been preserved. They started a bed-and-breakfast boom, whereby they could earn the income to keep up the maintenance of these properties.

The result is an unprecedented number of former estates and even utilitarian buildings being saved. In this book, I have covered some of those styles from Early American to Victorian and Country European. Also, we see in the Main Street Revival section how schools, churches, train stations, and even jailhouses were saved in the name of bed-and-breakfast! How romantic, for example, to stay in an old schoolhouse with the memories that flood in from childhood days. How romantic still, to be able to take some of Vicki and John Ott's decorating ideas to keep reminding you of those pleasant thoughts. Or, how about buying a smaller schoolhouse yourself and turning it into a home or guest cottage.

Stories such as David and Marcia Braswell's from **The Corner George Inn** will inspire you, as you learn how their bed-and-breakfast was the catalyst for making everyone else want to fix-it-up in a tiny Midwest town.

It's all part of a silent preservation movement but a powerful one for which the keepers of small inns are responsible. Innkeepers go to great lengths to make history come alive in the 20th century. Their inns are showcases for America's past—mellowed antiques and collectibles that are part of a living museum—in which we, the visitors, can look and touch. We are encouraged to sit in the rockers passed down from their great-grandmothers, to sleep in the bed that was original to the house but has been lovingly restored, and even try on some of the vintage clothing that is part of the inn's very special collection.

And anything you want to know from how to purchase a historic building, move it to your property, and then decorate it, is no secret. Innkeepers are willing to share, as you will see in my potpourri of tips and ideas in the Take-Home Tips and Inn the Workshop sections.

▲ *A woven rug at **Antrim 1844** displays a date from the inn's past as a plantation.*

Living the Romantic Inn Life at Home

Innkeepers teach us that the romantic past can be very much a part of our present. They find ways to make 200-year-old items work in a space-age society. To get private baths into rooms, for example, some inns have placed tubs right in the room, just as they were years ago. Many inns have made antique double-bed frames work for modern queen-size mattresses, without compromising the integrity of the *objet d'art*.

▲ *French toast sundae at* **Round Barn Farm.**

And so, I have brought you a glimpse of some of the thousands of inns nationwide where you can learn how to create romance—a sense of the past with the joy of the present and the hope of the future. I have provided a representative sample of styles and ideas from inns in all regions of the country. Creating romance does not just happen with the decor. Innkeepers show that pampering, hospitality, and good food are what's needed to close the loop on romantic living. Thus, I have added some of their recipes to help you complete the picture at your home.

The beauty of a home is not just skin deep. Decorating extends beyond the obvious. I think innkeeper Shash Georgi of **Back of the Beyond** said it well when she wrote to me some years ago, "The beauty of your home includes environmental and other concerns. They are as much a part of making your rooms welcoming as are the pretty linens, lovely curtains, and beautiful room arrangements."

This is a book about inns, but also a book that celebrates life at home with a little help from our innkeeping friends. History is in the making. Years from now, it will tell how innkeepers had a major effect on lifestyles, not just on preservation and travel.

Inns remind us that we can all live a gentler, more enriching, more adventurous life. For me, they remind me to make time to pamper and play; to take dinner in the dining room with our good china, crystal, and silver, even in the middle of the week when we don't have company over; to take my editorial work to a stuffed chair with a knit throw and a cup of tea; to have friends over for breakfast; and to permeate the air with the scent of sweet flowers—special occasion or not. All of this takes a bit of an effort, but there is no debating the rewards.

Living the romantic inn life at home is not only possible, but within your reach. I hope this book inspires you to go for it and create—at least in spirit—your own little bed-and-breakfast at home.

Gail Greco

The Romance of
COUNTRY
INNS

❖ ❖ ❖

Early American

To be happy at home
is the ultimate result of all ambition—
the end to which all enterprise
and labour tends.

—SAMUEL JOHNSON, 1750

◄ *The Captain Lord Mansion*

❖ ❖ ❖

PERIOD INDULGENCES FROM AN OLD SHIPBUILDER'S HOME

The Captain Lord Mansion
Kennebunkport, Maine

ONCE at sea, a ship is at the mercy of nature's fickle moods. I wouldn't have made a very good mariner. In the days when Nathaniel Lord and family built sea-bound vessels controlled by rugged swashbucklers, I would have remained in port and let the braver navigate the forces of undulant waters. At **The Captain Lord Mansion,** built in 1812 by Nathaniel for his wife, Phebe, you are only an observer in safe harbor aboard rooms such as the Ship Ophelia, the Schooner Champion, and the Bark Dana—guest quarters named after sailing craft built by the Lords.

Some guest chambers feel as though they are luxury cabins on an old vessel for they have low ceilings and are reached by way of anterooms where you can stow away personal cargo, i.e. your luggage. Needlework samplers, stitched by innkeeper Bev Davis, identify each "cabin" along with a line-drawing of the actual ship and its anatomy.

Bev designed the rooms with seafaring treasures such as Oriental porcelain and wooden chests that explorers might have gathered from exotic lands. A tapestry of fabrics from chintz to homespun abounds in an alchemy of good taste, fine design, and comfort.

Rick Litchfield, Bev's husband, is at the helm of this ship. He taps a gentle fugue of notes on antique chimes to summon all to breakfast. The xylophone-like instrument was used in similar fashion during the mansion's early days. Rick often presides over the morning fare, served in a galley-style kitchen, complete with a black coal stove. To-

▲ *A period bathroom with a print by artist K. Richards graces the Mary Lord Room. Don't fret, the antique potty chair is only a decorative accessory!*

◄ *A spiral staircase sweeps romantics to the belvedere. More than a century ago, those going up to the top of the house were looking for their seafaring relatives.*

❖ ❖ ❖

day, the stove is a sideboard for serving guests afternoon tea. Breakfast is family-style on maple tables with painted Windsor chairs.

The gathering room is bathed in elegance with crystal and china plus folk-art portraits of the Lords adorning the raised-panel woodwork. It is too bad that Nathaniel hardly had a chance to enjoy the opulence he created. The mansion took three years to build, and he died in 1815 at age 39, just as it was being completed. Phebe lived another 49 years, and Bev and Rick have honored her in another bed-and-breakfast across the street called **Phebe's Fantasy.**

Bev and Rick are pioneers in America's bed-and-breakfast movement. Having purchased the mansion in 1978, they helped propel the industry and inextricably wove themselves into American history by their ardent preservation. They, too, endured the rough waters that such an undertaking entails, not unlike those who steered the Lord's fleet many years ago.

▶ *A wealthy sea captain would be at home in the worldly Brig Merchant Room. A wallpaper of cream and raspberry scalloped trompe l'oeil fabric established the colorway for this room. The crowning touch is the bowed canopy bed of Honduran carved mahogany, dating back to 1830. Reproductions of this bed and any at the mansion can be ordered for your home. See J.J. Jenkins Beds in the Resource Guide.*

▶ *Rick and Bev also own **Phebe's Fantasy,** a smaller bed-and-breakfast across the street. The decor is less formal and more fanciful, as evidenced by this confident move to use black wallpaper. The arched window nooks have built-in closets. The room also hosts a built-in highboy and window seat.*

▶ *The Harvest Room is filled most curiously with dated objects, including a well-worn cobbler's bench and a wooden wheel of fortune. Lucky indeed are we who can gather ideas from this room. Bev wasn't afraid to use bold colors. And Rick added a seafaring mural of Kennebunkport in the 1800s, painted on a removable canvas. Shaker pantry baskets are silhouetted against the window, while a reproduction Moses Eaton stencil adds color. An 1847 daguerreotype of the mansion depicts children playing with a rocking horse, similar to the one in the corner. A few pieces of antique furniture from the inn were reinterpreted by the Thomasville Furniture Company (See Resource Guide.) for inclusion in the company's bed-and-breakfast line.*

▶ *Another hearth graces the dining room at Phebe's. Soft apricot walls accent a tiger maple chest surrounded by two windows, one of which is covered to show the house's original Indian shutters.*

❖ ❖ ❖

▲ *Whether at* **Phebe's** *or* **The Captain Lord,** *anyone wanting an old-fashioned soft-boiler gets it served in an egg cup. The cook snaps off the top of the hot egg with a nifty gadget that makes a spoon-size opening in the shell. The mansion sells the egg toppers because guests wanted to do this at home. I confess, I left with several of them myself.*

◄ *The crescent moon-and-star stencil was applied to all four walls of Phebe's kitchen, which also boasts a large cooking hearth. Bev found the tin stencil at an auction. It's a real antique. For the pattern, see page 247.*

❖ ❖ ❖

MAKING A FEDERAL CASE OUT OF IT

▲ *Clifton chef Craig Hartman turns confectionery architect at holiday time.*

Clifton Inn

Charlottesville, Virginia

HERE, why don't you look through these before-pictures and see if you can guess what came after," quizzed Mitch Willey. During a recent visit, the owner of **Clifton** was challenging my perceptive powers. But thanks to his dramatic renovations to this former Federal-style property, I was at a virtual loss. Who would guess that the three garden cottages overlooking a river beyond the pines had once been a drooping, shed-roofed livery stable? The Carriage House, now with its spacious living room and loft bedroom, was unrecognizable, as were many rooms in the main house.

The Honeymoon Cottage was once the law office of attorney Thomas Mann Randolph, the husband of Thomas Jefferson's daughter, Martha. Randolph was governor of Virginia and a member of the U.S. Congress, and **Clifton** was their home. The hilly land was once part of the Shadwell Plantation, birthplace of our third president. Thomas Jefferson's home at Monticello is nearby, sometimes visible through the treetops.

Like the home's original owner, Mitch Willey is also a lawyer. He has placed the inn in the capable hands of Donna and Craig Hartman, who do whatever it takes to maintain **Clifton's** stellar reputation. One day, I watched Donna on hands and knees in the library, repairing a slit in the centuries-old wide-plank floors. Later, she hosted dinner guests for the meal her husband had been preparing all day.

The gustatory reverie at **Clifton** has been critically acclaimed in such magazines as *Gourmet*, and Craig was known as one of the top

◀ *Small and intimate, the Garden Room is blanketed in soft vanilla wainscoting with a built-in bench seat, striped in periwinkle and white damask to match the fireside chair. An appliquéd quilt in shades of pink and jade completes the colorway. A quaint wood stove fires up a cozy afternoon for reading. Shutters fly open to a washroom that makes you want to linger.*

❖ ❖ ❖

▲ *The Christmas tree of all-natural trim carries nut-filled baskets of dried orange skins hung by copper wire. Besides the baskets and lights, lady apples and gingerbread are all that grace the tree but for an angel at the top. For more Clifton holiday art, see pages 275 and 276.*

▶ *A fresh slice of watermelon teams with cool mint on the walls, in the scatter rug, and in the framed pictures over the mantel. Afternoon sun streams past the bedroom into a sitting area where the color pattern follows in reverse.*

chefs on North Carolina's Outer Banks before he came to **Clifton.** Craig's food is full of flavor, great taste, imagination, and sincerity.

The chef welcomes his diners in the parlor, while they sample Virginia wines and listen to the strains of a Celtic harp played by Eve Watters. He introduces the menu and explains his repertoire of culinary ingredients and methods. Discussing the succulent items and preparations in this, the chef's opening act, sets the tone for anticipation of an enchanted evening ahead. Craig shows how an interlude about the food at your own dinner parties can establish the mood for a romantic evening.

Dinner is served in the historic dining room or in the white-parchment-painted, brick enclosed porch. A wall of windows fronts woodlands and two resident sheep. It was holiday time when I last visited the inn. But I have also been to the inn in summer when the property is abloom with bountiful gardens. It all makes you glad that Mitch, the present-day lawyer/owner, decided to make the rebirth of **Clifton** a Federal and very important case. Those old pictures he and his wife, Emily, proudly pass around are no longer the status quo, but rather the quid pro quo!

◀ *Dusted in grainy shades of oatmeal, even the beam oozes charm with its aged stress marks in the Meriweather Room. The support column doubles as a nighties butler with wooden hangers, decorative items when not in use. Rhubarb and crème fraîche stripes, Norman Rockwell illustrations, plus a touch of flowers in a table skirt, complete the look.*

Early American

▶▶ *French doors shepherd you from the bathroom to the living area of the simple but romantic Honeymoon Cottage. A wooden ladder pilots the way to a loft-for-two. Soft light on original bricks painted birch-white and maple hardwood floors flushes the room in natural tones. A beam conceals a beacon of light directed at the heart of entwined blooms and twigs.*

▼ *An Oriental rug supplements the peacock, claret, peony, and pine tones in the tapestry wing chairs in the parlor. A fresh Advent wreath surrounds the white Star of Bethlehem. An antique ladder offers a unique repose for the poinsettia.*

▲ *The inn's Federal dining room is decorated in Colonial taupe and cardinal and shows how to integrate two colors by delineating them with molding. The mantel decor is chock-full of magnolia branches, evergreens, and Villeroy and Boch's Petite Fleur pattern soup terrines filled with fruit.*

Above, a sagging livery was turned into guest cottages. The photo at left takes you to a sitting area in one of them.

❖ ❖ ❖

WILDFLOWER JEWELS PAINT THE LANDSCAPE

Gardens of Eden

Lancaster, Pennsylvania

TUCKED into a wooded dale where the Conestoga River pours past an old mill, a bed and breakfast nourishes its visitors with gifts from its gardens. From dining table to bedside table, delicate flowers meet with earthy containers, baskets, and wreaths twisted and turned by the skilled hands of an impassioned innkeeper.

Gardens of Eden is what its name implies. The book *A Place on Earth* offers this explanation: "In rivers and pools . . . swamplands and woodland glens across the dunes and in the sunlit meadows . . . life with all its beauty its achievement over adversity . . . its promise of eternity is taking place."

As you stroll about the wildflower paths, you get a sense that all things in life have come together and that "a river runs through it," borrowing from a movie by that name. The gardens are freckled with tiny wildflowers, peeking up from the renewed ground of spring and the fully restored earth of summer, with fairy-tale names—Shepherd's Purse and Shooting Star. They also illuminate the forest floor in jeweled array. Along with other petite flowers, many no larger than a ring finger, they find their way to sunlight between curiously gnarled tree roots, dried bramble and winter-beaten thickets.

Marilyn Sanko-Ebel oversees the gardens with her husband/innkeeper, Bill. Marilyn knows where the wild flora nest whether in bloom or not. By the time you leave the inn, you know some of the secrets of the gardens, too.

Edible garnishes tell part of the story at breakfast. Even the jelly,

◄ *Flowers surround Gardens of Eden. The Lesser Celandine (bottom right) arrived at the inn's doorstep from a hurricane that left seeds behind after the waters subsided.*

❖ ❖ ❖

made with violets or lavender, is revealing as are the innkeeper's gardening tales. Marilyn, a naturalist floral designer, is well-schooled but keeps on learning. Flowers will suddenly root at the inn, sending her to the botany books for identification. The sometimes ebullient Conestoga River gives even more variety to this enriched hollow with seeds deposited from rising waters.

Named after the Conestoga Indians of the region, the river was the inspiration for naming a vehicle of transportation and commerce. The Conestoga wagon, built in the area to haul grain to Philadelphia, took its name from the river. Bill tells how Conestoga drivers traveled with bells attached to horse harnesses. If their vehicle broke down and someone helped them, it was understood that they would give the helper the bells in return for the assistance. The expression, "I'll be there with bells on," was derived from the Conestoga teams who were assuring those at the other end that they intended to have an unimpeded trip; the same as Marilyn and Bill wish you when journeying to their **Gardens of Eden.**

▼ *Breakfast is served in the dining room where the innkeepers managed to fill a long wall attractively with an assortment of frames.*

❖ ❖ ❖

A bear and book are nearly always waiting on the bed in this guest room. Marilyn loves to style her decor as though she were painting a picture. The half-moon spray on the window was made by Marilyn, who holds wreath-making and natural floral arranging classes at the inn. See page 272 to learn how to make a similar one for your own window, door, or fireplace mantel.

❖ ❖ ❖

◀◀ *The Conestoga River flows past the inn. Lancaster's tobacco-growing fields once yielded rolled cigars smoked by Conestoga wagon drivers. This gave cigars their nickname of stogies.*

◀ *A wildflower jewel peeps through a curious tree trunk.*

▼ *The luggage at the foot of the bed is not a guest's. Marilyn put it there for decoration and as a way of telling guests they may move it and use the rack for their own luggage. The room is simply stated with blues and creams and two of everything.*

American Country

Don't worry
about the garden next door.
Just take care of yours and it will
bloom with individuality
just like you.

—ALMA BARNES

◀ *Maple Leaf Cottage Inn*

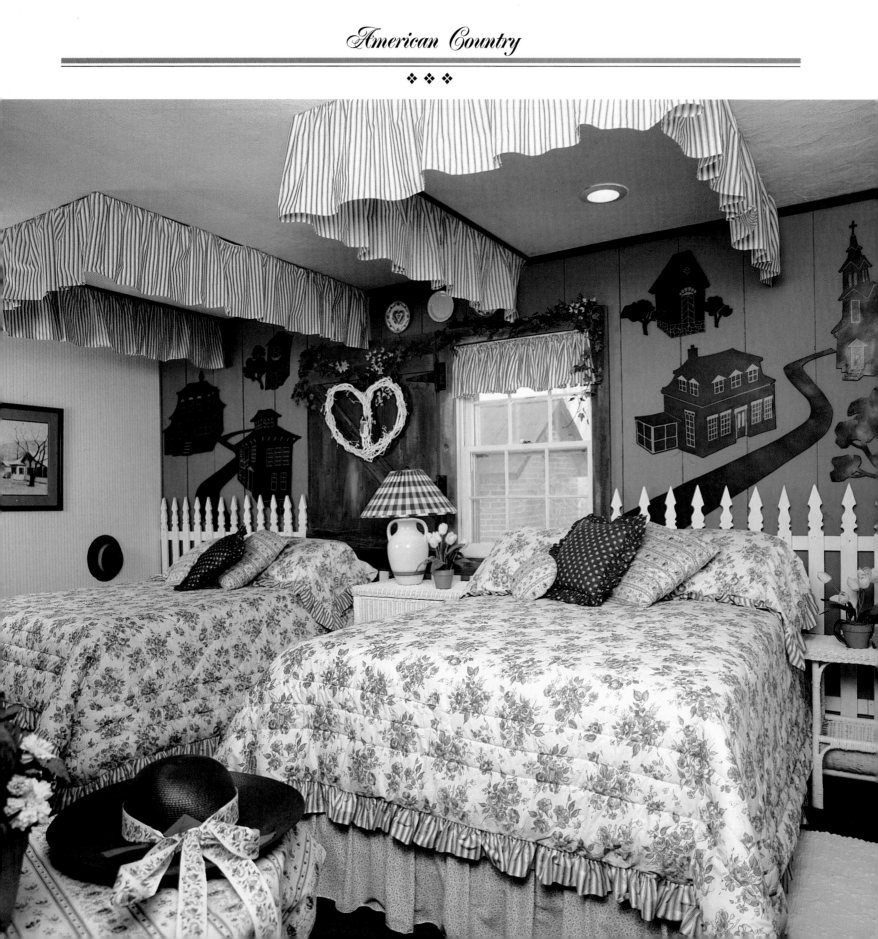

❖ ❖ ❖

ENCHANTED COTTAGES THROUGH THE LOOKING GLASS

Maple Leaf Cottage Inn

Elsah, Illinois

*"I knew by the smoke that so
gracefully curl'd above the green elms,
that a cottage was near. And I said,
If there's peace to be found
in the world, a heart that was humble
might hope for it here."*
—THOMAS MOORE

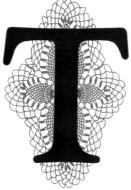

HIS describes what I felt, arriving at **Maple Leaf Cottage Inn** in a tiny hamlet off the Mississippi. Here resides the 1853 village of Elsah, snugly wrapped in time and history. Peace can be found here where the imagination reigns—and all seems larger than life. I felt as though I had just tumbled into Wonderland where everything is unusual and fascinating.

It happened that way for innkeepers Patty and Jerry Taetz. A friend happened to take them by Elsah, just up the road from Alton—a town Jerry frequented for years, never scouting beyond its borders. On their very next visit to Elsah, the couple fell in love with a stone house for sale. On the way back to St. Louis, where Jerry had just excitedly signed a new lease on "the most marvelous apartment ever," he and Patty stopped the car, called the Elsah real estate agent from the road, and put a hold on the house. Their whole world went topsy-turvy into adventureland.

"It was the craziest thing I ever did," recalls Jerry. "I don't know

◀ *The Maples Cottage features the inn's signature—the white fence. Here, Jerry used the Gothic pickets that once embroidered the former estate for the headboards by mounting them to the wall. To the left of the window is an original gate, also mounted to the wall. Building cutouts were designed by Patty and done by K. J. Anderson. (See Resource Guide.) Patty chose buildings of Elsah for this decoration. The cross-stitch sampler was made by a friend. The pattern is on page 254.*

❖ ❖ ❖

▶ *The enchanting dining room in the Garden House is set for breakfast, but the inn also serves intimate dinners. Vines of roses, intertwined with tiny white lights, are mounted on trellises. To make the unusual shade effect and turned-up fabric curtains, see page 264.*

what possessed me." But sometimes that's just what's needed to make dreams come true. As Patty and Jerry somersaulted into a new world, they did so with open minds and curious hearts, never knowing what lay ahead.

Jerry and Patty kept their big-city jobs while starting their new life in Elsah, until one day when another adventure fell into their laps. Longtime resident Alma Barnes announced she was selling her beloved Maple Leaf Cottages (which she had established from a former estate in 1949) and had selected the people she would "allow" to take over. A few weeks later, she told her very good friends, the Taetzes, that they were the chosen ones. Patty, a medical administrator, and Jerry, a well-traveled marketing rep, were shocked. Once again they didn't know what hit them, but answered the calling from Elsah. In 1985, they began the new **Maple Leaf Cottage,** turning it into a bed-and-breakfast.

Patty re-interpreted the property, keeping alive the heart of the property—Alma Barnes's swirls of English flower gardens, winding about the cottages and brick walkways. Patty complemented her friend's work by also planting gardens inside, so to speak. The main cottage, where a sumptuous and elegant breakfast is served, was named the Garden House and is one of six cottages budding with earthly reminders. From sheets to the inn's china, Patty likes to say, "Everything here remains *inn* bloom all season." It's kind of like it is through the looking glass where it is always 4 o'clock and time for a tea party. Time does seem to stand still at this charming little inn where your own tumble into wonderland awaits.

> . . . *The city house may be*
> *our grand stage for living,*
> *but the country cottage is the dressing room—*
> *a place for taking off our many faces*
> *and putting up our feet. It's where we go*
> *to be ourselves, or the people we dream of becoming.*
> *So we decorate with simple ambitions*
> *with objects that tug at the heart,*
> *then the eye . . .*

—Carol A. Crotta, *Home* Magazine, April 1991

42

Maple Leaf Cottage Inn

❖ ❖ ❖

◀ *The Wash House was once the summer kitchen for the early 1800s estate. Sometime after World War I, the kitchen was damaged by fire so the family turned it into the laundry. Saluting its former use, Patty decorated the cottage in the laundry theme with a clothesline full of wash-day nostalgia. An old mangling board serves as a side table, complete with copper boiler underneath. The wallpaper border depicts wash day. But the focal points of the room are the fluffy featherbed and the gingham curtains tied back with miniature clothespins. A pair of vintage pantaloons is just one of the many artful hangings complementing the cottage.*

❖ ❖ ❖

▶ *The lobby of the Garden House bursts with a trellis of blooming posies, some of which are for sale in the inn's gift area. Rooms at the inn were designed as European secret gardens, each with its own story. The overall idea was to decorate them with bright colors to keep rooms cheerful inside throughout the winter. Old plaster walls were bathed in raspberry and stenciled by Patty.*

An atypical doorway painted injudiciously by Patty with wipes from a dry paint brush leads the way to the Attic Room at the Garden House Cottage. Everything you might find in grandma's trunk is displayed in this bedroom, where Patty sewed up a rectangular piece of fabric and stapled it to the ceiling as a canopy for the bed. The fabric culminates in a circular drop, formed by tucking a fabric tie up through the center and attaching it to the ceiling. The sewing machine table serves as a night stand.

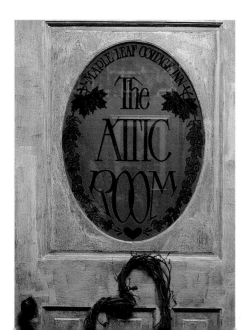

◀ *Wisps of grapevine encircle a window in the dining room, culminating in a wreath of bittersweet. To make these fold-back tab curtains, see page 265. Herb E. Moss, the Santa (above) made of all dried and natural grasses and flowers, can be ordered at the inn.*

❖ ❖ ❖

VIGNETTES OF AFFECTION FROM A HOUSE OF COLLECTIONS

Riverwind

Deep River, Connecticut

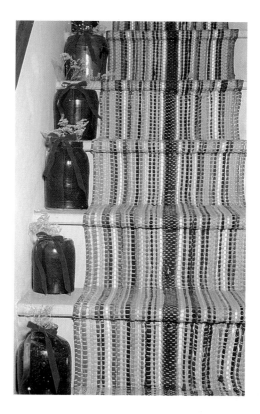

▲ *Jugs jog up the stairs, brightened by the interlocking cottons of a colorful country runner.*

WHILE admiring another's possessions, you are actually looking into the soul of the collector—his or her sense of humor, hopes and dreams. The charms of the collector's past, present, and future are on display for you to share. What a privilege!

That's why innkeeper Barbara Barlow's guests return. They see the innkeeper through her treasures, finding comfort and a fresh perspective in the things she offers to share. Purity and whimsy are found in the imperfect world Barbara has created at **Riverwind** through her shelves of folk art.

The Hearts and Flowers bedroom is filled with sweet sentiments from the old tin heart-shaped baking pan hanging on a wall to the heart pin cushion, and the heart peg rail. In the Americana Room, there's a sepia portrait of a soldier in uniform among the red, white and blue homespuns and stenciling. Who could he be?

Another sitting room reveals a soft-sculptured checkerboard with stuffed cats as game pieces. There are seven gathering rooms plus eight bedrooms at the inn—nearly one common area for each guest room. This is unusual. The innkeeper could turn some of those rooms into paying ones, but she wants to keep the inn small for her guests.

Breakfast, consisting of flaky piglet biscuits and Smithfield ham, derives from Barbara's native Virginia. (See recipes on pages 211 and 217.) The daughter of a hog farmer, and herself a learning disabilities teacher, Barbara left the Shenandoah in 1983 in search of a new adventure. She found it in the circa 1635 picture-postcard Connecticut

◄ *This antique table, across from the keeping room, is usually set with Barbara's china. But we show off her pottery during an afternoon snack.*

❖ ❖ ❖

► *An antique rake is employed as a quilt rack with patches of red in the quilt complementing a lamp shade, flag, and even the sherry in the decanter.*

River Valley settlement of Deep River. She bought an early 19th-century home, restored it and turned it into an inn.

Barbara's bed-and-breakfast was a success, so she doubled the size of the house, complementing its post-and-beam structure with salvaged barn-board ceilings and wide-plank floors. You cannot tell which side of the house is older because the materials in the new annex truly date from an earlier time. Even a stone fireplace in the new keeping room seems to be wearing the ash of centuries—for the stone was actually excavated from the home's original foundation during the expansion project. (See page 234 for **Riverwind's** tips on doing an old addition.) It was during this time that Barbara met her husband, Bob Bucknall, a contractor on the addition.

The signature of Barbara's inn is a simple ball-and-arrow weathervane, a symbol found throughout the house. Each one points you in the right decorating direction—the one that tells you to just follow your heart, as Barbara did.

◀ *The gingerbread was formed with a traditional cookie cutter but interpreted by Barbara's friend. Each cookie was given its own character by the turn of a foot or the bend of an arm before baking.*

▼ *A keeping room at* **Riverwind** *is decorated for the holidays with a chorus line of gingerbread cookies, strung up along an iron bar. Although it seems to be 200 years old, the fireplace is new! Cider is kept warm in an antique iron kettle. If you do this at home, have a crane installed to hang the pot. The cider takes on an appealing smoky flavor as it simmers.*

◄◄ *Barbara enjoys her small kitchen with an antique flour bin as her counter and a glowing candle, her only light. Breakfast is both prepared and served by candlelight.*

◄ *The Willow Room is painted in off-white and a Colonial muted turquoise. An 18th-century birdseye maple bed is flanked with black accents from the sconces on the wall to the antique pressing irons. These offer a contrast to the softness of the creamy lace canopy and the collection of vintage apparel on the wall.*

◄ *A favorite room at Riverwind is done in hearts. Barbara commissioned an artist to craft this window for the bathroom.*

❖ ❖ ❖

▶ *A wooden bunny casts a long, playful shadow in a* **Riverwind** *hallway, conveying the spirit of all the folk-art collections at the inn.*

◀ *Suggesting the mysterious and sultry life of the author and wife of F. Scott Fitzgerald, Zelda's Room is accented with silk shawl, raucous feather boa and an old starched collar with black tie. The picture is completed by framed vintage sheet music with the title, "You Made Me Love You. I Didn't Want to Do It." Barbara painted the floors in Zelda's Room in antique white and then a six-inch border in forest, using porch and deck floor paint. Her original stencil was then used to bring the floor to life and accentuate the era of* The Great Gatsby. *See page 248 for stencil pattern. I went home and borrowed library books by Zelda!*

❖ ❖ ❖

PORTRAIT OF AN INNKEEPER'S ART

The Southern Hotel

Ste. Genevieve, Missouri

THE MIST off the Mississippi River shrouds the innkeeper as she snips fresh herbs and segues to the cook stove through a kitchen door. A feast for groggy heads will be prepared by Barbara Hankins and husband Mike, owners of the inn since 1986.

Barbara was a photo stylist and theater manager in St. Louis, and she is a multi-faceted artist. She has staged the inn with artistic excitement in the garden, in the cooking, and in the decor.

The Fan Room showcases a collection of Victorian breeze makers above the fireplace mantel. The fans are mounted to the wall, and to keep them dust-free, the innkeepers enclosed them in plexiglass. The Gentleman's Room adds a touch of sophistication and whimsy with a wooden butler holding bathroom tissue. A yellow rubber duck resides in every tub at the inn. I guarantee you will want one for your own bathing at home.

Yards of woodwork at **The Southern Hotel** was stripped and regrained by Barbara to the way it was when steamboat travelers and gamblers visited. Missouri's earliest settlers came to Ste. Genevieve between 1725 and 1750, leaving behind transitional French-American structures, Georgian Colonials, log and prairie houses and German-brick gabled homes. In the early 1800s, **The Southern Hotel** was a swank stop for travelers en route to St. Louis. The building continued as a hotel and was later divided into apartments. Barbara and Mike—who left his job as an executive for Ralston Purina—brought it back to its original form.

While the Hankins did most of the handiwork—laying out 5,200 bricks for a walkway and 4,200 feet of copper pipe for more in-

◄ *Barbara likes to start planning a bedroom by first selecting a headboard. When she couldn't find one for this room, she decided to concoct her own in honor of artist Charles Wysocki. Barbara borrowed his folksy style and cut out the two-dimensional houses and town buildings, not at all unlike the Wysocki puzzle on the bed. The room's tub has a Wysocki motif, as does a dresser in decoupage.*

❖ ❖ ❖

▶ *The former summer kitchen is a gift shop in the garden. To bring in sightseeing tourists, Barbara crafted a portable sign. Every day she wheels out her antique hand truck, with circles crafted to form a man's body—snowman style. Each of the circles points the way to the shop in back. Nothing falls beyond the realm of Barbara's artistic creativity.*

door plumbing—a professional stone company did the exterior tuck-pointing and repaired chimneys.

One night while I was visiting, an unrelenting thunderstorm rolled in with furious lightning bolts that created eerie shadows on the windows. I shivered slightly but was able to lay my head to rest once I remembered that the building had been standing for 200 years. It was very unlikely that it was to go down on this very night. So, I pulled the covers over my head and fell asleep, only to awaken to the smell of something sweet baking in Barbara's kitchen. (See pages 212 and 214 for recipes.) I hadn't even heard her go out the back door for her morning ritual in the garden.

I left the inn with my comments and signature to be etched someday in thread. Barbara and Mike's guest book is a quilt. Visitors sign their names on fabric that rests in a stand-up hoop in the parlor. Later, Barbara hopes to finish embroidering all of the names. So far, she is done with one quilt. There are seven more to go and counting!

❖ ❖ ❖

◀ *A rosewood bed is center stage in Barbara's Buttons 'n' Bows Room. The heirloom was passed down to fellow artist and Ste. Genevieve resident Dolly Dufour from her Aunt Effie. Enhancing the bed with Effie's picture is most appropriate. The room showcases old buttons in a glass case. The buttons are strung with knots, leaving space between each so they stand out. Several strands hang from the top of the case.*

▼ *Painted wooden shoes designate rooms.*

CABBAGE ROSE

❖ ❖ ❖

▶ *More of the innkeeper's art, in the guise of "Truffles" the pig, is painted on the kitchen door to the back garden. At far left is a lemon soup with blackberries as a garnish, dollop of ice cream, and mint. (See recipe, page 214.) Also on the menu are asparagus crêpes, a fanciful quiche, and a pound cake with a glazing of raspberry sauce. Butter (center heart) is always flavored with equal portions of honey to unsalted butter and pressed into a mold. You can do this with large molds or candy molds and freeze until ready to serve. The Four-and-Twenty Blackbirds Pie is always available at the inn. But only the birds have dared to descend into the faux dough. (For instructions on how to make your own faux pies, see page 271.)*

❖ ❖ ❖

▲ *What a clever thing to do with hammer handles! The soldiers were made by Dolly Dufour, who often works with Barbara on art at the inn. Dolly took one look at the pile of hammers and said, "I saw soldiers." The artist found them at a yard sale for 50 cents, but you can buy the headless handles at a hardware store. The dummy boards are also Dolly and Barbara's creations (See Resource Guide.) and make terrific fireplace screens.*

There are 24 quilts in the small Quilt Room at **The Southern Hotel**. The schoolhouse quilts came from Barbara's grandmother. Two are tucked into club chairs, doubling as slipcovers. More quilts hang from rods. Wooden spools form the basis for this unique chess set, which Barbara made as a gift to Mike. To make your own, simply glue together wooden sewing spools (and other wooden thingamabobs) and paint on faces and clothing.

◄ *Guest rooms at* **The Southern Hotel** *have open bathing areas. Clawfoot tubs and pedestal sinks are secluded by decorative screens in the bedrooms. This is a good way to add such conveniences at home where space may be at a premium and you want more bathing facilities. The tubs are all hand-painted with Dolly's help. Each complements the theme of the room. Before painting your own tub, use a zinc primer to hold the top layers of paint.*

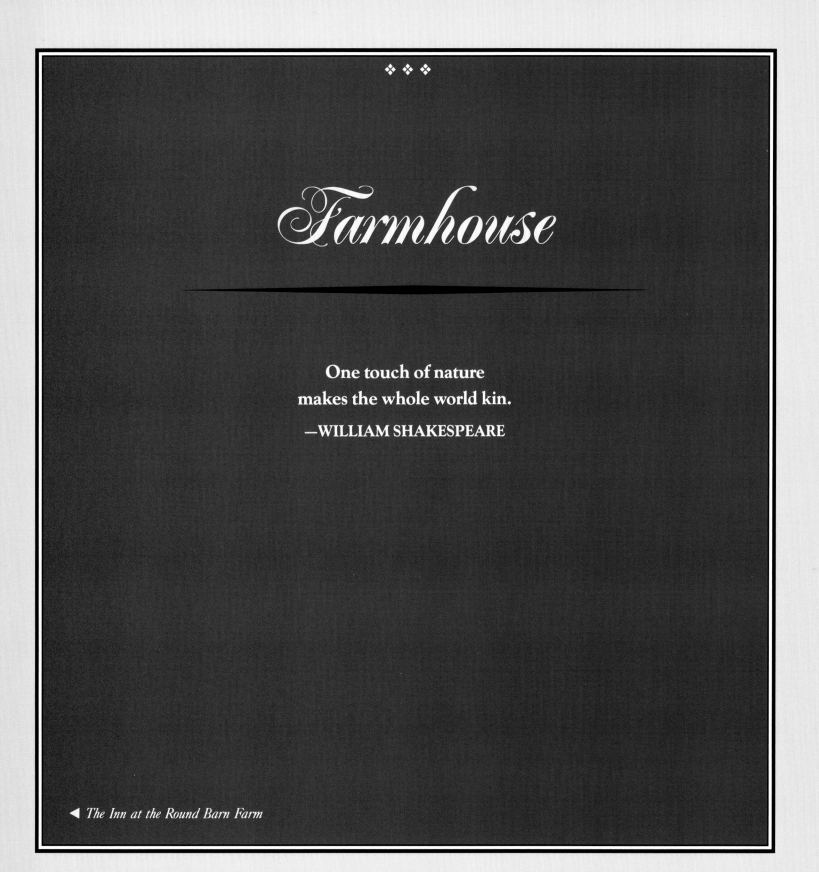

Farmhouse

One touch of nature
makes the whole world kin.

—WILLIAM SHAKESPEARE

◀ *The Inn at the Round Barn Farm*

❖ ❖ ❖

A CAMEO OF PRESERVATION COMES FULL CIRCLE

The Inn at the Round Barn Farm
Waitsfield, Vermont

▲ *A menagerie of metal sculptures, formed from farm-tool scraps, such as this whimsical bovine grazing 'neath a weeping cherry tree, shape the farm with interest in every season.*

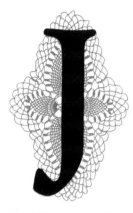

ACK AND Doreen Simko have a penchant for bringing things to life. That helps explain why the former New Jersey floral business owners took on the seemingly mad idea of restoring an enormous hulk of a round barn with twelve crumbling sides and a faltering foundation as a "retirement" project. Even diehard restoration experts would have thought twice about raising the twelve-sided, 16,000-square-foot barn from its floor. But not the Simkos.

They are, after all, rejuvenators (of flowers). Perhaps it was a desire to give new birth that eclipsed logic. The farm in the Mad River Valley (not a pseudonym for the inn, but mad because the river flows north instead of south) came up for sale and the Simkos penned their name to the contract within twenty-four hours.

You amble out of the town, over a narrow covered bridge, winding past quiet barnyards, apple trees, and sugar maples to reach their round barn—the focal point of a pastoral canvas on 85 idyllic acres. The Simkos' 1910 round barn is one of eight remaining in Vermont. In their heyday, round barns made it easier for maneuvering farm equipment on and off the fields.

It's not every day that someone refurbishes such an architectural rarity. The family relied on the help and resources of Arnold Graton, who rebuilt a round barn at the Shelburne Museum in nearby Burlington. The work took nearly two years before the inn opened in 1988.

The round barn sports interior white-washed, plank walls and a

◀ *The Simkos converted the attached carriage barn into luxurious guest rooms for bedtime rituals. The contrast of the barnyard ceiling and crisp white accents creates a comfortable renaissance look, demonstrating the reward of considering textures when you decorate. A soft waterfall of chiffon flows over a modern iron bed frame. To duplicate this look, see page 260.*

❖ ❖ ❖

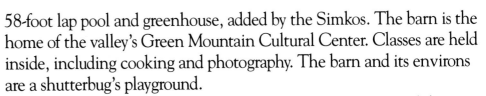

▼ *Beautiful hooked rugs such as this one don't have to be relegated to the floor. Hang them on a wall or use them as a table cover. (See Resource Guide.) It was the man of the house's idea to take a cutout of the complementary wallpaper and add an accent (see above). Doreen says everyone laughed at Jack. But the guests love it, and so do I.*

58-foot lap pool and greenhouse, added by the Simkos. The barn is the home of the valley's Green Mountain Cultural Center. Classes are held inside, including cooking and photography. The barn and its environs are a shutterbug's playground.

The 1810 farmhouse, which the Simkos also renovated, houses guest rooms, as does the horse barn, renovated and opened in 1992. The Simkos' daughter, AnneMarie DeFreest, worked with her mother on the decorating and has been Round Barn's innkeeper and cook.

Saving such a barn and running an inn is no easy feat for anyone, no less the "retiring" Simkos. But Jack and Doreen, with the help of their grown children, just keep going. They recently converted part of the horse barn into their own private quarters. And on my most recent visit to the inn, Doreen had just pulled up in a station wagon full of flowers. No, this couple isn't about to let any grass grow under their feet. From flowers for the inn to added rooms, the Simkos keep bringing new life to the world. The latest addition is something else round—a bundle of joy: AnneMarie's first child. Perhaps Elizabeth Ann will inherit the barn someday and keep it alive in the spirit of her grandparents.

▶ *A burst of funky floral fabric brightens an antique sleigh bed in the Sherman guest room. The intensity of the wallpaper is subdued by warm woods and the coordinating striped paper in the bathroom. Note the box-pleated skirt. It's simply stitched as if it were a curtain and hung on a rod across the foot of the bed frame. One problem when buying an antique bed is that the largest are usually double-mattress size. Innkeepers such as Jack Simko have solved that problem. To see how to support a queen-size mattress on an antique bed, see Jack Simko's instructions on pages 238 and 239.*

▶ *A hint of sunlight washes a period room complete with whirligig. The window treatments are easy to make and show versatility. Sew together a solid fabric and lace, then back it with Velcro. (Add a Velcro strip to the window trim as well.) Pull back the inside corners with a decorative tie and you have a new curtain. To preserve the wide-planked yellow pine floors at the inn, guests are asked to remove their shoes. Slippers, such as those at the foot of the bed are provided. It's a good idea if you ask the same of your guests, as friends of ours ask even if we're over for dinner—only they're concerned about their wall-to-wall carpets.*

▶ *A splash of the broad-shouldered Sugarbush Mountain decorates the awesome view in this bathing room. A friend carved and then painted the forest of flowers on otherwise uninteresting paneling. The rubber duck reminds the bather not to get too lost in the elegance of it all and forget to have fun.*

❖ ❖ ❖

◀ *These two doors represent the floral talent of the Simko family. I asked Jack Simko to help us learn how to make the inn's beautiful Christmas doors. See his instructions on page 274.*

▼ *The farmhouse feel is certainly evident in this room. The Simkos wanted a swirl of windows to surround breakfasters with food for thought. The simple curtain treatments add color and texture without distraction. P.S. The porcine with the pretty floral skin is harmless.*

❖ ❖ ❖

A Fantasia of Leaf and Bud Plays a Posy Rhapsody

Blue Lake Ranch

Hesperus, Colorado

Y OU CAN hear the thistle in the thickets going to seed, the peonies promenading left and right as bachelor buttons curtsy in a round and scarlet poppies sashay under breezy azure skies. There's a choreography of nature here—a profusion of melody and movement with the unrivaled designs and nonpareiled colors of boisterous flowers. The land bursts into rainbows of color and symphonies of sound—sheep bells in the meadows and wind chimes on the cottages. Your toes tap and your heart hums.

Blue Lake Ranch could have been the inspiration for Walt Disney's *Fantasia*, if only it were older. The pioneering movie that paired the notes of Bach, Beethoven, Tchaikovsky, and Schubert with animation truly comes to mind. The ranch is a combination of poetry and art in motion. Only, the flowers in this garden are under the spell of innkeeper David Alford, not the orchestral wand of Leopold Stokowski and the Disney artists.

The language of flowers—that's what this bed-and-breakfast speaks. Tucked into the hills of southwestern Colorado, not far from an ancient Indian reservation and the La Plata mountains, this retreat among the jewels of nature must be seen to be believed. Since David purchased the former tumbleweed-swept cattle ranch, he has brought an impressionistic canvas of flowers and heirloom bulbs to the 100-acre, lake-bound property.

David, who presses his waterproof garden clogs down gently as

▲ *"She loves me. She loves me not." David and Shirley Alford pick flower petals apart for their dried floral garnish. The garnish goes on salads, soups, pasta, cereal, and you name it.*

◄ *Powder the face of a new or old piece with trompe l'oeil. This "fool-the-eye" version was done for David and Shirley by an artist friend. Note the innkeepers' heirloom quilt.*

71

he pads about the giving earth—pointing to this variety and that, has given his guests the chance to see what one can do with a garden.

You will find flowers for gathering, for pressing and even for eating. There are many posies for the palate, which David and his wife, Shirley, package and sell. At first, they put them on cereals for the guests, but then realized that the uses of the petals are endless: soups, salads, sprinkles for toast. Whenever they get the chance, they spend hours fiddling with the petals—picking them for drying and packing into jars they ship all over the world with a Blue Lake Bed-and-Breakfast seal. They have yet to find the conclusion to the age-old aphorism, "She loves me. She loves me not." My guess is they never will.

Inside **Blue Lake**'s three cottages and the guest rooms in the main house, the mien of the outdoors mirrors the indoors. Artistic friends hand-painted trompe l'oeil above beds, over beams and under windows. A "waltz of the flowers" is everywhere, and you don't need the Tchaikovsky classic of that name to remind you to take the ideas of **Blue Lake Ranch** home with you as a prelude of great things to come.

❖ ❖ ❖

▲ *Hollyhocks crane for a peek through a Dutch door at a* **Blue Lake Ranch** *guest room. The florabunda add pattern to the room's simple lines. The trip-around-the-world quilt on the chair and the chain-of-diamonds quilt on the bed are from Shirley's collection of antique homespuns. A woven cotton tablecloth envelops the bed's framework.*

❖ ❖ ❖

The inn is surrounded by David's plantings—from giant sunflowers to tiny posies.

❖ ❖ ❖

SPINNING YARNS AND DRYING FLOWERS WHILE THE SHEEP PLAY

Sweet Basil Hill Farm
Gurnee, Illinois

▲ *Country accents are the welcoming greetings in the mud room of mellow yellow clapboard.*

TERI AND Bob Jones own this bed-and-breakfast on nearly eight acres of wooded and barnyard property. Here, they show you how to "go placidly amid the noise and haste." First, let me tell you about Teri. Teri has always been a naturalist at heart. Books on the contemplative life abound in the country living room her guests enjoy. She spins here, usually in winter when the only sounds are made by a blazing fire and the rhythm of the wood gently clacking as the yarn is tugged. Ah, how she shows us to "remember what peace there may be in silence." The room is finished in English and American scrubbed pine antiques, so befitting her gentle nature.

Teri is also a photographer. Her framed photos grace the inn, portraying not only her talent, but the environs at **Sweet Basil Hill.** Teri is also serious about flower-drying and using herbs in her cooking. An entire room is devoted to keeping these supplies on hand. Guests partake in classes and go home with their own bundles of flowers and herbs. And Teri, is of course, an innkeeper. The world knocks on her door to experience more of those lines from the poem, "The Desiderata."

Bob is a commercial actor, which means he spends time in a studio when he's needed by Madison Avenue types and time at the farm when his two llamas and 35 sheep are calling out for nutrition and exercise. He works out, too—writing his own book and at the piano composing tunes.

Together, they left the rat race in search of more meaning. They

◀ *You can dry your own flowers even if you don't have the small cottage like this one that serves as Teri's drying room. Hang yards of chain links, as Bob did, in a relatively dry room. Bunch flowers into bouquets with rubber bands. Use paper clips as wire to secure the rubber bands to the links.*

77

❖ ❖ ❖

and their guests find it every day at **Sweet Basil Hill Farm.** Even the bedrooms are inviting escapes. The Basil Room showcases a canopy bed and hand-stenciling. The Burgundy Room was painted a wine color to contrast brighter accent pieces.

Teri and Bob live the life many of us dream about. But a sign at the inn reminds us that we can have it all if we simply think a bit differently. Here, let Henry David Thoreau explain: "If the day and night are such that you greet them with joy, life emits a fragrance like flowers and sweet-scented herbs—more elastic, more starry, more immortal—that is your success."

▼ *Living rooms for the '90s are taking on more casual personalities. The sideboard and hutch plus all-purpose table at the inn, make this room most inviting. The bench on the opposite side of the table was made from an old headboard. The key ring (shown on the bench up close) is a carved wooden sheep.*

❖ ❖ ❖

◀ *Teri shares a spinning wheel with guests as some innkeepers do a piano! Anyone is allowed to go for a spin with Teri's help.*

▲ *Teri and Bob's inn looms behind the farm bell.*

► *Teri antiqued this yard-sale purchase by painting the chest pink and then gently sanding away some of the new paint to reveal the aged green paint. The sponge-painted walls are a perfect backdrop for the piece. (See how she did it on page 250.)*

❖ ❖ ❖

*Bob tends to his sheep and llamas. All the animals at **Sweet Basil Farm**—including Johann Sebastian Baa—have delightfully whimsical names. But I cannot even tell the difference between Fernando and the Dali Llama.*

Victorian

Happiness consists of
a little fire, a little food,
and an immense quiet.

—RALPH WALDO EMERSON

◀ *The Chicago Pike Inn*

❖ ❖ ❖

NEW IMPRESSIONS FROM A BYGONE ERA

The Chicago Pike Inn
Coldwater, Michigan

I MAGINE Asbury Buckley's task. In 1903, the famed Midwest architect was hired to build a Colonial reform house for Morris G. Clarke of Michigan. The owner of a prosperous mercantile in Coldwater wanted a stately building that would reflect his position in the community. Little did Buckley know when he put pencil to drafting board that this house would someday also embrace weary sojourners with the hospitality of his own era.

The Clarke home required cherry and walnut hardwoods and a pediment was artfully designed to outline the roof. An imposing twin stairway—upon which to take flight—was built, as well as a window seat and a buffet in the dining room. Almost instinctively, Buckley added those amenities of luxury and grace befitting a special visitor.

Every detail was addressed by Buckley, an architect known and respected for the grand buildings he designed on Michigan's Mackinac Island. For the Clarke home, it wasn't all glamor, however. Some 706 feet of natural gas pipe was installed, for example, making it the longest length of such material to be laid in a residence of Coldwater. The home took a year to build.

Such a supreme house is no longer in the hands of its original family. But the talents of Asbury Buckley and the vision of Morris G. Clarke have teamed up with the ambitions and abilities of Harold and Jane Schultz and their daughters.

Between the time the Clarke family finally sold the home to an outsider in 1936 and the Schultzes bought it in 1989, three other fami-

◀ *Cherry hardwoods form the grand twin staircase. Note the double wallpaper border treatment used to punctuate the underside of the stairs. The floor is uniquely comprised of thousands of inlaid oak end-cuts.*

❖ ❖ ❖

lies cared for it. When Harold and Jane acquired it, they renovated the house and gave it a face-lift orchestrated by Jane, (See her portrait on page 228.) who, in her decorating, has the splendor of a Mario Buatta and the warmth of a Mary Emmerling.

That translates into rooms of variety that are genteel but inviting. Jane's innate gift is assisted by a knowledge of paints and wallpapers that stems from being around her father's wallcoverings store. Overall, she approached the decor with a pastel palette to contrast the dark wood trims. Guest rooms are left open when not occupied, "so that everyone can see and feel the entire house," says Jane.

But that's not all that's inviting at this inn. Jane's daughter Becky is the full-time innkeeper and she, along with her sister, Jody Willard, prepare scrumptious three-course breakfasts and afternoon tea on china and crystal. It's just the way it was years ago, right down to the smorgasbord of confections—the penny-candy store style sweets that are left out for all to enjoy in the library. Buckley and the Clarkes would be right at home, just as I was.

▶ *A decorous mix of wallpapers complements the elegant dining room where breakfast is served. The papered ceiling helps define the room's architectural beauty. Pinks and green in the kilim-style rug on the floor pull the room together.*

◄◄ *A square piece of hemmed fabric looks daintier on this table with tied ribbons at each corner.*

◄ *Youthful paintings and vignettes such as this one adorn the room. The pretty mugs are part of the elegant but unusual collection from which guests drink morning coffee.*

▼ *By dropping the feeling of height in the room with a border of wallpaper and then paint, the sweet repose of the Grandchildren's Room is cut down to size. This is a useful technique for any room you may want to cozy up a bit. Two lace curtain panels, wrapped around nails, form the soft bed toppers. Vintage christening gowns decorate each bed's footboard.*

► *A charming bathroom sports a faux marble floor in honor of early days of real marble. Reproduction gas lanterns were also hung to recall the home's previous life.*

▼ *One wooden curtain rod and two brackets mounted to the wall form this lovely fabric headboard. Nail the pieces and sew up a full-length curtain panel. Wrap it around the rod and brackets. The dainty inner bed skirt hides the bare box spring when you fold down the comforter at night.*

❖ ❖ ❖

◀ *The embroidery atop the dresser says it all.*

◀ *A rosy way to rise 'n' shine each morning is by accenting a bedroom in red and white. Jane chose the Cranston plaid pattern for the walls and comforter to offer this small room reason to look important. Petite wall shelves serve as end tables and save space. Colors are carried into the sitting room in a basket of yarns and the quilt. Notice the turkeywork on the pillowcase. Turkeywork evolved from Colonial days when seamstresses wanted to recreate Turkish carpet designs on linens. The pattern from the inn was influenced by German stitchery.*

❖ ❖ ❖

OH, HOW THEIR GARDEN GROWS

Twin Gates

Lutherville, Maryland

WHEN I first stopped by Bob and Gwen Vaughan's Second Empire home, Bob was repairing a cross-bow fence that embroiders their corner property. When I visited the second time, the innkeeper was fencing again, this time building a new Gothic rail to enhance one of the many gardens Gwen tends. Bob's handshake left me with saw-dusted palms and the desire to jump in and help. But Bob, who was working without blueprints, was successfully rolling along with sure-footed assistance from wooden horses and a circular saw.

"I thought I'd end the fence at a 45-degree angle. What do you think?" he asked. Sounded fine to a carpentry amateur, but I asked him to draw a fence and garden sketch of what he was building for your own backyard. (See page 206.)

Finding **Twin Gates,** as it was historically named, waxed symbolic for the Vaughans. "Things happen to us in twos," notes Gwen, beginning with her twin daughters. The inn was originally home to Benjamin Sadtler, principal of a Lutheran female seminary. When Abraham Lincoln was debating Stephen Douglas, **Twin Gates** was under construction, complete with a secret room to hide runaway slaves.

Gwen relinquished her job as a medical secretary to open the inn in 1987. The innkeeper steadfastly worked on establishing gardens as she and Bob restored the home's three floors.

When they began work in the kitchen, they added a window box and Gwen planted seeds to sprout in view of the window. "Place your gardens where they can be seen from the inside, as well," she advises. (See Gwen's gardening tips on page 205.) The gardening theme was also carried inside in the Greeting Room, or family room. Creamy

▲ *Trailing vines inch up an arched trellis, creating a romantic nook for soaking up those lazy days of summer.*

◀ *The elegant dining room is softened with a gentle wallpaper above the chair rail. An artificial ficus tree helps to hide the old-fashioned plumbing, leaving just a hint of the pipes to bow to the past. The mirror helps reflect more of the outdoors.*

❖ ❖ ❖

summer peach-and-white windowpane check and crisp winter navy highlight the room that is filled with gardening books, ceramic bunnies, and earthenware cherubs. Inside a nook sits a table for board games or afternoon tea.

Bedrooms, such as the Cape May Room, reveal Bob and Gwen's travels. "I like rooms to wrap around you," notes Gwen, whose artful touches summon a mohair shawl to a chaise lounge as though someone is resting; starched bows to brass mounted lamps; and peg rail for old, frayed toys.

Gwen never compromises comfort for style. It's the same with her breakfasts, which look and taste delicious but are nutritious, too.

From the rapturous gardens to flower-enhanced sitting areas under age-old spreading trees and new trellises, this is a giving inn in so many ways. Gwen likes to share her garden and send new friends off with precious keepsakes—clippings from her plants. She tells us how on page 203. It's Gwen's way of spreading the love of her inn wherever she can. What a good idea for our own gardens.

▼ *The Cape May Room is complete with seaside furniture, pictures of inns in that Victorian town, and brochures of the area. Adding companion literature to a room helps reinforce any theme you are trying to convey.*

❖ ❖ ❖

◀ *Guests are often served breakfast in the gazebo. The sun spreads across a scrumptious table laden with warm scents and bursting with the colors of Gwen's heirloom china and budding perennials. To replicate her perennial garden, see the plot on page 206.*

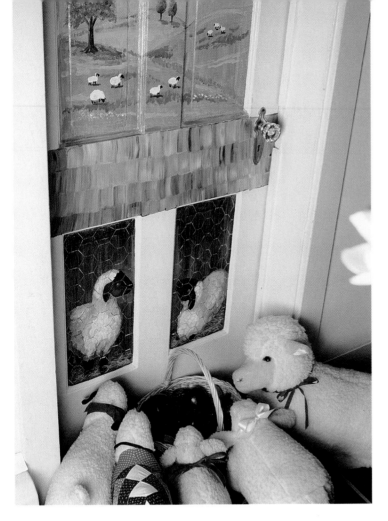

▲ *Gwen had an artist paint the grazing scene to brighten up the pantry door in the kitchen. The addition of the stuffed sheep and basket of fruit complements the scene and creates a vignette.*

▲ ▶ *The Hunt Room is complete with red-vested fox, rider's hat and horn of the hunt. Double-faced curtains seem to flair out like the lapels of a rider's jacket, blowing in the breeze of the ride. The curtain treatment is simple and a good idea to dress up any room.*

▶ *The garden theme continues inside on the mantel in the Greeting Room.*

BUKOVNIK/WATERCOLORS · ADI GALLERY/SAN FRANCISCO · JANUARY 17, 1980

❖ ❖ ❖

◀ *Grinning bears flaunt summer shades. Gwen changes the bears' apparel according to the time of year. Bursts of trompe l'oeil floral bouquets as an extension of the wallpaper pattern bring the garden to the hall.*

❖ ❖ ❖

ROOMS THAT BLOOM WITH "HART" AND SOUL

Walnut Street Inn
Springfield, Missouri

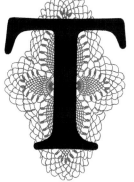

THE INNKEEPER takes you to your quarters—the Danzero Room. You are just about to set down luggage when you find there's already baggage in the lodger's respite—two steamer trunks. Your mind drifts across the ocean a century earlier as you eye maps and an outdated camera. A young man, Domino Danzero is crossing the Atlantic at 19 from his native Turin, Italy.

Suddenly, he's bent over, washing dishes at a Chicago restaurant. He becomes a citizen, a chef, and he marries. He then moves to Springfield where he opens his own restaurant, a bakery, and a macaroni factory. You see him laughing with his nine children, but just as quickly, he is ill and at only 42, doctors give him six months to live. The Danzeros sell the family businesses. Domino takes up photography to pass whatever time is left, and sells inventions to Kodak, changing photo history.

Thirty-eight more years pass by and Domino is still at work. The weight of your luggage shakes you out of your daydreaming. "Here, let me get that for you," the innkeeper offers. "Yes, we named this room after my grandfather. Let me know if there's anything else I can get you," she adds on her way out the door.

But what more could one want than to be surrounded by history and an immigrant's trinkets of hope, promise, adventure, and success? **Walnut Street** is owned by Gary and Nancy Brown, Domino's granddaughter. The Browns purchased the 1894 Victorian with its hand-painted Corinthian columns and immediately started renovation. The

▲ *Wood paneling highlights the innkeeper's check-in desk. A watercolor of the inn is bordered not only in its own gilded frame but also by a cutout of a rope pattern from a wallpaper border. That same wallpaper cutout was used to accent a window and a clock (not shown). Find a wallpaper border to make your own curious cutout. Adhere it to the wall according to normal paper-hanging directions. Trim with a flower, decorative bow, or other accent that may also be found in the paper pattern.*

◄ *Creamsicle colors dusted with hints of pink and blue make up the colorway in the Jewell Room. A collection of old hatboxes serves as a side table for family photos and a jewelry box. (See instructions on sponge painting on page 250.)*

❖ ❖ ❖

Springfield Symphony selected it as the site for their designer showhouse. Domino's photographs now embellish the decor throughout the inn. The Browns own a furniture store that has been in Nancy's family for years, and is where Nancy received most of her design inspiration. (See Resource Guide.)

More innkeepers than not name their rooms. Naming a room at an inn, or home, adds a sense of discovery and education and helps develop a decorating theme. The Thomas Hart Benton Room, for example, was done as if it were an artist's studio, and includes Benton's works.

When I last visited, Nancy walked me through Springfield's gem of a new attraction across the street from the inn. The Juanita K. Hammons Hall for the Performing Arts seats 2,500 and features music and Broadway traveling shows.

It is worth going to Springfield and the inn even just for a weekend to hear the music at the great hall, sit on the inn's front porch swing, or read a book by the fire. See if you don't reflect, as I did, just how proud Domino Danzero would be to see what he really started such a long time ago!

▲ *A mantel and gas firebox with faux logs were added to the Jewell Room. (See more on installing gas fireplaces on page 201.)*

▶ *Painted chairs decorate the dining room at Walnut Street. Brave colors of apricot, mint green, and powder blue are enhanced by hand-painted scenes taken from the castles and buildings that appear in the wallpaper. A gingerbread trim frames the dining room and the parlor.*

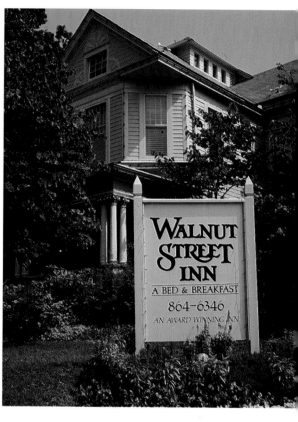

◀ *The inn's carriage house is supported by upper cross beams and support posts. When designing the Jewell Room in the former buggy shelter, beams were boxed in with wood to become the four posters for a new bed. Paneling and a shelf of dentil molding were designed for the headboard. An easy-to-sew gathered curtain was attached with a rod on each side of the bed to form a canopy. Recessed reading lights were added—one over each pillow, on separate switches.*

❖ ❖ ❖

▶ *The cabaret atmosphere of the Robertson Room is underscored by the clever design of bricks showing through patches of plaster that were pulled away from the wall. Old instruments serve as decor and a steamer trunk serves as a knick-knack table and reminder of the musician's way of life. You can create this backstage look in any appropriate room at home.*

▶ *The Maschino Room is topped by skylights that bring in the outside. It was a clever way to open up the closed feeling an angled and dormered room can give. The curvaceous dried ivy seems at home creeping up from the handmade lattice headboard. Birdcages and birdhouses also decorate the room, attractively tied together by the colorful quilt. The nightstand belonged to Nancy Brown's grandfather, who owned a bakery. Pies and cakes were kept free of dust for the day behind the glass doors.*

❖ ❖ ❖

◀ *An antique sink vanity is the focal point of the bathroom in the McCann Room. The drawers are fixed, but the doors open to private storage.*

◀ *This is not a real bookcase. The inn's decor fools the eye in the Carver Room. The hand-painted library wall and Missouri books invite you to read in this room, complemented by jewel-tone colors on the bed and other fabrics. The flame-stitch chair adds a dramatic contrast to the bookcase. Such artistic foolery is a great substitute when space won't provide for the real thing.*

❖ ❖ ❖

THE CURTAIN RISES ON TODAY'S VICTORIAN

Arsenic & Old Lace

Eureka Springs, Arkansas

▲ *Jeanne Simpson Johnson*

J EANNE Simpson Johnson offered me an afternoon libation from a wine decanter in the parlor at **Arsenic & Old Lace.** Peering suspiciously around the parlor, I edged forward, reaching eagerly for the crystal glass, but suddenly shrank back.

"Could this be elderberry wine?" I wondered. "How silly," I thought. "Why should I hesitate? Oh, come on, certainly that endearing Cary Grant flick wasn't conjuring up unseemly images. Or was it?

"This dear sweet innkeeper was interested in my comfort after a long journey. Wasn't she? Not that I might be presumed lonely and could be put out of my misery with one swift gulp—a fate that befell the unsuspecting victims in the play and movie. Right?"

Remembering the many accolades written in the guest book, I realized that more than one guest must have had fun with similar musings. They had lived to tell about their stay in glowing terms. And that's just the way the innkeeper wants it.

"Some said my name for the inn was, well, 'terrible.' But you've got to have a sense of humor," Jeanne explained, as if reading my hesitation. I accepted the glass. "That's one of the reasons why I named the inn after the movie. I don't mind having fun with the topic."

The choice of name for the inn was also wise, as there are a bevy of inns in Eureka Springs and the title of this one gets attention. So does the design and setting of the home, looking out from high on a hilltop. **Arsenic & Old Lace** shows that you can have a new Victorian home built from the ground up, as Jeanne did in Queen Anne style,

◀ *A reproduction of an old tin ceiling accentuates this elegant dining room. It goes to show how you can create many architectural features of the past in a new home. Jeanne didn't have room to hang her entire collection of butterfly art until she thought of mounting the works between two picture frame moldings all around the room. A cordial glass of sherry sits on the table of warm woods and inlays. Does anyone dare take a sip?*

103

complete with turret and sweeping verandas. The three-story home, where Jeanne also lives, is complete with five bedrooms, a parlor, library, dining room, and breakfast room.

Jeanne is a patron of the arts and has decorated the inn with original paintings. Lace cascades abundantly from windows in the common areas. Bedrooms contain reproduction antiques as well as items from Jeanne's personal collections. One octagon-shaped room is virtually built into the trees with windows on three sides revealing branches up two stories high.

The inn is lovely outside as well. I enjoyed breakfast with a patio view of a sloping embankment dotted with new shrubs and flower gardens. The morning energy boost is great for exploring the area.

Eureka Springs is an exciting town in the famed Ozark Mountains, filled with curious shops and art galleries, that bows to a mystical past when its waters were said to heal. And to think I might have thought just the opposite! Hiccup!

▲ *Jeanne had the architect build a window seat like the one in the movie. A picture of Cary Grant sits on top of the seat, surrounded by yards and yards and yards of lace Jeanne has hung around the inn. You'll have to visit to find out what's in the box!*

◄ *Breakfast is served overlooking a country kitchen and glass doors to outdoor gardens. The teapot totem is from England.*

❖ ❖ ❖

Main Street Revival

There's Main Street.
Why, that's Mr. Morgan's drugstore. . . .
And that's the livery stable.
Oh, that's the town I knew as a little girl.
And, look, there's the old white fence
that used to be around the house.
Oh, I'd forgotten that!
Oh, I love it so!

—*OUR TOWN,* THORNTON WILDER

◀ *Christmas Farm*

❖ ❖ ❖

❖ ❖ ❖

A STEEPLE IN THE MARSHES RISES AGAIN

Christmas Farm
Wittman, Maryland

N THE midst of a bountiful cornfield and a snug, bullrush cove of the historic Chesapeake Bay, I stumbled upon a working farm with a charming old house and a white-steepled church that welcomes sojourners for much more than a passing tithe. You might say I entered paradise, but eternity proved to be only a fleeting weekend. I wondered later if the visit to **Christmas Farm** wasn't all just a miracle in the marshes.

But the sheep grazing in the field—symbolic of the many who have flocked to this unusual bed-and-breakfast—reminded me that it was all very real. **Christmas Farm**—named for the time of the year that its owners decided to take on a new life—is a sanctuary from the stressful rigors of daily life.

You cannot help but wax ecclesiastical when you enter the "parish" innkeepers Beatrice (Bea) and David Lee formed in 1985, five years after they bought the Colonial farm on a 50-acre plowman's parcel. Located just outside the tiny bayside hamlet of St. Michaels, **Christmas Farm** is comprised of a main farmhouse, a church for guests and several out-buildings for barnyard animals from colorful Rhode Island Reds that tender fresh eggs each morning to peacocks and a miniature horse.

The farmhouse is a rambling one that includes several additions and is where the Lees live and offer two guest suites. The house dates to circa 1800 when it was born a 12x12-foot all-purpose room with cooking hearth and sleeping loft. Over the years, the house grew with vari-

 The Brother Palmer's Still is the name of this guest suite with a Belgian wood stove and French doors that open to a porch with a view of the cornfields and the water.

► *In 1893, St. James Church first welcomed parishioners to its humble house of worship. Today, the 20x40-foot building has been preserved and turned into a B&B. It is one of the few such accommodations in America and was moved to the property. For house-moving know-how, see the innkeepers' tips on page 234. Just inside the front door is the church vestibule with an original pew. See the Resource Guide to order one of these church seats. Innkeeper Bea Lee often throws on a wool shawl on cold mornings to gather fresh eggs from her hens for breakfast.*

ous additions and when the Lees came, they attached a centuries-old dining room to the farmhouse. It happened one day when they spotted an old home for sale. They only needed a large wing from the end of the house. So, they bought the entire home and had the one room moved and added to their farmhouse.

The bell-towered clapboard church, which houses the other two guest quarters, was also moved onto the property as were eight or so other small buildings the couple wanted to preserve. St. James Church traveled less than a mile to its new resting place where it now offers a separate peace to those who spend a few days at **Christmas Farm.**

To maintain the B&B, all these buildings and a two-tenths-of-a-mile gravel driveway onto the property, David and Bea have other jobs during the week. David is a ship cargo broker based in St. Michaels and Bea is an international lawyer, who commutes two hours one way, each week, to an office in Washington, D.C.

It is the sacrifice they have decided to make to satisfy their passion to preserve architectural history and provide the means for others to enjoy it, too. Amen to that.

❖ ❖ ❖

▲ *Guests usually enjoy breakfast in their spacious suites, but sometimes Bea serves in the farmhouse dining room, which the Lees moved to the property. China from Bea's grandmother graces the table along with cards created by David, who is a wonderful artist. The cards depict the farm at night and are available from the inn as note card sets.*

▲ *Cheviot and Barbados sheep make their home at the farm, which raises corn, soybeans, and winter wheat crops. The farm's Chesapeake waterfront can be seen in the distance.*

▶ *Here's a look from the bedroom into the breakfast and sitting area of one of the two suites in the former church. Sunlight catches the window mullions in such a way as to form a cross.*

❖ ❖ ❖

◀ *The innkeepers live in this farmhouse, a few feet away from the church. They added the section on the far right. The board-and-batten structure was once a waterman's house, which the Lees converted into a two-story guest suite.*

▼ *Burgundies, blues, and greens color the other suite inside the church.*

❖ ❖ ❖

AT THE HEAD OF THE CLASS WITH SCHOLARLY COMPOSITION

The School House Bed & Breakfast
Rocheport, Missouri

S A GUEST at **The School House Bed & Breakfast,** you get caught up in the nostalgia of it all. During my first visit, I was assigned to the Schoolmaster's Room and thought of visits to the principal's office. On a second visit, I had made the Honor Roll (Room) but was glad there was no longer a roll call. Busy researching other parts of the inn, I would not be in my seat. The Spelling Bee Room, for example, is alight with spring fancy—yellow, green, and pink. (I remember when I was in a real bee, circa third grade!)

Naturally, I have been tardy each time I visited **The School House**—as much as 78 years! But that's okay, as there are still many lessons to learn at Rocheport's 1914 red-brick school. The first and foremost tenet is that nearly any building can be turned into a home. In fact, when innkeepers John and Vicki Ott purchased the school in 1988, it was operating as an antiques emporium. They intended to reconfigure the interior into a contemporary New York loft home. "But as we began to live in it, we realized that we wanted to preserve what was here," recalls Vicki, "and we wanted to share the beauty of the structure with others."

The "structure" includes 12- and 13-foot-high ceilings, beaded baseboards with king's corners, arched passageways, 90-inch-tall schoolhouse windows; and brick and plaster walls—so thick that all of the electrical outlets had to be installed in the floors.

The upstairs—which was once the assembly room, principal's office, and high school—is now three bedrooms and a breakfast area/

▲ *Except for built-in blackboards, the mighty bell was the only artifact left in the schoolhouse when the Otts purchased it. And that was because the boards couldn't be removed easily and the brass bell was so heavy that it was left in the attic when the school closed in 1972!*

◄ *An original blackboard serves as the welcome mat at the inn. Vicki and John scribe the names of each guest arriving that day. The blackboard presides over the inn's living room, once a high school classroom.*

❖ ❖ ❖

living room. Downstairs—where primary grades learned reading—are more bedrooms, a crisp and airy hallway with 22 steps to the second story, and a display of sepia photos from the original school.

As soon as the Otts had studied up on innkeeping, the school bell rang again to the peal of a different clapper. The primary-through-secondary school was transformed into a nine-bedroom B&B. Out came the rulers, pencils, and T-squares once again, but not for geometry. John had walls to move, trims to paint, and Vicki had curtains and bed coverings to sew. (See how to make her easy-release bed skirts on page 259 and designer-padded hangers on page 255.)

Vicki cooks up delicious breakfasts at the head of the class in the large common room and kitchen. The inn is decorated with just the right amount of educational trinkets. Let your imagination do the rest, remembering happy childhood antics, favorite teachers, and of course, life's little embarrassing moments, such as that elementary school spelling bee. I was disqualified on the word *business*. Business is the very thing you leave behind as soon as you walk through the swinging front doors of **The School House Bed & Breakfast** to enjoy a break from your everyday routine.

▼ Three-year-old Mackenzie, in her overalls and Peter Pan-collar blouse, reminds us we should all be kids in our own home. Here, the Otts' daughter does like Sally from the Fun with Dick and Jane *reader series, adding her own interpretation in this life-imitates-art photo. Several original pages from the well-known reading primers hang about the inn. Coincidentally, John tells us that the author graduated from the nearby University of Missouri in Columbia.*

▲ *The plaster walls in the Show-and-Tell Room were in such disarray that Vicki decided the only way to cover them would be with fabric. Some 90 yards were sewn together and installed over batting in this popular room with heart-shaped tub. (See page 251 for in-* structions.) *Coordinating Waverly fabric enrobes the bathroom while a kindergarten chair holds a basket of flowers. The T-shirt, with its* **School House Bed & Breakfast** *logo, is often purchased by guests as sleepwear.*

❖ ❖ ❖

▶ *Lengthening shadows mirror the transom windows and cast drama into the front foyer. Vicki's smart choice of pastel shades in the quilt and walls gives the hallway a soft, unintimidating look. The unusually long deacon's bench (nine feet) offers a seat for musing about school days and is believed to have come from a railroad depot. The Otts left the front doors intact but added polished brass handrails and hung a Victorian chandelier. The 1890s rocking horse is constructed of burlap and leather on wood. The horse has warm glass eyes and comes from an antiques shop in the basement of the inn.*

Traditional schoolhouse windows are intriguing architectural features of the inn, allowing abundant light to be part of the decor. Such heights might have been a real decorating worry, but Vicki chalks up her bravery to years in college as an ardent cliff rappeller! The custom-made wooden plantation shutters enhance light patterns and provide privacy. The Schoolmarm's Room also instructs us that putting a tub into a bedroom gives your home more bathing space. Vicki makes her bed dressings, including dust ruffles devised for easy removal. For directions, see page 259.

❖ ❖ ❖

▶ *The community hall (through the window) is one of the reasons Rocheport, with all of its 13 blocks, resembles a quaint New England town. The hamlet borders the Katy trail—an abandoned railroad that is being turned into a delightful 250-mile walking and biking path. The Honor Roll Room boasts wine walls, contrasting lace curtains and floral "underwear."*

▲ A painted wooden mantel suggests a fireplace boarded up and adds a decorative accessory to this room called The Graduate. Vicki chose black as the pivotal color for the room, thinking of the traditional black mortarboard. But the centerpiece here is a charming voyager's chapeau with flowers that match the room's fabrics.

▲ An antique wardrobe hides the other half of an original built-in chalkboard in the Schoolmaster's Room. The jeweled afghan was crocheted by John's great-grandmother.

❖ ❖ ❖

INNKEEPERS' PASSIONS AWAKEN AN OLD HOTEL

Corner George Inn
Maeystown, Illinois

HIGH on a hill in an old stone church built more than a century ago by German masons, Marcia Braswell paced in front of her altos, baritones, and sopranos. With humble heads bowed, a chorus of busy lips gave rise to a crescendo of notes in preparation for Sunday services the next morning. It was Marcia's night for choir direction, one of the many roles she and innkeeper husband, David, fill in their quest to return a town to its origins.

David and Marcia came to Maeystown in 1988, renovating what was once a hotel into a bed-and-breakfast. Ever since then, they have been hailed for bringing about a renaissance in a village where electricity was some 30 years late; where running water had not been installed until 1978; and where flagstone gutters still line the streets.

Maeystown, Illinois. As I ambled into town over a stone bridge and rounded the corner into a genteel country village of beautiful stone houses, I knew this was a *Brigadoon*. Not many have heard of this Bavarian hollow founded in 1852 by German immigrant Jacob Maeys. It doesn't exactly make daily headlines. But what goes on here every day is a matter of national priority and that is the saving of America's small towns—an effort that usually takes a catalyst and a will on the part of inhabitants.

Both those elements came together as music teacher Marcia and German-language teacher David purchased the rundown hotel and began pouring out all they had in time and money to bring Maeystown's cornerstone back to life.

◄ *I love the bathing beauty of a room featuring a clawfoot tub. Marcia saw the tub for sale on someone's front lawn and had to bid for it! The lovely stone building, visible through the bathroom window, gives added texture to this simply understated room, and is also being restored by the Braswells, who will add two more guest rooms and a German bakery.*

123

Historian Gloria Bundy (granddaughter of Jacob Maeys) and some 150 others who make up the town's population, were hoping for just that. The Braswells were ripe for another rehabilitation and the undertaking of the 4,000-square-foot hotel and attached general store was a perfect match. It took 18 months before they were ready to reopen the **Corner George** with its grand ballroom, four guest rooms, and honeymoon hideaway in the summer kitchen/sausage smokehouse out back.

The Braswells also dug out an old brick wine cellar with its arched ceiling, and left virtually untouched the old technique of beer-staining woodwork, throughout the building. Decorating was done by Marcia, who wanted to make the rooms seem as they were when the hotel was the town hot spot.

The couple also gave the inn its curious name. Between 1907 and 1914, there were four men living side by side on Mill Street with the name George Hoffmann. To keep their identities, each acquired a nickname: Laughing George, Schmitt George (a blacksmith), Fat George and Corner George, for the man who lived at the corner of Mill and Main Street. The whimsical name has brought many visitors to the inn—seeking the secrets of Maeystown, including a man named George Corner—honest!

A first-floor bedroom is done in a muted-mauve wallpaper of stripes and floral cameos, and opens out into the main hallway. The butternut-colored door and staircase were finished in a technique that used beer as part of the staining of the wood. The result is a soft, bubbly look to the wood grain. The Victorian high-back matches the walnut marble-top bureau. The white painted wood floors add a hint of contrast and brightness.

❖ ❖ ❖

▼ The grand ballroom, where Maeystown residents once danced the night away, is now a combination breakfast/living room. Sun filters through the windows during the day, enlightening the ballroom with natural sparkle. Note the lovely detail of the blue and deep pink wallpaper and how (see photo top right) it matches the inn's china, Rose Chintz by Johnson Brothers. That's the real Corner George in his wedding day photo.

▲ *The summer kitchen is lit by western-style lanterns and is warmed by wood floors and its exposed stone foundation.*

◀ *Shrimp and salmon highlights on hunter green wash the Hoffmann Room with old-hotel charm. The hand-painted kerosene lamp with decorative wrought-iron base complements the room's colors so well. A green poinsettia that keeps its blooms all year offers the right color balance.*

◀◀ *The inn's kitchen is done in a simple German country style of blues and white. The cabinet doors were being discarded when the Braswells rescued them and had cabinets built to suit.*

◀ *Ardent preservationists, the Braswells like to leave things intact, such as the way they found the door to their McRoberts Room. Note the way time aged the door at the far right, behind the bed, to a black-ened patina. Marcia liked the texture it provided, and so she left it and designed the color scheme around the door. Arched transom doors lead to a bathroom and powder room.*

❖ ❖ ❖

BEAUTY BEHIND THE BARS: AN INNMATE'S ESCAPE

The Jailer's Inn
Bardstown, Kentucky

THE JAILER'S INN is a prime example of what I mean when I say innkeepers are responsible for saving so many old and significant buildings in America. What else could you do with a former eight-cell-block jail with 30-inch-thick walls, but turn it into another shelter—this time, one for those who come free of handcuffs. And that is just what Fran and Challen McCoy did in 1988 when they purchased the building at auction and began inviting tourists to spend a night in jail. Only a year earlier, misdemeanor offenders were sleeping on hard bunks against the cool (native Kentucky) limestone of the jail's walls.

Now, visitors who descend upon the small town—made famous partially by the Jim Beam distillery—sleep in one of five decorated guest bedrooms in the jail, whose origins date to a small cell built in 1797. A permanent limestone jail was built in 1819, and in 1874, a jailer's residence was added to comply with a new Kentucky mandate that a jailer reside on the property.

The former jailer's residence now houses all but one of the guest bedrooms. The other is an actual former cell. Guest rooms are on two floors and wedged between them is an upstairs dungeon, which the McCoys have kept intact.

"We thought about turning it into a bedroom," explains Fran, "but we are trying to preserve the building's history." The inn has a room full of jailhouse memorabilia, including a gun carved out of soap, which was used in an escape by an inmate in 1986. The prisoner

◀ *The Colonial Room features the jail's natural limestone walls plus the exposed jailhouse ceiling beams that are random widths but 18 inches thick. The beams also form the floor of the "dungeon" directly upstairs. The deep windowsills are a hallmark of the inn and the McCoys added bars for a whimsical touch. Fran stenciled the pineapple symbol of welcome, just in case anyone had second thoughts about the type of hospitality offered here.*

131

❖ ❖ ❖

▼ *The Victorian Room is filled with antiques and Fran's touches. I like the idea of the sheer curtains hung on a rod with valance and jabots over the top to accent the headboard. Many of the antiques were passed down from the innkeeper's grandparents. The walnut roll-top desk is similar to one used in the jailer's residence years ago. I love the way the cobalt blue kerosene lamp base adds color and character.*

painted the soap with black ink, making a guard think it was the real thing. There are also photos of hangings that took place in the jail's rear courtyard where B&B guests now savor breakfast in warm weather and beautiful wedding receptions are a common occurrence.

Most inmates, who were usually no more than 25 years old, spent short sojourns—usually fewer than six months. Today, during tours given at the B&B, guides sometimes hear former prisoners tell their wives and children, "This was my bunk and cell . . . ."

Today, spending a night in the slammer means being surrounded by Colonial and Victorian furnishings while in another part of the building, the peeling paint of the decades serves as a historic reminder.

Bardstown is full of antiques and specialty shops and is home to the Stephen Foster amphitheater. And just across from **The Jailer's Inn** is Hurst Pharmacy, where all your childhood dreams can be relived as you sip a butterscotch malt and bite into a burger at the drugstore's Norman Rockwell-style soda fountain. I don't think being in jail ever felt this good.

► *The former women's cell is now a comfortable guest room you might call Jailhouse Rock. The bottom bunk is a waterbed and the room is decorated in black-and-white except for the color television, so they joke. By the way, breakfast at the inn is anything but bread and water. Fresh fruit, juice, homemade muffins, and a baked dish are the order of the day.*

▼ *The Garden Room used to be an office but is now a lovely bedroom that makes you forget where you are.*

▲ The "dungeon" is just off the second-floor landing. It is certainly a study in contrast. A breakfast table is visible here as part of the dining room that is across from the old cell. Fran used the blue "wallpaper" throughout the inn's common rooms. It is made of brown paper! You crinkle and adhere to the walls. To achieve this elegant, textured, and very inexpensive look, see page 251.

❖ ❖ ❖

DECORATING FROM THE OTHER SIDE OF THE TRACK

Trout City Berth & Breakfast
Buena Vista, Colorado

ALL ABOARD! Train buff or not—this one's for you. It's the ultimate in model railroading: over-nighting in rail cars or a train station at a B&B, or, consider assembling one of your very own such accommodations at home.

When we drove up to **Trout City** in the midst of a mountain pass on a sunny Southwestern day, Irene Kjeldsen was trying to beat us up the hill to extend her hospitality. But let's face it, how fast do you think she can travel the track, pumping her way up the hill in a narrow gauge Victorian hand car?

Her husband, Jules, was with a suspicious group of cowhands—men in leather chaps—and ladies in fancy satin hats and high-button shoes. They were hanging out at the kerosene-lit, mahogany-studded saloon, looking for who killed . . . well, it doesn't matter, we weren't interested in murder (of the mystery-weekend kind), just a few theme decorating ideas to throw in our saddlebags and be off.

As the innkeepers caught up with us, they shed the 19th century and served us a sandwich with a side order of **Trout City** history. Jules was a high-powered Houston oil executive who traded his desk for the Rockies here at Trout Creek Pass in the San Isabel National Forest. As he learned more of the local history, he decided to rejuvenate the former McGee station that once served the nearby mining town of Leadville.

Rather than buy old rail cars that once traversed the Denver South Park and Pacific Railroad, Jules built his own, because he found it

◀ *Twin built-in beds flank either side of the parlor with its beveled windows. There's even a private bath with an organdy-ruffled shower curtain. Bed pillows are crocheted family heirlooms, finished in satin and generous trims of lace and ribbon. Roses are the accents and are even stenciled on the window shades. Maroon velvet berth covers and drapes trimmed in gold fringe complete the Old West bedroom in the Pullman car. The doll on the wicker chair is from a collection displayed in a mercantile store at the inn.*

❖ ❖ ❖

▶ *The breakfast room is in the former ticket area of the old train station. Breakfast is cooked up behind the counter and served with crystal, china, and antique silver by the innkeepers, who wear Old West Victorian costumes. The station also includes two bedrooms. Walls are papered with railroad bonds. A bay window that overlooks the tracks was the ticket agent's domain with telegraph, candlestick phone, and station clock. Mozart and Vivaldi compositions are usually playing in the background.*

too expensive to renovate retired rail cars. So, like any good train aficionado, Jules created the engine, Pullman cars, and caboose in the basement of his mother-in-law's home in Colorado Springs, then hauled them to the site. To ensure accuracy, he worked from authentic railroad-car building plans and Irene took her decorating cue from pictures of period rail cars.

The train station houses two bedrooms. The caboose has four bunks, gingham curtains, and a pot-bellied stove. Visible up the hill is a wooden water tower where laundry dries in the breeze a la "Petticoat Junction."

Trout City pumps its own water and the inn is solar powered. Guests have become accustomed to retiring their hair dryers for this sojourn. We had to hook up a generator for the photography lights and that source drew from solar panels that store energy in the generator's batteries.

But there are many benefits outweighing the minor inconveniences. You can pan for gold, watch the wildlife, and ride up the track in the hand car to work off breakfast and get in some aerobic exercise. And, who knows, you may get side-tracked and decide to build a life-size railroad house for yourself.

❖ ❖ ❖

▲ *On weekends, guests may choose to participate in making a movie with the Old West set Jules built. Usually, it's a comedy. What else?*

▼ *Jules' reproduction of a steam train is now guest quarters. Rooms are fashionably Old Western with dried arrangements in camp coffeepots and needlework pictures of period subjects. Irene made most of the quilts on display and on the beds.*

▲ *Sometimes, breakfast is served outdoors cowboy style from an authentic, 100-year-old (restored) chuck wagon. Granite pots, tin cups, and lots of barbecue sauce are the order of the day.*

❖ ❖ ❖

Regional

The root of all reform
lies in the individual and that
the life of the individual is shaped
mainly by home surroundings.

—GUSTAV STICKLEY

◄ *Casa Benavides*

BLUE SKIES, RED PEPPERS, AND THE GOOD LIFE

Casa Benavides

Taos, New Mexico

THE PERFECT circle of a translucent moon shimmered above the distant hills. Clouds formed like shadows against an indigo sky, creating what might be a design for a Navajo blanket. We were edging toward one of the Land of Enchantment's most scenic, most charming towns—Taos—and one of the Southwest's most spectacular inns—**Casa Benavides,** the "house of good life."

Like the mystical connections they make here between the land, the heavens, and the people in Taos, this bed-and-breakfast brands a colorful pattern in your mind as it weaves together those same elements in its decor and hospitality.

At the center of it all is innkeeper Barbara McCarthy, who never knew that the house she passed every day on her way to school would one day be hers to share with the world—maybe even the universe. "I used to pick blossoms from the trees—these same trees," she explains on a tour of the adobe compound she named **Benavides,** after her family.

Likewise, she never imagined that Tom McCarthy, one of the boys who teased Barbara and her coterie of friends on the way to school, would one day be her husband. But in 1989, Barbara and Tom, who own three shops in town—brimming with all things Southwestern (See Resource Guide.)—decided to buy the old house and restore it. They have also enlarged it to 22 rooms, each distinctly different.

Painted Desert, Aztec, Rio Grande, and Chimayo are a few room names that certainly conjure up regional images. The Georgia O'Keefe Room, with its simple, clean lines typical of the artist's works,

▲ *Although most of its history is lost, this genteel, hand-carved* santos *(saint) of solid wood shows the character of the ages. The statue, draped with crystal rosaries from Barbara's mother, has been in the family since it was crafted sometime in the 1600s. Relics are commonly found in Southwestern decor, and this is one of the innkeeper's most cherished pieces of art.*

◀ *Vivid colors and designs give this small room great presence. A bedspread (just like the one on the bed) forms the curtain, resting on two nails at each end of the window frame and one in the center. The spreads are from Bob Timberlake's line of home furnishings. The Navajo rug is part of Barbara's extensive collection (See Resource Guide to order rugs.) An antique pressing iron acts as a bookend on the bedside desk.*

❖ ❖ ❖

features primitive furniture and pine board floors. The Doña Tules Room, named after a bordello resident, is frilly with crocheted lace curtains and a white iron bed. The San Tomas Room is ecclesiastical—quietly lit and decorated like a chapel with *retablos* and other antique religious art. The Rio Grande Room of natural *viga* ceilings and native log-turned furniture breathes the fiery red tones of hot chili peppers.

"I had the building painted the colors of the earth and sky," Barbara says of the sandy adobe walls and the warm blue trim. Once again, the elements come together. Native American carpenters work at the inn, adding rooms and maintaining others. Barbara's father, Carlos, was one of the Taoseños who built the adobe structure in the early 1900s. The Benavides family lived in one of the buildings in the complex.

A fiesta of good feelings washes over your stay at this inn. I came home longing to do what I've wanted to do for a long time—decorate one of our spare rooms in a Southwestern theme. Armed with fresh ideas from **Casa Benavides,** I was inn-spired.

Casa Benavides

❖ ❖ ❖

◀ *Mexican tiles abound at Casa Benavides and have been used generously in shower stalls and over sinks. Not a bad idea to consider at home to brighten a bathroom.*

◀ *This beautiful sitting area at Casa Benavides is highlighted by Navajo rugs on the floor and one on the oversized chair. The blues in the landscape painting coordinate with dishware on the bountifully carved Mexican hutch. Barbara's flour tortillas and salsa sit with Indian artifacts on the glass table (See Salsa recipe on page 212.)*

❖ ❖ ❖

► *An exciting symmetry of color and design makes this such an inviting sitting area off one of the inn's suites. The winsome peasant in the portrait sets the tones of turquoise, raspberry and dark sienna accents, against the scrubbed pine table. Even the props of hand-woven Indian baskets and the wooden santos fit right in.*

▲ *A gate leading to a courtyard at* Casa Benavides

❖ ❖ ❖

◀ *The walnut headboard is actually a door that dates to the early 1800s. Barbara couldn't resist its simple carvings and even left the black metal lock in place to remind everyone of its original use.*

▲ *A delightful cabinet, filled with ebony pottery and Indian artifacts, has no glass. Barbara never got around to replacing the glass when she refinished the piece. There are a few such cabinets around the inn, which show up the objects inside much more distinctly without glass panes.*

❖ ❖ ❖

ROMANCING THE STONES

Canyon Villa
Sedona, Arizona

THE SKY was a cornflower blue and the sun a brilliant spotlight on the rich red rock formations of Sedona. We were looking for a new inn in the foothills of one of nature's most curious and intriguing regions. Here, fiery terra-cotta ridges, formed at a time I cannot even comprehend, are sculptures with telltale names: Cathedral and Courthouse Rocks, to name a few.

We wound our way through Sedona's swanky but quaint shopping village and soon reached the inn. And what a site! One of the famous formations, Bell Rock, stood majestically in back of the inn. **Canyon Villa,** washed in sandy vanilla walls, appeared with its mission-style peaks and dark, Spanish roof, as if it were a cutout in a 3-D picture, chiseled out of the rock.

Canyon Villa is one of America's newest bed-and-breakfasts, built from the ground up by Chuck and Marion Yadon. As new kids on the block, these novice innkeepers opened in June 1992 and are already role models not just for hospitality and decorating ideas, but as innkeepers. If you're thinking about opening a B&B and want to see how it's done with sophistication yet charm, professionalism yet freshness, and talent yet unpretentiousness, this is the place to tutor yourself through observation. Or, if you're not interested in being an innkeeper but want to be surrounded by some of the neatest rooms and best breakfasts in America, buy your plane ticket now. **Canyon Villa** has it all and then some.

Marion and Chuck named their ten guest chambers after native flowering bushes, which were drawn by an artist, framed and hung on

◀ *The inn's signature cinnamon rolls and red rocks*

149

❖ ❖ ❖

▼ *The tiles of **Canyon Villa**. Miles of decorative tiles accent this lovely inn.*

room doors. Indian Paintbrush, Claret Cup, Gold Poppy, and Strawberry Cactus are a few examples.

"Whenever you think about building a home, location is everything," says Chuck, "and even more so if you want to open a bed-and-breakfast."

No kidding, Chuck took his own pontificating quite literally. Chuck and Marion, who were in property sales and management in their native Tulsa, Oklahoma, searched for years for just the right piece of land. Imagine living with views of these historic rocks right in your living room, dining room, and bedrooms. That's just the way it is at the inn whose south wall is practically all glass with clerestory and arabesque windows stretching everywhere.

Bedrooms were decorated with the rocks in mind. Colors and styles were chosen to complement the outdoors. Marion loves all styles and added Victorian as well as American and French country with accents of family heirlooms and fine art.

When you aren't looking at the rocks, you may well be raising one of Marion's sumptuous cinnamon rolls in your hand. (See recipe, page 220.) Either way, how sweet it is!

◀ *Colors for the inn were chosen to comple-*
ment the view of red rocks outside each
window. This gathering of breakfasters sits
on tapestry chairs, selected for their earthy
tones and the fiery purples and blues that
echo the sunsets beyond the rocks.

▲ *No, this is not a postcard. Famed Bell*
Rock sits smack in the middle of the patio
door from this vantage point in the Spanish
Bayonet Room (so-called in honor of a
native wildflower). The painting above the
mantel sets jewel tones for the room.

▶ *Creating vignettes in decorating is fun, such as this one that includes red hot chili peppers and bright lemons. Even the gold around the picture frame meets its match in the brandy on the table.*

▶ *The soft arch of this folk art room at the inn complements the half circle of the watermelon at the window. A geometric twist on the bedspread just makes this a happy room to visit, and the bathroom tiles carry out the look.*

Canyon Villa

❖ ❖ ❖

◀ *A touch of Santa Fe makes its way to* **Canyon Villa** *in this contemporary rendition. Very little in the way of curtains are hung at this inn to allow for complete views. To make this simple tailored and versatile Stagecoach Valance for any style room, see page 267.*

❖ ❖ ❖

'ARTS AND CRAFTS' AT AN INN WITH A MISSION

The Pebble House
Lakeside, Michigan

TOWARD the end of the 19th century, America was changing its attitude, and along with it, its ideas on decorating the home. The frills of the Victorian era were being replaced with simpler designs by many who were seeking what they called an "honest" craftsmanship, particularly celebrating nature. Out went the frills and in came straight lines, simple muslin and embroidered fabrics, and matte-finished pottery.

A new breed of thinker was searching for changes at home while at the same time espousing a need for better working conditions, health reform, nutrition, and exercise. What emerged was the so-called Arts and Crafts Movement, also called Mission style because the furniture was said to have a "mission" to make the world a better, more egalitarian place. The look had as much emphasis on aesthetics and elevating crafts to an art form as it did on social reform. Handmade furniture and thrown pottery painted in earth tones became hallmarks of the style, which has been heartily embraced by innkeepers Jean and Ed Lawrence.

The Lawrences have been collecting antique Mission furniture for nearly two decades, and probably have the best example of a complete Mission-style inn in America. **The Pebble House** is certainly different from most country inns, and with that difference comes a freshness and a new appreciation for this unusual design period.

The Pebble House challenges your perspective. The style has had its critics who see it as stark, with function over form. Yet you can-

◀ *Just as the exterior is faced with local river rock dating to 1912, so too is the fireplace in the inn's gathering room, where wine and cheese are served every evening.*

155

❖ ❖ ❖

▲ *Arms from two Mission chairs, characteristic of the style.*

▶ *Coved ceilings add to the geometric flair of Mission decor in the inn's breakfast room, which overlooks the parlor (left) and the library (rear). Roycroft revival china in sleek lines of red, black, and white sets the table at* **The Pebble House.** *(See Resource Guide.) Note the wall hanging above the mirrored sideboard. Jean is an artist and complemented the inn with this pebble depiction. It was not uncommon for wall hangings to be positioned to the right or left instead of in the middle of an arrangement, as Jean has done here.*

not help but rejoice in the Lawrences' interpretation. It may even send you running to introduce the line into your own home . . . here it is a millennium later, and as we move toward the turn of another century, history is repeating itself. Mission style is in again. Manufacturers have introduced goods with the Mission theme. Sherwin Williams paint company offers "Roycroft Arts and Crafts," a palette of American interior colors. Ethan Allen, Thomasville, and other furniture companies are selling Arts and Crafts-inspired furniture lines.

Jean, who first took a liking to the style in Wisconsin where her Girl Scout camp was furnished with craftsman pieces, displays handsome accents such as her collection of bright vases and unusual stained-glass lamps, all true to the period.

The Pebble House invites long, lingering hours of conversation among guests, or folding up by a bright, sunny window in the privacy of a good book, or a walk across the street to Lake Michigan. Everything you do at this wonderful little bed-and-breakfast seems perfectly natural, as it was designed to be.

◀ *The lovely and rare antique bookcase lamp serves form as well as function in* **The Pebble House** *living room.*

▼ *The* Arts and Crafts *look includes furniture pieces enhanced by stained glass as is this slim end table at the foot of the Stickley-style bed. The bath of muted yellow on the walls allows for a canvas of dark wood, typical of the period.*

❖ ❖ ❖

CHERISHED LONGINGS FOR THE LOG LOOK

Log Cabin Guest House
Galena, Illinois

FEATURED are three authentic log cabins and a coach house suite (circa 1830). Forgivably, central air conditioning, heat, and modern plumbing have been added. So reads a blurb from the brochure for the **Log Cabin Guest House.** The owners, the Bernard family, apologize for having to add twentieth-century amenities to their outdated but much-in-style log houses.

Log cabins and small lodges are a sought-after design craze again, some say brought on by the popularity of the television series, "Northern Exposure." Others say they are the last bastion of ultimate escape. So it's understandable why we are even doing faux log-cabin finishes in family rooms and spare bedrooms at home to get the look.

We can't all go out and buy a log cabin. For one thing, there are very few authentic ones left. But nothing is more American in housing than a log cabin, and a visit to this enclave of three cabins was a step back in time to the Land of Lincoln.

The working farm has been home to one cabin since 1865 when it was built by a Civil War veteran. Two more cabins, built around 1859, were found in Wisconsin, dismantled and brought to the farm for guest quarters.

Visiting the **Log Cabin Guest House** inspired me to look into doing a room with chinked logs and then filling it with Adirondack-style furniture and other outdoorsy pieces. I bought my first accent for the room as a gift to my husband. It was a slate plaque with a hand-painted scene of a log cabin on the edge of a small lake in the midst of

◀ *An old water pump and antique ironing board are accent pieces in a rustic cabin that is softened by lace curtains.*

159

❖ ❖ ❖

tall pines. "Welcome to the Lake" it says. I found out where I can purchase old barn-wood beams and we plan to sink them in plaster all around the room. Unless, in the meantime, we find our dream log cabin on a lake somewhere!

▼ *Simply decorated, this cabin retains its original flavor. Steps at left lead to a modern whirlpool-tub bathroom loft with simple decoration, including the grapevine wreath.*

❖ ❖ ❖

▼ *The inside of another cabin is white-washed, giving the cabin a brighter look, while still retaining its charm. Red and blue add to the color in the room, which is also brought out in the sofa throw and corner cupboard in the sitting area of the cabin. The stone floor adds texture and character, with a braided rug providing warmth.*

Country European

... once you have traveled,
the voyage never ends, but is played out
over and over again in the quietest chambers,
that the mind can never break off
from the journey.

—PAT CONROY, *THE PRINCE OF TIDES*

◀ *The Inn at Summer Hill*

❖ ❖ ❖

IN EVERY ROOM A FLOWER BLOOMS

The Inn on Summer Hill
Summerland, California

*"Nature like a great poet,
knows how to produce the grandest effects
with the fewest materials. You have only
a sun, trees, flowers,
water, and love."*

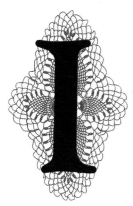

▲ *A vial of posies is held by Cupid in this unusual vase, available from the inn. A missive on inn stationery awaits the finishing hand of what must surely be a romantic greeting! Fresh pansies were picked from the inn's container gardens.*

I N 1890, Margaret MacDonald Pullman penned those words in a book called *Summerland.* Although she was referring to the coastal village along the Pacific, just outside of Santa Barbara, she may as well have been talking about Mabel Shults, an innkeeper who, as a matter of fact, not only did as nature did in Pullman's eyes, but also paid tribute to nature, with her **Inn on Summer Hill.**

Every guest chamber at the inn bursts with the tokens of nature. Flowers in patterns spread out on the beds, climb upon the walls, and tiptoe about dhurrie and hand-hooked rugs. Even keepsake antique trunks and covered lampshades sprout the nosegays of a gardener's day in the sun. The pick of the floral crop abounds in vials by the bedside and even in a glass vase whose suction cup allows it to actually hang upon the face of a mirror.

Mabel Shults planted and sowed each room to enrapture its inhabitants in their own secret garden. Furniture is primarily warm, light pine woods, most of which Mabel had designed in Europe. Each room seems like a French country cottage.

The European feel is also evident in the inn's dining room. Its

◀ *A European chef serves fervent morning fare in the intimate breakfast room. Farmhouse animals on iron chairs with soft cushions pop up above the table. Mabel's collection of old and new teapots crowns the dining room, while Battenburg placemats hosting Bread Pudding (See recipe, page 211.) await fresh-eyed guests.*

▶ *Fireplaces are romantic and the inn has a gas-powered one in every room. Even the mantels were decorated to enhance the room, and notice how the stack of black-bound books accents the wallpaper border.*

▲ *Every room at the inn features an antique trunk, refurbished and hand-painted to match colors and textures in the room. This detail of one of those chests shows that any trunk—even one with slats across the top—can be brought to artistic life.*

casual, family-style seating, fireplace, and candlelight give you the sense of a friendly farmhouse.

The inn itself is a mix of California craftsman style and seaside bungalow. Latticed trellises reach toward the sky and glorify the gardens. Tiny buds of kalanchoes adorn window boxes and garden patches are highlighted by sculptures.

Four o'clock is time for hors d'oeuvres, dishes filled with crudités and tasty spreads. And if that isn't enough, after going out to dinner on the town, the inn has dessert waiting upon your return.

Mabel is the owner of an interior design firm in Santa Barbara that specializes in inns and hotels. Although her training was in music, her natural desire to put colors together and make shapes work in harmony propelled her into the design business. That's why when you see some of the rugs at the inn and notice how well they match with the draperies, you will understand that the rugs were made in Europe to match the fabric.

Romance is what Mabel has created at **The Inn on Summer Hill.** You walk into a guest chamber and classical music is playing softly, but I defy you to find the hidden speakers. A heart doormat leads guests through every room and, in the morning, you find a card outside your door informing you of the day's predicted weather. But who cares what the forecast is. It's always sunny in your room.

▲ *"Innterior" designer Mabel Shults shows how perfectly at home walls of floral wallpaper are with a boisterous checked sofa and a floral side chair.*

▲ *A restored Victorian trunk was painted with flowers, the symbol of the inn. There's no shortage of fabric in guest chambers that ooze with floral textiles.*

▼ *Patterns of hydrangea spread like wildflowers in this seductive room at the inn. The colors were chosen to complement the view outside. If you look beyond the French doors, you can see the Pacific Ocean. The canopy was made by weaving slats of sewn fabric straps, leaving hemmed pockets on the ends to slide onto the canopy rails. The fabric belt tie-back offers a contrasting fabric as well as a great idea for any tie-back. "Belt" buckles are available at sewing-supply shops.*

❖ ❖ ❖

An Inn of Many Lands Embraces a Traveler's Interlude

Hillbrook Inn

Charles Town, West Virginia

*"At the end of a flat,
grassy clearing, a table for two
had been set in the shade of a sprawling scrub oak—
a table with a crisp white cloth, with ice buckets,
with starched cotton napkins, with bowls of fresh flowers,
with proper cutlery and proper chairs . . .
All my misgivings had vanished. This was as far away
from a damp bottom—and ant sandwiches—
as one could possibly imagine."*

UTHOR Peter Mayle's description of an elegant picnic, although written of France in his best-selling book, *Tojours Provence*, couldn't better describe the culinary forays on the misty and magical grounds of **Hillbrook Inn.** Yes, there are grassy clearings, in fact, ones where geese waddle to a gently flowing stream. Yes, there are oaks, but willows and ferns too. And yes, the fine linens and fresh flowers are there. But what is proper is not just cutlery and chairs. **Hillbrook** is also properly pretentious, gracious, and distinct.

When diners wish to be outside, the extremely talented chef, Christine Hale, prepares a sumptuous feast that may be taken at outdoor garden tables or on the grounds, which, for some, is even more romantic. Inside, the intimate dining room is splashed with candlelight and polished brass, and the food ranks as some of the best in the region. Even the coffee is special, served in a gentrified manner in demitasse cups.

▲ *Gretchen Carroll has a knack for pulling a room together. The wallpaper is unusual in color and design and yet the innkeeper found the most complementary painting, with, of course, the ubiquitous face. Although from different eras, the woman in the painting and the Whistler-inspired Madame Mieux on the dummy board add the same sense of mystery to the room. Dummy boards hail from the 19th century when they were used as fireboards to thwart chimney drafts. (See Resource Guide.)*

The main house nestles terrace-style along a limestone ridge surrounded by Impressionistic gardens. Behind the English country stucco and stone house, a wooden walking bridge and a fresh-water spring house punctuate the landscape.

Innkeeper Gretchen Carroll is part of a family of diplomats, and so she has traveled widely. Residing in so many exotic lands, including Turkey and Thailand, helped her formulate the decor at the inn. Common rooms such as a library, parlor, and tavern (that was once a garage) are filled with objects of unusual shapes, adding excitement and color. The main thread that runs through her collection is the motif of faces that appears on the pottery, canvasses, and carvings of countries all over the world.

"One day, it hit me that I am drawn to art with faces," Gretchen tells me. The resulting decorating scheme is most individual and harmonious—which seems to carry over into everything they do at **Hillbrook.** Once in awhile, when the inn is quiet, you can even hear melodious voices. The chef and innkeeper have been known to strike up a chorus of serious song as Christine peels the turnips and shaves the carrots. Of all faces, these are two of the most lively. And you will put on your own new face—an enlightened and satisfied one—before you leave Gretchen Carroll's corner of the world.

Hillbrook Inn

❖ ❖ ❖

▼ *Gretchen's much-traveled curios in the living room at* **Hillbrook** *show you how a room can take on a global presence. Burnished red walls are a great color for contrasting a room's architectural as well as decorative features. Here, an elliptical table hosts an assortment* *of foreign brass. The loveseat in the foreground picks up the blues and red-oranges. Adding to the drama are a luminous picture window and wooden beams that sculpt the room and lead to the Locke's Nest guest room upstairs.*

❖ ❖ ❖

▶ *Sometimes the best decorating solutions turn up instantly after you have spent hours looking for just the right accent. When Gretchen was getting ready to open the inn, she realized at the last minute that her long search for just the right piece to hang above the sideboard had been fruitless—until a friend's sketches of pears saved the day. At least, Gretchen deduced, she could hang them temporarily. But the pears went so perfectly that to her surprise, she needed look no further.*

▲ *Romantic picnics for two are often taken on* **Hillbrook's** *grounds. An alternative to a picnic blanket on the grass is a rug.*

❖ ❖ ❖

THE FRESH FEEL AND TENDER TOUCH OF GEMÜTLICH

Swiss Woods

Lititz, Pennsylvania

He went to the fireplace . . .
sat down on the three-legged wooden stool with the
round seat and kindled a bright fire. Almost immediately
the kettle began to boil, and the old man held over the fire
a large piece of cheese at the end of a long iron fork.
He moved it this way and that until it was golden yellow on all sides . . .
When the grandfather brought the toasted cheese to the table,
it was already nicely laid with the round loaf of bread,
two plates, two knives, for Heidi had noticed the cupboard,
and knew that all would be needed for the meal . . .
the grandfather filled the bowl (with cheese) again to the brim
and placed it before the child, who looked
quite content as she began to eat her bread,
after it had been spread with the
toasted cheese, soft as butter.
—Johanna Spyri, Heidi

THE LINES from the classic story of a little orphan and her grandfather describe fondue, before it evolved into what it is today. The passage also sets the scene for what Switzerland reminds us of—cheese, open spaces, hilltops, and friendly people—all of the things the visitor finds at **Swiss Woods** today.

At first it may seem unlikely for an ethnic bed-and-breakfast to be in rural America. But the inn is a part of the Pennsylvania Dutch community. **Swiss Woods** is tucked into a back country road, on a hilly 30-acre plot, and was built by Debbie and Werner Mosimann, who live there with their children.

◀ *On special winter evenings,* **Swiss** *Woods guests cozy up to a dining room table, in view of a winking fire, and enjoy a pot of melting cheese and French bread. On this table, knick-knacks from the inn—a leather milking cap, authentic cow bells, antique accordion, and carved wooden animals from Switzerland—add to the festivities. Even the guest book is from another land. (See page 219 for fondue recipes.)*

177

▲ *Breakfast is about to be served, but not until Debbie has gathered morning flowers. When the Mosimanns built their inn, they planned that every room would look out onto a garden. The inn's breakfast plates also reflect the Appenzell region, but Debbie found the Swiss-made plates in America. They look similar to the rug hanging above the raclette. (See photo, page 180.) A print of Swiss life in the 1900s by Debbie's favorite artist, Albert Anker, hangs above the morning table.*

▲ *"Nordish schlafen" describes how guests sleep at the inn—without a top sheet. An all-weather natural comforter is covered with a duvet and that's your top sheet. "Sleeping northern" as the translation implies, means not having to get tangled up in a sheet. Debbie says so many guests write to tell her they have changed their bedding at home, because they never slept so soundly as at Swiss Woods.*

Swiss-born Werner met Debbie when she was working as a missionary in Belgium. Debbie, although American, spoke Werner's language, in more ways than one. The couple was soon married and lived in Switzerland when they started having children. They later decided to come to America where the kids could be close to their grandparents.

In 1986, the Mosimanns built a Swiss-style chalet with a dark wood roof and an imposing stone fireplace. A Swiss ambassador has stayed here as well as other dignitaries, looking for a piece of their homeland.

Guests usually spend the day shopping and sightseeing or in a seasonal sports activity. The inn is decorated in light woods and clean lines. You will hear foreign languages spoken here and, once in awhile, eat fondue. (See recipes, page 219.)

The flag that flies along with the American banner is Werner's Canton Bear, signifying his town of origin. But to **Swiss Woods** guests of all backgrounds, it has become a symbol of warmth, good cheer, and a place to experience a European *auberge*.

❖ ❖ ❖

▶ *Hand-hooked rugs make great decorations. The colors in this one are the key to the decor in the facing living room. The colors and design of the costume indicate the area called Appenzell, from which Werner and Debbie's ancestors hail. On the table is raclette, a style of cooking served to skiers in the Alps. It was originally titled after a cheese of that name. Now, Gruyère, Muenster, Tilister, and Monterey Jack are cut in thick slices and melted in individual little trays over a burner. The cheese is scraped with wooden spatulas onto boiled or fried potatoes, and I can testify that it is delicious.*

▼ *The teepees in the garden are for white pole beans growing next to curious onions. Werner takes care of the inn's gardens, which yield asparagus, elderberries, raspberries, blueberries, zucchini, carrots, tomatoes, Indian corn, and pumpkins, to name a few items. Werner sells much of the produce to area open markets.*

Swiss Woods

❖ ❖ ❖

◄ *Six different woods in the inn plus 64 colors in the needlepoint by Debbie's mom, add color to* **Swiss Woods.** *Cherry, oak, ash, walnut, pine, and cedar in the ceilings and furniture offer texture, color, and design. The hydrangea or purple snowballs on the sideboard in this light and airy gathering room were just picked from the gardens. A round wooden cheese box serves as footstool.*

❖ ❖ ❖

OLD WORLD PRESENCE SPINS NEW IDEAS

Antrim 1844
Taneytown, Maryland

▲ *Ferdinand, the inn's resident mascot, waddles down a snowy lane at Antrim, past the ice house guest cottage in a scene reminiscent of a quiet lane in the French countryside.*

IF YOU want to know how to do your home with style, character, and personality, you will be inspired by innkeeper Dorothy (Dort) Mollet's unintimidating approach to decorating.

Although Dort has what you would expect of a decorator's vitae, she is anything but typical. Instead of a lot of money and design rules, she invests adventure, excitement, and a free spirit in her decorating. The results are show-stopping rooms that have reason but no rhyme. Harmony but no chorus.

Much of her secret wizardry is in her approach to fabrics. "They must be mounted to a wall naturally," she says. "Fabrics fall so individually that artists even have a hard time capturing their essence in paintings." That's why Dort rarely uses curtain rods. For her, they represent unnecessary structure. Instead, she fastens and forms—even the longest and most luxurious of window treatments—with the mere tap of a staple gun.

Dort suggests approaching decorating with the confidence to try most anything. She advises, "If you love a certain item—a painting, a fabric—start to plan the room around that source and everything will fall into place."

Knowing her fearless approach to decorating and to life, it is no surprise that she and husband Richard took on the massive restoration of **Antrim,** a 24-acre plantation built by Andrew Ege from county Antrim in Ireland. Dort and Richard left their jobs to open the inn in 1990. It took everything they had. The inn comprises a main house and several out-buildings.

◀ *The Clabough Room in the main house features an Empire-style bed and more of Dort's easy-to-design window treatments.*

183

It was probably also Dort's undaunted spirit that propelled her and Richard to check, one day in 1992, on a wreck of a house in town that was about to be torn down. Amidst snickers from those touting them as foolhardy, the Mollets had the 1861 home (they guessed the date from a bottle burrowed in a basement wall) moved less than a mile to **Antrim** where they brought it back to life as their own home and living quarters. It seems as though the petite four-room house was always part of the plantation. It stands pertly but majestically in the center of a formal European boxwood-maze garden.

The main house, with its Greek columns and high ceilings, embodies a playful mix of stately Colonial and whimsical decor. Hepplewhite-style furnishings with yards of flowing fabrics work well with Dort's spontaneous style. "I never order anything." Instead, she scours auctions for antiques and discount stores for designer fabrics.

After you visit **Antrim,** you go home with a new, unbridled attitude about everything, especially home decorating.

▲ *The 1861 home the Mollets saved from destruction by moving it to the inn*

▶ *The Ryan Room (named after one of the Mollets' teenage sons) bursts with garden taste. A wooden frame was mounted to the wall, batting glued to the wood and fabric, wrapped like a present, to form this Breath-of-Spring Lace Cornice. (See directions on page 269.)*

◀ *Bold colors accent the Brandon Room (named after the Mollets' other son). Note what you can do with a make-from-scratch headboard and how to treat a window with an awning effect. (See page 262 for instructions.)*

▲ *In The Cottage, which was once the plantation office, the look of Versailles is captured with cascades of lace and a canine dummy board. The room began with nothing more than a mattress and a box spring. Once Dort dug in, she created a regal throne with a layered canopy. (See page 260 to make the canopy.)*

In the ice house, a tablecloth with a lace napkin at each post forms the canopy. The Angel-Wing Swag at the head of the bed is one piece of fabric, gathered on a bracket and tied at the sides. (See directions, page 268.) The stone foundation was re-shored, adding texture. Dutch doors bring the outside in.

The ice house never had floors—as storage was 12 feet below ground level. In addition to wide boards, Richard installed the newel posts from an old front porch he bought at auction. The posts grace the entry to the bedroom and the whirlpool-bath area.

Puffy clouds on the ceiling were painted by Dort to complement the rare 18th-century French mirrored vanity (to the right of the fireplace) and its painted porcelain sinks. These heavenly cherub bowls have no drain. Years ago, they discarded water—at the flip of the bowl—into buckets which the servants later removed. It works much the same way today for guests, who enjoy the experience of another lifetime.

They don't call this the Carriage Room for nothing. Dort and Richard wheeled the old prairie buggy into the restored barn one day and never took it out. Why not a carriage in a house? *wondered Dort.* Its black chassis and red wheels determine the room's rich colors. The Crunch 'n Pouf curtain with valance is wired so that you can turn up the edges and see a complementary fabric. (See directions on page 270.) The carriage hides a mini-bar and stereo in the sitting room. The stairs lead to a bedroom. In the Sleigh Room next door, there is—what else—a Currier-and-Ives-style sleigh in the bedroom!

◄ *The library at the main house features a dance-out-to-the-front-porch window. The Scalloped Swag window treatment is one example of the innkeeper's no-rod curtain mount. (See directions on page 266.)*

◄ *Who would ever think to put a ceramic fish and a dainty Victorian umbrella together—in a bathroom, no less! The innkeeper's zany approach to decorating shows how stepping aside and seeing what works pays off. To make these lovely curtains, mount a small continental rod and add a hemmed curtain with a wide pocket. To get the double-dipped effect, bring florist's wire up through the middle. Fasten at the back. Add complementary fabric and drape over the top of the rod. Bunch up with florist's wire and secure to the wall.*

Take-Home Tips from the Innkeepers

The housewife . . .
was up by sunrise everyday,
making the rounds of the kitchen, the smokehouse,
the dairy, the weaving room, and the garden,
with a basket of keys on one arm,
and of knitting on the other;
and who, as the needles flew, would attend to
every one of the domestic duties,
preside at a bountiful breakfast table,
resume rounds to visit the sick . . .
and then sitting down to her
books and music . . .

—*THE SEASONAL HEARTH*

◀ *Poor Farm Country Inn*

❖ ❖ ❖

MORE INNTERIOR DECORATING

QUICK DECORATING TIPS

Painted Stairs

Steps and risers at **The Southern Hotel** were painted red and topped with trompe l'oeil treads painted by the innkeeper. Not only does it make for an interesting stairway, but it keeps you alert as it fools the eye.

Wallpaper Those Flower Pots

At the **Inn at Fordhook Farm** in Doylestown, Pennsylvania, the Burpee family (yes, they are the family who started the seed company), has dressed up colorful throw pillows by tacking down an attractive handkerchief—on the diagonal so that it appears as a diamond. They also make plain flower pots special by gluing wallpaper around the top of the pot or around the entire pot.

Small Night Tables

Plant stands make great night tables for tight spots. —**Hersey House**

◀ *Many of us would love to have a wall of bookcases with the romantic rolling ladder we've seen in aristocratic mansions. It was Poor Farm innkeeper Dottie Hoestler's dream also, but her Colorado inn didn't have such a luxury. Suddenly a light went on and Dottie figured out how she could have one, too. The innkeeper commissioned a local carpenter to design the ladder, incorporating her idea to install a garage door track and wheels so the entire apparatus would glide across the bookcase. Now she and her guests' (B. J. Robinson from Oklahoma in this photo) favorite "reads" are only a step and a slide away. (In the mid-19th century poor farms cared for the penniless.)*

Decorating a Staircase

A basket attached to a balustrade can add interest to a staircase. Fill it with complementary flowers. Add a grapevine wreath to a hallway wall and keep a small electric candle in the middle of the wreath to find your way up those stairs. —**The Homeplace**

Dispense with Paper Cup Holders

Forget those ugly plastic paper cup holders for a bathroom. At **The John F. Craig House** in Cape May, New Jersey, antique mugs and cups are more decorative and will keep demi-paper cups from flying around the room.

Decorating for Security Reasons

Glass displays can be deterrents to burglars. That's why Marguerite Swanson decorated a threshold window at her **Durham House** in Houston, Texas, with blue glass knick-knacks. The glass reflects colorful light inside and is also a known precaution. Thieves prefer not to risk entry, even if the location of the window would make it easy. Shattering glass creates unwanted noise.

Hide Facial Tissues with a Bag

Use a decorative gift bag from a card shop to hide facial tissue boxes. The cost is less than a plastic holder and the result more interesting. Make sure the top of the bag is within one inch of the top of the box. If the bag is too deep, place a half brick or small bowl in the bag to boost the box to the proper level. —**Durham House**

❖ ❖ ❖

Making Use of Old Iron Floor Grates

Many of us have adapted old sewing tables by gutting the cabinets and adding glass and other tops. But not many have done what **The Anniversary Inn** has done. Located in Estes Park, Colorado, the inn suggests that a heavy ornate iron floor grate from an old house's heating system may also be used for a table top.

Creating a Canopy

Hang a lace curtain panel on each of the four corners of a tester bed instead of using a canopy cover. Add a nosegay to the inside of each corner, so that you have appealing decoration on the inside of the bed as you sit up and read before turning lights out. (See photo page 199.)—**The Southern Hotel**

Rehab an Old Lampshade

Upgrade or change a lampshade, simply by dyeing it another color and adding trims around the base with a glue gun.

A Desk in the Bathroom

Many people have converted old bureaus to sink vanities. **Manor House** has used old desks for that purpose as the desks have a knee-hole space, making them more serviceable, plus drawers for toiletries.

▼ *The romantic front parlor at* **Park Avenue Guest House** *is accented by pieces of vintage clothing from the innkeeper's fashionable collection.*

❖ ❖ ❖

The Innkeepers' Ten Keys to Successful Decorating at Home

❀ Begin decorating a room on paper first to avoid costly and unsatisfying mistakes. —Karen Owens, **The King's Cottage.** (See the Room Designing Planner for your use at home on pages 241–244.)

❖

❀ Buy only what you truly like; then it will always work in your home. —Gretchen Carroll, **Hillbrook Inn**

❖

❀ When you hear yourself saying, "wow" over a color or a pattern, go with that first impression. You will tire less of something that is interesting and exciting than you will of something you settle on because it is more conservative. Don't be afraid of following your emotions when decorating. —AnneMarie Simko Defreest, **Inn at the Round Barn Farm**

❖

❀ Decorating does not need to be intimidating. Whatever your personal style, it's okay. Let your home really reflect who you are, and you will never be unhappy with it. —Dort Mollet, **Antrim 1844**

❖

❀ You don't need a fortune to decorate beautifully. Consider all resources available, including discount stores and consignment and antiques shops for hidden gems. —Diana Trembly, **Manor House**

❖

❀ If you have trouble fully visualizing a room, visit decorator showhouses or furniture shops that have room displays and you will gather confidence as well as ideas. —Jane Schultz, **Chicago Pike Inn**

❀ When decorating a historic home, it is important to consider the structural elements of the building to complement your decorating efforts. Keep in mind history, architectural characteristics, ambient light, and your own personality. Allow the building to speak to others through your decorating. —Marcia Braswell, **Corner George Inn**

❖

❀ Hiring a decorator doesn't mean that you aren't involved in your home. The designer is a great resource for finding furniture and decorative accessories. A decorator takes away a great deal of the confusion and frustration of decorating, especially when you are doing more than one room at a time. You actually save more in the long run. —Marion Yadon, **Canyon Villa**

❖

❀ Color strongly influences how you will feel in a room, even to affecting your appetite. When decorating a room, consider the influences of color, not just for its obvious characteristics, but for its inward effects. Pink, for example, enhances food, so it is good for dining rooms. Blue in a bathroom reflects poorly on skin. Green evokes peacefulness. —Carlton Wagner, **The Bayberry Inn** (Note: Innkeeper Carlton Wagner is also a color consultant to major corporations. See Resource Guide for his books.)

❖

❀ Decorating is a process. A house may be built and decorated quickly, but creating a home happens over time. —Jean Lawrence, **The Pebble House**

▲ *Maple Leaf Cottage innkeeper Jerry Taetz recycled this old roof gable into a decorative headboard in one of the cottages.*

Hat Decor

Hats are an interesting decorative accessory. Now is the time to start collecting hatpins and add them to the hats to increase interest and have a suitable place to collect this jewelry.

Speaking of hats, they may also be used as flower pots for artificial greenery or house plants. **Walnut Street** has employed an old felt derby to host a Boston fern. And I love the inn's idea of making a hat a part of a framed and hanging picture. A prairie man's straw hat, for example, could complement a folk-art farm scene. A cloche could top a 1930s scene. Hang the hat on the wall at one of the corners of the frame, making sure that the brim overlaps the frame by several inches.

Fabric Border

Instead of wallpaper as a border, you can create a warm look by using fabric that coordinates with the colors and other fabrics in the room. The fabric is edged between strips of wood or decorative molding. Here's how:

1. Cut long lengths of fabric in desired widths (probably no more than 6 inches wide). Set the fabric aside.
2. Measure out the wall to position the fabric. Make pencil marks so that you can line up the fabric per-

▼ *Underneath the glass tabletop in the dining room at* **Maple Leaf Cottage Inn,** *guests find lace, fabric, and botanical seed packets, adding to the room's decor. (See photo on page 43 for a larger picture of the dining room.)*

▲ *Park Avenue Guest House innkeeper Sharon Fallbacher likes to use the things she collects. Here in the inn's breakfast room, general store merchandise and kitchen collectibles are both useful and practical.*

fectly straight. If mounting the border at ceiling height, be sure to leave room to add the molding. Staple the fabric in place, making sure it is pressed flatly against the wall.

3. Cut and stain or paint the molding. Mount the fabric to the wall with a staple gun.
4. Mount the molding on top and bottom edges of the fabric with nails. To learn how to cover an entire wall with fabric, see page 251.

Sewing Table Idea

When transforming an antique sewing table into a kitchen island or table, consider spray-painting the wrought-iron base a bone white. It looks smashing and shows off the fancy grill in an artistic, delicate way.

Dish Towel Shower Curtain

New dish towels, sewn together, can make an interesting patchwork quilt drape for the bathtub with shower.

Guest Towels

Another way to leave towels out for visiting friends or relatives is to fold them and tie with pretty ribbon or fabric in a bundle and leave them at the foot of the bed or on a generous-sized bathroom countertop.

▲ *Postage stamps and stenciling make for easy screen decorating at* **The Southern Hotel.** *Safeguard the stamps in plastic shields before gluing to the wood.*

Planning for Decorating

Even if you are finished decorating a room, always keep paint chips, fabric swatches, wallpaper samples, or any colorways of your rooms in a handy envelope stored under the front seat of your car. This way, if you are out somewhere, you will have your patterns with you when you least expect you will need them. Or, get yourself a printed folder with pockets for each room, such as is available from Marcia McAllister in the Resource Guide.

Tub Talk

Dress a clawfoot tub with a lace border mounted underneath the lip by stringing ribbon through the lace and tying it at the front of the tub with a bow hanging down.

Shower Convenience

Attach a strong strip of plastic or wood to a shower door jamb. It puts your towel within reach after you shower.

▼ *Walnut Street Inn had antique dining room chairs painted to match vignettes in the room's wallpaper. (See photo on page 98 of the entire dining room with other chairs.)*

❖ ❖ ❖

Fabric Scrap Decor

Roll and tie those bundles of fabric scraps you have been saving and place them in a glass bowl or large pickle jar and add coordinating color to a room.

Old Shoes

I love innkeeper Linda Busteed's collection of high-button and other darling antique shoes at her **Windham Hill Inn**

▼ *Lace curtain panels form the bed dressing in the Gentleman's Room at* **The Southern Hotel.** *The nosegay accents the panels and offers a decorative touch you can enjoy when sitting up in bed.*

in West Townshend, Vermont. Linda stuffs her shoes with a pouff of complementary printed fabric popping out of the tops. You can also do this with pretty papers or colored soft tissue paper.

Table Runners for Curtains

Lace table runners can make lovely window treatments for those slender windows on each side of the front door. Mount with heavy straight pins or flat thumbtacks. You may want to pinch the centers by tying with a decorative ribbon or a velvet tassel.

Armoire Decor

Wardrobes, especially some antique ones that may be in poor shape, can be spruced up inside as well as outside. Cover the backs and/or sides of the "closets" with wallpaper. A brighter paper will eclipse the darkness inside. Or, if you display the piece with open doors, the paper makes an attractive addition to the room.

Artistic Print Warning

Beware of prints that are signed by artists and read *Limited Edition.* Some artists also come out with the same print unsigned in open stock. Know what you're buying.

Scenting the House

For a natural home deodorizer, they get out the old crock pot at **Garth Woodside Mansion.** Innkeeper Irv Feinberg fills the pot with water and any used rinds from breakfast. He adds a few drops of potpourri oil and lets the mixture simmer all day.

Wet Towel Alert

If you have ever had guests who put their wet towels on your furniture, consider blaming yourself. There needs to be a place for the guests to put them. At **Herr Farmhouse,** there are large baskets with a dainty sign that says, "Wet Towels."

▲ *In her decorating philosophy of bringing the outdoors in,* **Maple**
Leaf Cottage *innkeeper Patty Taetz employed a cornice of ginger-*
bread to highlight the room's curtain treatment.

Keeping Notes Organized

Small baskets on doorways are receptacles for guest messages
at **The Wooden Rabbit.** What a clever idea. This way, no
one can blame you for having lost an important message.

Keep a notepad in the pantry for jotting down a food item
you have just depleted, suggests Deb Lintner of **Hillside**
Farm.

Mount a Curtain with Clothespins

You can use an assortment of unconventional means for
mounting curtains as we have seen at **Antrim 1844.** But to
add to that list, consider hanging cafes or valances with
clothespins or clips of any kind. At **Gardens of Eden,** you
will see a window treated with a piece of pocket-hemmed
muslin resting on a thin dowel that is hung on the window
with string.

A Table-Napkin Tablecloth

Add a small fabric accent topper to a round side table by
sewing together four cloth napkins. Add a lace trim between the napkins as you sew them together.

Kitchen Chair Cushions

Make mismatched kitchen chair cushions. Try different
colors of the same pattern or different patterns that work
together.

Easy-to-Make Potpourri Balls

Buy foam balls the size of an orange. Cover with craft glue.
Dip in finely-mashed potpourri, covering the ball completely. Spot decorate by gluing on snippets of ribbon or
lace. Add a ribbon to hang and place in the closet. —**The**
Palmer House

Bench Those Shoes!

Guests follow the far eastern custom of removing their shoes
when entering **Alaska's 7 Gables B&B.** It reminds me to

❖ ❖ ❖

put a small bench in the foyer where guests can remove shoes to keep dirt off the floors and the noise of our hardwoods throughout to a minimum. The inn's owner, Paul Welton, also suggests adding a basket of slipper socks next to the bench. "Buttons or lace, shoes off at this place," reads a sign over the inn's bench. A warm idea from cold Fairbanks.

Egg Crates for Small Objects

When reorganizing his garage, Vic Mangini of **The Greenfield Inn,** uses empty egg cartons to sort scattered nuts and bolts—great also for organizing a desk drawer full of paper clips, thumbtacks, and such.

Fireplaces

Fireplaces are practical as well as decorative. Here are some tips for enjoying yours at home.

■ Today, anyone can have the cheer of a fireplace at home with the convenience of gas. **Walnut Street Inn** explains that there are fireboxes for certain gas units that may be directly back-vented outside the building so there is no need to go through the roof. A variety of pre-fab firebox sizes, coupled with gas logs, give great flexibility of installation. Designs range from traditional to contemporary. Contact the inn's store, Maschino's, listed in the Resource Guide, for more information.

■ Al and Annie Unrein in Alaska, spatter one-half cup of number two diesel fuel over the ashes before starting the fire at their **Glacier Bay Country Inn.** This procedure helps burn the wood that isn't dry so that you don't need kindling, they report. Don't try this after you've started the fire. You can also do this with charcoal lighter fluid when you're too tired to go out and forage for kindling.

■ George Pavloff oversees seventeen fireplaces and three wood stoves at his **Goose Cove Lodge.** He suggests keeping tarps off your wood piles, contrary to popular belief. Aging wood still needs air, he contends, and if it gets rained on, it will dry quickly. The innkeeper encourages anyone using a tarp to secure it in a way that air may circulate.

■ If smoke enters the room, John Colbey Stone of **The Captain Whidbey Inn,** tells us to roll up a newspaper, light it as though a torch, and hold it up the flue for a few seconds, to draw the down-draft of smoke up through the chimney again.

■ Collect and store fireplace ashes to use outdoors as fertilizer and also to combat slugs.

■ The aroma is nicest in your fireplace when burning such woods as apple, beech, hickory, and pecan.

■ The closer to the front of the fireplace you lay your fire, the more heat will enter the room.

■ Do not let ashes accumulate above two inches in height, or they will hamper the flow of air and the fire will burn less efficiently.

■ Split-wood seasons faster than whole logs. Store with the split side down to protect from moisture.

■ During the off season, empty fireplaces are great spots for fluorescent-light greenhouses and they brighten the firebox during warmer months.

■ Creosote in the chimney may be caused by burning large loads of wood at a time, not necessarily by the moisture content of the wood. The air and fuel need a good balance so that there isn't more smoke than there is available air. Burn a gentle fire.

■ All of these fireplace suggestions are moot ideas if one does not respect the environment. I think this passage in an article in *Country Living* magazine (October 1990), by Richard Stevens, says it all:

"Wood is without a doubt, the 'greenest' fuel . . . The carbon dioxide produced by wood burning would in any case have been released into the atmosphere when the wood rotted, and so does not alter the balance of carbon dioxide in the atmosphere . . . or make a net contribution to the greenhouse effect. This, however, is not a license to fell healthy trees. Firewood is by definition wood that is suitable for no other purpose. It is dead wood, thinnings, loppings, toppings, and forestry residues."

Addresses for the inns providing these tips can be found in the Inn Directory beginning on page 280.

❖ ❖ ❖

INN THE GARDEN

SHARING YOUR GARDEN

INNS are famous for sending guests home with clippings and divisions of plants that are growing prolifically in their gardens. As Gwen Vaughan of **Twin Gates** Bed and Breakfast says, it is an ideal extension of your hospitality. Here, she offers you her tips on how to treat your own family and friends to your good and prosperous earth.

Giving Away Divisions

KEEP clean plant containers on hand for divisions.

DIG up a large section of the plant you are dividing, bringing along with it plenty of the soil that surrounds the roots, but making sure to keep it free of weeds and bugs.

WRAP damp newspapers around the roots of the plant and place in the pot. If transporting in a plastic bag, sprinkle the overall plant with water and then fasten the bag, leaving air inside. You are creating a greenhouse effect, but plant it almost as soon as it gets home.

ADD a touch of liquid vitamin B-1, found at garden centers, as well as some garden fertilizer when planting the division.

Clippings

IF GIVING out a clipping that will have to take its own roots, place it into a plastic bag, sprinkle some water over all and fasten the bag, leaving some air inside.

USE wooden tongue depressors to label your plants, once in the ground. It helps to paint the color of the bloom onto

the wood, so you do not forget which flower you planted where. This comes in handy, especially when you want to think about adding flowers later and nothing is in bloom.

▼ *Wooden twigs—parading as snakes—guard against any mischief among the flowers at* **The Southern Hotel.** *Innkeeper and snake artist Barbara Hankins attached telephone wire to form the serpents' tongues.*

◄ *Purple tops of Stately Spires and Yellow Nicotina at* **Twin Gates**

▲ *An English dovecote provides a picture-perfect roost for a variety of small birds and is an eye-catching piece of garden architecture at* **The Inn on Summer Hill.**

Remembering Your Garden

Gwen suggests that you buy a small blank book with a garden scene on the cover and write out where your clippings came from and what date you planted them, as well as anything about the person who gave you the flowers.

"Sharing my garden," she says, "helps me make way for new plants." And the innkeeper suggests having a garden tea party where participants swap clippings and divisions.

GARDEN VARIETY OF TIPS

Vine Support from Kids' Playthings

When those outdoor gyms and other backyard playthings are outgrown, literally give them new life by letting vine-type plants, such as cucumbers, beans, and morning glory, grow up around them. It's worked for the Burpee family of the **Inn at Fordhook Farm.** Furthermore, tie the vines to the playthings with old nylon hose as it will stretch as the plants grow.

▼ *The combination of weathered tree trunk, tin pail, spindly wagon wheel, and rustic barrel make for art in the front garden at* **Davidson's Country Inn.**

Ten Secrets to Starting and Maintaining a Garden

Twin Gates Bed and Breakfast, whose gardens swell with rich color and floral variety, offers this guide to helping your garden grow.

❀ When you decide where to put a flower garden, choose a spot that can be seen from your kitchen window so that you can always enjoy the view. Plot everything out first, remembering to project areas where sun and shade fall.

❖

❀ When planning your garden, however large or small, it is best to sketch it out on graph paper, using 1/4 inch to the foot. Note also where you might place garden furniture and accent pieces.

❖

❀ Choose perennials that bloom at different times so you always have color in the garden.

❖

❀ Buy quality bulbs and position them in raised beds as much as possible, so that water drains away and prevents bulbs from rotting.

❖

❀ Go slowly when building your garden. Don't try to do it all at once. Better to take a few years, deciding what will work best as you go along.

❀ Accept the limitations of your environment. Don't try to grow flowers that cannot make it in your surroundings. Use potted plants to enhance your garden if you must have certain flowers that are not indigenous.

❖

❀ Throw used coffee grounds in the garden. Plants love them better than commercial fertilizer, and what a way to recycle the grounds.

❖

❀ Use old newspaper to keep out weeds. The paper is more environmentally friendly than plastic liners. Moisten 6 to 8 sheets of paper per plot. Place paper around holes, plant flowers, and cover all with topsoil.

❖

❀ Find a handy tool caddy, such as an old golf bag that has room for long-handled tools such as rakes and hoes, and smaller pouches for hand tools.

❖

❀ Share your garden, dividing plants as they become overgrown. At **Twin Gates,** many a guest has left with clippings to plant at home. It is an extension of the inn's hospitality and can express the same at your home. Besides, creating a perennial garden can be expensive, so sharing clippings and divisions is a nice thing to do. (See Sharing Your Garden on pages 203 and 204.)

Twin Gates' Perennial Garden Plot

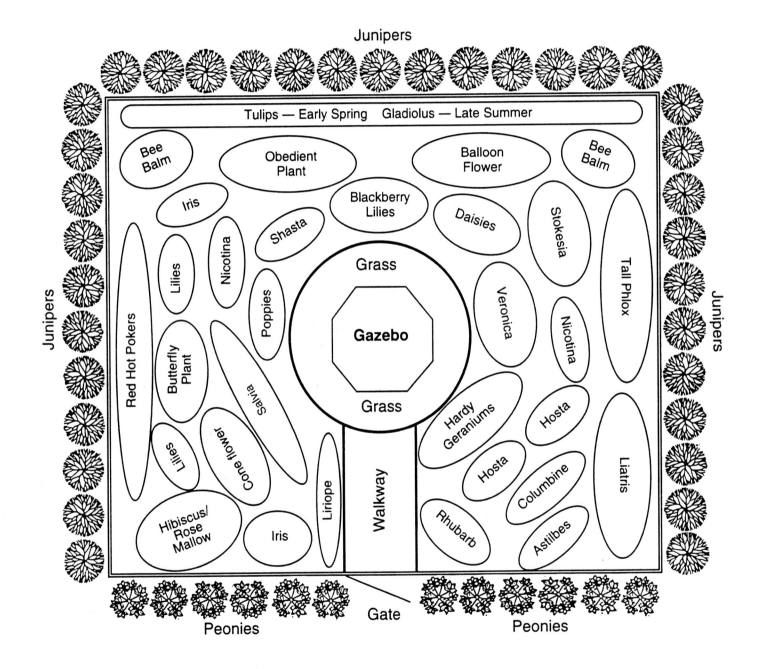

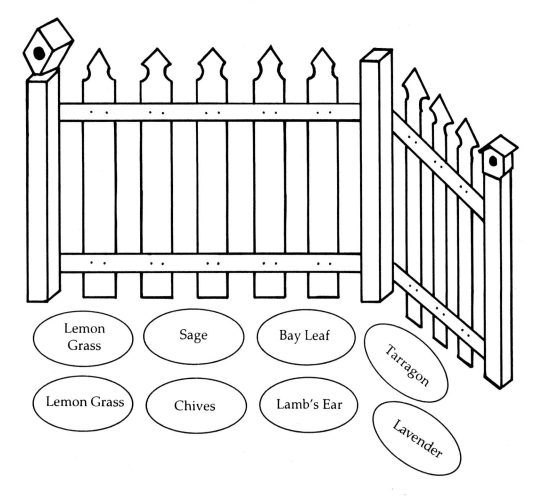

TWIN GATES' HERB GARDEN

THROUGHOUT the blooming season, flowers show their blossoms and colors at various times so that something is always in bloom in the inn's backyard. That's what makes having a perennial garden so special.

Surrounding the **Twin Gates** gazebo (page 93) where guests often take breakfast or relax with a good book, is Gwen Vaughan's perennial garden. I asked Gwen if we could get a bird's eye view of her garden so that we could understand what to plant where. It is on the previous page.

Gwen's plot shows where to place various flowers so that they are not hidden by others. The peonies are one of Gwen's favorite plants and they make for a show-stopping

entryway. The garden is framed with hearty juniper bushes with brushes of color from larger bordering perennials such as Tall Phlox and Hibiscus.

This plot is good for a garden that is anywhere from 18 to 25 feet square. It houses a gazebo that seats up to six people comfortably. You can plant a much smaller version of **Twin Gates'** garden if you do not have as much space to devote in your backyard.

On this page is a drawing of the Twin Gates fence I mentioned on page 91 that the innkeeper was building on my arrival. Note the placement of herbs that offers a visual accent for the fence. Gwen has planted the herbs in such a way as to provide full view of the tasty garden treats here at the inn just north of Baltimore.

Killing Weeds Organically

To kill grass and weeds the natural way, Donna Justin of **Just-N-Trails** spreads animal feeding salt around borders. The salt, says Donna, draws moisture from the roots and kills the unwanted plants.

When the Bulb Goes Out

When tying up bulbous plants that are past their bloom time, I use the fronds from those plants, instead of rubber bands or string.

▼ *Davidson's Country Inn* recycled an old milk can and a tractor seat and fused them together to make a terrific garden stool.

▲ *Blackberry lily* (Belamcanda Chinensis) *from the Orient, grows prolifically at* **Twin Gates.**

It Will Curl Your Hair!

I once saw a lovely fresh flower arrangement at a friend's house. She just couldn't wait to tell me that she had them anchored in the vase in plastic hair rollers that she had kept together with a thick rubber band!

Drying in Bunches

Teri Jones at **Sweet Basil Hill Farm** recommends tying bunches of fresh flowers with rubber bands for drying. This way, as the flowers contract during the drying process, the rubber goes along with them and keeps the bunch tight and together.

▲ *Hummingbirds look for nectar in the gardens of* **The Inn on Summer Hill.**

▲ *Hydrangea season at* **Swiss Woods**

Dried Hydrangeas

A guest who attended a talk I was giving about inns last year in Washington, D.C. asked me to include in my next book a way to dry hydrangeas, especially so that they keep their brilliant colors. I thought it was a good idea as I wondered about this myself. Barbara Barlow, at **Riverwind,** says she picks her blooms at the point at which she likes the color and fullness, and then places them in a vase (rather than in the usual upside-down position) without water and lets them dry.

❖ ❖ ❖

COUNTRY INN RECIPES

Breads 'n' Spreads

Victorian Bread Pudding
The Inn on Summer Hill

Bread puddings are romantic dishes to serve. Somehow, they recall kinder, sweeter, more sentimental days. The serving of bread pudding has appeared in many old English novels, for example, and it is found in many antique down-home cookbooks, especially those from Europe.

This version was assembled by native French chef Pierre Sirra, who serves it to **Summer Hill** guests frequently, along with an egg or crêpe dish, fresh fruit, and assorted breads. It is a completely different bread pudding from any I have ever cooked because you use sweet breads and muffins as opposed to crusty and heavier yeast breads. Pierre devised this recipe as a way to use leftover muffins and breads. You will have to determine how much seasoning to add as it will depend on the sweetness and flavors of the breads you are using. Prepare this recipe the night before. (See photo page 212.)

Bread preparation:

> 10–12 *cups of coarsely chopped sweet breads, cakes, croissants, or any combination—or more to fill a 9 x 13 x 2-inch baking dish*
> 10 *eggs*
> 1 *quart whole milk*
> *Sugar and cinnamon to taste*

Vanilla Sauce:

> 4 *egg yolks*
> 2 *tablespoons vanilla extract*
> 1/2 *cup sugar*

◀ *Riverwind Piglet Biscuits and Country Breakfast Bake with Artichokes and Cheese in the dining room*

> 2 *tablespoons all-purpose flour*
> 2 *cups milk*

Coat the baking dish lightly with a no-stick spray. Add sweet breads. Mix together the 10 eggs and the quart of milk. Add seasonings and sugar, if desired. Pour over breads. Cover and soak overnight in the refrigerator.

Next morning, preheat the oven to 375°. Bake the pudding for 45 to 60 minutes, or until it is set and lightly browned.

Prepare the vanilla sauce. Beat together the egg yolks, vanilla, sugar, and flour. Set aside. Over the stove in a small double boiler pot, bring the milk to a gentle boil. Add the egg mixture and slowly cook the sauce until thick but pouring consistency, stirring constantly. Keep warm until ready to serve. Pierre puts the sauce in a pitcher for easy pouring over individual servings. **Yield: 12 servings**

Piglet Biscuits
Riverwind

You can use any cookie cutter shape you want, but pigs are in the **Riverwind** tradition.

> 2 *cups self-rising flour*
> 1 *cup shortening*
> 3/4 *cup milk*

Preheat oven to 450°. In a large mixing bowl, cut shortening into the flour (it's gooey) with a knife. Add milk. Form into a ball and place on a floured board. Knead about 6 times, adding more flour each time, to work off stickiness. Smooth dough and roll out with your hands to about a 1-inch thickness. Cut into shapes. Place on ungreased cookie sheet. Bake for 8 to 12 minutes or until golden brown. **Yield: 16 biscuits**

▶ *Breakfast goes romantic with this sumptuous bread pudding recipe in a warm vanilla sauce from* **The Inn on Summer Hill.** *(See recipe page 211.)*

Green Tomato and Cinnamon Marmalade
Trout City Berth & Breakfast

A delicious blend of sweet and sour, serve this spread on buttermilk biscuits, warm homemade yeast breads or plain crackers.

4 *pounds green tomatoes, washed, seeds removed, chopped*

8 *cups sugar*

2 *lemons, diced*

1 *teaspoon each cinnamon and allspice*

In a medium saucepan, bring tomatoes to a boil. Lower heat and stir in remaining ingredients. Cook mixture over medium heat, stirring often, until thick. Pour into heated, sterile ½-pint jars. Seal. Place sealed jars in a hot water bath (with water coming up to the top of the jars) to boil for 10 minutes and further sterilize. **Yield: 8 half pints**

Jalapeño Salsa
Casa Benavides

Serve with flour tortillas, chips, or with eggs.

1 *(28-ounce) can whole tomatoes, drained (reserve liquid)*

1 *medium onion, skinned and quartered*

1 *or more fresh jalapeños (depending on desired flavor)*

½ *bunch fresh cilantro*

  Juice of 1 lemon

2 *fresh medium tomatoes, diced*

Place whole tomatoes, onion, jalapeños, and cilantro into a food processor. Process for a few seconds, until well chopped. Add reserved liquid from canned tomatoes, lemon juice, and fresh-cut tomatoes. Store in glass jars in the refrigerator. **Yield: About 2 quarts**

Rose Geranium Jelly
The Southern Hotel

Chemical-free, scented rose geraniums grow prolifically in **The Southern Hotel's** garden. This is a great jelly for your table or for gift-giving. For the latter, top each jelly jar with a piece of fabric, cut in a circle that is 1½ inches larger than the jar's cap. Tie the fabric on with thin ribbons and top with a dried sprig of flower or herb. Another variation is to top the jar with a paper doily and ribbon, or use both. You will need twelve 4-ounce canning jars for this recipe.

5 *cups apple juice*

1 *package pectin (1¾ ounces)*

4 *cups sugar*

15 *rose geranium leaves, plus an option of 1 whole leaf per jar*

In a medium saucepan, bring juice and pectin to a boil. Add sugar. Continue cooking until the mixture comes to a hard boil that cannot be stirred down. Cook for 2 minutes at a hard boil. Turn off heat and add the geraniums. Let steep about 15 minutes. Pour into jars, adding 1 fresh leaf per jar, if desired. Seal and store. **Yield: 48 ounces**

❖ ❖ ❖

▶ *Offer your guests a taste of elegance by serving fruit cups or fruit soups a la **The Chicago Pike Inn**. Simply mount two cakestands on top of one another.*

From the Fruit Bin

Raisin and Fruit Breakfast Soup Compote
The Chicago Pike Inn

The innkeeper's daughter, Jody Willard, prepares many of the dishes served at the inn. When this one was set before me in a crystal, wide-mouthed antique champagne glass, I felt royally treated. I heartily recommend you do the same for your guests.

½ cup minute-tapioca, uncooked

1 cup dark raisins

1 cup golden raisins

½ cup small pitted prunes

½ cup dried cherries

½ cup dried mixed fruit

½ cup dried apricots

2 large cinnamon sticks

6 cups hot water

4 cups apple juice

In a large saucepan, combine all of the ingredients except the apple juice. Over medium heat, blend the ingredients until smooth, a minute or so. Reduce the heat and simmer until the tapioca is transparent, about 30 to 35 minutes. The soup will be thick and clear. Add apple juice. Heat through. Remove cinnamon sticks and serve. **Yield: 10–12 servings**

❖ ❖ ❖

Baked Cinnamon Pears with Fruit and Yogurt Sauce

Twin Gates

Tasty and moist, this fresh-fruit breakfast appetizer may be made the night before. (See photo page 216.)

Pears:

> 4 very green pears
> 1/2 teaspoon raspberry jam per pear
> 2 1/2 cups cranberry, apple, orange, or a blend of juices
> 1/2 cup of blackberry brandy (optional)
> Ground cinnamon

Yogurt Sauce:

> 8 ounces lowfat vanilla yogurt
> 1 tablespoon brown sugar

Preheat the oven to 350°. Spray a 2 1/2-quart baking dish with non-stick vegetable coating.

Peel and core the pears, leaving the stem on, if desired. Trim the bottom of the fruit so that the pear will stand up.

Place small amounts of jam into each pear cavity. Place the pears in the baking dish and bathe with the juice. Add brandy if desired. Sprinkle with cinnamon. Bake for 1 hour or until pears are just slightly tender. Let cool. Cover and refrigerate.

Next morning, preheat oven to 350°. Uncover pears and bake for 30 minutes or until heated through. Meanwhile, prepare sauce. Mix the yogurt with the brown sugar and pour on top of each baked pear. Serve immediately. **Yield: 4 servings**

Danish Lemon Soup

The Southern Hotel

The real name for this dish is "Buttermilk Soup" but Barbara has adapted it from the original recipe and swears that no one would eat it if she called it according to tradition. This tangy dish is so soft and gentle to the palate for breakfast, afternoon tea, dinner, or dessert. Make ahead. (See photo page 58.)

> 2 large eggs
> 1/2 cup sugar
> 1/8 teaspoon vanilla extract
> 2 tablespoons lemon juice
> Grated peel of 1 lemon
> 1 quart buttermilk
> 1/2 cup vanilla ice cream, plus more for garnish
> Shredded lemon peel, mint, and raspberries for garnish

In a large mixing bowl, beat eggs and whisk in sugar and vanilla. Whisk in lemon juice and peel. Gradually add buttermilk and ice cream. Whirl mixture in a food processor until well blended. Cover and chill overnight. Serve cold in individual bowls, topped with a melon-baller-size scoop of ice cream, mint leaf, and raspberry. **Yield: 8 generous servings**

Hot and Cold Cereals

Wild West Granola

Davidson's Country Inn

> 42 ounces old-fashioned oats
> 1 cup wheat germ
> 1 1/3 cups canola oil
> 1 1/3 cups honey
> 1/2 cup sunflower seeds
> 1/2 cup walnuts, chopped
> 7 ounces flaked coconut (sweetened or unsweetened)

Preheat oven to 350°. In a large mixing bowl, stir all ingredients until oats are moistened by the oil and honey. Spread granola onto the bottom of a large baking dish. Bake for 30 minutes or until light golden brown, stirring often so that granola cooks evenly. Remove from oven and cool. Store in an airtight container. **Yield: About 4 pounds**

❖ ❖ ❖

◀ *Why reach for a box of cereal, when you can start your day with a romantic basket full of hearty grains? It was a cheerful eye opener to walk down to the dining room at **Davidson's Country Inn** and find this basket waiting, plus a fabulous hot breakfast. Line a favorite basket and lid with fabric, adding batting to give the inside cover a stuffed look. Tack on lace trim.*

Preheat oven to 350°. In a medium-size camp kettle (large saucepan, no-stick preferred), combine rice, raisins, and 2 cups of the milk. Bring to a boil. Reduce heat. Cover and simmer over low heat for about 20 minutes. Remove from heat. Stir in margarine. Blend remaining 2 cups of the milk, eggs, vanilla, and sugar in a separate bowl. Add egg mixture to the rice. Pour into a camp kettle (or a 9 x 9-inch baking pan) and bake for 30 minutes until custard initially sets. Sprinkle with your choice of granola, cinnamon, nuts, or other crunchy cereal. Bake another 20 minutes or until custard is firmly set. **Yield: 4–6 servings**

Sweet Rancher Porridge
Trout City Berth & Breakfast

A chuck-wagon breakfast at **Trout City** may consist of Irene's warm and nourishing custard.

¹/₂ cup uncooked brown rice

1 cup raisins

4 cups milk, divided

¹/₄ cup margarine

4 eggs

2 tablespoons vanilla extract

¹/₂ cup brown sugar

 Granola, cinnamon, nuts, or cereal

Sweet English Breakfast Porridge
The Captain Lord Mansion

4 cups water

1 teaspoon salt

2 cups quick-cooking oats

5 tablespoons butter

¹/₄ teaspoon cinnamon

¹/₄ teaspoon nutmeg

1¹/₈ cups brown sugar

2 ounces maple syrup

4 ounces condensed milk

In a 4-quart saucepan, bring the water and salt to a boil. Stir in the oats and cook for 1 minute, stirring constantly. Remove from heat and add remaining ingredients, mixing well. Serve piping hot. **Yield: 6 servings**

❖ ❖ ❖

◀ *Breakfast at* **Twin Gates** *often includes a Three-Cheese Herb and Crabmeat Puff with Baked Cinnamon Pears with Fruit and Yogurt Sauce.*

Preheat oven to 350°. In a large mixing bowl, beat together with a fork, the eggs, chilies, milk, seasonings, and half of the cheese. Pour into a large heated iron skillet that has been coated with non-stick spray. Top with the other half of the cheese. Place skillet into the oven and bake for 30 minutes or until eggs are set and cheese is runny. At the inn, they like to bring the eggs sizzling in the iron skillet to the table where they serve their guests. "It's much more romantic that way and shows your guests just how fresh they are," says innkeeper Barbara McCarthy. **Yield: 6–8 servings**

Three-Cheese Herb and Crabmeat Puff
Twin Gates

Super creamy and super low-fat best describes this filling egg omelet dish, which can also be served for lunch or dinner.

2 *tablespoons margarine*

1 *cup Egg Beaters (or 4 eggs)*

2 *cups low-fat cottage cheese*

½ *cup low-fat cheese such as Gouda, Swiss or Monterey Jack, grated*

2 *ounces low-fat cream cheese*

1 *tablespoon or more mixture of herbs such as chives, oregano, and dill*

½ *cup chopped crabmeat*

Fresh tomato wedges for garnish

Preheat oven to 350°. Spray two 4-ounce ramekins with a non-stick vegetable coating.

In a blender, whirl together margarine, eggs, cheeses, and herbs until smooth and creamy. Mix in crabmeat. Pour mixture into ramekins, leaving half an inch or so of space to allow for mixture to rise.

Bake for 30 minutes or until egg is puffed and golden. Garnish with tomato wedges before serving. **Yield: 2 servings**

Eggs and Entrées

Mexican Eggs
Casa Benavides

Serve these eggs over flour tortillas and a sauce of Jalapeño Salsa, on page 212.

1 *dozen fresh eggs*

1 *(4-ounce) can green chilies*

⅓ *cup milk*

Salt and pepper to taste

1 *generous cup cheddar cheese, shredded*

▶ *Study The School House Bed & Breakfast's Lilliputian Cheese-Egg Puffs recipe to get an "A" from your family!*

Country Breakfast Bake with Artichokes and Cheese

Riverwind

When the innkeeper makes this dish, she adds a floral vegetable bouquet, fitting atop the entire casserole, made with asparagus spears as stalks, quartered cherry tomatoes as petals, and roasted red pepper strips as the bow. Barbara insists that any fewer than 17 eggs will make a difference.

6 ounces seasoned croutons

4 medium tomatoes, sliced

1 pound Swiss cheese, sliced

8 ounces fresh mushrooms, sliced

1 8½-ounce can unmarinated artichoke hearts, drained and quartered

17 large eggs

¾ to 1 cup half-and-half

½ cup Parmesan cheese

Garnish with asparagus stalks (fresh-cooked or canned), roasted red pepper strips and cherry tomatoes.

Preheat oven to 450°. Line a 9x13-inch greased casserole dish with the croutons. Follow with a layer of tomatoes, Swiss cheese, mushrooms, and artichoke hearts. Break eggs (including the yolks) over the top, to cover the entire casserole. Drizzle with half-and-half. Bake for 20 minutes, adding the Parmesan halfway through baking. Make the garnish, if desired. **Yield: 16 servings**

Lilliputian Cheese-Egg Puffs

The School House Bed & Breakfast

You make these in mini-muffin tins and they are perfect served as a breakfast entrée or as an hors d'oeuvre at brunch.

2 tablespoons butter

½ cup milk

¼ teaspoon salt

⅛ teaspoon pepper

1½ cups all-purpose flour

2 eggs

½ cup cheddar cheese, shredded

¼ cup chopped ham

Preheat oven to 350°. In a medium saucepan, heat to boiling the butter, milk, salt, and pepper. Remove from saucepan, add flour, and pour into a mixing bowl. Add eggs—beating in one at a time. Add the cheese and ham. Pour into a no-stick mini-muffin tin. Bake for 25 minutes or until golden. **Yield: 12 muffins**

❖ ❖ ❖

Red Rock Artichoke and Salsa Bake

Canyon Villa

To make this dish ahead of time, assemble all ingredients except eggs and sour cream. Cover with plastic wrap and refrigerate until the morning. Prepare the egg mixture, pour over the top, and bake.

1½ *cups salsa*

1 *8½-ounce can unmarinated artichoke hearts, liquid drained and artichokes chopped*

2 *4-ounce cans sliced mushrooms, liquid drained*

⅔ *cup Parmesan cheese*

2 *cups shredded Monterey Jack cheese*

2 *cups shredded cheddar cheese*

12 *large eggs*

2 *cups sour cream*

Preheat oven to 350°. Spray a 9x13-inch glass baking dish with a no-stick vegetable coating. Spread salsa on the bottom. Layer with the artichokes, followed by the mushrooms, and each of the cheeses.

In a large mixing bowl, whisk together the eggs and the sour cream until smooth and well-blended. Pour the mixture over the casserole. Bake for about 50 minutes or until casserole is set. **Yield: 8–10 servings**

❖ ❖ ❖

French Toast Sundae

The Inn at the Round Barn Farm

At **The Inn at the Round Barn Farm,** they call this a Fruit-Drenched French Toast. But I can't help but rename it and I'm sure you will agree as you read the recipe. At holiday time, the inn makes this with eggnog instead of the milk and cream. Feel free to sprinkle nuts on top of your "sundae."

  8 *eggs*
1½ *cups milk*
 ½ *cup heavy cream*
  1 *tablespoon vanilla extract*
 ⅛ *teaspoon freshly ground nutmeg*
12 *slices Italian bread, sliced 1-inch thick*
  1 *cup cornflakes, crushed*
     Assortment of fresh sliced fruits in season
     Maple syrup
     Powdered sugar
     Whipped cream

Preheat griddle to 375°. In a large mixing bowl, whisk eggs, milk, and heavy cream until well combined, about 3 to 4 minutes. This allows the heavy cream to almost whip for a light batter. Add the vanilla. Pour mixture through a strainer to remove egg excess. Add nutmeg. Dip bread into mixture but do not soak. Dip one side of the bread into cornflakes. Repeat with all slices.

Grease griddle and cook bread with the cornflakes side down first. Flip when golden brown. Place two slices on a plate and top with fruit and maple syrup. Dust with powdered sugar. Add a dollop of whipped cream, if desired. **Yield: 6 servings**

◄ *French Toast Sundae welcomes breakfasters. The hand-painted napkin ring vases are a signature of the inn as is the Round Barn pottery. The Simkos sell Round Barn's pottery filled with Vermont maple syrup. What perfect souvenirs!*

Classic Cheese Fondue

Swiss Woods

There are so many varieties and recipes for fondues. Serve this dish with a green salad and the chocolate dessert fondue, and you have a meal. (See photo page 176.)

  1 *clove garlic, halved*
  2 *cups very dry white wine*
1½ *pounds coarsely grated Gruyère or Emmenthaler (Swiss cheese) or ¾ pound each*
  3 *tablespoons all-purpose flour*
 ¼ *cup kirsch*
     Nutmeg
     Cubes of French, Italian, or sourdough crusty bread

Rub the inside of the pot generously with the garlic halves. Discard garlic. Heat the wine in the pot until almost boiling. Dredge the cheese in flour. Add it slowly, allowing it to melt, before adding more. When the cheese is all melted and the mixture is smooth and thick, stir in the kirsch. Sprinkle with nutmeg. Serve with the bread cubes for dipping. **Yield: 4 servings**

Chocolate Fondue

Swiss Woods

  3 *3-ounce Toblerone Swiss chocolate bars (or other good quality chocolate)*
 ½ *cup heavy cream*
  2 *tablespoons cognac*
     Pound cake and/or bananas, strawberries, or other fruits for dipping

Melt the chocolate in the top of a double boiler over low heat. Stir in the cream and cognac. Transfer to a fondue pot and serve. **Yield: 4 servings**

❖ ❖ ❖

Suite Cakes

Canyon Villa Cinnamon Rolls

Canyon Villa

See photo page 148

At **Canyon Villa,** cinnamon rolls are the signature dish of the inn and I have never tasted ones so good as Marion Yadon's. The innkeeper has been using this recipe for many years and more often than not they make their way to the inn's tables. Rolls may be prepared for baking and refrigerated overnight. The next morning, before baking, cover and let rise in a warm place for 1 hour or until doubled in size. Bake as directed.

Marion bakes the cinnamon rolls and then wraps them in foil and freezes them. Before serving, she defrosts them overnight at room temperature. In the morning, she places them—still wrapped in foil—in a 350° oven for 15 to 20 minutes. She then glazes and serves them.

Rolls:

   1 *cup milk*

   1 *cup water*

  ¹/2 *cup butter*

   1 *egg, slightly beaten*

   6 *cups all-purpose flour (or more) divided*

  ¹/2 *cup sugar*

   3 *packages dry yeast*

   2 *teaspoons salt*

Filling:

  ¹/2 *cup brown sugar*

 1¹/2 *tablespoons cinnamon*

  ¹/3 *cup butter, melted*

Glaze:

   2 *tablespoons butter*

   1 *tablespoon milk*

   1 *teaspoon vanilla extract*

 2–3 *cups sifted powdered sugar*

In a small saucepan, combine milk, water, and butter; heat until very warm (about 120°) and butter melts. Add egg.

In a large mixing bowl, combine 2 cups of the flour with the sugar, yeast, and salt. Stir well. Add milk-egg mixture to the flour mixture. Beat at medium speed with an electric mixer until batter is smooth and elastic, about 5 to 8 minutes. Place in a greased bowl, turning once to grease the top of the dough. Cover with a damp tea towel and let rise in a warm place for 1 hour or until doubled in size.

Meanwhile, combine brown sugar and cinnamon in a small bowl and melt the butter. Set aside.

Return to dough. Punch down. Cover again and let rest 10 minutes more. Divide dough in half and set one-half aside. Roll the other half out on a floured surface to form an 18x12-inch rectangle; brush with half the melted butter, leaving a ¹/2-inch border. Sprinkle with half of the brown sugar and cinnamon mixture. Beginning at the long side, roll up jellyroll fashion; moisten edges with water and press together to seal. Cut roll into 1¹/2-inch slices to form rolls; place cut sides of slices down in a greased 9x13-inch baking pan. Cover with a damp tea towel and let rise in a warm place for 45 minutes to an hour or until doubled in size. Repeat with remaining half of the dough.

When rolls have risen, bake them in a preheated 375° oven for 20 minutes or until golden brown. While rolls are baking, prepare the glaze.

In a small saucepan, heat together butter and milk until butter is melted. (You can use a glass measuring cup in the microwave to do this.) Add vanilla and enough of the powdered sugar for desired spreading consistency. Apply glaze when rolls have cooled slightly. **Yield: 2 dozen**

Blueberry Cinnamon Crumb Cake

Canyon Villa

Topping:

  ¹/2 *cup sugar*

  ¹/3 *cup all-purpose flour*

  ¹/2 *teaspoon cinnamon*

  ¹/4 *cup butter*

Sift together sugar, flour, and cinnamon. Cut in butter until mixture becomes crumbly. Set aside.

❖ ❖ ❖

Cake:

¼ cup shortening

¾ cup sugar

1 egg

2 cups all-purpose flour

2½ teaspoons baking powder

½ teaspoon salt

¾ cup milk

2 cups fresh or frozen blueberries (thawed)

Preheat oven to 375°. Cream together shortening and sugar. Beat until fluffy. Add egg and beat well. In a separate large mixing bowl, stir together flour, baking powder, and salt; add to creamed mixture alternately with milk. Fold in blueberries. Pour batter into a greased and floured 9-inch round or square baking pan. Sprinkle cinnamon crumb mixture over top. Bake for 45 to 50 minutes or until cake tester inserted in center comes out clean. (Note: For high altitudes, add 1 to 2 tablespoons more flour and decrease baking powder to 2 teaspoons.)

Persimmon Muffins

Walnut Street Inn

Muffins come and muffins go at bed-and-breakfasts. But this recipe for tasty and more unusual little sweet breads, is rarely found on the tables of America's small inns.

½ cup persimmon pulp (about 2 seeded and peeled persimmons)

1 egg, beaten

½ cup milk

¼ cup butter, melted

1½ cups all-purpose flour

½ cup sugar

3 teaspoons baking powder

½ teaspoon cinnamon

1 teaspoon nutmeg

¼ teaspoon ground cloves

Preheat oven to 400°. In a medium mixing bowl, beat persimmon pulp, egg, milk, and butter until smooth. In a separate, larger bowl, mix together flour, sugar, and spices. Stir persimmon mixture into flour mixture just until moistened. (Batter will be lumpy.) Spoon into ungreased muffin tin. Bake for 15 to 18 minutes or until golden. **Yield: 12 muffins**

Maple-Baked Pears in a Jiffy

The Inn at the Round Barn Farm

This recipe is a snap and a wonderful starter for a leisurely breakfast or brunch.

4 ripe seasonal pears (any variety)	Maple syrup
4 tablespoons butter	Brown sugar
⅛ cup white sugar	Heavy cream

Preheat oven to 325°. Peel pears and remove seeds with a spoon. Set aside. Grease the bottom of an 8x8-inch square baking dish, leaving extra butter in the dish. Dust with the sugar. Place pears in the dish, flat side down. Drizzle tops of pears with maple syrup and brown sugar. Bake for 15 minutes. The juice from the pears will mix with butter and sugars to create a caramel coating. Serve on individual dishes. Round Barn Farm tops the pears with a splash of cream and an edible pansy. **Yield: 4 servings**

❖ ❖ ❖

BRINGING IT ALL HOME
WITH THE AUTHOR

WELCOME to my home, The Country White House. No, Tom and I do not own a B&B, although some of our friends have accused us of such. We have a guest book, a few spare guest rooms, and an outpouring of pampering; so our guests like to make believe we run an inn. Tom and I have always named our homes and this moniker was chosen because of its color as well as its proximity to the president's home, only a few miles away.

We do not have an old home. Our circumstances at the time we purchased The Country White House made it

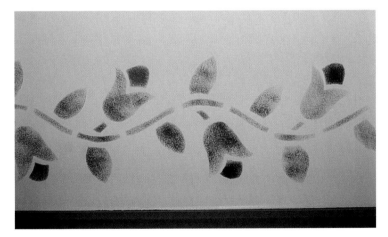

Stenciling has always been a part of our home decor. I stenciled the front hallway of this home with a trailing vine pattern. I had the stencil custom cut to match the design of the quilt on the wall. The quilt set the color scheme for the foyer—pink and a soft green, the latter of which is a color said to immediately spell "welcome." To learn how to cut your own stencil and to stencil a wall, see page 245. See Resource Guide for a custom stencil artist to make your very own pattern if you would rather not do it yourself. Oh, the mouse that ran up the clock is only a stuffed one! I like to mix whimsy with formality.

impossible to acquire such a venue. While it is still our dream to own one some day, we wanted our home to reflect a vintage ambience despite its vinyl siding and plastic window grilles. I decided to include some of the things I have done here as a way of showing you how ideas from the inns can spark your imagination.

No matter what style home or apartment you live in, you can bring the atmosphere of an old home or a bed-and-breakfast to your humble abode. Stop agonizing and longing and make it happen with what you've got right now. Don't wait until you can have that old rickety place to fix up.

Step back and realize that anything is possible, depending on what you are prepared to spend in time and money. The first thing we did was put in a brick country walkway to the front entry. Then, practically before we had boxes unpacked, we called **The Brafferton Inn** and asked innkeepers Jim and Mimi Agard for the name of the artist who had done their mural, as we wanted one in our dining room. (See Resource Guide.) Already things were shaping up a la country inn.

We quickly mounted brass towel racks on the back of the doors to our spare bedrooms and placed fluffy towels over the bars, as we had out-of-towners that first month. Thinking about what innkeepers told me when setting up their inn, we slept a night in each room to determine what more a guest might need—better reading lamps, magazines suitable to the personalities, and a letter sorter just as **The Inn on Summer Hill** has, to keep a pad and pen handy by the bed (only we used an antique English breakfast toast holder). We added a bookmark, which we encourage our guests to take home.

In the kitchen, we wanted a brick floor, but our modern builder would not oblige at any cost. We got the old look by selecting a floor covering with a very realistic brick-and-

223

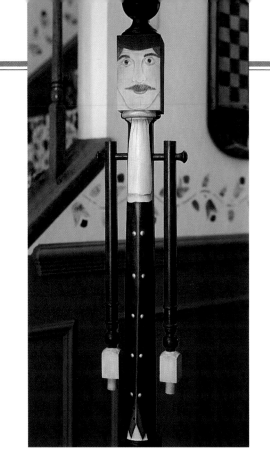

▲ *A clever piece of folk art, created by a local artist out of a recycled newel post, is our innkeeper, Jefferson, who greets guests. (See Resource Guide.)*

(See Resource Guide.)

❖ ❖ ❖

Many a quiet evening or rainy afternoon, my guest book beckons me to tiptoe through its contents. I pensively oblige, hearing the voices of its myriad authors, encouraging me to go ahead and bathe myself guiltlessly in its unbridled felicitations. I turn the pages, reading randomly, catching comments that force a smile: *"We love you madly,"* or *"The conversation was so memorable and inspiring."*

"Thank you for showing us the begonias," trumpets one poetic entry. These are memories that not only bespeak my guests' enjoyment but also my own. If it weren't for these frequent visitors, I might altogether forget to seek the pleasures of either flower or fancy. Their presence forces me to make time for play. A guest book for your home will do the same.

". . . And over the main table cover was a crisply starched and embroidered heirloom cloth, a curious complement to the sparkling champagne flutes . . ." observes a scribed reminder of a sentimental evening presented to two most deserving

mortar pattern. We hung an antique wooden ladder for baskets. Well, I could go on and on, but my point is this: when you see what innkeepers have done with old buildings, you realize there is the potential for creating such a world at your place. It's the inn thing to do, of course.

THE GUEST BOOK IS
THE POETRY OF OUR HOME

MY VISITOR'S book is perched on a plate holder so that it faces out, and sits on top of a 19th-century school desk in the foyer. The desk's unskilled youthful carvings from the past are forever etched into the oak grain, but it is the warm scribbles in ink on the pages from the present that longingly and endearingly summon me.

▼ *I love yo-yo quilts and decided that the little medallions could be sewn together to form placemats. I have provided instructions on page 256. That's our guest book off to the right and the bread is fresh from a mail order company as I had no time to bake it for the photo. (See Resource Guide.)*

I have provided instructions on page 256. ... *(See Resource Guide.)*

❖ ❖ ❖

friends. What a great reward, knowing that they truly savored the cosseting.

"*Particularly enjoyed the game of checkers,*" offers another fleeting inscription. Ah, I recall that day now. It was a raw winter's afternoon—brightened by the sight of a tole-painted checkerboard, a gift from my mother's untrained but artistic hand. That day, I used the colorful geometric canvas to entice a rigid visiting scholar into matching competitive wits at one of the world's oldest amusements. I don't remember who won. It doesn't matter. But the words on the page of my guest book remind me of his beguiling expression when I suggested he turn his focus to the little red and white heart-shaped disks. The whimsical checkerboard had charmed this most astute of academicians away from his mountain of textbooks.

My visitor's book, as humble as its contents may be, represents the soul, the passion, and the poetry of my home, just as an inn's guest book does for its innkeeper. I once watched innkeeper Crescent Dragonwagon eagerly reach for the guest book she leaves in every room at her **Dairy Hollow**

▼ *We knew we wanted to do a mural in our dining room, as that would certainly give our new house an "older" look. When we had seen it done at* **The Brafferton Inn***, we asked the innkeepers how we could do it too. They put us in touch with artist Virginia McLaughlin. (See Resource Guide.) Virginia is a prominent American mural painter, who was approved by Mrs. Robert E. Lee (the fourth) to do murals in the restaurant at George Washington's Mount Vernon estate. This scene was done for us in the style of 19th-century itinerant artist Rufus Porter.*

▼ *This closeup of the mural, which includes a scene from our region, is set for tea-time with* **The Bailiwick Inn's** *wonderful reversible tea cozy for keeping the afternoon beverage warm. See directions to make the cozy on page 256.*

▲ *Innkeeper Bobby Boals of* **The Veranda** *sent me instructions on how to make this butterfly napkin ring. I made these with wallpaper from our Victorian room. See directions on page 273.*

why an open hand hasn't offered a pen for some closing remarks.

It makes sense to have a guest book in your home for other reasons as well. One is forced to think about poetic things to say and descriptive words to use, to look inward and think aloud in verse or rhyme as they did in the letters of years ago. Guest books have been around for some time, and writing about one's visit to someone's home (or inn) has been going on for centuries. I am amused by Charles Skinner Matthews' very Cambridge description in 1809 of a sojourn with Lord Byron at Newstand Alley:

"Our average of rising was one and it was frequently past two before the breakfast party broke up . . . there was reading, fencing, single-stick, or shuttle cock in the great room; practising with pistol in the hall; walking and rising; cricket; sailing on the lake or teasing the wolf."

▼ *I like to enhance picture frames with fabric. See directions for making fabric bow hangers, and another way to mount them, on page 257. Or see the Resource Guide to order them.*

House. As she showed me the rooms at the inn, she reached for the books with childish delight to read what the room's most recent inhabitants had left behind. Crescent and so many innkeepers never tire of hearing the joys their guests have experienced while under their roof. You won't either.

My treasury of who has come and gone for an overnight stay, dinner, brunch, or tea-time, offers me many restorative gifts. The reinforcing comments remind me that I am indeed giving back as well as taking. *"Because of your gracious hospitality, parting is not easy."* Such propitiousness is emblazoned in my heart and propels me to serve up those pleasures once again.

When initially I had asked departing guests to pen their sentiments in the visitor's journal, I wondered if my requests were out of turn. After all, mine is a private home, not a publick house. The generosity of their comments, however, told me to keep it going. Now, if a repeat visitor isn't asked to sign the book, he or she demands to know

❖ ❖ ❖

I don't think the precious recollections in my guest book will ever be so documented in history. However, they will forever be first-rate in my book.

❖ ❖ ❖

Be sure when selecting a guest book that there's plenty of room for comments. A book that merely has Name and Address doesn't invite guests to pen their remarks as well. Look for one that has a column marked Comments. They can be found in stationery stores and card shops. If you don't find a book commercially that you like, make your own as they did at **The Peppertrees B&B.** Put together your own visitor's ledger by using a loose-leaf binder. At **Peppertrees,** you note your profession, your favorite city and restaurant, movie, play and hobbies, and comments, of course.

Many inns leave a fabric-covered bound book with blank pages in the bedrooms. Here, guests have plenty of time to write in their thoughts.

▲ *The Country White House*

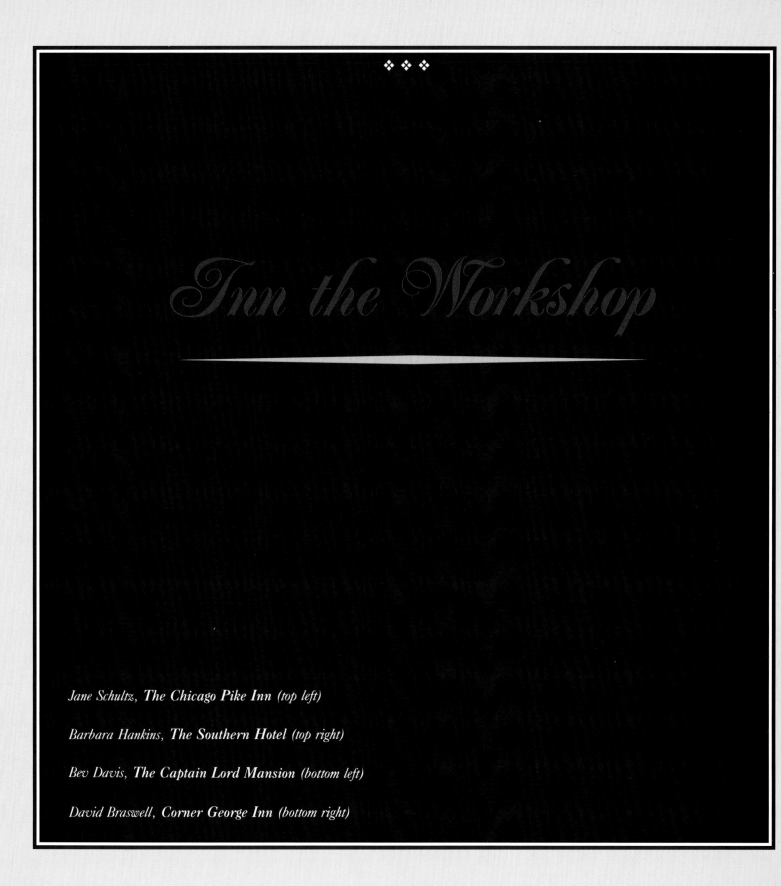

Inn the Workshop

Jane Schultz, **The Chicago Pike Inn** *(top left)*

Barbara Hankins, **The Southern Hotel** *(top right)*

Bev Davis, **The Captain Lord Mansion** *(bottom left)*

David Braswell, **Corner George Inn** *(bottom right)*

❖ ❖ ❖

RESTORATION AND RENOVATION

THE TEN COMMANDMENTS OF RESTORATION

—Tim and Maureen Tyler, **Russell-Cooper House**

THE **Russell-Cooper House** is a gracious 1830 home that has been faithfully restored by the Tylers who are restoration consultants. I asked Tim to give us these commandments, so that we may be inspired to do a restoration, even if we have never done one before. Here is his most candid, most enjoyably written guide to fixing things up in the bibli-, I mean—historical sense. (See PastForward in Resource Guide.)

I. THOU SHALT NOT SKIMP

As you plan your "labor of love" restoration, labor is about the only part of the project that won't directly cost money. Whatever you cut corners on in the beginning is bound to cost twice as much or more to do the right way down the road. While you may be forced by expense to pursue your restoration project in a series of phases, you will have the peace of mind which comes from a job well done; an opportunity to relax periodically and show off your remarkable transformation to friends and family; and time to squirrel away enough money for the next phase.

II. THOU SHALT NOT UNDERESTIMATE

You have devoted countless hours investigating, estimating, researching, reference-checking, comparison shopping, measuring, evaluating, crunching, and re-crunching numbers. You've used geometric logic and the best spreadsheets available for your calculations. You've even bartered a few plum deals with a supplier or two. Now that your budget is done, you are ready to get to work. Right?

Wrong. You have forgotten the most important element in restoration—financing. Before you reach for the tool belt, go back to your final budget figure. See that nice round, well-crafted number? Take out your calculator (or use your head if it is still functioning at this point) and multiply that number by 1.5. If you cannot afford this new budget figure, then you have only a few choices: Scale back the project to accommodate the new multiplier or wait until you have the additional cash. But please do not go ahead based on your original budget.

The best way to create your restoration budget is to use the multiplier for each facet of the project, whether on the cost of two pounds of ten-penny nails or the estimate of the plasterer who is doing the ceilings (only the most foolhardy plaster their own ceilings!). You may then keep track of the project as it grows. By the way, this same technique is highly recommended when figuring the amount of time it will take for you to complete a restoration task—except in that case the total number of hours you have estimated should be multiplied by 3.

◀ *Park Avenue Guest House*

231

❖ ❖ ❖

III. THOU SHALT NOT OVERESTIMATE

That is, thou shalt not overestimate the following:

■ The extent of your own or another's abilities
■ Your energy level and pain threshold
■ Your capacity to live with dust and debris
■ The strength of your marriage or relationship if not working alone

Restoration cries out for a healthy blending of two otherwise opposing forces—informed reality and creative idealism. Being able to visualize a project's completion before it begins will give you something to dream about and work toward. Being honest with yourself will enable you to build the sturdy foundation necessary to make the dream a reality.

IV. THOU SHALT PUT NO OTHER PROJECT BEFORE ME

Speaking of foundations, walls, floors, rafters, chimneys, and roofs; plumbing, wiring, insulation, weatherproofing, and drainage—maybe you are one of the lucky ones. Maybe none of these terms fills you with a queasy sense of dread. Maybe only one or two of them do. If so, this is very good, because before you can contemplate any of the fun restoration projects, like stripping paint and wallpaper, refinishing floors or tearing out a dropped ceiling, you must take care of your infrastructure.

In any rehabilitation, but especially in pure restorations, the most serious structural problems always come first. Start with the roof and the basement or foundation. Can you detect any visible signs of water damage? How many layers of roofing material are present? Does the basement have an odor reminiscent of wet, worn socks accidentally left in the hamper too long? These are but a few of the interesting questions you will have to answer and resolve, for only after the building is sound can you begin confronting the next big area of your restoration—the mechanicals.

Do lights dim when a blow dryer is turned on? Did you have a hard time finding an outlet to plug into in the first place? Can you flush the commode and get a cold drink of tap water at the same time?

V. THOU SHALT NOT COVET THY NEIGHBOR'S LIFE

Working and living in a home or building under restoration can cause the mind to play tricks on a person. It is not uncommon for the most carefully prepared and organized people to lose track of their goals during the hubbub of restoration work, and to say, for instance, "Why are we doing this?"

When confronted by the reality of this love-hate relationship, it is important to remember as you look across the street at your neighbor's greener grass—that before long, your project will bear its own fruit as well as the respect and admiration of future generations—yes, future generations! So, relax. Take your time. Take a walk. You are doing just fine.

VI. REMEMBER THE HISTORY: KEEP IT WHOLLY

Take the time to live with your environment during its evolution. This way, you may be able to make some modifications to accommodate the impressions and feelings you have about your space, especially in a kitchen or bathroom. Unless the historic fabric of your building—the doors, windows, floors, and other architectural elements—has been obliterated from years of wear, you will be hard-pressed to justify its removal. When only a portion of an element survives, remember that in restoration work, imitation is a sincere form of flattery and the only way to go.

❖ ❖ ❖

VII. THOU SHALT NOT COMMIT REMUDDLING

Many people believe that demolition is more acceptable than remuddling, a term applied to rehabilitation work which obscures, removes, or otherwise obliterates the original architectural form or fabric of the building. We're some of those people. Chances are that you agree or you would not be reading this.

VIII. THOU SHALT NOT BEAR FALSE WITNESS

Record all your restoration work copiously. As the memory of your achievement grows less clear with the passage of time, you don't want to forget the breadth of your achievement. Photographs, videos, blueprints, and the written records you compile detailing every step along the way will always remind you and those of future generations of a job well done.

IX. HONOR THY TOOLS AND THY EQUIPMENT

The care and maintenance of your tools of restoration cannot be overstated. Advanced technology has provided an array of specialized restoration implements, which will serve you well. Proper cleaning after use is imperative. Read the instructions that come with those tools and make safety a priority. Have a place for everything and everything in its place; the right tool for every job; keep your edges sharp; duck when you have to; and avoid old "saws" unless they make good sense.

X. THOU SHALT NOT GO IT ALONE

When the going gets rough (and it probably will), you can take solace in knowing that you are not alone. Although your project is unique, for no two restorations are exactly alike, the challenges you face can be successfully confronted by applying the vast source of knowledge and ingenuity compiled over the years, and which is available—literally at your fingertips!

For one thing, your state preservation office is at your service. Headquartered in state capitals, they are only a phone call away. Better yet, an area representative will come and consult with you personally if you request the assistance . . . at no cost.

Restoration is like any other subject. Knowledge is power. Perhaps the most valuable source of information available to you is your public library. Your state preservation office also maintains a reference library as well as complementary and reasonably priced preservation how-to publications. The same can be said of the National Trust for Historic Preservation.

Then there is *The Old House Journal* and *Traditional Building*, which provide detailed information about products, techniques, and solutions for restoration projects.

Finally, if tackling a restoration project personally is too daunting, but the desire for that old building is passionate, there are professional restorers of historic structures. You can find them through some of these sources mentioned, or in many telephone books and local newspapers. There is no excuse not to follow your passion and have that charming old structure. Follow these commandments and your heavenly home in history will follow.

❖ ❖ ❖

On Moving a Building

THESE tips are from Bea Brickell Lee and David Lee of **Christmas Farm Inn,** who moved the small church on page 110 to their farm. The couple moved at least 12 buildings and once they removed only a wing of a house and moved it (page 113). They suggest you don't let anything stop you from having a building you want. Here are a few of their ideas to help you get started.

ONE DAY you may see a "For Sale" sign on a building but it is in the wrong place for you. Ask the owner if you could buy it and move it, without having to purchase the land.

CONSULT the Yellow Pages under "House Movers" to find a reputable mover. If there is no listing, call a local or state historical society. Interview several, as this work requires special skills and equipment and prices vary.

THE HOUSE mover will lead you through most of the steps to moving the building, such as telling you that power lines will have to be moved, perhaps. Consult with local utility companies about what must be done. This can be the most expensive part of the move.

IF THE house or other building is to be transported along a state road, you may need a special permit. Check with the local branch of the Department of Transportation.

STRIP the building down to the drywall or plaster to prepare for the move.

LET THE house mover know that you will want to keep the building jacked up on oak timbers while the foundation is being poured. Consider using a brick or stone foundation which replicates the building's original foundation.

BE PREPARED for many questions. People are often surprised, awed, or astonished to learn that you have moved a building. It may help to point out that in days past, moving buildings was quite common. Houses were not only moved over land, but in sea-bound areas, they were often jacked up and floated on barges to new locations on a mainland or up or down the coastal region.

CONSIDER yourself a hero or heroine. And don't stop after moving one building. Perhaps you will find additional structures—tiny barns, cabins, smokehouses, or a church—as we found—which will complement your house. As buildings from the past are usually so well built, they are worth saving and moving. With a fresh coat of paint and minor repairs, they are ready to provide you with years of service.

How to Build a New/Old Addition

AT **RIVERWIND,** innkeeper Barbara Barlow built an addition that doubled the size of her home/inn. A focal point of that addition is the stone fireplace on page 49. She made it so authentic that it actually looks older than the original part. She did it all with the help of Bob Bucknall, a contractor on the job who later became Barbara's husband.

Here are her funny, renegade and most candid instructions for doing this at home:

❀ **Hire no architect whatsoever.** The plans I took to the zoning board were in pencil, sketched on the back of an envelope.

❀ **Don't hire the cheapest builder.** Hire the old-timer who cares.

❀ **Insist on building the addition by taking down as few old trees as possible.** If you have a good crew, they'll hang from the trees to do the work!

❀ **Learn the current building codes by heart. Then work around them by interpreting them to work**

❖ ❖ ❖

for your building. For example, load-bearing beams can span a greater distance if they are bigger than the joists (box them in with molding and paint them the trim color in your fancier rooms—great for hanging stuff) or have a knee brace on the ceiling—which is legal.

❀ **Buy 200-year-old barn wood for ceilings.** Clean it with a wire brush.

❀ **Floor Magic.** Use regular 1 x 8, 10, or 12-inch-wide boards for flooring. Put black roofing paper over plywood sub-flooring and space the boards a bit, keeping in mind that they may shrink a bit. Finish with rose-cut (reproduction) head nails. Lay floor as soon as possible so subsequent movement about the building will age the floors quickly.

❀ **Design windows to butt right up to corners of ells.** That's what old houses looked like as they were added onto over the years. This gives the building that old farmhouse look.

❀ **Have interior and exterior moldings and trim hand-milled to your exact specifications for a perfect external match.**

❀ **Use old or reproduction hardware everywhere.**

❀ **Look for a stone mason who has been around for a long time and has the patience, say, to remove a 1-ton lintel stone because the side you like was put on the inside.**

❀ **Dig up old foundation walls to obtain stone for your fireplace.** I had an entire stone foundation wall in my basement removed to use on my fireplace. (See page 49.) I had to have a lot of bourbon for this event. Be brave.

❀ **Make your stone man carve a piece of wood "like they used to" to point (tuckpoint) all bricks and stones instead of using a modern metal pointer which gives the tuckpointing a new, not an old look.** He will complain about this suggestion, but he will be happy when it's done.

❀ **Use wooden lattice panels to hide modern exterior concrete foundations as was done years ago for porch foundations.**

❀ **Have all your paints mixed by someone willing to toss all paint chips put out commercially and mix it your way.** Just make sure you keep a file on the color recipe for every room for future use and admirers who will want the recipe.

❀ **Use grey-white paint on walls rather than a warm white as it looks older—like plaster.** For a really old look, slap joint compound on drywall with a wide putty knife. It's a great old look and you don't even have to paint it.

❀ **Marry a member of the crew.** After all, he already knows all there is to know about the building and you. If he is planning to marry you—you know the building is sound.

❖ ❖ ❖

QUICK RESTORATION/ RENOVATION TIPS

The Before-and-After Snapshots

Most people think of taking one or two pictures of the dilapidated area or room before the reconstruction begins. But at **The King's Cottage,** they advise taking several "progress" photos as the job continues. Take photos of open walls, ceilings and floors. A new electrician on the job will know where wiring is, for example. Later on, they will serve as a reminder of how much you accomplished when the work is still incomplete and you're getting impatient to finish.

Wallpapering Over Old Plaster Walls

When wallpapering over old plastered walls, cover the cracks with small pieces of old nylon curtain, secured with a light coating of wallpaper paste. Jan and Gene Kuehn of **Victorian Bed and Breakfast,** have done a great deal of wallpapering in their gracious Queen Anne home and inn.

If you encounter a bad stain which continues to bleed through the old plaster walls, you can solve the problem as the Kuehns have, by adhering aluminum foil over the stain with wallpaper paste before hanging the wallpaper.

Easing the Pain of Painting the Ceiling

Wear a neck collar (brace) when painting, wallpapering or plastering a ceiling. The folks at **Captain Mey's** learned that after ornamenting the dining room ceiling with gold leaf trim and large swatches of fabric. That's the way they often decorated ceilings in Victorian times. The fabric overhead was a sign of wealth—that the family had traveled overseas and brought back exquisite wares for everyone to see, just in case they hadn't noticed the dresses and other garments.

Do Something with Those Old Newspaper Finds

When Jan and Bobby Boal found pages from early 1900s newspapers between floors and sub-floors, put there probably for insulation purposes, they had them laminated so that visitors could read about events occurring as **The Veranda** was built. Making such papers readily available for people to read adds to the sense of history of a house.

Making it Easier to Restore Hardwood Floors

Here's how from **The Country Haus:**
- ❀ Remove everything from the room, including wall hangings and window treatments.
- ❀ Cover duct work with masking tape.
- ❀ Open windows but close all doors to the room.
- ❀ Rent a large power sander. First, go over the floor with a coarse grade of sandpaper, then a medium, and finally, finish sanding with a fine grade of paper. Sand floor evenly, taking care not to leave the sander running in one spot for too long. Use a sanding block to smooth the corners of the rooms.
- ❀ Vacuum the entire floor thoroughly, removing all dust. Stain the floor, using a small brush for corners and a clean paint roller for the other area. Always apply stain in the direction of the wood grain.
- ❀ After the stain has thoroughly dried, apply clear polyurethane. You may need to apply a few coats.

Air Conditioning an Old House Attractively

Innkeepers at **Cedarcroft Farm** kept their home's character by hiding a new cooling system. Since installing conventional duct work for upper floors causes you to tear out walls and ceilings, it's no wonder many opt for window units when putting air conditioning into an old house.

Bill Wayne says that when he and wife Sandra tackled this problem, they were also putting on an addition. But they say, "The concept would work in any old home. We mounted the air handler unit in the attic of our addition and then ran duct work straight through the wall into the upstairs rooms, put on directional grills to get circulation, and then boxed in the small protrusion made by the duct work. Then, we covered the top with fabric to make an attractive permanent lamp-stand about two feet high." Bill and

❖ ❖ ❖

Sandy's guests frequently ask, "Where's the cool air coming from?"

To supply air to the lower level, the Waynes mounted directional grills flush into the ceiling where they are unobtrusive yet still do the job. The majority of the duct work is in the attic, with a few hoses running through the walls to the basement and outside to the compressor.

Framing Wallpaper Memories

When they completed renovations at **Walnut Street Inn,** the innkeepers saved the layers of old paper they kept stripping from each room. They then placed pieces of the paper in a collage and framed it. Several rooms have such a tribute to the way the walls used to be.

When Mildew Creeps in . . .

Combat mildew and paint peeling off ceilings by using cedar wood planks (³⁄₈-inch thick and random lengths) as a ceiling finish in lieu of paint, suggests **Manor House.** Not only does the cedar resist mildew, but the wood adds a warmth to the room, and the wood planks tend to make the room appear larger.

Hiring Help

When hiring a contractor to handle a reconstruction project, make sure this person is someone with whom you can communicate. Does he or she understand what needs to be done and ask questions to clarify directions? Is he or she a good listener?

Be accessible. Only you know the big picture and you have to communicate well also. Tour the work area at least once a day. Contractors will solve problems in ways you would not have chosen. Try to stick around for any problem-solving that needs to be done. **—The King's Cottage.**

❖ ❖ ❖

How to Convert a Double Bed to a Queen Size

THE antique (56-inch-wide) sleigh bed in the Sherman Room at **The Inn at the Round Barn Farm** (See page 67.) was equipped to support a 60-inch-wide, queen-size mattress by innkeeper Jack Simko. Here are his instructions, which you can adapt to your own antique bed:

Materials:

1 sheet ¾-inch plywood, cut to 60 inches wide by 80 inches long. If you can't special order a five-foot-wide piece of plywood from your local lumber store, you can join two pieces with a good carpenter's glue and H-shaped metal plywood clips.

2 pieces of high quality 1 x 4 wood for side rails, mi-
tered at a 45° angle to frame the plywood where it returns to the bedpost. (The 1 x 4 will be approximately 3¼ inches wide by ⅞ inch deep and should be of a length determined by measuring from the headboard to footboard—about 80 inches.)

4 (2 to 2½-inch-long) pieces of the same high-quality 1 x 4 wood, also mitered at a 45° angle. (These short pieces will be used as returns at each of the four corners of the plywood base.)

20 wood screws

8 nails

Directions:

1. Cut plywood length to fit between the headboard and footboard of the bed (approximately 80 inches). This creates a base to support the mattress. Rest plywood on existing bed boards.

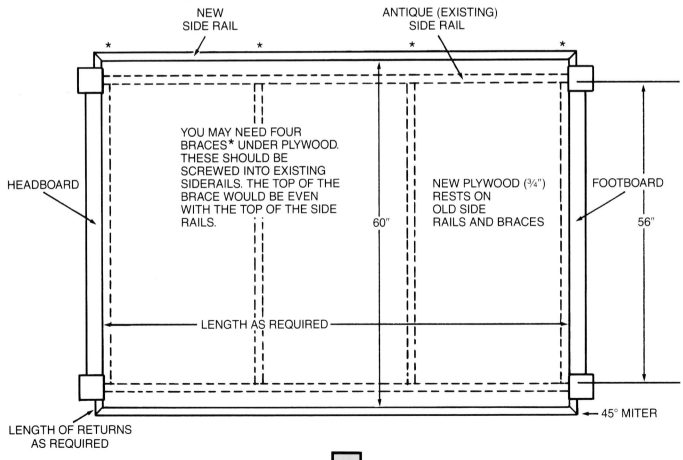

NEW SIDE RAIL

ANTIQUE (EXISTING) SIDE RAIL

YOU MAY NEED FOUR BRACES* UNDER PLYWOOD. THESE SHOULD BE SCREWED INTO EXISTING SIDERAILS. THE TOP OF THE BRACE WOULD BE EVEN WITH THE TOP OF THE SIDE RAILS.

HEADBOARD

NEW PLYWOOD (¾") RESTS ON OLD SIDE RAILS AND BRACES

FOOTBOARD

60"

56"

LENGTH AS REQUIRED

45° MITER

LENGTH OF RETURNS AS REQUIRED

2. Using the high-quality 1 x 4 wood boards to match the wood of the existing bed, create side rails to cover the sides of the plywood. Using a good carpenter's glue, glue and then screw the rails into the plywood, using six screws per side and pre-drilling each hole to prevent the plywood from splitting. Fill and finish the holes for aesthetics.

3. Use the eight remaining wood screws (two per corner) to secure each of the returns to the side rails. Fill and finish the holes. Nails (two per return) can be used to further secure the returns to the side rails. Screw the wood screws first through the side rails and then into the returns, and hammer the nails first through the returns and then into the side rails.

4. Stain the boards to match the original bed finish.

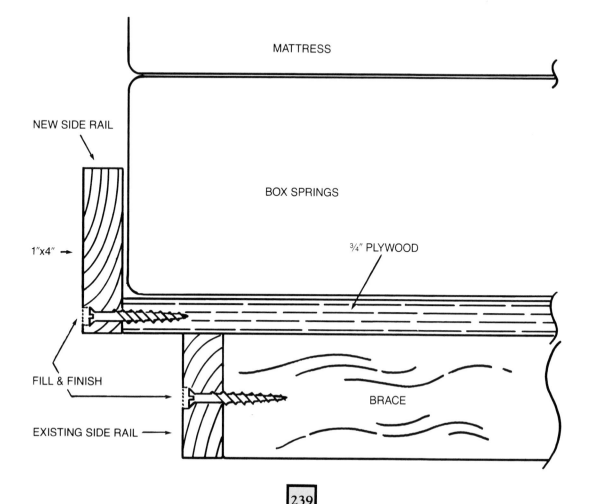

MATTRESS

NEW SIDE RAIL

BOX SPRINGS

1"x4"

¾" PLYWOOD

FILL & FINISH

BRACE

EXISTING SIDE RAIL

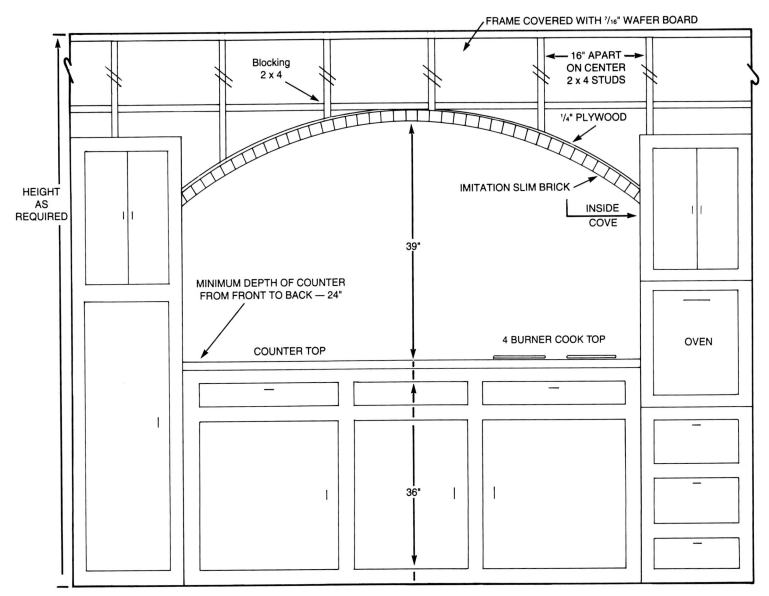

FRAME COVERED WITH ⁷⁄₁₆" WAFER BOARD

Blocking
2 x 4

16" APART
ON CENTER
2 x 4 STUDS

¼" PLYWOOD

HEIGHT
AS
REQUIRED

IMITATION SLIM BRICK

INSIDE
COVE

39"

MINIMUM DEPTH OF COUNTER
FROM FRONT TO BACK — 24"

COUNTER TOP

4 BURNER COOK TOP

OVEN

36"

Blueprint for a Brick Kitchen Alcove

See photo page 190

DURING my travels for this book, I stopped at **Poor Farm Country Inn,** a former shelter for the homeless and frail, which innkeepers Dottie and Herb Hoestler rejuvenated and turned into a delightful bed-and-breakfast. One of the many interesting features of the inn is the kitchen, which Herb renovated with a brick cooking alcove. This is something I have always wanted in my kitchen, and so I asked Herb for a blueprint. As every kitchen size is different, you will need to adapt this blueprint to your own kitchen measurements. Or, you could set aside an area of your room where the exact blueprint from the inn will fit.

❖ ❖ ❖

DECORATING TECHNIQUES

ROOM DESIGNING PLANNER

- Make photocopies of the planner on this page and page 242 and of the grid on page 243 so that you keep your book intact.
- Each square on the grid equals one square foot.
- Mark off the size of your room on the grid and pencil in places where there are windows and doors that open into the room.
- Cut out the furniture templates for the room and place them on the grid to determine where all your furniture will go. Keep in mind walking areas and furniture that extends or opens out. If necessary, make up your own furniture templates as I did with the pieces marked "credenza" and "plant."
- Use rubber cement to adhere the templates to the grid. This adhesive allows you to pull off the furniture without tearing the paper. Simply rub old glue off the grid with your fingers. Now you're ready to rearrange the room again.

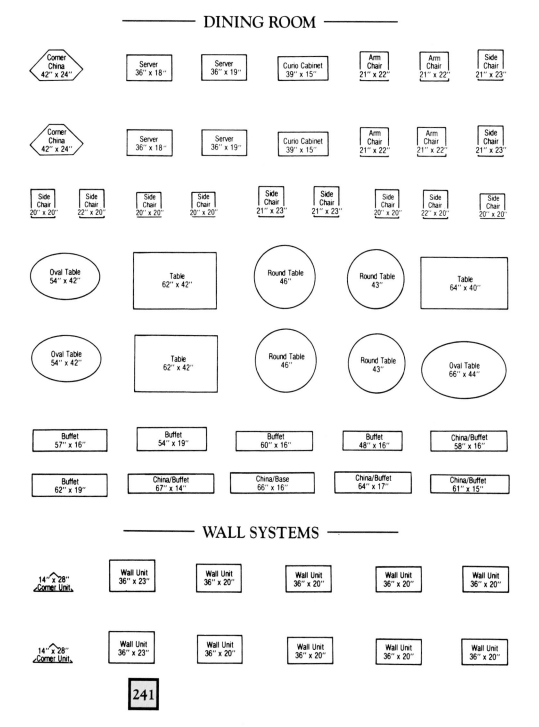

DINING ROOM

WALL SYSTEMS

Inn the Workshop

❖ ❖ ❖

——— LIVING ROOM ———

Lamp Table 16" x 24"	Desk 48" x 26"	Kneehole Desk 54" x 28"	End Table 15" x 28"	87" Sofa	Lamp Table 16" x 24"	Desk 48" x 26"	Kneehole Desk 54" x 28"	End Table 15" x 28"

Butler's Tray Table 34" x 21"

Table 21" x 25"

Coffee Table 28" x 44"

Tea Table 20" x 30"

82" Sofa

Butler's Tray Table 34" x 21"

Table 21" x 25"

Coffee Table 28" x 44"

Tea Table 20" x 30"

Sofa Table 48" x 16"

Table 21" x 20"

Butler's Tray Table 34" x 21"

Table 21" x 20"

59" Loveseat

Coffee Table 38" x 38"

Lamp Table 21" x 27"

77" Sofa

59" Loveseat

Coffee Table 38" x 38"

Lamp Table 21" x 27"

Armless Chair 24"

Armless Loveseat 49"

Left-Facing Loveseat 57"

Right-Facing Loveseat 57"

66" Loveseat

Right-Facing Loveseat 57"

66" Loveseat

77" Sofa

Corner Unit 32"

Accent Chair 26" x 29"

Wing Chair 28" x 32"

Round Chair 31" x 32"

Table 25"

82" Sofa

87" Sofa

Corner Unit 32"

Accent Chair 26" x 29"

Wing Chair 28" x 32"

Round Chair 31" x 32"

Table 25"

Plant

Fireplace

Armless Chair 24"

Armless Loveseat 49"

Left-Facing Loveseat 57"

——— BEDROOM ———

Dresser 63" x 18"

Dresser 58" x 18"

Nightstand 24" x 16"

Nightstand 22" x 14"

Highboy 41" x 20"

Dresser 63" x 18"

Dresser 58" x 18"

Nightstand 24" x 16"

Twin Size Bed

Full Size Bed

Queen Size Bed

King Size Bed

Twin Size Bed

Full Size Bed

Queen Size Bed

Dresser 67" x 19"

Chest on Chest 40" x 19"

Armoire 40" x 18"

Highboy 41" x 20"

Chest on Chest 35" x 18"

Dresser 67" x 19"

Chest on Chest 40" x 19"

Armoire 40" x 18"

ROOM DESIGNING GRID

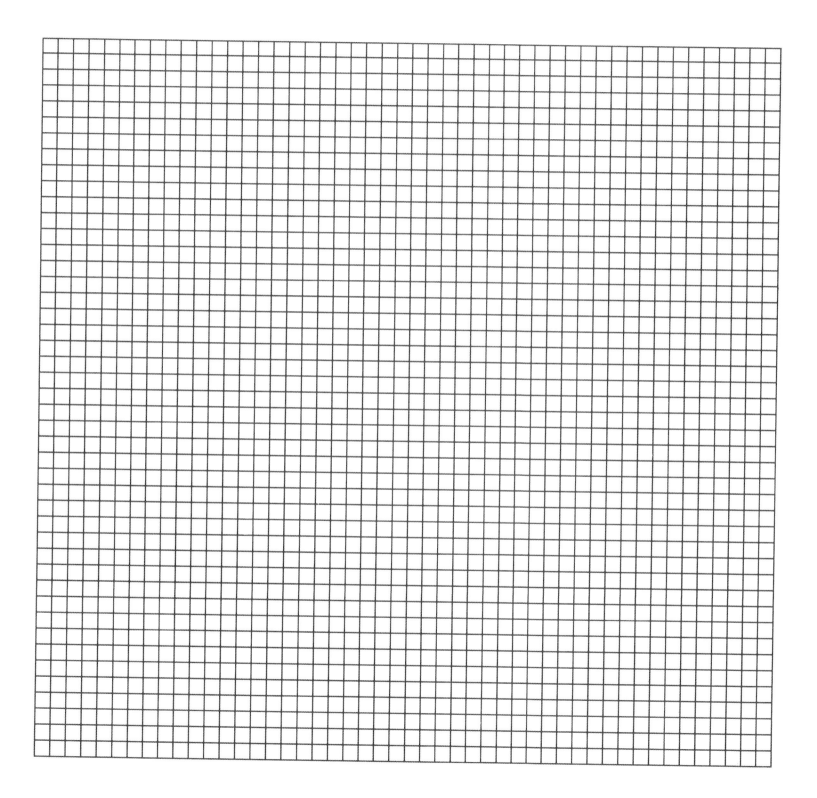

Inn the Workshop

❖ ❖ ❖

SAMPLE ROOM LAYOUTS

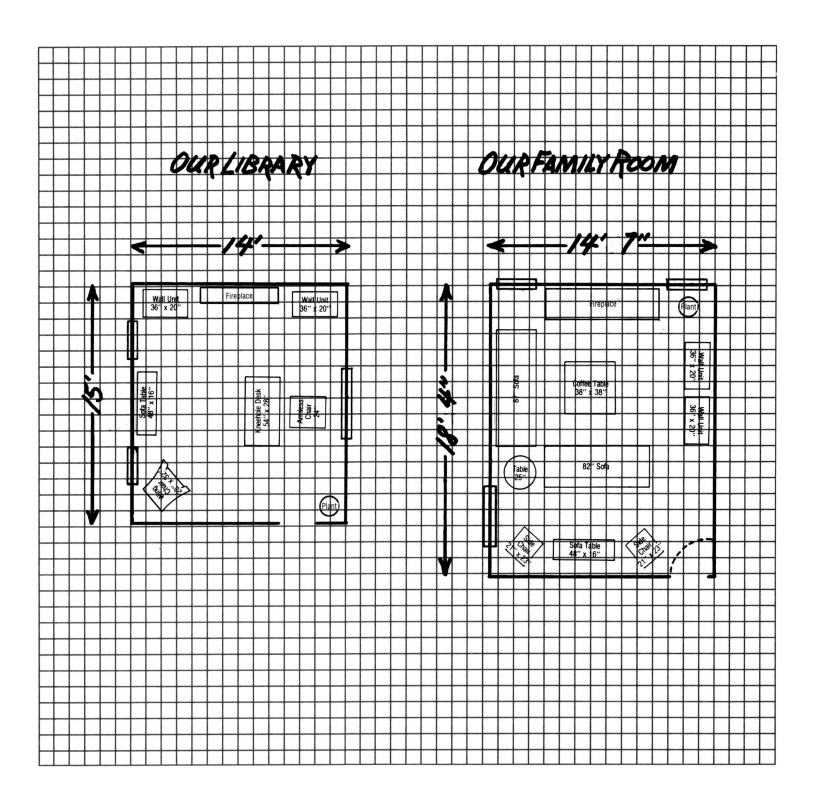

❖ ❖ ❖

The Art of Stenciling

BEFORE wallpaper, there was stenciling, the itinerant artists' way of decorating homes with nature from flowers to fruit and trailing vines. They painted friezes (stenciling below the ceiling line or crown molding), dabbed paint through a stencil above a chair rail or baseboard, and even decorated the floor. They used stencils made of wood and tin and paints they made or mixed on their own. Some early stencil designs have survived and you will see them restored at many inns across the country.

Stenciled walls provide rooms with color, texture, and design, and are an added choice besides wallpaper. Stenciling has certainly witnessed a comeback in America as we search for our roots in design as well as lifestyle.

The patterns that follow are from the inns except for one from my own collection. When I stencil, I do not follow the conventional rules of measuring. I feel that stenciling is an art done by eye and at best is imperfect. Even when a stencil design calls for placing a motif in the center of the wall with a coordinating border stencil, I do not measure but let the eye do it all. In my travels, I have yet to find an innkeeper who measures first, the way stencil books tell you to do. So, here are my basic instructions for stenciling. Usually, when you buy stencils, they are pre-cut. Since you will have to photocopy and then trace these stencils onto mylar, I have provided instructions on cutting your own.

STENCIL PATTERN: Splashes of Daisies
FROM: *Riverwind Inn*

❖ ❖ ❖

HOW TO CUT YOUR OWN STENCIL

Materials:

Tracing paper
Mylar or clear acetate (a heavier gauge)
Medium tip permanent ink marker
Utility knife with replaceable blades
Glass surface
Masking tape

Directions:

1. Make a photocopy of the stencil from this book, enlarging all patterns to 125 percent except Talking Tulips which should be to 250 percent. There are two patterns for Talking Tulips, pattern #1 for stenciling the vine and leaves in one color and pattern #2 for stenciling the center of the flower a second color. On pattern #2 the dotted lines are for positioning on pattern #1.

2. Trace the enlarged stencil design onto a piece of tracing paper.

3. Cut a piece of the clear plastic 2 inches larger than the design. Note: If you are working with more than one color, you will need a separate sheet of acetate for the second color and template. To cut a stencil for the second color, tape another piece of acetate over the first stencil, aligning them exactly. What you traced in solid line on the first stencil, mark with dotted lines on the second stencil. Than trace in solid lines everything to be stenciled for your second color. Repeat for additional colors.

4. Place the plastic over the design and secure with masking tape.

5. With marking pen, trace the outline of the pattern, so that all shapes can be cut.

6. Place on a glass cutting surface and cut the stencil with the knife, following the marked shapes.

STENCIL PATTERN: The Dogwood Patch
FROM: *Riverwind Inn*

❖ ❖ ❖

HOW TO STENCIL

Materials:

Acrylic paints in desired colors

Stipple brush (for medium-size wall stencils, use a medium stipple brush)

Paper plate (not plastic-coated)

Newspaper

Paper towels

Masking or drafting tape

Directions:

1. Using masking tape, secure the stencil to the wall, starting in a corner. Adhere with a small piece of tape on all four corners of the stencil.
2. Pour about 1 tablespoon paint atop the surface of the paper plate.
3. Hold stipple brush between thumb and pointer finger and practice a few stipple movements without paint by pouncing the brush or tapping it perpendicular to the flat surface. After a few practice pounces, dip the brush in the paint, allowing only the tips of the bristles to touch the paint. Then, the idea is to work with a dry brush, so tap most of the paint off the brush by dabbing it onto a newspaper or paper towel. Gently pounce the brush to the wall, filling in the open stencil areas with a speckled coat of paint. (Be careful not to build up too much paint.) Add more paint by the tablespoonful onto the paper plate as needed.
4. If working with a second color, complete the first color, moving the stencil around the room and adhering it each time with tape. Then go back and apply the second paint, using the other part of the stencil you cut.
5. Be sure to clean brushes and stencil carefully in soap and water after you are done.

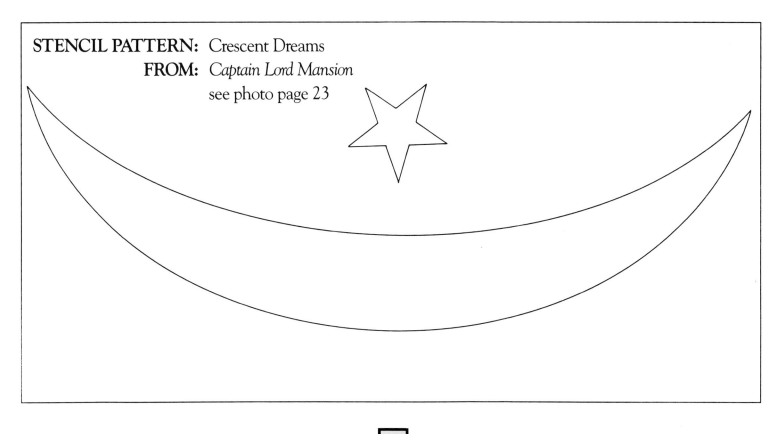

STENCIL PATTERN: Crescent Dreams
FROM: *Captain Lord Mansion*
see photo page 23

❖ ❖ ❖

STENCIL PATTERN: Dimples
FROM: *Riverwind Inn*
see photo page 53

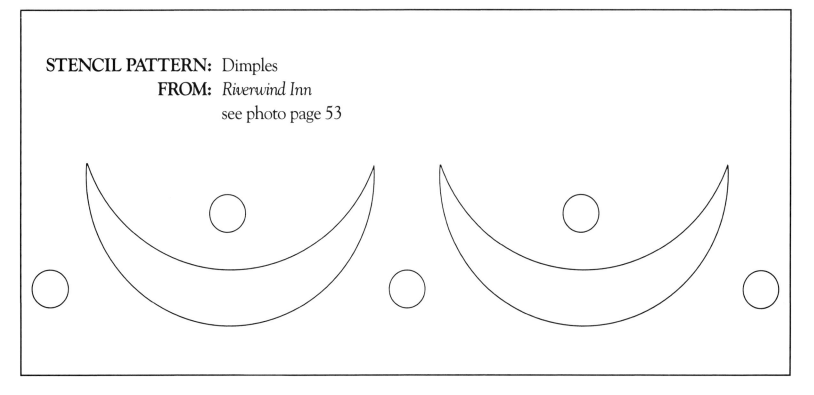

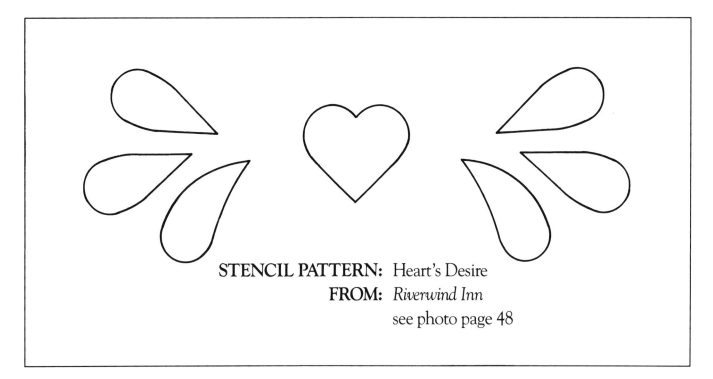

STENCIL PATTERN: Heart's Desire
FROM: *Riverwind Inn*
see photo page 48

STENCIL PATTERN: Talking Tulips
FROM: *Author*
see photo page 223

#1

#2

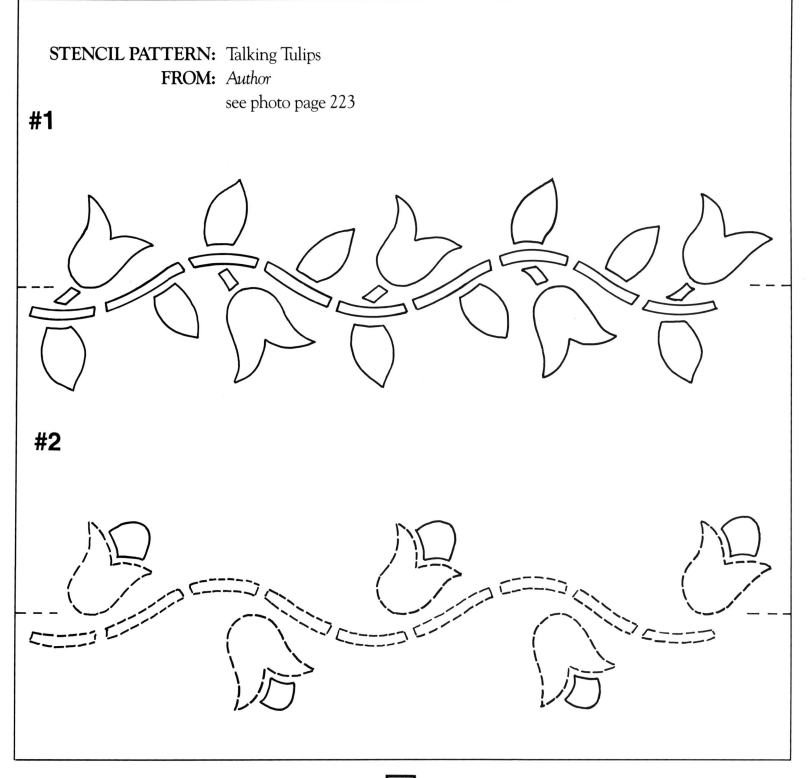

❖ ❖ ❖

Sponge Painting

See photo page 80

YOU CAN choose any combination of paints or textures to do your walls at home. This step-by-step photo sequence shows you how it works using **Sweet Basil Hill Farm** innkeeper Teri Jones' deep and light pink tones as an example.

Materials:

1 base coat paint; 2 top coats paint; one shade slightly lighter than the other; 2 medium-sized natural sponges; newspaper, paper dish and towels, stirrer.

Directions:

▼ *After painting a base coat onto the walls and allowing it to completely dry, drizzle some of the well-stirred top coat onto the paper plate. Soak some of the paint onto the sponge. Remove excess paint from the sponge by dabbing it onto newspaper.*

▼ *Dab paint onto the wall, hitting it once and trying not to overlap, as you don't want to lift up any paint already sponged to the wall. Go around the entire room, using your eye as judge on how much to cover. (Sponging is a technique that allows you to be free and do what is personally pleasing.) Then, using the lighter shade of paint, dab in between the darker shade.*

❖ ❖ ❖

Decorating Walls Elegantly with Brown Paper

See photo page 135

FRAN McCOY of **The Jailer's Inn** saw crinkled walls done in a designer showhouse. She inquired about how to do it and was surprised to learn how easy it is to master this technique. Fran papered the common areas of the B&B with this easy, elegant and inexpensive technique. This can be an especially effective way for covering scarred or damaged walls as there are no straight lines to match and the crinkles hide a lot of sins.

Materials:

> 1 large roll of brown wrapping paper, or more if needed
> Wallpaper paste
> Interior wall paint of your choice

Directions:

1. Tear off brown paper about a foot or more longer than the height of your wall as the crinkles shrink the paper. Crumble the paper into a ball. Set the ball aside.
2. Paint the walls with a heavy wallpaper paste. Then, pat the crinkled paper onto the walls, starting at the top, aligning the edge of the paper with the top of the wall. You do not have to worry about overlapping paper, matching, or keeping anything straight. Cut off any excess length of paper at the bottom, with a straight edge and cutting blade.
3. After you have covered the walls, you can paint over the paper with a color of your choice.

How to Cover Interior Walls with Fabric

See photo page 117

FABRIC ON walls is not only decorative, but it can provide sound-proofing as well as cover unsightly old walls that are not easily repairable. Here is how **The School House B&B** suggests you cover your walls.

Materials:

> Fabric, enough to cover all wall surfaces
> Raw cording for welting (see directions below)
> 5/8-inch polyester batting, enough to cover wall surface
> 5/32-inch cording, enough to make double-welting as trim along outer edges of the fabric
> Staple gun and staples
> Glue gun and glue
> Single-edged razor blades

Additional Materials Required for Plaster Walls Only:

> 1/2-inch-deep wood furring strips, enough to run along top of walls and down both sides of corners (to create a stapling surface)
> Moisture Barrier Acrylic Sealer
> Spray Adhesive

Directions:

Determining fabric required:

1. Measure each wall from ceiling to floor and across from corner to corner. Allow 3 inches additional for each wall-length of fabric required; allow for 1/2-inch seam allowance between each fabric panel. Allow extra fabric for prints that require pattern matching. (Your fabric store can assist you in figuring yardage required.)
2. Measure for batting as with fabric. Extra batting is not required for pattern matching.
3. To determine the length of cording required, measure along the top and bottom of the walls, around all doors and windows, and down both sides of every corner. Add up all amounts and multiply this figure by 2.

❖ ❖ ❖

Preparation of walls:

1. Be sure that sheetrock wall surfaces are free of nails. For plaster walls, scrape down and paint with the acrylic sealer; nail or screw furring strips along the tops of the walls and down both sides of the corners.
2. Remove all outlet and switch plates.

Cutting:

For wall covering, cut fabric panels according to wall measurements (remember to add 3 inches to the length of each cut panel measurement). Cut 3-inch-wide strips of fabric, enough to cover the entire length of cording you measured for previously.

Padding application:

Measure and cut batting to cover all wall surfaces. For sheetrock walls, attach batting with staple gun, stapling every 5 or 6 inches to secure. Leave a 1-inch gap between the batting and the edge of ceiling, corners, baseboard, and moldings. (For plaster walls, attach batting with spray adhesive.) Cut out batting at outlet and switch-plate openings.

Fabric preparation. Pin fabric panels together for each wall separately, taking care to match pattern. Sew together using 1/2-inch seam allowance. Press open seams.

Fabric application. Start at the top middle of one wall. Mark the center point on the first fabric panel. Place the center of the panel at the center top of the wall. Turn fabric under 1/2 inch and begin stapling along the top in both directions, close to the corner so that the staples will be covered by the welting. Pull the fabric taut as you go. Continue stapling along the bottom, just above the baseboard trim, stretching the fabric across in both directions. Then, pull fabric and staple along corner edges.

Trim excess fabric along baseboard with single-edged razor blade.

Do each wall like this, making sure fabric will match at the corners. When you come to a window or door, carefully cut fabric to the size of the opening; then stretch and staple around the window or trim. Do the same for any electrical outlets or switches, making sure to staple the fabric where the cover of the switch plate will hide the staples.

Note: It is very important to staple at the very edge of the fabric so that the welting will hide the staples. It is extremely important that fabric is stretched in every direction. You may need to pin some areas before stapling to assist in getting the fabric securely taut and straight.

If you happen to prick your finger and blood gets on the fabric, immediately wet a clean finger with your own saliva and wipe stain away. (Innkeeper Vicki Ott learned this lining walls at the B&B.)

Welting application. Sew fabric over cording to form covered welting. With glue gun, attach double welting around all edges where fabric was stapled, thus hiding staples. (See photo below.)

❖ ❖ ❖

SEWING PROJECTS

Home-Sweet-Home Cross-Stitch Sampler

See photo page 41

I LOVE the soft and curvy lines of this sampler from the **Maple Leaf Cottage Inn** and the lovely way the design is balanced and softened with trailing vines. The one at the inn was made for the innkeeper by a friend's grandmother, and so the pattern is an old cherished one. It triggered the color scheme in the Maples Room at the inn. It was adapted for this book by noted stitchery expert Patricia Moore who often gives classes at inns.

Materials:

½ yard glazed cotton fabric—off-white
0.50 quilters lead pencil
Embroidery hoop
#24 sharp needle
D.M.C. stranded floss in: #312 blue, #726 yellow,
    #3348 leaf green, #725 gold, #783 orange/gold

Directions:

Photocopy the pattern on page 254, enlarging it if you wish. Tape the photocopy onto a hard surface. Tape the glazed cotton right side up over the pattern and with the lead pencil, trace the design onto the fabric. Mount into a hoop and stitch as follows:

Lettering—3 single strands #312 blue, stitch all the x's in cross stitch.

Blue Flowers—2 single strands #312 blue, stitch 4 cross stitches, and center with a french knot.

Yellow Flowers—2 single strands of #726 yellow. Each flower consists of 5 petals (lazy daisy stitch) in a circle. Add a french knot in the center of each flower.

Green Leaves—2 single strands of #3348 leaf green. Each leaf consists of 3 straight stitches clustered together. Stitch #1 and #2, then add #3 between the 2 stitches.

Curls—3 single strands of #725 gold worked in satin stitches. Follow the diagonal slant of the satin stitches as shown on the pattern. Outline stitch all the satin stitches in #783 orange/gold with 2 single strands.

Spinning Wheel—Satin stitch in 3 single strands of #725 gold. Cross stitch x's on the wheel with 3 single strands of blue #312. Outline stitch with 2 strands of #783 orange/gold.

Yarn on the Spinning Wheel—Satin stitch with 3 single strands of #3348 leaf green.

CROSS-STITCH

STRAIGHT STITCH

LAZY DAISY STITCH

OUTLINE STITCH

FRENCH KNOTS

SATIN STITCH

❖ ❖ ❖

Padded Hangers

ONE OF the most symbolic amenities at bed-and-breakfasts is padded hangers. **The School House** teaches us how to make them, using pretty cotton print fabrics. These directions are for a 16-inch-wide hanger with a thin hook.

Materials:

> ¼ yard 45-inch wide fabric
> Thin wooden coat hanger
> Glue gun and glue
> Quilt batting (1½-inches thick)
> Matching thread
> ½ yard (³⁄₈-inch wide) coordinating decorative ribbon

Directions:

Cutting:

Cut one piece of fabric 1¾ x 14 inches for gathered hook cover.

Cut two pieces of fabric 3½ x 10 inches long for bottom piece of hanger cover.

Cut two pieces of fabric 3½ x 15½ inches for top of hanger cover.

Cut two pieces of batting, each 8 x 12 inches for hanger padding.

Sewing:

1. **Hook cover:** Using fabric piece for hook cover, turn fabric under ¼ inch to the wrong side at the short ends. Press. Turn under ³⁄₈ inch to wrong side on long ends and press. Fold fabric in half lengthwise, wrong sides together, and press. Topstitch long side of fabric, ¼ inch from folded edge.
2. **Hanger cover:** Begin with one of the hanger top pieces. Machine baste, ³⁄₈ inch from fabric edge along three sides, rounding at corners and leaving one short end open. Repeat with second top piece. Pull threads to gather fabric down to a 10-inch length on each piece.

With right sides together, pin one top piece to one bottom piece. Sew together using ½-inch seam allowance, rounding at corners and leaving one short end open for turning. Turn right side out. Repeat with second top and bottom pieces.

Assembly:

1. Slip the hanger hook strip over the hanger hook with stitched edge to the outside, gathering all fabric onto the hook. Touch the end of the hook with a small amount of glue, pinching the end of the fabric to cover the end of the hook. Hold it in place for several seconds until glue begins to dry. Distribute gathers evenly along the hook.
2. Paint glue around half of the hanger; wrap and glue one of the batting pieces (at the 12-inch side), securing it around the hanger. Fold over the excess batting at the end of the hanger and glue in place. Repeat the process with the other half of the hanger.
3. Slide hanger cover pieces over each hanger end, easing the fabric over the batting. Turn under raw edges at the hanger center and hand-stitch together, placing the hook—cover end inside—with all the batting.
4. Tie ribbon around the base of the hook, making a bow, and tack it to the fabric.

❖ ❖ ❖

Tea Cozy

See photo page 225

AFTERNOON tea is served daily at **The Bailiwick,** and since guests like to linger, the inn keeps teapots warmed with cozies. Sandra R. Ruefer, who is also a Virginia historian and docent, makes these for use and for sale at the inn where she is an important member of the staff.

The cozy is completely reversible, so in sewing this up you are composing two units for one cozy. The possibilities are endless. You can use the cozy practically or decoratively, to match a fabric in a room, or to cover an old chipped teapot, turning it into a knick-knack.

Materials:

> 1/3 yard each, two complementary fabrics
> 2 pieces batting, each cut into rectangles 6½ x 14 inches
> 2/3 yard ribbon, ½-inch wide
> 1/3 yard elastic, ¼-inch wide

Directions:

1. Cut fabric into 4 pieces—11 x 14 inches.
2. With right sides of the fabric together, iron a crease 2 inches down from the top (11-inch) edge.
3. Center batting in the space between the crease and the bottom edge. Note: It won't fit the space.
4. Using a ¼-inch seam allowance, assemble all 3 pieces (two fabrics and batting) for each component, leaving a space open ½ inch below the crease and ¾ inch up from the bottom.
5. When stitching across the bottom, be sure to leave a 3- to 4-inch opening, so that you will be able to turn the piece right side out.
6. Turn piece right side out. Square the corners and iron them flat.
7. Edge stitch along the bottom, catching the opening.
8. Stitch ½-inch from the first line of stitching, creating a channel for the elastic at the bottom.
9. Stitch along the crease.
10. Stitch ½-inch down from the crease, creating a channel at the top for the ribbon.
11. Pull elastic through the bottom channel and stitch ends together.
12. Pull ribbon through the top channel and tie ends into a bow.

Yo-Yo Quilt Placemats

See photo page 224

THE first thing I ever learned to sew when I was a young girl was a yo-yo quilt, which I remember my mother teaching me on a cold winter's day. Fond memories of learning by my mother's skillful hands has made this a favorite style of quilt for me. And recently I devised a new way to use the colorful sewn rosettes as placemats.

I must admit that I could not remember how to make them, so I turned to Mom again and watched once more her gentle and tender approach to an age-old craft. Here is how she told me to put my placemat together. Feel free to make more and more rosettes and go on to make a quilt. Here, you are making 70 rosettes for an approximately 12 x 17-inch placemat. But you will need about 900 rosettes for a twin bed-size quilt. If you do a quilt, it is fun to stuff each finished rosette with cotton or batting.

Materials:

> An assortment of colorful fabrics, preferably all cotton and pre-washed
> An assortment of complementary spools of quality thread—quilting thread is the best as it is strong enough to withstand pulling as you gather the rosettes
> Sewing needle
> 1 (4-inch diameter) cardboard circle template

Directions:

1. Cut 70 fabric circles, using the cardboard template.

❖ ❖ ❖

2. Take one circle and turn a ¹/₈-inch hem all around the circle, using a running stitch. When you get to where you started, pull the thread to form the rosette. Take the needle and thread and push through the center opening of the rosette, fastening it in the back with a few stitches to hold. Cut thread off and repeat the process with remaining circles. Note: The finished size of each circle should be about 1³/₄ inches in diameter.

3. When all rosettes are completed, attach them to each other, sewing right sides together with whip stitches. Sew 10 circles across to form the width and 7 down to form the length.

Picture Frame Bow Hanger

See photo page 226

JUST as a picture frame may embellish a painting, a print, or a decorative mirror, so too, can a pretty fabric bow. These bows can be made in a variety of sizes, styles, and fabrics. Moiré is most commonly used because its subtle pattern makes a picture come to life, almost sparkle, and it is available in a wide assortment of colors. Brocade, damask, velvet, and chintz are also good choices as they have enough weight to hold the shape of the bow.

The directions below are for a 48-inch-long, double bow hanger. If you decide not to take the time to make these wonderful decorative accents, see the Resource Guide (Tied to Tradition) for ordering them finished.

Materials:

> 1 yard (54-inch wide) decorator fabric
> Matching thread
> Small plastic ring or pin-style hook for hanging
> 1 1-inch nail for hanging

Directions:

Cutting:

> Cut 1 piece of fabric 11 x 34 inches for the bow.
> Cut 2 pieces 7 x 54 inches for the tails.
> Cut 2 pieces 4¹/₂ x 5 inches for bow assembly.

Sewing:

1. Start by making the bow. Fold the bow piece in half lengthwise, with right sides together. Stitch along the long edge, using ¹/₂-inch seam allowance. Press the seam open and turn the fabric right side out. Center the seam on the back of the fabric and press.

2. With right sides together, fold—short end to short end—and stitch a ¹/₂-inch seam along short end. Turn fabric right side out and crease at the seam. Measure more than 9¹/₂ inches from the seam and mark. Stitch down the width of the bow at the mark through all layers of fabric.

3. Open out the fabric with the first seam centered at the back and the second seam placed directly over it, to create a small bow on top of a larger one. (See illustration next page.) Center fabric on each side of the seams. Stitch along the center through all layers of fabric to secure the double bow.

Sewing the Tails:

1. Fold each tail piece in half lengthwise, right sides together, and stitch along long edges using ¹/₂-inch seam allowance. Press seams open and center seam on back of each tail. Measure 2 inches up from the short edge and draw a diagonal line to the opposite corner (¹/₄ inch from the raw edge). Stitch along the line to make a diagonal tail edge. Trim to ¹/₈ inch. Repeat with the second tail piece, but reverse the diagonal so that when assembled, the tails face in opposite directions.

2. Turn tails right side out and iron flat. Press under ¹/₂ inch on top raw edge of one tail. Trim ¹/₂ inch from the top raw edge of the second tail. With right sides face down,

❖ ❖ ❖

place the shorter tail on top of the longer tail so that the bottom of the tails are even and the ½-inch flap of the longer tail folds over the edge of the shorter one.

3. Fold both tails over—4 inches from the fold at the upper edge—and stitch ¼ inch from the first fold through all layers of fabric.

Bow Assembly:

1. Fold in and press raw edges of bow assembly pieces to make 2 (1½ x 5-inch) finished pieces. Pinch the bow at the center and wrap one of the finished pieces around it. Turn under raw edges and hand-stitch to secure.

2. Pull the second bow assembly piece through the first at the back of the bow. Pinch the tails 4 inches from the upper edge. Hand-stitch the second assembly piece around the tails, turning under the raw edges.

3. Hand sew the plastic ring and secure the pin-hook to the tail piece 1 inch from the top.

Hanging:

1. To hang, nail a 1-inch nail, centered on the wall 7 or 8 inches above the picture or special mirror so that the bottom edge of the bow sits about 2 inches above the frame. Hang the bow from its ring, then drop the tails behind the picture, separating them around the hook on which the picture is hanging.

2. Another way to use the bow is to hang it as described above; but instead of dropping the tails behind the picture, softly bend each tail accordion style and rest them slightly behind the top of the frame on each side of the bow. (See photo page 226.)

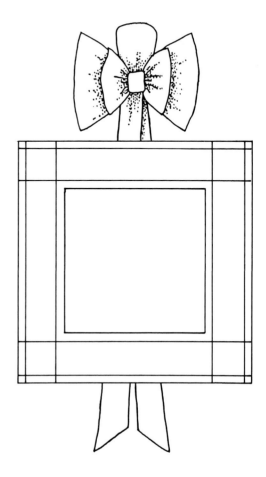

❖ ❖ ❖

The Best-Ever, Easy-to-Remove Dust Ruffle

THE beauty of this dust ruffle or bed skirt from **The School House Bed & Breakfast** is that you do not have to remove the mattress and unmake the bed in order to remove the skirt for cleaning or seasonal changing. The skirt is attached to the box spring in three separate sections so that if one gets soiled, you can remove only that section for cleaning.

Materials:

> 6½ yards (54-inch wide) decorator fabric for the dust ruffle
> 6½ yards (48 to 54-inch wide) lining fabric (a lightweight cotton can be substituted)
> Matching thread
> Straight pins
> 20–22 large safety pins (at least 1½-inches long)

NOTE: Yardage and directions are for the standard queen-sized bed. Additional fabric and larger measurements would be required for larger beds or higher bed frames.

Directions:

Cutting:

1. Cut 2 pieces of decorator fabric 161 x 15½ inches, for the bed's side ruffles. Cut two pieces of lining fabric the same size.
2. For the ruffle at the foot of bed, cut 1 piece of decorator fabric 120 x 15½ inches. Cut 1 piece of lining the same size.
3. For tabs on side ruffles, cut 2 strips of decorator fabric, each 81 x 9 inches. For foot ruffle tab, cut 1 strip of decorator fabric 61 x 9 inches.

Sewing:

1. To make ruffles, begin with one of the side pieces of decorator fabric and a matching piece of lining fabric. With right sides together, sew a ½-inch seam along three sides, leaving one of the long sides open for turning. Press seams open. Turn right side out and press. Machine baste along raw edge through both fabric and lining ⅜ inch from the edge. Machine baste another seam ⅝ inch from raw edge. Repeat the process for the remaining side ruffle and then for the foot ruffle.
2. Pull on basted threads to gather each ruffle piece. Gather the side pieces to a length of 80 inches and the foot piece to 60 inches, distributing gathers evenly.

Assembly:

To attach fabric tabs to the ruffles, turn under ⅝ inch to wrong side of fabric on all short ends of tab pieces and press. Start with one side tab and one side ruffle. Pin right side of tab to wrong side (lining side) of ruffle along raw edge. Sew along raw edge using ½-inch seam allowance. Press seams open. Fold under ½ inch on remaining raw edge of tab and press. Open out the tab and bring the folded edge to the front of the ruffle to cover the raw edge and basting stitches. Pin in place, then topstitch ⅜ inch from folded edge of tab.

Placing Bed Skirt onto the Bed:

When all 3 sections are completed, pin the bed skirt to the box spring. Place the tab part of each ruffle piece on top of the box spring, letting the ruffle fall to the floor. With large safety pins, pin through tab onto top of the box spring. Place pins at ends and approximately 8 to 12 inches apart, all along the tab.

❖ ❖ ❖

Sleeping Beauty Canopy

See photo page 64

THIS beautiful canopy can be made with any fabric that matches your decor. Innkeeper AnneMarie Simko De-Freest of **The Inn at the Round Barn Farm** notes that you may also cover the chains with a fabric tubing and you may add tissue paper inside the material to pouf it and create a fuller look. The directions here are for a ceiling that is 15 feet high. Extra fabric can pool at the foot of each post, or you can use less material for shorter panels, according to the height of your own ceilings.

Materials:

> 1 metal hoop, about 18 inches wide
> 3 lengths of chain, 18 inches long per chain
> 28 yards of chiffon or desired material (48 or 54 inches wide)
> 1 2-inch steel screw-hook
> 4 tiebacks or tassels to match fabric as desired

Directions:

1. Purchase a metal hoop. (They are available at some department stores.) **Round Barn** used one that was from an old sap bucket in their defunct sugarhouse.
2. Drill three holes in the hoop (if not buying a pre-made one) at equal distances (6 inches apart).
3. You are going to need four panels of material, one each to drape over the four bedposts. Divide the yardage. Cut into 7-foot lengths and stitch 1-inch hems on all four sides of each panel around the hoop by folding it over to make a hem, hand-stitched around the hoop.
4. Screw the hook into the ceiling. Gather the three chains with fabric, suspending it by linking each chain to the hook.
5. Drape the material to each of the bedposts, poufing the fabric if you choose (with tissue paper) as you tie it back.

A Crowning Bed Chamber

See photo page 186

DON'T be intimidated by the seemingly complex beauty of this bed treatment designed by **Antrim 1844** innkeeper Dort Mollet. Actually, Dort has employed several simple curtain construction techniques here. The fabrics are not sewn, but stapled to wood furring strips at the ceiling. As you repose in bed, you look up at billows of gathered fabric and veils of lace. Dort often merely turns raw-edged fabric rather than sew. Here, I have presented the hemmed version so that you can decide to do either.

The fabric elements of the treatment include:
- Lace drape panels to be hung from each of the bed's corners and down the width of the bed at the headboard side
- A lace-lined valance panel to be hung from the molding at the ceiling around the perimeter of the bed
- A ceiling panel with lace overlay to be shirred and hung horizontally across the ceiling directly over the bed

Materials:

> 1 x 3-inch furring strips*
> Wood or polystyrene crown molding (determine size)
> Miter box (optional)**
> 48- or 54-inch-wide decorator fabric
> Decorator lace (at least 48 inches wide)
> Decorator paint for crown molding
> Matching thread
> Florist's wire
> 1⅝-inch drywall or plaster screws for furring
> Finishing nails (size appropriate to molding)
> Staple gun and staples

❖ ❖ ❖

Directions:

Measuring/Cutting Wood and Decorative Molding:

1. *Cut 4 lengths of furring strip, 2 the same length as the mattress length and 2 the same length as the mattress width minus 1½ inches.
2. Cut lengths of crown molding to mirror the size of the bed's frame, adding a few extra inches to allow for mitering of corners. (If your bed sits against a wall, you will not need to cut crown molding for that side of the bed.) Cut mitered angles so that the pieces join together at the corners. **NOTE: Some lumberyards will cut mitered angles for you on wood or polystyrene you purchase from them.

Measuring/Cutting Fabric:

1. For **shirred ceiling panel,** cut decorator fabric the same length as the mattress length plus 4 inches. Since the panel must be 2 to 2½ times the width of the mattress to allow for shirring, cut additional pieces the same size (to be sewn together later), according to the width of your mattress. For lace overlay, cut decorator lace pieces the same size.
2. For **valance** width, cut decorator fabric twice the measurement of the perimeter of the bed frame (excluding the side against the wall). Cut the length of the valance according to your own taste, taking into consideration the height of your ceiling and remembering to add 1 inch for seam allowances. For **lace valance liner,** cut decorator lace pieces the same size.
3. For **lace drape panels** at the headboard and corners, measure the distance from the ceiling to the floor and add 8 inches. Cut the appropriate number of lace panels this length. (Since lace comes in a variety of widths and styles, the number of panels you cut will depend on the lace you choose and the desired fullness.) Cut panels as appropriate.

Painting:

Paint cornice with decorator paint.

Sewing:

1. **Shirred ceiling panel.** With right sides together, sew fabric pieces along the long raw edges, using ½-inch seam allowance. (This will make one wide panel piece.) Make ½-inch double hems on all sides of the panel. Repeat the process for lace ceiling panels.

   Lay decorator fabric panel on large surface, with right side facing up. To create lace overlay, place the lace panel on top of the fabric panel, with right side facing up. Pin together. Machine baste two rows of stitches ⅜ and ⅝ inches from each of the long edges. Pull on basting threads to shirr fabric to the width of the bed.
2. **Valance.** To make one very wide valance piece, sew individual valance pieces together at short ends, right sides together, using ½-inch seam allowance. Repeat the process for lace valance lining. Make ½-inch double hems on short ends of the fabric and lace panels.

   Pin fabric to the lace, right sides together. Sew along both long edges, using ½-inch seam allowance, leaving short ends open for turning. Turn right side out and press. Sew a seam ¼ inch up from bottom finished edge to create a pocket for inserting florist's wire. Machine baste two rows of stitches ⅜ and ⅝ inches from the top finished edge of the valance. Pull on basted threads to gather fabric down to the size of the perimeter of the bed frame.

   Insert florist's wire in the hem pocket. Once the valance is mounted on the canopy, you can bend the wire to achieve a wave-effect and give the valance body.
3. **Lace drapery.** Make 1-inch double hems on the top and bottom of each panel. Make ½-inch double hems on the sides of each panel. Machine baste two rows of stitches ⅜ and ⅝ inches from the top finished edge of each panel. Pull basted threads to desired width.

Assembly:

1. **Mounting furring strips.** Screw furring strips to the ceiling directly above the perimeter of the mattress (outside edge of wood should line up with outside edge of mat-

❖ ❖ ❖

tress). NOTE: The strip over the headboard should be mounted slightly away from the wall to allow stapling of lace drapes to the side of the strip.

2. **Attach shirred ceiling panel.** Staple shirred panel to the face of furring strips on the ceiling, along the headboard and footboard side of bed, hiding staples in between folds of fabric. Then staple at the sides, putting staples in inconspicuous spots.

3. **Attach lace panels.** Staple lace drapes to the outside of the ceiling furring strip across the headboard area and around the corners.

4. **Attach valance.** Staple valance around the perimeter of the furring strips, over top of the lace.

5. **Mount crown molding.** Nail crown molding pieces to the ceiling directly above the perimeter of the bed frame, taking care to assure mitered joints fit together neatly.

6. **Finishing touches.** Fluff out valance and bend wire into soft curves to your taste. Tie back or pin up lace panels at corners, as desired.

Good Morning Awning Headboard

See photo page 185

WHILE THE treatment in the photo taken at **Antrim 1844** is supported by a wooden frame, you can achieve almost the same look using conventional curtain rods.

Materials:

48- or 54-inch-wide decorator print fabric
Contrasting solid fabric, same width as decorator fabric, for lining and trim
Matching thread, regular and heavy-duty
1 ¾-inch curtain rod the width of the bed plus 20 inches, with a 2-inch return and a center support
1 ¾-inch curtain rod the width of the bed plus 20 inches, with a 12-inch return and a center support
Staple gun and staples
Thumbtacks
2 ready-made coordinating tie-backs with hooks

Directions:

Installing rods:

1. Install rod with 2-inch return first. Center on the wall above the bed, and mount brackets so that the rod will sit as close to the ceiling as possible; but remember to leave enough clearance for mounting the rod onto the brackets.

2. To install rod with 12-inch return, measure down 15 inches or so (depending on the height of your ceiling and your personal taste) from the first brackets. Mount brackets and center support.

Measuring/Cutting:

1. **Valance panel:** Measure the distance from the ceiling to the bottom of the bottom rod and add 15 inches to determine the cut length. To determine the cut width, measure across the width of the bottom rod and add 40 inches for fullness, returns, and seams. Cut decorator fabric according to these measurements. (Since the measured width will be wider than the fabric, you will need to cut and sew together several pieces to make the valance panel.) Cut the lining the same size in the solid fabric.

2. **Valance trim:** Cut a strip of the solid fabric the width of the valance panel by 11 inches long.

3. **Back curtains:** Measure the distance from the ceiling to the floor and add 10 inches. Cut 2 full widths of print fabric this length.

4. **Side curtains:** Measure the distance from the top of the bottom rod to the floor and add 11 inches. Cut 2 full widths of print fabric this length. Cut 2 full widths of solid fabric the same size.

❖ ❖ ❖

Sewing:

1. **Valance:** Starting with the print fabric for the valance, make ½-inch double hems along short side edges only. For the solid lining piece, make ½-inch double hems along 3 edges, leaving one long side raw. With right sides together, pin print fabric to the lining at the top raw edge and sew along the top raw edge only, using ½-inch seam allowance. Press seam open, turn right side out, and press again along seam. Determine the size header you need by measuring from the ceiling to the top of the top rod. Create a header and a rod pocket at the top of the panel. NOTE: Fabric and lining are separate below the rod pocket.

    Make ½-inch double hems on side edges of solid fabric valance trim strip. With right sides together, pin strip to bottom raw edge of valance print fabric and sew together using ½-inch seam allowance. Press seam open, turn fabric out, and press again along seam.

2. **Back curtains:** Make a 1-inch double hem on the side and top edges of the (2) back curtain panels. Make a 2-inch double bottom hem on each.

3. **Side curtains:** Make a 2-inch double bottom hem on each of the side curtain panels and contrasting lining. Attach print fabric to the lining and make a rod pocket with a 1-inch header at the top of each panel.

Mounting:

1. **Back curtains:** Find the center of the wall above the bed, and mark lightly at the top, by the ceiling. Place one curtain panel on each side of the center point and staple along the top of each panel, close to the ceiling. Tie back the panels to desired position and staple to the wall, hiding staples between folds of fabric. Use thumbtacks if necessary.

2. **Side curtains:** Slip each end of the bottom rod into the rod pocket of the side panels. Hang rod on brackets. Hand-gather the fabric to desired position. Use tie backs to hold in place.

3. **Valance:** Slip the top rod through the rod pocket of the valance panel and hang the rod in place. Bring the front flap of the print fabric out in front of the bottom rod. Let the contrasting fabric fall in back of the rod. Starting in the center front, bring the lining fabric together with the print fabric, and hand-gather the fabric and the lining together, bringing it up toward the rod. Hand-stitch in place, using heavy-duty thread. Place the needle through the front of the print fabric (above the rod), out the back of the lining fabric, and around the rod to the front. Repeat several times to secure in place. Repeat this process at the side and back corners of the valance.

4. **Other trim:** Decorate the center front of the treatment with a fabric bow or other decorative element of your choice.

❖ ❖ ❖

CURTAINS

Shady Lacy

See photo page 43

FOR a permanent shade look on the window, this version from **Maple Leaf Cottage Inn** is simple to make. The key to this treatment is the use of tension rods. An inside mount is what makes it all work. Directions assume you are treating a double window, as in the photo. Make adjustments for single windows accordingly.

Materials:

Ready-made lace panels to fit lengthwise in bottom half of windows
48- or 54-inch-wide decorator floral fabric
48- or 54-inch-wide decorator striped fabric
Lining fabric, same size as decorator fabric
Decorative curtain rod with finials and hanging brackets to fit width of window and beyond
8 tension rods (4 for each window)

Directions:

Installing lace panels and decorative rod:

1. Slip the lace panels onto the tension rod and put in place at the bottom half of the window.
2. Mount decorative rod brackets on the outside of each window, at the window's midpoint.

Measuring/Cutting:

1. **Shades:** Measure the distance from the inside top of the window to the top of the lace panel and add 4 inches. Measure the width of the window and add 1 inch. Cut 2 panels of floral fabric and 2 panels of lining fabric, this size.
2. **Valance:** Cut 2 pieces of striped fabric, 11 inches long by the width of the window, plus 2 inches.
3. **Café rod and panels:** Measure the distance from the decorative rod to the windowsill and add 15 inches. Cut 3 panels of the striped fabric this length by 19 inches wide.
4. **Rod pockets:** Cut strips of fabric for rod pockets to cover the rod pole between the café panels. You will need to determine the width of each pocket based on the overall length of the rod, minus the width of each café panel.

Sewing:

1. **Shade pieces:** Attach floral fabric to the lining fabric and make rod pockets at the top and bottom.
2. **Valance pieces:** Make 1/2-inch double hems on the short sides of each piece. Fold pieces in half lengthwise and sew a 1/2-inch seam along the raw edge. Press the seam open. Turn right side out and press.
3. Fold one café panel in half lengthwise, right sides together, and sew a 1/2-inch seam along 3 sides, leaving one short side open for turning. Press seams open. Turn right side out and press again. Turn raw edge under 1/2 inch to the inside and press. Topstitch to secure 3/8 inch from the edge. Repeat the process for the remaining panels.

   Hang the panel lengthwise on the decorative rod, bringing the topstitched edge to the front and letting it hang down 8 or 9 inches. Remove from the rod. Tack down the overhang along the right edge, leaving an opening for the rod. Fold back the bottom left corner of the flap and tack in place to form a triangle. Sew across the width of the panel, just above the folded triangle, to complete the rod pocket.

❖ ❖ ❖

Mounting the treatment:

1. Insert tension rods into the top rod pockets of the shades. Hang the shades in the top of the window, placing rods as far back into the window as possible. Turn under the bottom tension rod to create a rolled-shade effect.
2. Insert tension rods into the valance pieces and hang in the top of the window in front of the shade pieces.
3. Slip 1 café panel onto the center of the rod. Slip rod pocket pieces on either side. Finish by slipping remaining café flaps onto each end of the rod.

Tab Tops Turn a New Angle

See photo page 45

WHILE these tab tops from **Maple Leaf Cottage Inn** are stationary and cannot be used to cover the window at night, their stacked-back panels are a great treatment to give the illusion of a bigger window. Their tailored look adds dramatic contrast to a room filled with curvaceous flowers and design.

Materials:

    48- or 54-inch-wide decorator striped fabric
    48- or 54-inch-wide decorator print fabric
    Matching thread
  1 ready-made lace panel for top of window
    Decorative rod (with finials and hanging brackets)
        long enough to allow stack back of curtains on
        each side of window
  2 tension rods

Directions:

Mounting the decorative rod:

    Hang the decorative rod brackets on the wall at equal distances from the center top of the window.

Installing lace panel:

    Slide lace panel onto tension rod and hang in the window at desired height.

Measuring/Cutting:

1. **Shade:** Measure the inside distance from the window top to the window bottom. Measure the width of the window and add 2 inches. Cut 1 panel of decorator print fabric this size.
2. For **curtain panels,** measure the distance from the bottom of the decorative rod to the floor and add 5 inches. To determine the cut width, figure 2 times the fullness of the area you want to cover. Cut the fabric accordingly. (You may need to cut and sew together several widths of fabric for each curtain side panel.) Cut a 3-inch-wide facing. The length of the facing should be equal to the width of each curtain panel.
3. **Tabs:** Determine the number of tabs needed for each panel by figuring placement as follows. Place one tab, 2 inches in from each panel edge, and one at the panel center. Space remaining tabs 6 to 8 inches apart. Cut the number of tabs needed (as figured above), each 8 inches long by 2 times the desired width.

Sewing:

1. **Curtain facing strips:** Press under 1/2 inch on one long side and both short ends of each of the curtain facing strips.
2. **Curtain panels:** Finish panel sides by making double 1-inch hems. Finish the panel bottoms with double 3-inch hems.
3. **Curtain tabs:** Finish each tab by folding in half lengthwise, right sides together, and sewing a 1/2-inch seam along the long raw edge. Press the seam open, and turn right side out. Center the seam on the back of each tab and press. With seam to the inside, fold each tab in half so that raw edges meet. Pin tabs in place on the right side of each curtain panel, with raw edge of the tabs meeting the raw edge of panel.
4. **Curtain assembly:** With right sides together, pin the raw edge of the facing strip to the raw edge of the curtain panel (tabs will be sandwiched between curtain and facing). Stitch along the raw edge, using a 1/2-inch seam allowance. Repeat with the second panel. Turn facing to

❖ ❖ ❖

inside of each curtain panel and press along the length of the facing. Tack facing in place at sides and several points on lower edges.

Hand-pleat the fabric between each tab by folding in half, wrong sides together, and pressing. Turn each pleated corner down to make a triangle and press, then tack in place.

5. **Shade:** Finish side edges of the shade piece by making double ½-inch hems. With right sides together, fold fabric in half so that raw edges meet. Sew along raw edge using ½-inch seam allowance. Press the seam open. Turn right side out and press. Sew small rod pocket for tension rod parallel to the seam.

Mounting the treatment:

Slip the shade piece onto the center of the decorative rod with the tension rod pocket at the bottom. Slip the tension rod through the pocket and place the rod in the window near the lace panel. Slip tabbed curtain panels onto the opposite ends of the decorative rod, and place the rod onto its brackets.

Scalloped Swag

See photo page 189

ELEGANT but simple, this treatment from **Antrim 1844** is done with 2 quick cuts of fabric, using the simple fabric railroading technique.

Materials:

1 x 2-inch wood furring strip cut to a length that is 1 inch less than the inside width of the window
48- or 54-inch-wide solid color decorator fabric such as silk, damask, or moiré
Matching thread
Fabric for lining, same width as decorator fabric (you may use the decorator fabric itself or choose conventional lining)
Coordinating fringe (to be topstitched to treatment)
Staple gun and staples
Decorative antique pin, button, or other decoration
Wood screws

Directions:

Measuring/Cutting:

1. **Cut furring strip.** Cut 1 furring strip as described under "Materials" section based on inside measurement of the window.
2. **Cut fabric.** Since you are working with a solid fabric with no up-and-down pattern, and the fabric has significant width, you can use the railroading technique. That is, turn the fabric sideways so that its width becomes its length. Cut 1 piece of fabric the length of the furring strip plus 5 inches. Cut 1 lining piece the same size. Cut fringe the same length as the cut fabric, minus 4 inches.

Sewing:

1. **Sew fabric panel.** With right sides together, sew the fabric to the lining along 3 raw edges, leaving one long edge open for turning. Press open the seams. Turn right side out and press. Sew a ½-inch seam along raw edge to secure.
2. **Attach fringe.** Find the center point of the fabric along bottom finished edged. Pin the center point of the fringe to the center point of fabric. Topstitch fringe along the bottom, turning fringe under at the ends. (NOTE: The fringe will not reach to the edges of the fabric since each end will return around the wood furring strip inside the window and will not be seen.)
3. **Attach fabric to mounting board.** Mark the center point on the top front of the mounting board. Mark center point on long raw edge of fabric. Matching center points, place about ¾ inch of raw edge of fabric onto the wide

❖ ❖ ❖

part of the board. Staple in place along the length of the board and the return.

4. **Creating swags.** Place the treatment on the edge of a table so that the fabric hangs down. Determine the number of swags you would like, allowing for equal distances between each. Hand-gather fabric vertically at each new swag point and each end of fabric, and hand-baste to secure.

5. **Mount treatment.** Simply screw the furring strip to the top inside of the window.

6. **Finishing the treatment.** Pin or sew decorative pin to the top center of the treatment.

Stagecoach Valance

See photo page 153

Directions from **Canyon Villa** are for a finished valance 12 inches long and 40 inches wide, which is suitable for a 35-inch wide window.

Materials:

1¼ yards 48-inch or 54-inch-wide decorator print fabric for valance and self-lining
1 yard 42-inch-wide solid color fabric for ties
Staple gun and staples
Fabric glue
2 wooden dowels, each 1½ inches in diameter and 40 inches long
2 1½-inch L brackets with 2 screws each for hanging

Directions:

Cutting:

1. Cut 2 pieces of the decorator print fabric, each 20 x 41 inches, for the front and self-lining parts of the valance.

2. Cut 4 (3-inch-diameter) circles of decorator print fabric, to cover pole ends.

3. Cut 6 pieces of solid fabric, each 5 x 28 inches, for the ties.

Sewing:

1. To make valance panel, place valance front and self-lining pieces right sides together and sew a ½-inch seam along each of the 20-inch sides. Press open seams. Turn right side out and press. Topstitch ½ inch from raw edge on both 41-inch sides.

2. To make ties, fold each tie piece in half lengthwise, right sides together, and press. With 2 of the tie pieces, sew a ½-inch seam along long raw edge of each. Trim seams, turn right side out, and press.

   To make pointed tails on each of the remaining 4 ties, draw a diagonal line at one short end of each tie. Stitch along long raw edge using ½-inch seam allowance, then turn fabric and stitch along diagonal line. Clip seams, turn right side out and press. Topstitch ½ inch from remaining short raw edge.

Assembly:

1. Using fabric glue, paint the flat end of 1 pole and 1 inch in from the edge. Place one decorator fabric circle on the glued surface, right side up. Wrap the edges of the fabric circle around the side of the pole and hold in place while glue dries. Repeat with remaining pole ends.

2. To mount valance panel on top pole, paint a 1-inch strip of fabric glue along the length of the pole. Place raw edge of valance panel, self-lining side down, on the glued surface and staple along the length of the pole ¼ inch from raw edge of fabric. (NOTE: Since this pole will be at the top of the valance, you will need to be sure you mount the fabric so that the design faces right side up.) Once glue dries, roll the pole toward the self-lining until fabric covers the entire pole and overlaps the stapled edge by ½ inch. To secure, staple along the length of the

❖ ❖ ❖

pole at the top where staples will not be seen once the valance is hung.

3. To attach the second pole, paint a 1-inch strip of fabric glue along the length of the pole. Place the bottom raw edge of the valance panel onto the glued surface, right side to the glue. Staple along the length of the pole ¼ inch from raw edge of fabric. Once the glue dries, roll the pole toward the right side of the fabric (in the opposite direction from the top pole) until the fabric covers the entire pole and overlaps the stapled edge by ½ inch. Staple along the length of the pole at the back where staples will not be seen once the valance is hung.

4. To attach ties to the valance, begin with one of the tie pieces that have raw edges at both short ends. Fold in half—short end to short end—and sew along short end using a ½-inch seam allowance. Turn right side out. Repeat with second tie piece. Slip tie pieces around the poles on each end of the valance with short seam at the back of the valance. Staple in place 5 inches from each pole end. Attach the remaining 4 diagonal-tail pieces, 2 on each side, by stapling the raw edge of each tail to the back of the top pole. This should be done in a way that, when the tails are brought down in front of the valance, they come diagonally down toward the center tie band. Using both tails at once, tie a Windsor-style knot around the vertical tie band.

Installing:

Hang a 1½-inch L bracket. (The top pole of the valance will sit on top of the bracket.) Drill two holes, on the underside of the top pole, 3 inches in from each end. Place the pole on top of the L bracket and use one screw in each bracket to secure the valance in place.

Angel-Wing Swag

See photo page 187

YOU don't need to wait for the sound of a bell ringing at Antrim 1844 to know that they consider you an angel who has earned his wings. When you sleep in the ice house cottage here, you do so with angel's wings above your head. This heavenly and functional treatment is characterized by fabric panels that gracefully flow from the center top of the window to the bottom and back up again to its corners. Simply unlock the tie-backs and let the panels fall for evening privacy.

Materials:

48- or 54-inch-wide decorator fabric
Fabric for lining, same width as decorator fabric
Ready-made decorative tie-backs
6-inch diameter drapery ring with self-mounting
    bracket
2 hooks for tie-backs
Thumbtacks

Directions:

Install ring over the center of the top of the window at desired height.

Measuring/Cutting:

Measure from the drapery ring to the top right corner of the window, down to the bottom of the window, and add 24 inches to this figure. Cut 2 panels of fabric this length, using the entire width of the fabric.

Cut 2 panels of lining fabric the same size.

Sewing:

Hem the bottom of the fabric and lining. Attach fabric to the lining, assuring that all raw edges are turned under.

Mounting treatment:

1. Hold one finished panel in front of you lengthwise and hand-gather it at the top. Fold the top over about 12 to 14 inches. Then stuff the folded fabric through the back of the drapery ring and pull through to the front, taking care to keep short ends of the folded piece at the back of the ring. Do the same with the second panel.

❖ ❖ ❖

2. Pouf the fabric in front of the ring into a button shape, and shape the short ends at the back of the ring into fans or other desired look.

3. Pull the outside edge of one fabric panel up to the top corner of the window, letting the fabric swag gracefully. Hook the panel in place. Repeat with the other side.

4. Attach tie-back hooks to the wall at the corners by actually pushing them through the fabric near the thumbtack. (This will hold the fabric in place when the tie-backs are done.)

5. Use tie-backs to pull up the curtain panel into "angel's wings." Hang the tie-backs on corner hooks to hold the panels in place.

6. Now that the panels are in place, use your creative talent to adjust the treatment to your liking.

Breath of Spring Lace Cornice

See photo page 184

Materials:

> ½-inch plywood or pine board for top, front, and sides of cornice*
> Decorator fabric to cover outside of cornice
> 1-inch cotton or polyester batting
> Lining fabric to cover inside of cornice
> Decorative lace to hang from cornice (in a length that is equal to the finished cornice's front and sides)
> Carpenter's glue
> Sixpenny finishing nails
> Staple gun and staples
> L brackets for hanging

Directions:

Measuring/Cutting:

1. *To determine the cut measurements for the wood cornice, measure the outside width of the window, including any moldings, and add 4 inches to this figure. Determine the desired height of the cornice (your personal taste) and record this figure. Determine the desired depth of the cornice (again, personal taste, but should be at least 3 inches deep) and record this figure.

2. For the cornice top, cut 1 piece of wood using the width and depth measurements. For the cornice front, cut 1 piece of wood using the width and height measurements. For the cornice side pieces, cut 2 pieces using the height and depth measurements, adding ½ inch to the depth measurement to allow for the thickness of the plywood when assembled.

Cutting fabric:

1. For the cornice front, cut 1 piece of decorator fabric 6 inches wider than the front plus the sides of the cornice board, and 6 inches longer than the height of the board. Cut 1 piece of lining fabric the same size.

2. Cut 1 strip of batting long enough to cover the front and sides of the cornice board.

Assembly:

1. Glue cornice top to cornice front. Nail to secure. Attach side pieces with glue, then nails.

2. Glue batting strip to front and sides of cornice, cutting away any excess.

3. Staple the lining to the inside of the cornice, cutting away excess fabric.

4. Attach decorator fabric to cornice board. An easy way to do this is to place the decorator fabric piece, right side down, on a table or on the floor. Place the front of the cornice piece on top of the fabric in the center. (Check the fabric pattern to assure that fabric will not be upside down when the cornice is turned over.) Wrap fabric around the cornice (much like wrapping a gift), turning under raw edges and stapling at the corners and other inconspicuous spots. (Be sure to keep the fabric taut and the pattern straight as you staple.)

5. Staple the pre-finished, hemmed lace to the inside of the cornice so it drops to form a well-proportioned treatment.

6. Secure the cornice to the wall with L brackets.

❖ ❖ ❖

Crunch 'n' Pouf Valance-Curtain

See photo page 188

A VALANCE and curtain all-in-one. Dort Mollet finds florist wire a versatile material when dreaming up curtain treatments on the spot as she usually does. The florist wire adds a new twist to curtain style.

Materials:

> 48- or 54-inch-wide decorator floral fabric for curtain
> Decorator striped fabric for valance, same width as floral fabric
> Lining fabric, same width as floral fabric
> 3/4-inch curtain rod with 2-inch return
> Florist's wire
> 1 ready-made coordinating tie-back and hook
> Tissue paper

Directions:

Measuring/Cutting:

1. Measure the length and width of the window. Cut floral curtain fabric the length of the window plus 22 inches, by 2 1/2 times the width of the window. (For wide windows, you may need to cut and sew together several widths of fabric to make a large enough curtain panel.) Cut lining fabric the same size.
2. Cut striped valance fabric 24 inches long by the same width as the curtain panel.

Sewing:

1. Sew together floral curtain pieces at the sides (if you have more than one) to make a single panel. Repeat the process with lining and with valance pieces.
2. Hem floral and lining panels. Attach lining to fabric at side seams. Turn right side out and press.
3. Fold under 1/2 inch along the top raw edge and press. Then fold under again, 12 inches, as though you were about to make an extremely large rod pocket. Stitch across the width of the panel along the first (1/2-inch) folded edge. To make a rod pocket at this unusual place in the fabric, sew a second seam parallel to the first and far enough from it to accommodate the thickness of your rod. (When hung on the rod, the curtain will have a large flap of fabric that will fall forward.)
4. To create a tiny pocket for the florist's wire, stitch along the width of the panel 1/4 inch from the top folded edge of the panel. (This is the edge of the flap that will fall forward when the curtain is mounted on the rod.)
5. For the valance panel, finish each of the sides by sewing small double hems, making sure that the finished valance panel is the same width as the finished curtain panel. With right sides together, fold fabric in half so that raw edges meet, and sew together at raw edges using 1/2-inch seam allowance. Press open the seams. Turn right side out and press.
6. Attach the valance piece to the curtain piece. Place the curtain panel, right side down on a table or large surface. Place the seamed end of the valance panel over the top line of the rod pocket stitching, and pin in place. Turn panel over and secure valance by stitching over the original rod-pocket stitching line. This creates a second flap that will hang down in front of the curtain.

Mounting:

1. Install rod, hanging brackets and tie-back hook at desired locations.
2. Slip rod through rod pocket and hang treatment, bringing both flaps to the front. Distribute fabric evenly across the rod. Pull curtain to the side with tie-back and hook in place.
3. Lightly crunch a few pieces of tissue paper and stuff them into the curtain flap and valance piece.
4. Insert wire into the small pocket on the curtain flap and lightly bend, using your eye to shape as desired.
5. Crunch and pouf both the valance and the curtain flap, and add or subtract tissue paper until you like what you see.

❖ ❖ ❖

CRAFT PROJECTS

Fee Fi Faux Pies

See photo page 58

ALL year long, innkeeper Barbara Hankins of **The Southern Hotel,** puts out pies. But some are for eating and others are just for decoration. Faux-dough pies sitting on a kitchen counter warm a country home and add color to your decor. Barbara's Four-and-Twenty Blackbirds pie is just one example. She added plastic birds, inserted in the pie after baking. You can do just about any theme pie with this basic recipe from the inn.

> Pre-baked fruit—cherries, blueberries, blackberries, or such*
> 4 cups all-purpose flour
> 1 cup salt
> 1 1/2 cups warm water
> Egg wash (1 egg mixed with 1 teaspoon water)
> Acrylic paints
> Acrylic spray

Mix together by hand the flour, salt, and water, kneading the dough until well combined. Shape into a ball. Let rest in a plastic bag for 30 minutes. Roll dough out to 1/4-inch thickness and press into an 8, 9, or 10-inch disposable foil pie plate. Cover with plastic wrap and place in refrigerator. Set aside.

*Preheat oven to 250°. Use leftover dough to form desired fruit. Bake fruit for 30 minutes to 1 hour or until totally dry. Paint fruit. Remove pie shell from refrigerator and fill pie shell with it.

Form remaining dough into lattice strips. Cut 1/2-inch-wide strips of dough with a knife or try cutting jagged edges with pinking shears, pizza cutter, or pastry roller. Weave the strips over top by placing strips over the fruit from left to right about 3/4 inch from each other. Fold back every other strip halfway. Place a strip across the unfolded strips from front to back. Unfold the strips. Fold back the alternates. Place the next strip 3/4 inch from the last. Continue until half of the pie is latticed. Then, repeat the process, beginning on the other side of the center line.

When the entire pie is latticed, attach the strips to the pie edge loosely to allow for shrinkage. Moisten the ends to make them stick. Cut them off before crimping the crust. Brush with egg wash and bake in a 250° oven for 1 to 2 hours, until pie is totally dry. Then using acrylic paint, poke through the lattice to add color to the fruit. Spray lightly with acrylic sealer to add a light sheen. **Yield: 1 pie**

❖ ❖ ❖

Half-Moon Branch Swag

ALTHOUGH pictured on page 35 on a window at **Gardens of Eden,** this swag can be hung anywhere. Its design is rather eclectic, allowing it to fit into almost any decor. You can personalize this project by selecting complementary ribbon, but preferably the slightly crinkled paper ribbon style, especially the ones with printed flowers as they enliven the natural branches.

Materials:

Enough bare and pliable branches to form a bunch that is 48 inches long by 5 inches in diameter
Florist's spool wire
Forsythia branches, blossoms removed to form three bunches that are 48 inches long and 3-inches in diameter
4 eucalyptus branches
6 yards paper ribbon, 3 inches wide
Optional—any dried or silk flowers

Directions:

1. Form the top of the swag first by wrapping the bare branches with the spool wire, four inches from each side of the center. Twist the wire together and cut. Do this for the remaining two forsythia bunches.
2. Secure each branch together by wrapping florist's wire around the bunches to hold them together. It is best to wrap the wire completely around the bunches in long sweeps.
3. Attach one bunch to the top support bundle you tied earlier, at each end so that it forms a half-moon shape.
4. Take the remaining two forsythia bunches you have secured together and form them into a heart shape. Wire them securely to the half moon as shown in the photograph. Repeat with remaining bundle.
5. Form the ribbon into a bow and wire it to the center of the swag. Weave the ribbon tails through the top of the swag, keeping a balance on both sides of the ribbon.
6. Tuck two eucalyptus stems on either side of the ribbon. NOTE: Glue anything in place you feel is not tightly secured. Feel free to further decorate the swag with other dried materials such as baby's breath or flowers.

◄◄ *Supplies for making the swag*

◄ *Forming the half-moon shape with the support branches at the top and the forsythia at the bottom.*

◄ *Form 2 heart shapes with each remaining forsythia bundle and attach to the half-moon.*

▲ *Add ribbon and eucalyptus and any other dried or silk flowers you wish.*

Butterfly Napkin Rings

ONE room of the inn is filled with butterfly gear, mementos, and even a butterfly kaleidoscope. In honor of the fragile insect, **The Veranda** decorates many a party with paper butterfly napkin rings.

These are a cinch to make and the possibilities for their use are endless. I've already made them out of wallpaper (See photo page 226.), contact paper, and fabric-covered cardboard.

Here's **The Veranda's** pattern. Simply photocopy this page and cut it out as a template. Then let your imagination run wild. Cut the slots and fit them together and use as a variation for your own party or dinner table. (NOTE: To suit the thickness of your napkins, you can make the ring larger by extending the shaft.)

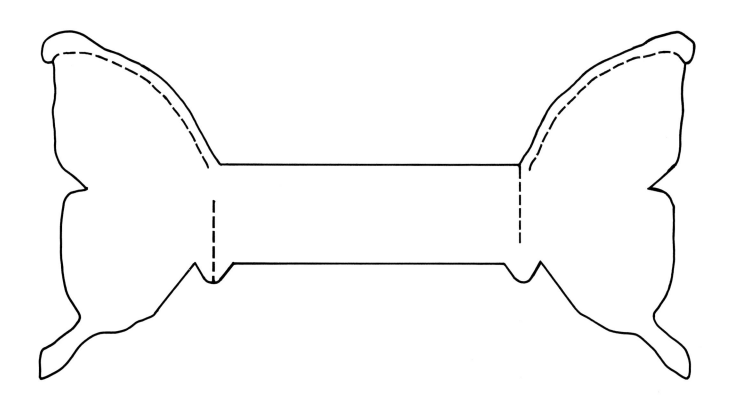

❖ ❖ ❖

Topiary Doors

See photo page 69

ALTHOUGH these doors from **The Inn at the Round Barn Farm** are for holiday decorating, you can decorate your doors for any time or season of the year, just as you would hang a wreath on the door.

Materials:

> 1 12 x 36-inch styrofoam block (2 to 3 inches thick)
> Fern pins
> Moss, fresh or dried
> Fresh balsam, boxwood, or other evergreens
> Tree branches, birch or other
> Bramble of sorts
> Colored foil
> Ribbon
> Apples
> Holly

Directions:

1. To make the flowerpot base, cut a 12-inch-high, pot-shaped wedge out of styrofoam.
2. Wrap the styrofoam pot in red or green plastic-backed florist's foil. Use fern pins to pin foil to styrofoam.
3. Apply strips of ribbon to decorate the pot.
4. To make the top balls of the topiary, cut 2 (12-inch) circles out of the remaining styrofoam. (Optional: You can use a holiday wreath to top your tree.)
5. Stick evergreens into each styrofoam ball, starting on the outside edge and working toward the center. Decorate with apples, holly, and the like.
6. Attach branch(es) to both the styrofoam pot and the top styrofoam balls with hot glue or nails. Decorate branches with bramble.
7. Use screws to attach branches to the door.

Hazelnut Pomander
The Clifton Inn

◀ Hazelnut Pomander (center). Make several pomanders to hang all over your home.

◀ Gather fresh moss (or visit the florist) to cover the size foam ball of your choosing. Cover the ball entirely with the moss and keep it in place by wrapping thin wire around the moss until it is secure. Then, using a glue gun, position hazelnuts (or acorns) around the ball, covering it completely. Attach a piece of ribbon and hang.

❖ ❖ ❖

Apple Wreath
The Clifton Inn

▶ *Designed as a rectangle, the apple wreath may be used as a centerpiece or a wall hanging.*

▶ *Cut a 2-inch-thick piece of styrofoam 8¹/₂ x 3 inches. Wrap it in any color foil. Pick magnolia leaves, cutting stems completely off the leaves. Attach them to the underside of the foil-covered rectangle with florist's pins or glue, gathering them in threes as shown here. Go around the styrofoam until you have a magnolia base. Pierce the lady apples with florist's picks (toothpicks won't hold the weight) and then press into the block in two lines. Fill in the open spaces with fresh boxwood by piercing the greenery through the foam.*

276

❖ ❖ ❖

COUNTRY INN RESOURCE GUIDE

Accessories

PATRICIA MOORE
67 Gold Road
Wappingers Falls, NY 12590
Custom stitchery artist and instructor who also holds "stitch-in" weekends at inns

SANDRA R. RUEFER
11705 Vale Road
Oakton, VA 22124
Tea cozies such as those at **The Bailiwick Inn**

TIED TO TRADITION
1030 Cox Avenue
Washington Crossing, PA 18977
Picture frame bows such as the one in the author's section

Antiques

White Horse Antiques
Third and Clark Streets
Rocheport, MO 65279
Rocking horse such as on page 118, and other special country and primitive artifacts

▶ *Mural artist Virginia McLaughlin*

East Road Gallery
14906 Red Arrow Highway
Lakeside, MI 49116
Arts-and-Crafts-era furniture and Roycroft china

Artists

K. J. Anderson, Illustrator
Sculpture Graphics Studio
2712 Melrose Place
Godfrey, IL 62035
Silhouettes such as those on page 40 and other art

Dolly DuFour
c/o Southern Hotel
146 South Third Street
Ste. Genevieve, MO 63670
Dummy boards

Virginia McLaughlin
133 Jacks Mountain Road
Fairfield, PA 17320
Mural artist as featured in author's section

Marcia Miller
R.D. 3, P.O. Box 119
Owego, NY 13827
Artist who designs stencils from homeowner's furnishings like those in author's section

❖ ❖ ❖

◄ *Casa Benavides innkeeper Barbara McCarthy at one of her Taos, New Mexico shops*

Project Planners
P.O. Box 520
111 W. Chestnut Street
St. Michaels, MD 21663
Eight-page bulletins from how-to project experts Gene and Katie Hamilton that help you plan home improvement projects

The Wagner Institute for Color Research
4000 West Fillmore Street
Chicago, IL 60624
Books on how color affects human responses

Clothing

All Akimbo
P.O. Box 385
Cape Girardeau, MO 63702
Handmade jumpers and buttons such as the one worn by Barbara Hankins on page 228

Crafts

The Fox's Den
3200 Jones Road
Woodbine, MD 21797
Custom banister art such as the innkeeper on page 224

Books

Marcia McAlister Enterprises
P.O. Box 381704
Germantown, TN 38183
With House In Hand, a decorating organizer book as used by **Chicago Pike Inn**

Herb E. Moss Sculptures
Susan Van Meter
c/o Maple Leaf Cottage Inn
P.O. Box 156
Elsah, IL 62028
See page 45

Floor Coverings

Claire Murray Rugs
P.O. Box 390
Ascutney, VT 05030
Hand-hooked rugs of bold designs like those at **The Inn at the Round Barn Farm**

Village Weavers
McCarthy Plaza
Taos, NM 87571
Hand-woven wool rugs, log furniture pieces such as those at **Casa Benavides,** *owner of the shop*

Food

Smithfield Packaging Company
P.O. Box 447
Smithfield, VA 23430
Specialty hams such as those served at **Riverwind**

Breads and Spreads
13Y Hillside Road
Old Greenbelt, MD 20770
Fresh breads and pastries shipped all over the country such as the bread on page 224

❖ ❖ ❖

Furniture

J. J. Jenkins Beds
(See *Reproductions*)

Maschino's Home Expressions
1715 S. Campbell
Springfield, MO 65807
Fireplace equipment and patio furniture, including decorative fabric outdoor umbrellas—shop is owned by **Walnut Street Inn**

Thomasville Furniture
Thomasville, NC 27360
Back Roads and Country Inns furniture collection with pieces inspired by such inns as **The Captain Lord Mansion**

Inn Sources

Inn Marketing
P.O. Box 1789
Kankakee, IL 60901
Newsletter reporting on new inns and news of the B&B industry

The Professional Association of
  Innkeepers International
P.O. Box 90710
Santa Barbara, CA 93190
Source for inn information and products, inn real estate

Kitchen Ware

Old Mexico Shop
McCarthy Plaza
Taos, NM 87571
Regional, tin ware, and dishes like those at **Casa Benavides,** *owner of the shop*

Reproductions

J. J. Jenkins Beds
600 Taunton Avenue
Seekonk, MA 02771
Reproduction antique beds such as those at **The Captain Lord Mansion**

Renovator's Supply
Miller Falls, MA 01349
Victorian hardware, fixtures, friezes, etc. Write for catalog.

W. F. Norman Corporation
Box 323
Nevada, MO 64772
New tin ceilings such as those found in **Arsenic & Old Lace**

Restoration

PastForward
Historic Preservation, Rehabilitation Analysis
The Russell-Cooper House
Mount Vernon, OH 43050

INN DIRECTORY

A

Alaska's 7 Gables
P.O. Box 80488
Fairbanks, AK 99708
907-479-0751

The Anniversary Inn
1060 Mary's Lake Road
Estes Park, CO 80517
303-586-6200

Antrim 1844
30 Trevanion Road
Taneytown, MD 21787
410-756-6812

Arsenic & Old Lace
60 Hillside Avenue
Eureka Springs, AR 72632
501-253-5454

B

Back of the Beyond
7233 Lower East Hill Road
Colden, NY 14033
716-652-0427

The Bailiwick
4023 Chain Bridge Road
Fairfax, VA 22030
703-691-2266

The Bayberry Inn
111 West Valerio Street
Santa Barbara, CA 93101
805-682-3199

Blue Lake Ranch
16919 Highway 40
Hesperus, CO 81326
303-385-4537

The Brafferton Inn
44–46 York Street
Gettysburg, PA 17325
717-337-3423

C

Canyon Villa
125 Canyon Circle Drive
P.O. Box 204
Sedona, AZ 86336
602-284-1226

The Captain Lord Mansion
P.O. Box 800
Kennebunkport, ME 04046
207-967-3141

Captain Mey's B&B
202 Ocean Street
Cape May, NJ 08204
609-884-7793

Captain Whidbey Inn
2072 W. Captain Whidbey Inn Road
Coupeville, WA 98239
206-678-4097

Casa Benavides
137 Kit Carson Road
Taos, NM 87571
505-758-1772

Cedarcroft Farm
Route 3, Box 130
Warrensburg, MO 64093
816-747-5728

The Chicago Pike Inn
215 East Chicago Street
Coldwater, MI 49036
517-279-8744

Christmas Farm
Route 33
Wittman, MD 21676
410-820-7125

Clifton Inn
Route 13, Box 26
Charlottesville, VA 22901
804-971-1800

Corner George Inn
Main and Mill Street
Maeystown, IL 62256
618-458-6660

The Country Haus
1191 Franklin Street
Carlye, IL 62231
618-594-8313

❖ ❖ ❖

D

Davidson's Country Inn
P.O. Box 87
Pagosa Springs, CO 81147
303-264-5863

Durham House
921 Heights Boulevard
Houston, TX 77008
713-868-4654

G

Gardens of Eden
1894 Eden Road
Lancaster, PA 17601
717-393-5179

Garth Woodside Mansion
R.R. 1
Hannibal, MO 63401
314-221-2789

Glacier Bay Country Inn
Box 5
Gustavus, AK 99826
907-697-2288

Goose Cove Lodge
Deer Isle, ME 04683
207-348-2508

The Greenfield Inn
Forest Road
P.O. Box 156
Greenfield, NH 03047
603-547-6323

H

Herr Farmhouse
2256 Huber Drive
Manheim, PA 17545
717-653-9852

Hersey House
451 N. Main Street
Ashland, OR 97520
503-482-4563

Hillbrook Inn
Route 2, Box 152
Charles Town, WV 25414
304-725-4223

The Homeplace
5901 Sardis Road
Charlotte, NC 28226
704-365-1936

I

The Inn at Fordhook Farm
105 New Britain Road
Doylestown, PA 18901
215-345-1766

The Inn at the Round Barn Farm
R.R. 1, Box 247
East Warren Road
Waitsfield, VT 05673
802-496-2276

The Inn on Summer Hill
2520 Lillie Avenue
Summerland, CA 93067
805-969-9998

J

The Jailer's Inn
111 West Stephen Foster Avenue
Bardstown, KY 40004
502-348-5551

The John F. Craig House
609 Columbia Avenue
Cape May, NJ 08204
609-884-0100

Just-N-Trails
Route 1, Box 263
Sparta, WI 54656
608-269-4522

K

The King's Cottage
1049 East King Street
Lancaster, PA 17602
717-397-1017

L

Log Cabin Guest House
11661 Chetlain Lane
Galena, IL 61036
815-777-2845

M

Maple Leaf Cottage Inn
12 Selma/P.O. Box 156
Elsah, IL 62028
618-374-1684

❖ ❖ ❖

The Maples Inn
16 Roberts Avenue
Bar Harbor, ME 04609
207-288-3443

Manor House
69 Maple Avenue
P.O. Box 447
Norfolk, CT 06058
203-542-5690

P

The Palmer House
81 Palmer Avenue
Falmouth, MA 02540
508-548-1230

Park Avenue Guest House
208 Park Avenue
Galena, IL 61036
815-777-1075

The Pebble House
15093 Lakeshore Road
Lakeside, MI 49116
616-469-1416

Poor Farm County Inn
8495 Country Road 160
Salida, CO 81201
719-539-3818

R

Richmond Hill Inn
87 Richmond Hill Drive
Asheville, NC 28806
704-252-7313

Riverwind
209 Main Street
Deep River, CT 06417
203-526-2014

The Russell-Cooper House
115 East Gambier Street
Mount Vernon, OH 43050
614-397-8638

S

The School House Bed & Breakfast
Third and Clark Streets
Rocheport, MO 65279
314-698-2022

The Southern Hotel
146 South Third Street
Ste. Genevieve, MO 63670
314-883-3493

Sweet Basil Hill Farm
15937 W. Washington Street
Gurnee, IL 60031
708-244-3333

Swiss Woods
500 Blantz Road
Lititz, PA 17543
717-627-3358

T

Trout City Berth & Breakfast
Highway 24/285
P.O. Box 431
Buena Vista, CO 81211
719-395-8433

Twin Gates
308 Morris Avenue
Lutherville, MD 21093
410-252-3131

V

The Veranda
P.O. Box 177
252 Seavy Street
Senoia, GA 30276
404-599-3905

Victorian B&B
425 Walnut Street
Avoca, IA 51521
712-343-6336

W

Walnut Street Inn
900 E. Walnut
Springfield, MO 65806
417-864-6346

Windham Hill Inn
R.R. 1, Box 44
West Townshend, VT 05359
802-874-4080

The Wooden Rabbit
609 Hughes Street
Cape May, NJ 08204
609-884-7293

INDEX

A

addition, building an, 234
air conditioning, 236
antiques
   bookcase lamp, 157
   buggy (four-wheel) as
      mini-bar and
      stereo, 188
   chuck wagon, 139
   clothing, vintage, 193
   flour bin, used as kitchen
      work surface, 51
   gable as headboard, 196
   hatboxes, 96–97
   iron floor grates as table
      tops, 194
   ironing board, 158
   lanterns, reproduction, 127,
      132
   mangling board as side
      table, 43
   pantaloons, 43
   pie safe as nightstand, 100
   pressing iron as
      bookends, 143
   rake, used as quilt
      rack, 48
   roll-top desk, 132
   sewing machine as
      table, 44, 197
   shoes, high-button, 199
   sink, painted
      porcelain, 187
   spinning wheel, 161
   trunk, 166, 168
   wardrobes, 114–15, 199
   water pump, 158

apple wreath, 276
artichokes, 217, 218
Arts and Crafts
      movement, 155–56

B

Baked Cinnamon Pears with
      Fruit and Yogurt
      Sauce, 214
ballroom, 126
bathroom(s), 19, 61, 68, 88,
      101, 117, 119, 122,
      123, 145, 187, 189,
      194
   with antique sink
      vanity, 101
   decorated with a
      desk, 194
   with faux marble floor, 88
   rooms with open bathing
      areas, 60
bathtub(s)
   clawfoot, 61, 198
   painting, 68
Beam, Jim, 131
bed(s)
   built-in, 99
   canopy, 44, 65, 169, 186,
      260
   converting a double to a
      queen-size, 66, 238–39
   decorative headboards, 87,
      88, 147, 196
   dressings for (see also
      bedskirts, canopies,
      headboards), 99
   Empire, 183

Honduran carved
      mahogany, 20
   rosewood, 57
   sleigh bed, 66
   Stickley style, 157
   18th-century birdseye
      maple, 51
bedrooms, 19, 61, 68, 87,
      88, 89, 92, 94, 97, 99,
      100, 101, 112, 113,
      115, 117, 119, 120,
      121, 122, 123, 125,
      129, 131, 132, 133,
      137, 143, 145, 151,
      152, 153, 157, 162,
      167, 168, 169, 172,
      183, 184, 185, 187, 189
bedskirts, 88, 116, 119
bed toppers (see also
      canopies), 67, 87
beer-staining, 125
bench(es)
   built-in window, 105
   church pew, 110
   cobbler's, 22
   deacon's, 118
birdcages, 100
birdhouses, 100, 204
biscuits, 210, 211
blackboards, 115, 121
Blueberry Cinnamon Crumb
      Cake, 220
bow hanger, for picture
      frame, 226, 257–58
bread, Victorian Bread
      Pudding, 164–65, 211,
      212

building, moving a, 234
buttons (collection), how to
      display, 57

C

canopy (see also beds)
   bed topper, 67, 87
   lace, 186, 260
   making your own, 194,
      260
Canyon Villa Cinnamon
      Rolls, 220
ceilings
   cloud-painted, 187
   coved, 156
   papered, 86
   painting, 236
   tin, 103
cereals
   granola, 214
   porridge, 215
chairs, painted, 98, 198
cheese fondue, 176, 219
chess set of wooden
      spools, 61
chest, tiger maple, 22
Chesapeake Bay, 109, 112
Chocolate Fondue, 219
Christmas tree, 26
church, 108–13
cider, 49
cinnamon, 149
Classic Cheese Fondue,
      219
clawfoot tub, 60, 123
closet, decorated with
      wallpaper, 199

❖ ❖ ❖

clothespins, using for curtains, 43, 200
cobbler's bench, 22
Conestoga wagon, 34, 37
cottages, 28–29, 31, 43, 44, 77, 186
Country Breakfast Bake with Artichokes and Cheese, 217
crabmeat, 216
crêpes, 58
cross-stitch sampler, 40–41, 253, 254
curtains (see also window treatments)
  made from a bedspread, 143
  made from dish towels, 197
  made from table runners, 199
  making, 264–70
  mounting with clothespins, 200
  tied back with clothespins, 43
  without a rod, 189

D

Danish Lemon Soup, 214
deacon's bench, 118
decorator planner, 198
dining rooms: 21, 30, 34, 42, 45, 69, 71, 86, 90, 91, 98, 103, 111, 126, 135, 140, 149, 151, 156, 165, 174, 178, 197, 211, 225
  garden, 42
  primitive, 110
  with a mural, 22, 223, 225
doors
  Christmas, 274

Gothic-style, 110
topiary, 69, 274
dummy boards (see also fireboards), 59, 186
dust-ruffle, making (see also bedskirts), 259

E

Eaton, Moses, 22
eggs, 23, 216, 217, 218

F

fabric
  decorating walls with, 117, 251
  decorating with scraps, 199
  headboard, 87, 88
  table top, 67
  wall border, 196
faux marble floor, 87
faux-dough pies, how to make, 58, 270
fence and garden sketch, 91
fence, made into headboard, 40
fertilizer, from coffee grinds, 205
fireboards (see also dummyboards), 172
flame stitch, 101
fireplace
  gas, 98, 166, 201
  made from river rock, 154–55
  mantels, 98, 121, 166
  tips, 201
Fitzgerald, F. Scott, 53
floors
  faux marble, 87
  inlaid oak, 84
  painted, 125

restoration of
  hardwood, 236
  stenciled, 53
flour bin, as kitchen work surface, 51
flowers
  displaying, 208
  drying, 77, 208, 209
  edible, 33, 71, 72
folk-art, 58, 59, 224
fondue, 176–77, 219
foyers, 84, 95, 97, 110, 118, 158, 222–23
French toast, 219
fruit (see recipes)
Fun with Dick and Jane, 116
furniture, painted, 80

G

gardens, 180, 202-09
  fence and garden sketch, 207
  gifts from the, 204
  plot, 206
  secrets of maintaining, 205
  sharing your, 203
  stool made from farm equipment, 204
gas lanterns, reproduction, 127, 132
gazebo, 93
gingerbread (architectural decor), 49, 200
granite-style pots, 139
granola, 214
grapevine, wreath-making, 35, 272
Green Tomato and Cinnamon Marmalade, 212
guest book, 56, 103, 177, 224–27
guest towels, 197, 223

H

hammers, made into soldiers, 59
hangers, making padded, 255
harp, 27
hats, decorating with, 196
hatboxes, 96–97
headboards
  awning-style, 185, 262
  decorative, 88
  fabric, 88, 185, 262
  made from a door, 147
  made from an old roof gable, 194
  made from picket fence, 40
  Wysocki style, 54
herb garden, 207
holiday decorations, 26, 28, 275, 276
house moving, 110, 111, 234
hydrangea, 181, 209

J

jail, 130–35
Jalapeño Salsa, 212
Jefferson, Thomas, 25
jelly, 213

K

keeping room, 46
kilim-style rug, 86
kitchens (see also summer kitchen), 23, 50, 56, 58, 94, 105, 128, 129, 140, 190, 197, 223, 240

L

ladder
  access to loft, 28
  antique, as flower stand, 28

❖ ❖ ❖

rolling on garage door
track, 192
lamp (see also lighting),
antique bookcase, 157
lampshade,
rehabilitation, 194
lanterns (see also lighting),
reproduction gas, 127,
132
lighting
antique bookcase
lamp, 157
recessed reading, 99
reproduction gas
lanterns, 127, 132
Lilliputian Cheese-Egg
Puffs, 217
living rooms, 38, 46, 48, 49,
78, 82, 94, 121, 126,
145, 146, 154, 173,
180, 188, 189, 193
log cabin, 159–61

M

mantels, 98, 121, 166
Maple-Baked Pears in a
Jiffy, 221
marmalade, 212
Mexican Eggs, 216
Mexican tiles, 145, 150
mildew, combating, 237
Mission-style decor, 155–
58
moving a building, 234
mud room, 77
muffins, 221
mural, 22, 223, 225

N

napkin rings
butterfly, 226
making, 273
Navajo rug, 143, 145
needlepoint, 181

O

Oriental rug, 28

P

painting (see also trompe
l'oeil)
bathtub, 60
chairs, 98
sponge, 80, 96, 250
parlor (see also living
rooms), 193
pears, 214, 221
perennials, 93, 206
Persimmon Muffins, 221
picture-frame bow
hanger, 226, 257–58
pies, faux-dough, 61
Piglet Biscuits, 211
placemats
Battenburg, 164–65
yo-yo quilt style, 224, 256
pomander, hazelnut, 275
porridge, 215
Porter, Rufus, 225
potpourri, 200
pudding, Victorian
bread, 164

Q

quilts, 20, 35, 49, 51, 61,
70, 119
guest-book, 56
schoolhouse, 61
trip-around-the-world, 73
yo-yo quilt placemats, 24,
224, 256
quilt rack, antique rake, 48

R

raclette, 178, 180
Raisin and Fruit Breakfast
Soup Compote, 213
Randolph, Thomas
Mann, 25

recipes, 211–21
Red Rock Artichoke and
Salsa Bake, 218
renovation, 236
restoration
10 Commandments
of, 231-33
of hardwood floors, 236
tips, 236
rocking horse, 1890s, 118
Rockwell, Norman, 27, 133
rolls, cinnamon, 148, 220
room-designing
planner, 241–44
Rooms (see also bathrooms,
bedrooms, dining rooms,
living rooms, kitchens)
Americana, 47
Attic, 44
Brandon, 185
Brig Merchant, 20
Brother Palmer's
Still, 108–09
Buttons n' Bows, 57
Cape May, 92
Carriage House, 25
Carriage Room, 188
Carver, 101
Clabough, 183
Colonial, 130
Danzero, 97
Fan, 55
Garden, 25, 134
Gentleman's, 55, 199
Graduate, 121
Grandchildren's, 67
Greeting, 91, 94
Harvest, 22
Hearts and Flowers, 47
Hoffman, 129
Honeymoon Cottage, 25, 28
Honor Roll, 115, 120
Hunt, 94
Ice House, 187

Jailhouse Rock, 134
Jewell, 97
McCann, 101
McRoberts, 129
Mary Lord, 19
Maschino, 100
Meriweather, 27
Quilt, 61
Robertson, 100
Ryan, 184
Schoolmarm's, 119
Schoolmaster's, 114–15
Sherman, 66
Show and Tell, 117
Sleigh, 188
Spanish Bayonet, 151
Spelling Bee, 115
Victorian, 132
Wash House, 43
Willow, 51
Wysocki, 55
Zelda's, 53
Rose Geranium Jelly, 212
Rufus Porter style, mural
scene, 225
rugs
hooked, 66, 180
kilim, 86
Navajo, 143, 145
Oriental, 28

S

santa, 45, 49
santos, 143, 146
schoolhouse, 114–21
seed packets as decor, 196
sewing table, 197
shoes, decorating with,
199
shower curtain, 197
soup, 58, 214
spinning wheel, 29
sponge painting
techniques, 250

❖ ❖ ❖

staircase
  decorating, 47, 193
  painted, 193
  twin, 85
stenciling, 223
  cutting your own, 246
  how to stencil, 247
  moon-and-star style, 23
  Moses Eaton style, 22
  on floor, 53
  on walls, 130–31
  patterns, 245–49
  tin, 23
summer kitchen, 56, 127
Sweet English Breakfast
    Porridge, 215
Sweet Rancher Porridge,
    215

T

table runners for
    curtains, 199
tablecloth, 200
tea cozy, 225, 256
  how to make, 226
Three-Cheese Herb and
    Crabmeat Puff, 216
tiles, 145, 150
tin
  ceiling, 103
  stencil, 23, 247

toast, French Toast
    Sundae, 219
tomato, Green Tomato and
    Cinnamon
    Marmalade, 212
tools, sculpture and whimsy
    made from, 65
topiary door-making, 69, 274
towels for guests, 197, 199
trains, 136–39
tree, Christmas, 26
trompe l'oeil
  bookcase, 101
  door, 94
  stairs, 193
trunks, hand-painted, 166,
    168
tub (see bathtubs)
turkeywork, 89

V

valances (see also curtains;
    window treatments)
  crunch 'n pouf, 188, 270
  stagecoach, 153, 267
Victorian Bread
    Pudding, 211

W

wainscoting, 25
wallpaper, 95

ceiling papered with, 86
collage, 237
cutouts, 66, 97
decorating plant pots
    with, 193
decorating an armoire
    with, 199
wallpapering over plaster
    walls, 236
walls
  decorated with a
    mural, 22, 223, 225
  decorating with brown
    paper, 135, 251
  decorating with
    fabric, 117, 251
  hand-painted (see
    stenciling and
    sponge painting)
  plaster decor
    techniques, 100
  sponge-painted, 80
weathervane, 48
weeds
  keeping out with
    newspaper, 205
  killing organically, 208
whirligig, 68
Wild West Granola, 214
window seat, 105
window treatments

Angel-Wing Swag, 187,
    268
Awning, 185, 262
Breath-of-Spring Lace
    Cornice, 184, 269
Crunch 'n Pouf
    Valance-Curtain, 188,
    270
  lace, 104
  Shady Lacy, 43, 264
  making, 264–70
  mounting curtains with
    clothespins, 43
  Scalloped Swag, 189,
    266
  Stagecoach Valance, 153
  tab-tops, 45, 265
wood stove, 109
wreaths
  Advent, 28
  apple, 276
  grapevine, making a
    half-moon swag, 35,
    272

Y

yogurt, Baked Cinnamon
    Pears with Fruit and
    Yogurt Sauce, 214
yo-yo quilt placemats,
    making, 256

MILLENNIUM PARTY GUIDE

CONTENTS

PARTY IDEAS

MM NIGHT ★ 21ST CENTURY PARTY ★ DRAGON PARTY

CARNIVAL NIGHT EXTRAVAGANZA ★ EXPLORERS & INVENTORS

RULERS OF THE MILLENNIUM ★ SPORTS HEROES PARTY

ECLIPSE PARTY ★ BEACH PARTY ★ TREE-PLANTING PARTY

2000-GUEST PARTY ★ TIME CAPSULE PARTY

MASQUERADE PARTY ★ STREET PARTY ★ MOGUL BANQUET

MILLENNIUM MURAL ★ TANGO PARTY

GLOBAL PARTY GUIDE

TONGA ★ FIJI ★ NEW ZEALAND ★ AUSTRALIA ★ ISRAEL ★ EGYPT

SOUTH AFRICA ★ UNITED KINGDOM ★ IRELAND ★ FRANCE ★ GERMANY

ITALY ★ NETHERLANDS ★ BELGIUM ★ SPAIN ★ SWITZERLAND

AUSTRIA ★ POLAND ★ NORWAY ★ FINLAND ★ ICELAND

UNITED STATES ★ CANADA ★ COSTA RICA ★ BRAZIL ★ SAMOA

642.9
MIL

PARTY IDEAS

FOR A MILLENNIUM PARTY TO
REMEMBER, CHOOSE A SPECTACULAR
LOCATION, OR TRANSFORM A ROOM
INTO A STUNNING SETTING. SET UP
A FUND FOR A DAZZLING FIREWORKS
DISPLAY, AND HAVE INVITATIONS
AND DECOR MATCH YOUR THEME.
FINALLY, TAKE TIME OVER FINISHING
TOUCHES SUCH AS LIGHTING,
FLOWERS, NAPKINS, AND GLASSES.

MM NIGHT

TWO THOUSAND IN ROMAN NUMERALS IS MM,
SO ENJOY AN MM NIGHT ON THE EVE OF THE
MILLENNIUM. ASK GUESTS TO DRESS AS CHARACTERS,
MOVIES, ANYTHING BEGINNING WITH THE LETTER "M."

Invite Send out with a request for each guest to donate
a firework of a set value, to be delivered before the party.

Costumes Ideas include: Mickey Mouse, Minnie Mouse,
Marilyn Monroe, *Mary Poppins*, the Marx Brothers,
The Munsters, Mighty Mouse, one of the Muppets,
Mad Max, or the millennium bug.

Decor Spray chairs silver, buy silver napkins and tie with
silver ribbon, spray fruit silver and attach to name tags.

Food Serve dishes that begin with "M" – try M&M's,
marshmallows, meringues, and marzipan fruits.

Drinks Moët & Chandon champagne.

Entertainment Erect a huge clock counting down
to midnight, then start the fireworks display.

Photograph © Lincoln Exley Designs Ltd. Created by Sarah Jones.

21st Century Party

INVITE GUESTS TO DRESS IN COSTUMES INSPIRED BY THE 21st CENTURY AND BY MOVIES SUCH AS *WAR OF THE WORLDS*, *INVASION OF THE BODY SNATCHERS*, *CLOSE ENCOUNTERS OF THE THIRD KIND*, AND *ALIEN*.

Invite Attach to camera shots showing a clock with both hands set at midnight.

Costumes Spacemen, martians, astronauts, and aliens.

Decor Create a moonscape atmosphere by hiring a dry-ice machine. Cover the windows with reflective silver paper, replace ordinary lightbulbs with blue colored ones, and hang streamers from every door frame.

Music The soundtrack from *2001: A Space Odyssey*.

Food Keep it simple: huge bowls of chips, dips, and canapés to graze on.

Drinks Add a little green food coloring to cocktails.

Entertainment Hand out party poppers, horns, whistles, and sparklers to set off at midnight.

Dragon Party

AS THE YEAR 2000 IS THE CHINESE YEAR OF THE DRAGON, CELEBRATE IN ASIAN STYLE.

Invite Write on colored paper fans.

Costumes Wear silk, or dress as a Chinese lion, dragon, or the animal of the Chinese year you were born in. Wear plenty of red, associated with joy and happiness in China.

Decor Hang kites, fans, and paper dragons from the ceiling and walls. Draw Chinese characters on large sheets of white paper, and hang from bamboo canes. Spread the dinner table with sheets of Chinese newspaper and decorate the area with paper lanterns.

Food Serve Chinese food from rice bowls and bamboo steamers. Eat with chopsticks and wash down the meal with Chinese beer or green tea. Finish the meal with sticky rice cakes, called *lin guo*, and fortune cookies.

Entertainment Set off firecrackers at midnight to scare off evil spirits. Give guests small gifts in red envelopes.

For a carnival atmosphere,

hang whistles from the ceiling

on long lengths of gold ribbon.

Paint containers of every shape

and size in bright colors,

fill with dried beans, and use

as drums and shakers.

CARNIVAL NIGHT EXTRAVAGANZA

THINK RIO, TRINIDAD, EVEN NEW ORLEANS, AND RECREATE THE THRILL OF THE SAMBADROME IN BRAZIL, WITH A STEAMY EVENING OF LOUD SAMBA MUSIC, RUM PUNCH, AND NONSTOP DANCING.

Invite Attach package labels, detailing the venue, time, and place, to long, brightly colored feathers.

Costumes Glamorous tall headdresses, feathers, and sequins; tiny bikinis (if you dare) for women; ruffled shirts for men.

Decor Decorate tables with African fabric and huge platters of tropical fruit piled into pyramids.

Music Soca and samba – played loud.

Food Easy food that's fun to eat with the fingers: offer rice and peas with fried fish and jerk chicken, plates of skewered vegetables and fish, and sweet potato and plantain chips. Dice and slice tropical fruit such as mango, pineapple, and papaya to make a fruit salad, then squeeze lime juice over it and lace with white rum.

EXPLORERS & INVENTORS

CELEBRATE THE EXPLORERS AND INVENTORS WHO HAVE HELPED SHAPE THE MODERN WORLD BY USING THEM AS INSPIRATION FOR COSTUME THEMES.

Invite Send on a cut-out photograph of possibly the most useful and oldest invention of all: the wheel.

Costumes Ideas for costumes include: Scott of the Antarctic, David Livingstone, Albert Einstein, Louis Pasteur, Alexander Graham Bell, Archimedes, Jacques Cousteau, Wilbur and Orville Wright, Thomas Alva Edison, Sir Walter Raleigh, Neil Armstrong, Abel Tasman, Marie Curie, Alexander the Great, Captain Cook, Marco Polo, Sir Isaac Newton, the Pharaohs.

Decor Paint a huge mural for the wall featuring inventions such as the telephone, television, clock, camera, bicycle, light bulb, chess set, airplane, and space rocket.

Entertainment Award a prize at the end of the evening for the most inventive costume.

PARTY VENUES

THE MILLENNIUM IS THE ONE OCCASION FOR WHICH THERE IS NO EXCUSE FOR NOT CELEBRATING TO THE HILT, SO REALLY GO TO TOWN AND HOLD AN ULTIMATE PARTY IN THE ULTIMATE LOCATION:

Paris, Amsterdam, or New York ★ *Hot-air balloon*
In a park ★ *Museum* ★ *Nightclub*
Art gallery ★ *Yacht club* ★ *Casino*
Restaurant ★ *Swimming pool* ★ *Fiji, Hawaii, or Goa*
Yacht ★ *Ski chalet* ★ *Double-decker bus*
Cabin in the country ★ *Beach*
Barn ★ *Riverboat* ★ *Vineyard*
Hotel ★ *Waterfall* ★ *Scuba-diving*
Swimming with dolphins ★ *Forest*
Desert ★ *Pier* ★ *Stately home*
Nile cruise boat ★ *Wine cellar*

RULERS OF THE MILLENNIUM

FOR A PARTY THAT TRAVELS THROUGH THE AGES, ASK GUESTS TO DRESS AS THE FAMOUS PERSON THEY FEEL SHOULD RULE THE NEXT MILLENNIUM, AND TO BEHAVE AS THAT PERSON FOR THE WHOLE EVENING.

Invite Send out plain paper crowns and invite guests to decorate them in keeping with their chosen ruler and wear them on the night.

Costumes Ask guests to dress as kings and queens, or as powerful figures from history or the present, such as Nebuchadnezzar, Joan of Arc, Genghis Khan, George Washington, Chairman Mao, and Nelson Mandela.

Decor Hang opulent drapes made from silk, velvet, or brocade on the walls. Embellish the cloth with gold paint, fake gems, and gold braiding.

Food Dress staff as attendants or servants, and provide a feast fit for royalty. Cover platters with vine leaves and offer mouthwatering canapés throughout the evening.

SPORTS HEROES PARTY

DRESS AS YOUR FAVORITE SPORTS HERO OF ALL TIME, AND SPEND AN EVENING DANCING TO RECORDS RATHER THAN BREAKING THEM.

Invite Attach to athletic running numbers.

Costumes Come as football, baseball, and athletic stars of today, or as Greek athletes from the first Olympics, Victorian tennis players, or golfers from the 1920s.

Decor Paint the five Olympic rings on white sheets and use them as tablecloths. Decorate food with paper flags from around the world, and illuminate the garden with flaming torches.

Music The soundtrack from *Chariots of Fire*.

Entertainment Hold competitive games: a sports trivia quiz, arm wrestling, and team games. Award medals or certificates to the winners.

ECLIPSE PARTY

A FULL ECLIPSE TAKES PLACE IN 1999, HAILING THE COUNTDOWN TO THE MILLENNIUM. CELEBRATE ALL THINGS CELESTIAL WITH A HEAVENLY PARTY.

Invite Written on glittery stars with a silver or gold pen.

Costumes Guests should dress in gold and silver and wear plenty of glitter makeup.

Decor Cut star, sun, and moon stencils from cardboard, and spray with silver and gold aerosol paint onto white or dark blue tablecloths. Spray old wooden chairs with gold aerosol paint. Hang up a glitter ball. Attach a net to the ceiling, and fill with gold and silver balloons to be released at midnight.

Music Bill Haley and His Comets, Ziggy Stardust.

Food Gild sweets and cakes with edible gold.

Entertainment Spray disposable cameras silver, and place on tables so guests can capture the evening. Hand out sparklers and hold a silver and gold fireworks display.

Illuminate an outdoor party by hanging tiny white lights in trees. Alternatively, paint empty glass jars with translucent glass paint, place votive candles inside and suspend with string.

BEACH PARTY

DRESS AS MERMAIDS AND MUSCLE-BOUND SURFERS, AND ENJOY ICE CREAM, FRUIT PUNCH, AND COTTON CANDY. IF YOU CAN'T BE DOWN AT THE BEACH, CREATE A BEACH INDOORS.

Costumes Dress in bathing suits, grass skirts, mermaid and lifeguard outfits.

Decor Build sandcastles, push flares into the sand, and decorate the area with large shells.

Music The Beach Boys, steel drum music.

Entertainment Toasting marshmallows, limbo dancing.

Instead of using glasses for drinks, offer guests hollowed-out coconut shells filled with delicious tropical cocktails.

TREE-PLANTING PARTY

LEAVE YOUR MARK ON THE PLANET BY JOINING WITH FRIENDS TO PLANT TREES FOR THE FUTURE.

Before the party, try to get additional funding for trees by contacting local businesses and inviting them to contribute. Ask a local council or wildlife group to designate an area that would benefit from more trees, seeking their advice on planting, too. After planting the trees, invite guests home for a delicious barbecue accompanied by baked potatoes with chili, sour cream, and grated cheese. Reward guests for their hard work by presenting them with bottles of pampering massage oil.

2000-GUEST PARTY

USE HEADS OF LOCAL SCHOOLS TO HELP ARRANGE THE
BIGGEST PARTY EVER – WITH 2000 PEOPLE AS GUESTS.

Invite Ask each school in your area to the party.

Decor Hold the event on the grounds of a large school.

Food Ask each school's PTA to supply a table of themed
food for a certain number of guests. Theme food
according to countries or colors.

Music Provided by school bands and choruses.

Entertainment Book a professional photographer to
photograph all the guests, and give a print to each school.

Organize a party where

you and your friends try

to break a world record for the

millennium, such as dancing

the world's longest conga.

TIME CAPSULE PARTY

INVOLVE ALL CHILDREN IN THE FAMILY, OR EVEN
IN THE STREET, ASKING THEM TO HELP FILL
A TIME CAPSULE FOR THE NEXT MILLENNIUM.

Invite every child to fill a blank page with a poem or
story about his or her life or about the millennium.
Include a snapshot of each child and his or her signature,
and bind the loose pages into an album. Other suitable
items for the capsule include: national and local
newspapers, fashion magazines, a pay stub, a car brochure,
and newly minted coins. Video the album being made
and the capsule being filled, and enclose in the capsule.

For striking party glasses, paint swirls of gold paint on plain wine glasses.

FANCY-DRESS THEMES

Dracula ★ *Superheroes* ★ *Cleopatra*
Mulan ★ *The Spice Girls* ★ Zorro
Star Trek ★ *Football legends* ★ Titanic
Fairy tales ★ Hollywood stars
X Files ★ *Pirates* ★ Guys and Dolls
On safari ★ Strictly Ballroom
Outlaws ★ *Carmen Miranda*
The circus ★ Oklahoma
Knights and maidens ★ Evita
The Great Gatsby ★ *Back to school*
Star Wars ★ Abba

MASQUERADE PARTY

SEND OUT INVITATIONS ASKING GUESTS TO WEAR SPECTACULAR MASKS.

Ask guests to choose any shape mask and to let their imagination run wild in embellishing the masks with paint, feathers, and sequins. Guests should wear the masks until midnight, when they then reveal their true identities. Award a bottle of champagne for the best creation.

STREET PARTY

JOIN TOGETHER WITH NEIGHBORS TO THROW A HUGE STREET PARTY.

Arrange to have the road cordoned off for the evening, then line the street with folding tables laden with delicious food. Book magicians, stilt-walkers, and fire-eaters to entertain guests, then encourage everyone to join in a torch-lit procession at midnight.

MOGUL BANQUET

ENJOY AN EVENING EATING DELICIOUS SPICY FOOD IN SUMPTUOUS SURROUNDINGS.

Decorate with silk screens, and drape brilliantly colored silk or muslin around the walls and ceiling to create a canopy effect. Scent the venue with jasmine incense sticks, and light the room with small votive candles. After a magnificent banquet, sound in the new year with drums and tiny bells.

Add glitz to party napkins by sewing on a shimmering ribbon trim.

MILLENNIUM MURAL

PAINT A HUGE MURAL to celebrate the millennium. First obtain permission and funding from local authorities. Invite a local artist to draw a design for the side of a local building such as a sports center, theater, movie, or shopping center. Divide the mural into sections and invite local nurseries, schools, colleges, and charity groups to complete a section each. Hold a party at the mural's official unveiling to thank people for their help.

TANGO PARTY

THROW A PARTY WHERE PASSION, GRACE, AND VERVE REIGN SUPREME IN A NIGHT DEDICATED TO DANCING THE TANGO.

Invite guests to dress in slinky evening wear. Decorate the venue to resemble an elegant dance hall of the 1920s. Hire a dance teacher for the night to teach guests the art of dancing the tango, and then dance until dawn.

FINAL TOUCHES

STYLE DECOR TO MAKE A STUNNING BACKDROP FOR THE ULTIMATE NEW YEAR'S EVE PARTY.

PERSONALIZED WINE BOTTLES

GIVE A PARTY GIFT to remember: print striking personalized wine labels celebrating the millennium. Include guests' names, the date, and the party location. Steam off labels from bottles of good red wine and replace them with your own labels. Guests can then keep the wine for the future.

MILLENNIUM PLATES

IMMORTALIZE YOUR PARTY by painting delightful millennium crockery to record the event. Paint inexpensive white china plates with each guest's name, the date of the party, and, if you are artistic, a picture of the venue or the guest. Use the plates during dinner, then offer the clean plates as gifts when guests leave.

TEQUILA TOAST

FOR THE ULTIMATE in stylish extravagance, add gold to tequila. Peel sheets of 24-carat edible gold leaf from the backing paper and place in a blender with a small amount of clear tequila. Blend the tequila for 20 seconds, then add enough ice-cold tequila to serve the number of guests present. Pour into small shot glasses and toast the new millennium in style.

GILDED LEAF NAPKINS

GLAMOROUS GILDED LEAVES are ideal for adorning napkins. Flatten pretty leaves between sheets of blotting paper in the pages of a heavy book. When dry, attach a short length of wire to each stalk and lightly spray the leaves with gold aerosol paint. Spray gold a wooden curtain ring for each guest and, using the wire, attach three leaves to each ring. Bind the ring with gold ribbon to hide the wire, and slip in a rolled linen napkin.

Spell guests' names out with red and green jelly beans, and use as festive place settings.

LUSTROUS PLACE SETTING

THESE WONDERFUL PLACE SETTINGS shine brilliantly on a party table. Write each guest's name on a small terra cotta pot using a glue gun or masking fluid. Spray the pot with gold aerosol paint and let dry. Peel off the glue or masking fluid to reveal the guest's name written in terra cotta. Place one terra cotta pot on each dinner plate.

PARTY DECOR TIPS

★ CREATE YOUR OWN dazzling millennium tablecloth for the evening by transforming velvet cloth with gold paint and ornate tassels.

★ ADD A BOLD, BRIGHT TOUCH to napkins: tie them with an attractive, wide ribbon and tuck a tulip or gerbera under each ribbon.

★ GARNISH COCKTAILS with delicious nibbles such as strawberry fans, melon balls, and cherries on stems.

GOLDEN PEAR PLACE SETTINGS

GILD A CELEBRATORY TABLE with glittering pear place settings. Wash fresh pears in soapy water and dry them well. Spray the pears with gold aerosol paint. When dry, push a small silk leaf into the top of each pear and tie on a handwritten baggage label with the guest's name on it.

GLOBAL PARTY GUIDE

THERE ARE FEW BETTER EXCUSES FOR A PARTY THAN TO WELCOME A NEW MILLENNIUM. COUNTRIES ACROSS THE WORLD WILL PARTY IN THEIR OWN STYLE AND AT THEIR OWN TIME. HOWEVER, ALL WILL BE UNITED IN WHAT PROMISES TO BE THE BIGGEST GLOBAL CELEBRATION IN HISTORY.

TONGA

★ **Tonga's** claim to be the first nation to see in the millennium has been questioned by the nearby Republic of Kiribati. Despite this, the island nation has great plans to celebrate, including a month-long millennium festival culminating in New Year's Day celebrations. The festival has both sports and musical themes, and will include fishing and golfing competitions, brass bands, and native cultural exhibitions. Web: www.tonga2000.net/

FIJI

★ **Fiji** is west of the international date line, but just misses out as the first nation to greet the dawn of the new millennium. Nevertheless, it is making much of the fact that the 180° meridian passes through the main island of Viti Levu. This is the venue of the primary New Year's Eve festivity, the "Dusk 'Til Dawn" concert. Web: www.bulafiji.com/2000.htm

NEW ZEALAND

★ **Gisborne**, on the eastern tip of the North Island, holds an annual First Light Festival, and claims to be the first city to see the sun of the new millennium. A larger than ever New Year's Eve festival is promised for 1999, with the Millennium and Town Clocks the focus of live entertainment through the night. Tel: (64) 04-495-7266.

★ **The Pacific Tall Ships Festival** reaches New Zealand in December 1999, and targets Gisborne in time to see in the new millennium, with some ships sailing to the international date line 100 miles (160 km) to the east. Web: www.enternet.co.nz/client/personal/steve/

★ **Te Mata Peak**, just outside the town of Hastings, is believed to be the first point in New Zealand to catch the rays of the dawn of the new millennium. A huge party is planned for New Year's Eve 1999, with dawn celebrations the morning after. Web: www.hawkesbay.com/millenn.html

AUSTRALIA

ALTHOUGH THE PEOPLE OF AUSTRALIA WILL BE FOCUSING ON THE OLYMPIC GAMES BEING HELD IN SYDNEY IN 2000, EACH MAJOR CITY PLANS TO CELEBRATE THE NEW MILLENNIUM IN STYLE.

★ **Sydney Harbor** will be the backdrop of one of Australia's biggest millennium celebrations. A huge fireworks display is planned to set the harbor alight, and up to two million people are expected to enjoy a variety of live entertainment and cultural activities.

★ **Sydney Opera House** is the stunning venue for a New Year's Eve masquerade party organized by the Millennial Foundation along with 30 other parties world-wide, and hosted by the Mayor of Sydney. Guests will have the best possible view of the huge fireworks display in the harbor. Web: www.yes2000.co.uk

★ **The Melbourne Millennium Committee** is organizing a community-based New Year's Eve party in 1999 featuring fireworks displays and street parties held in various venues in the center of the city.

★ **Cape Byron**, the easternmost tip of Australia, will be the first place in the country to greet the new millennium. As such, big celebrations are planned to see in the new year.

ISRAEL

★ **The Holy Land** will be a major focus of celebration and pilgrimage, with over four million visitors expected to converge on Israel and Palestine at the turn of the millennium. Numerous special events to commemorate the 2000th anniversary of the birth of Christ are planned, in particular, in Jerusalem, Nazareth, and Bethlehem. Tel: (972) 22-741-323 or (972) 22-742-224.

EGYPT

★ **Cheop's pyramid** in Giza will have a 9ft (3m) golden cover set on it from dusk of December 31, 1999, to the dawn of the new millennium. There will also be a 12-hour light show directed by Jean-Michel Jarre. Tel: (20) 02-391-3454.

SOUTH AFRICA

★ **In Cape Town** in December 1999, the Council for the Parliament of the World's Religions will convene. The Parliament is asking groups, nations, and religious communities to donate strategic millennium gifts that will benefit "our planetary community." Tel: (1) 312-629-2990.

★ **Table Mountain**, above Cape Town, is the imposing venue for a New Year's Eve "Trance" party planned for New Year's Eve 1999, featuring leading psychedelic trance bands, with the aim of blending nature with technology. Web: www.southafrica2000.com

UNITED KINGDOM

ENGLAND

THE ARRIVAL OF THE MILLENNIUM WILL BE MARKED BY A NATIONWIDE PEALING OF CHURCH BELLS. OVER 400 CHURCHES WILL ALSO HAVE NEWLY INSTALLED FLOODLIGHTS SWITCHED ON.

★ **Greenwich, London**, the historical location of the prime meridian, which dictates the time zones of the world, is the focus of British millennium celebrations, with The Millennium Experience. On New Year's Eve 1999, the opening ceremony of the huge Millennium Dome on the Greenwich Peninsula will herald a gala night for 35,000 people, including the Queen, the Prince of Wales, and the Prime Minister, as well as members of the public. Tel: (44) 0171-808-8200. Web: www.dome2000.co.uk

★ **Greenwich Meridian 2000** revolves around a New Year's Eve party in Greenwich Park for 50,000 people, featuring a huge musical spectacular. A 24-hour global telecast on giant screens will show parties as they happen around the world. Tel: (44) 0181-312-6745.

★ **Trafalgar Square** is a traditional London venue to celebrate New Year's Eve, and a record number of revelers are expected to gather to see in the new millennium.

★ **The South Bank of the Thames**, opposite Westminster, is the location for the British Airways London Eye, the biggest Ferris wheel ever to be built. It will be 450ft (135m) high, and will take 30 minutes to complete one full rotation. Tel: (44) 0171-229-9907.

★ **Newcastle's** millennium celebrations on New Year's Eve, 1999, will feature a huge sound and light spectacular, involving local artists and highlighting the city's rich cultural heritage. A grand parade featuring lanterns of hope will travel through the city center to the dockside and along the river, where music, fireworks, and laser shows will greet the new millennium. Tel: (44) 0191-261-0610.

SCOTLAND

★ **Hogmanay in Edinburgh** has become one of the largest outdoor events in Europe, attracting crowds of over 350,000. The millennium party is guaranteed to be the biggest yet. Tel: (44) 0131-473-1999.

★ **Glasgow's Hogmanay celebrations**, held annually, are inevitably overshadowed by the scenes in Edinburgh. Nevertheless, the organizers of the 1999 celebrations are determined to put on an event to rival their compatriots'. Tel: (44) 0990-992-244.

★ **The Millennia airship**, launched by Virgin from Edinburgh on New Year's Eve 1999, will attempt a record-breaking world tour, stopping at Greenwich, Paris, Moscow, Hong Kong, and, finally, Sydney, in time for the 2000 Olympics. Web: www.edinburghshogmanay.org

WALES

★ **Cardiff's 75,000-seat Millennium Stadium**, with retractable roof, is the venue for the Rugby World Cup Final in September 1999. The huge New Year's Eve party planned, to be held in the arena after the tournament, promises to be the biggest millennium celebration in Wales. Tel: (44) 01222-232-661.

★ **Cardiff's "Calennig"** will be a community-based millennium celebration, featuring fireworks displays, light shows, carnival rides, and musical stages, set around four of the city's main landmarks. Tel: (44) 01222-227-281.

NORTHERN IRELAND

★ **The Strangford Stone** is a huge granite monolith to be erected in Delamont County Park, Killyleagh, in June 1999. It will be a monument to the teamwork of the divided communities that have united to plan it together.

IRELAND

★ **In Dublin**, "Mile Atha Cliath Teoranta" has been formed with the assistance of Dublin Corporation. It is headed by the Lord Mayor of Dublin, and acts as a focal point for projects to mark the millennium. Web: www.dublin-2000.com/

FRANCE

DESPITE FEARS OF A POSSIBLE CHAMPAGNE SHORTAGE, THERE SHOULD BE PLENTY OF NONVINTAGE BUBBLY AVAILABLE: CURRENT STOCKS STAND AT 1 BILLION BOTTLES.

★ **The Eiffel Tower**, standing in the Parc du Champ de Mars, Paris, is the venue for France's biggest millennium party. After the scheduled sound and light spectacular, the Tower will lay a giant luminous "egg" which will crack open to show images of millennium parties around the world. The Tower will also be fitted with over 1000 spotlights to bathe the area in light as the dawn of the new millennium arrives. Tel: (33) 01-49-525-354.

★ **The Tour de la Terre** (Earth Tower) in central Paris will be 650 feet high with an over 32,000 square-foot platform housing bars, restaurants, and exhibition areas, with the environment being a central theme. The tower will form an impressive landmark, and aims to emulate the Eiffel Tower by representing France's modernity.

★ **The Seine River** will be filled with 2000 brightly colored plastic fish visible from the banks. There are also plans to perfume the Seine for the millennium.

★ **The Pompidou Center**, the Grand Palais, and the Louvre, are all undergoing major renovations for Paris's 2000 celebration.

★ **The Millennium Countdown Clock** will be centered on the Place Charles de Gaulle, Paris, where twelve avenues, marking the points on the clockface, converge. A powerful laser will form the second hand, sweeping around from the top of the Arc de Triomphe.

★ **The Boulevard Périphérique**, Paris's main road, will become a vast concert venue for many different bands and musical events on New Year's Eve 1999.

★ **Marseille** is the starting point for La Course, a round-the-world boat race, which sails on December 31, 2000.

GERMANY

★ **Berlin** is competing with the rest of the world to host the biggest party to mark the beginning of the new millennium. A major spectacle is planned for the center of the city on New Year's Eve 1999, involving an hour-long fireworks display at the Brandenburg Gate, which will also be the venue for bands and theatrical performances.

★ **Dusseldorf Fair** will be the venue for one of Europe's biggest, and possibly longest, millennium celebrations. In addition to the fairground's rides and attractions, a variety of live music and entertainment will be offered. The party is scheduled to start on New Year's Eve, 1999, and will continue through the next two days, making what the organizers hope will be the longest New Year's Eve Party ever. Tel: (49) 211-9523-2000.

★ **Oberammergau** will host over 100 performances of the famous Passion Play, commemorating the life of Christ, from May to September 2000. Tel: (49) 08822-92310.

ITALY

★ **Rome** is bracing itself for a record number of visitors for the Great Jubilee. From Christmas 1999 to January 2000, over 13 million tourists and pilgrims are expected to visit the city and its basilicas to celebrate the 2000th anniversary of the incarnation of Christ and the start of the third millennium of Christianity. Tel: (39) 06-49711. Web: www.roma2000.it/

★ **Bologna** has been designated one of nine European Cities of Culture, and exhibitions and festivals are being held throughout the year. Tel: (39) 051-204-606.

NETHERLANDS

★ **Den Helder's Fort Kijkduin** hosts the Netherlands's largest New Year's Eve celebration, featuring live musical acts, various entertainment, and themed bars in its labyrinth of tunnels. Tel: (31) 223-642-305. Web: www.trefnet.nl/kvnh/entree-2000

BELGIUM

★ **Brussels** is one of the nine European Cities of Culture that are coordinating their programs to create "a European cultural space for the year 2000." Brussels 2000 is organizing a large range of activities throughout the year, with a focus on the visual arts, theater, and dance. Tel: (32) 02-214-2000.

SPAIN

★ **Madrid's** Puerto del Sol is the traditional venue for New Year celebrations, and the millennium celebrations in 1999 promise to be the biggest ever. The thousands of people who are expected to turn up to hear Spain's most famous clock strike midnight will first enjoy a spectacular fireworks display and musical extravaganza. Tel: (34) 91-429-4951.

★ **Santiago de Compostela** has good reasons to celebrate the new millennium. 1999 marks the Jubilee of St. James, its patron saint, while it has been designated one of nine European Cities of Culture in 2000. The town has wide-ranging celebration plans, including festivals, art exhibits, and building programs. Tel: (34) 981-584-081. Web: compostela2000@corevia.com

SWITZERLAND

★ **Geneva's** New Year's Eve celebrations, organized by Signe 2000 on December 31, 1999, will be based on the theme of the four elements: fire, water, air, and earth. Web: www.swisstin.com/

AUSTRIA

★ **Vienna's Hofburg Palace**, the venue for The Imperial Ball on New Year's Eve 1999, offers one of the most sophisticated millennium eve parties in Europe. A gala banquet is followed by dancing in the magnificent state apartments, with bands and orchestras set to take guests into the New Year. Tel: (43) 587-366-623.

★ **The New Year's Trail** in downtown Vienna features a mile-long stretch of festivities ranging through the center of the city. The Millennium Eve celebrations promise to be the best ever, with bands, dancers, and street entertainers.

POLAND

★ **The Kraków 2000 Festival** builds upon the city's status as one of nine European Cities of Culture and its increasing popularity as a vacation destination. The theme for the festival, "Spirituality – The Faces of God," featuring various theatrical and musical events, reflects the city's traditional religious diversity. Tel: (48) 12-422-6091.

NORWAY

★ **Bergen 2000** aims to be Norway's largest cultural celebration, with exhibitions, shows, and entertainment centered around the new Frescohall, Norway's biggest information center. The theme of the celebrations will be "Art, Work, and Leisure." Tel: (47) 5555-2000.

★ **Oslo** enjoys a double celebration at the turn of the millennium, with the arrival of its 1000-year jubilee. There are plans for a massive fireworks party in the city.

FINLAND

★ **Helsinki Arena 2000** plans to celebrate with a virtual Helsinki in cyberspace. The project has widespread national support, and plans will culminate in the year 2000 with a completed three-dimensional model of the city. Web: www.helsinkiarena2000.fi

ICELAND

★ **Reykjavik** is a European City of Culture in the year 2000 and promises a "nonstop" program of festivities. Among these are the Reykjavik Millennium Art Festival, the Millennial Celebration of Christianity, and the Millennial Celebration of the Discovery of America from Iceland. Tel: (354) 575-2000. Web: www.reykjavik2000.is

UNITED STATES

THERE ARE CURRENTLY BIG PLANS FOR NEW YEAR'S EVE MILLENNIUM PARTIES IN ALL THE MAJOR US CITIES. EACH WILL BE TRYING TO MATCH THE TRADITIONAL CELEBRATION IN NEW YORK'S TIMES SQUARE.

NEW YORK CITY

★ **Times Square 2000** is set to attract over one million people on New Year's Eve 1999, with a similar celebration expected a year later. The 24-hour celebration will salute the coming of the new millennium by linking each of the world's time zones through giant TV screens. It will start at 7.00 AM (EST), when the New Year first arrives in the Pacific Islands, and will then broadcast live scenes from each of the world's 24 time zones. Tel: (212) 768-1560. Web: www.igc.apc.org/millennium/events/mega.html

BOSTON

★ **The First Night group**, based in Boston, promotes alcohol-free celebrations on New Year's Eve, supported by 170 communities across the US and Canada. First Night parties are usually community-based and include street parades and entertainment, music, theater, and fireworks displays. Tel: (212) 617-542-1399. Web: www.firstnight.org/

WASHINGTON DC

★ **The White House Millennium Program** will highlight projects that recognize the creativity of the American people. These include funding for the arts, culture, scientific exploration, technological discovery, education, and preserving the environment. Web: www.whitehouse.gov/initiatives/millennium/index.shtml

MIAMI

★ **New Year on South Beach** is promoting itself as the New Year's Eve warm alternative to New York. There will be a huge party with fireworks, and music and video towers along the beach. Web: www.southbeach.org

NEW ORLEANS

★ **Jackson Square**, at the heart of New Orleans' French Quarter, will be packed with revelers seeing in the millennium. The traditional combination of jazz musicians, artists, and street performers, as well as a huge fireworks display, will keep the crowds entertained.

CALIFORNIA

★ **Exposition 2000**, a three-day event beginning at sunset, December 31, 1999, is expected to attract over 250,000 people to San Diego's Balboa Park. The park is to be transformed into a cultural extravaganza, with a mix of music, fireworks, entertainment stages, hospitality tents, and craft activities, with local museums participating.

★ **The Mojave Desert** witnesses a two-day spiritual event from New Year's Eve 1999. Organizers hope to create the world's largest drumming and chanting circle. Web: www.WhisperedPrayers.com/

★ **Party 2000** is to take place on 4000 acres of land between Palm Springs and the Arizona border. Organizers claim they will host the largest fireworks display ever held. The party will last for three days, with live entertainment on five stages, and should feature many big-name bands. Web: www.party2000.com/

CANADA

★ **Cape Spear** in Newfoundland is the easternmost point on the North American continent, and will be the first place in North America to see the dawn of the new millennium. A "First Light" party is being organized at the point to welcome the millennium's dawn.

★ **Toronto 2000 – An Urban Odyssey** consists of a series of celebrations and a New Year's Eve gala on December 31, 1999. Tel: (416) 292-0206. Web: www.torontomillennium.com/

★ **Halifax, Nova Scotia** also celebrates its 250th birthday on New Year's Eve 1999. Organizers are planning a variety of cultural events and entertainment. Tel: (902) 420-4724.

★ **The Montreal International Jazz Festival** will feature a huge millennium party on New Year's Eve 1999, with a series of performances promised by some of the jazz world's biggest stars, on outdoor stages and in indoor clubs. Tel: (514) 523-3378.

★ **In Vancouver**, the ongoing MV 2000! event culminates in New Year's Eve celebrations in 1999. All-night parties are planned along with a time-capsule project, a Futurist's Festival, and a Festival of Time. Tel: (604) 618-5825.

COSTA RICA

★ **Costa Rica's** six-day millennium celebration, starting on December 27, 1999, promises to be a high-profile affair, with the United Nations peace conference as its centerpiece. Many of the world's leading politicians and environmentalists will be present, and celebrations will include a giant fireworks display and a series of live bands.

BRAZIL

★ **Rio de Janeiro's Copacabana Beach** is the glamorous setting for one of the world's biggest free parties, with over 2.5 million revelers expected to attend. The countdown to the new millennium will feature a bigger-than-ever carnival on the eight-mile stretch of beach, with a variety of live bands and a huge fireworks display.

SAMOA

★ **The 20th century** and the current millennium finally come to a close in Samoa, the nation closest to the international date line on its eastern side. Celebrations, thanks, and blessings will be centered in the capital of Apia, on the island of Upolu. The ultimate millennium countdown will culminate in a nationwide pealing of church bells at the strike of midnight, and a huge fireworks display and festival. Web: www.samoa.co.uk

THE
MILLENNIUM
PARTY BOOK

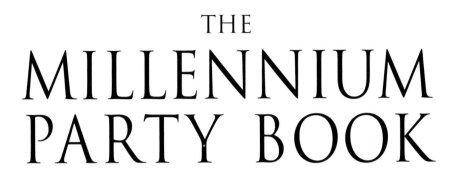

THE
MILLENNIUM
PARTY BOOK

PARTY IDEAS
LAUREN FLOODGATE

FOOD & DRINK
LUCY KNOX & SARAH LOMAN

PARTY PLANNING
SARAH LEVENS

PHOTOGRAPHY
SIMON SMITH

DK

A DK PUBLISHING BOOK
www.dk.com

A DK Publishing Book
www.dk.com

Project Editor Monica Chakraverty
Editor David Summers
Art Editor Lisa Goldsworthy
DTP Designer Bridget Roseberry
Senior Art Editor Tracey Ward
Managing Editor Susannah Marriott
Deputy Art Director Carole Ash
Production Controller Martin Croshaw
Stylist Clare Louise Hunt
US Editor Iris Rosoff

First American Edition, 1999

2 4 6 8 10 9 7 5 3 1

Published in the United States by
DK Publishing, Inc.,
95 Madison Avenue, New York, New York 10016

*This book is dedicated to my mom,
for all we've been through together.*

Library of Congress Cataloging-in-Publication Data
Millennium Party Book – 1st American ed.
p. cm.
Includes index.
ISBN 0-7894-4181-0
1. Entertaining. 2. Cookery.
TX731.M47 1999   98-54600
642'.4–dc21   CIP

Reproduced in Singapore by Colourscan
Printed and bound in Italy by LEGO.

CONTENTS

INTRODUCTION 6

COCKTAIL PARTIES 8

OUTDOOR PARTIES 14

Summer Parties 16 ★ Barbecues 18

Picnics 20 ★ Garden Parties 22

Parties Afloat 23 ★ Beach Parties 24

BANQUETS & WEDDINGS 26

Banquets & Balls 28 ★ Weddings 32

FESTIVE PARTIES 36

Halloween 38 ★ Fireworks 39

Thanksgiving 40 ★ Christmas 41

New Year's Eve 45 ★ Party Games 47

SPECIAL OCCASIONS 48

Birthdays 50 ★ Anniversaries 53

Theme Parties 54

INTIMATE PARTIES 56

Valentine's Day 58 ★ Parties for Friends 59

TEA PARTIES 62

Tea Parties 64 ★ Easter 67

CHILDREN'S PARTIES 68

Children's Parties 70 ★ Baby Parties 73

FINISHING TOUCHES 74

Invitations & Paper Crafts 76

Napkins, Plates & Glasses 78

Fabric Ideas, Tables & Chairs 80

Flowers & Fruit, Lighting 82

FOOD & DRINK 84

Canapés & Drinks 86 ★ First Courses 92

Main Courses 96 ★ Vegetables & Salads 104

Desserts & Cakes 108

PLANNING A PARTY 118

Essentials 120 ★ Planning 121

Checklists 122 ★ Countdown 124

Hints & Tips 125

INDEX 126

ACKNOWLEDGMENTS 128

INTRODUCTION

I HAVE ALWAYS LOVED PARTIES AND CAN STILL REMEMBER THE THRILL AND EXCITEMENT OF GOING TO MY FIRST REAL PARTY AS A LITTLE GIRL AGE FIVE. MY ENTHUSIASM WAS HARD TO CONTAIN – DRESSED UP IN A LONG DRESS, MY HAIR IN BRAIDS AND RIBBONS, I SPENT THE AFTERNOON PLAYING GAMES, EATING POTATO CHIPS AND CAKE, AND DRINKING LOTS OF SODA.

TODAY, I PREFER TO DRINK A LARGE GIN AND TONIC AND THE FOOD I'M SERVED AT PARTIES NOW RANGES FROM TACOS AND MEATBALLS TO SOPHISTICATED CANAPÉS, WHILE THE PARTY GAMES ARE MOST LIKELY TO BE PLAYED AFTER DINNER. BUT HOWEVER MUCH THE DETAILS HAVE CHANGED SINCE I WAS A YOUNG GIRL, MY SHEER ENJOYMENT OF A GOOD PARTY REMAINS THE SAME.

WHATEVER THE OCCASION OR TYPE OF PARTY – A LARGE-SCALE BALL FOR A WEDDING, A FORMAL BIRTHDAY DINNER, AN INFORMAL BARBECUE WITH FRIENDS, OR A SPUR-OF-THE-MOMENT PICNIC ON THE BEACH – THE KEY TO A SUCCESSFUL CELEBRATION

IS THAT FRIENDS AND FAMILY ENJOY THEMSELVES. I HOPE THIS
BOOK WILL HELP YOU ACHIEVE JUST THAT, AND CREATE A DAY TO
REMEMBER. YOU CAN PLAN AN ENTIRE PARTY FOLLOWING THE
IDEAS FOR INVITATIONS, MENU SUGGESTIONS, AND GAMES, OR
TAKE JUST ONE IDEA OR THEME AND ADAPT IT TO YOUR TASTE.

WHEN I WAS ASKED TO WRITE THIS BOOK, THE CHALLENGE WAS
TO COME UP WITH PARTY SUGGESTIONS THAT WERE PRACTICAL,
AFFORDABLE, AND WORKABLE WHILE STILL BEING FUN AND
ORIGINAL. THE IDEAS FEATURED CATER TO ALL AGES AND EVERY
OCCASION. I HOPE YOU WILL HAVE AS MUCH FUN
PLANNING AND ENJOYING YOUR PARTIES AS
I HAVE HAD WRITING THIS BOOK.

Lauren Floodgate

CELEBRATE IN STYLE WITH A COCKTAIL PARTY, WHETHER YOU ARE PLANNING AN INFORMAL SOIRÉE OR HOSTING A FORMAL EVENING PARTY. BE IMAGINATIVE – CHOOSE A THEME SUCH AS GLAMOROUS HOLLYWOOD GLITZ OR A TITANIC-STYLE NAUTICAL NIGHT, SELECT DRINKS AND FOOD TO MATCH, AND SUGGEST

COCKTAIL PARTIES

GUESTS DRESS TO SUIT THE OCCASION. SERVING COCKTAILS FROM THE RIGHT GLASS SEEMS TO IMPROVE THE TASTE. DRINK CHAMPAGNE COCKTAILS IN TALL FLUTES, MARTINIS AND MARGARITAS IN TRIANGULAR GLASSES, AND PUNCHES AND DAIQUIRIS IN ROUNDED GOBLETS. GARNISH COCKTAILS WITH CITRUS FRUITS AND STAR FRUIT AND WITH EDIBLE FLOWERS OR FRUIT-FILLED ICE CUBES.

SPAGHETTI WESTERN ▷

AN EVENING OF BANDITS, OUTLAWS, AND NE'ER–DO–
WELLS. CREATE A SALOON SETTING, OR, IF HOLDING
THIS PARTY OUTDOORS, BUILD A CAMPFIRE.

Invite Take a picture of yourself wearing a false moustache
and sombrero and use it to make up a "wanted" poster,
inviting your guests to come in disguise.

Costumes Ponchos and sombreros, cowboy boots and
spurs, big moustaches and three-day stubble.

Music The Gipsy Kings, the soundtrack to *The Good, The
Bad and The Ugly*, mariachi music, or a little Latin rumba.

Table Paint terra cotta pots with poster paints, and plant
with baby cacti (*see right*). Use a bright tablecloth.

Food Bandits love a feast, so cook spicy chorizo sausage
and meatballs with red sauce (*see page 93*). Serve with
refried beans, nachos, tacos, and red-hot salsa.

Drinks Start with Tequila Sunrise (*see below*). Later, serve
margaritas (*see page 90*) or "sour" tequila (*see below*). Arriba!

DRINKS FOR BANDITS

Tequila Sunrise Pour 1oz (30ml) tequila into a tall
glass filled with crushed ice. Top with orange juice, and
drizzle grenadine syrup into the center of the drink.

Tequila Sour Pour 1oz (30ml) tequila into a tall glass
and top with lemonade. Place your hand over the glass,
bang it carefully on the table, and drink.

SEAFARING COCKTAILS

Beachcomber Shake 1½oz (45ml) light rum, ½oz (15ml)
Triple Sec, ½oz (15ml) grenadine, and 1oz (30ml) sour mix
with ice. Garnish with lime.

Blue Lagoon Pour 1½oz (45ml) each of Blue Curacao
and vodka over ice. Top with lemon-lime soda.

Sex on the Beach Stir 1oz (30ml) each of vodka and
peach schnapps and 2oz (60ml) each of orange and
cranberry juice into a tall glass half filled with ice.

WHAT WERE YOU DOING WHEN
THE SHIP WENT DOWN?

INVITE GUESTS TO SPEND A NIGHT ON THE OCEAN WAVES,
PLAYING QUOITS AND CROQUET, GAMBLING IN YOUR
CASINO, OR PLAYING CARDS. FINISH THE EVENING
SINGING SEA SHANTIES BY MOONLIGHT.

Decor Set plenty of hurricane lamps around the room and
cover surfaces with pebbles and seashells. Deck the walls
with lobster pots and fishermen's nets.

Music Play a soundtrack of whale, dolphin, or seagull cries,
or a record of accordion music.

Food On the captain's table, serve a seafood buffet of
oysters, shrimp, lobster, and crab on an ice tray (*see page 78*).

Drinks Welcome your passengers with Beachcomber, Blue
Lagoon, or Sex on the Beach cocktails (*see left*). Finish the
evening with hot buttered rum: heat 2oz (60ml) rum, 2½oz
(75ml) water, and 1 tsp sugar in a pot. Add a small cinnamon
stick, 4 drops of vanilla, 1 pinch of nutmeg, and 1 tsp butter.
Serve when the butter melts.

JAMES BOND ▽

SERVE BLINI WITH QUAIL EGGS AND SMOKED FISH (SEE PAGE 89). THEN TOAST THE QUEEN WITH VODKA MARTINI (SHAKEN NOT STIRRED) OR WITH A GLASS OF CHAMPAGNE.

Invite Set the scene by sending each guest a toy water pistol attached to a baggage label (*see below*).

Costumes As every Bond fan knows, he is nothing if not impeccably dressed. As an option to wearing black ties and Armani suits, guests could dress as their favorite character, maybe as a Bond Girl scantily clad in a bikini, or as Odd Job, Jaws, Q, M, Moneypenny, Dr. Nos or Drax.

Decor Place a hatstand by the front door for bowler hats; hang Union Jacks on the walls.

Music Play anything by John Barrie or a compilation soundtrack of the Bond films.

Table Serve the meal using your best china, glasses, and silverware. After dinner, cover the dining table with green baize and set up a toy roulette wheel. Invite guests to gamble with piles of chocolate money.

To make a martini, shake together 3oz (90ml) gin, 1oz (30ml) dry vermouth, and crushed ice. Strain into a martini glass and add an olive.

1950s HOLLYWOOD

FOR AN EVENING OF GLITZ, ASK GUESTS TO DRESS AS MOVIE STARS FROM THIS GLAMOROUS ERA.

Invite Send out invitations attached to photographs of Hollywood stars of the 1950s, or to pictures of old cars, such as Buicks and T-birds.

Costumes Invite guests to don their slingbacks, dig out their seamed stockings, apply some lipstick, and go for glamour. Guests should dress as favorite movie stars of the era, such as Marilyn Monroe, Grace Kelly, Clark Gable, and Cary Grant.

Decor Project old movies onto the wall, and put up Hitchcock movie posters.

Music Ask guests to bring along their favorite oldies. Find an old phonograph and let the music of Elvis Presley, Buddy Holly, and Jerry Lee Lewis set the tone for an evening of nostalgia.

Drinks Pink gins (*see page 91*), champagne, and rum punch.

COCKTAIL FOOD

SALMON PINWHEELS
(SEE PAGE 86)

CARAMELIZED ONION QUICHES
(SEE PAGE 86)

PUFF PASTRY PIZZAS
(SEE PAGE 88)

CHEESE TWISTS (SEE PAGE 88)

GARLICKY MIXED OLIVES
(SEE PAGE 89)

COME AS A COCKTAIL

THROW A COCKTAIL PARTY, INVITING GUESTS TO DRESS UP AS THEIR FAVORITE DRINK.

Inspiration for costumes could come from: Bahama Mama, Black Russian, Bloody Mary, Blue Lady, B-52, Adam and Eve, Green Devil, The Morning After, Moulin Rouge, Moscow Mule, Pink Pussy Cat, TNT, or a Zombie.

BALLROOM DANCING

THIS IS A GREAT PARTY FOR A LARGE GROUP OF PEOPLE WHO DO NOT KNOW EACH OTHER.

Send invitations attached to large paper numbers that guests can pin to their clothes. Send matching numbers to different guests, who must introduce themselves at the party to the person wearing the same number and ask for the first dance. Dance the rumba, salsa, waltz, and bossa nova.

For a double-strength gin and tonic, use premixed and frozen G&T ice cubes set with lemon slices.

◁ VODKA SHOTS

★ Freeze flavored vodka shots for six hours or longer. The alcohol level prevents the vodka from freezing solid.

★ Mix pitchers of vodka-based Sea-breezes (*see page 90*), Bloody Marys, and Moscow Mules in advance. Just add ice to them as your guests arrive.

★ Set Jell-O® made with vodka in pots or tequila shot glasses (*see left*). Cool in the refrigerator and serve with spoons.

COCKTAIL PARTY TIPS

★ Try some more unusual cocktail garnishes: cut lily flower shapes out of kumquats; tie citrus knots from thin slices of peel; twist slices of fruit, then secure the shape using cocktail sticks.

★ Make sure your corkscrew is not waylaid: tie it to elastic and secure it to the door of the refrigerator.

★ To keep drinks cool, bury bottles in a tub or clean trash can part-filled with ice.

BRING A COCKTAIL PARTY

PHOTOCOPY SOME FAVORITE COCKTAIL RECIPES AND ASK GUESTS TO BRING ALONG THE INGREDIENTS.

Reduce the cocktail recipes to the size of a postcard, paste them to the back of tropical scenes, and send them out as invitations. You supply the garnishes, ice cubes, umbrellas, stirrers, fruit, and, of course, the food.

CUTLERY-FREE DINING

THE BEST TYPE OF FOOD to serve at a cocktail party is small, bite-sized items that can be easily eaten without a knife, fork, or plate. Offer canapés (*see menu, above*), one-bite sandwiches, melon or figs wrapped in prosciutto, satay sticks, crudités, chips, and dips. Serve food on trays garnished with vine leaves, and hand out napkins as you circulate.

HOT TODDIES

GLÜHWEIN, JÄGERTEE, SWEDISH GLOGG (*SEE PAGE 43*), MULLED WINE (*SEE PAGE 91*), AND IRISH COFFEE ARE THE PERFECT DRINKS TO SERVE AT AN APRÉS–SKI PARTY.

To make Irish coffee, add a single measure of whisky to a cup of black coffee. Then float the cream on top by holding a teaspoon, bowl side up, just above the coffee and slowly pouring the cream over it into the cup.

ON THE ROCKS ▷

ONE OF THE SIMPLEST WAYS TO GARNISH A COCKTAIL IS WITH DECORATIVE ICE CUBES. TRY SOME OF THE FOLLOWING IDEAS:

Stir a little food coloring into the water before freezing. Use shaped ice-cube trays. Add slices of olive, strawberry, orange, lime, mint leaves, and edible fresh flower petals to the ice-cube tray (*see right*), or simply present ice to guests in a pretty ice bucket (*see page 66*).

BOOZY POPS

COOL YOUR SUMMER GUESTS WITH ALCOHOLIC ICE POPS.

Stir together in a bowl a mixture of champagne, sugar, water, and a little black currant vodka to taste. Pour into ice pop molds and freeze. Variations of this can be made using piña colada, daiquiri, or margarita (*see page 90*) that has been made up, sweetened to taste with sugar, and then frozen.

To make crystal-clear ice cubes, always use filtered or bottled water in an ice tray.

FROSTING GLASSES

DRINKS SUCH AS MARGARITAS ARE TRADITIONALLY SERVED IN GLASSES WITH FROSTED RIMS.

To frost a glass with salt, dip the rim of the glass in lemon or lime juice before lightly dipping it in salt. For sugar- or sherbet-frosted glasses, dip the rim of the glass in beaten egg white, then into superfine sugar or sherbet. Look for brightly colored sherbet in the supermarket.

FRILLS & FLOUNCES

HOMEMADE COCKTAILS LOOK MORE COLORFUL AND PROFESSIONAL IF THEY ARE SERVED WITH A GARNISH, STRAW, OR STIRRER.

Stirrers are vital for some cocktails because alcohol and soft drinks do not mix and must therefore be stirred well. Always stir and serve Bloody Marys with a celery stick.

PINEAPPLE SHELLS

GIVE COCKTAILS A TROPICAL FEEL BY SERVING THEM IN HOLLOWED–OUT PINEAPPLES OR COCONUT SHELLS.

To make a pineapple shell, trim off one third of the leafy end of a pineapple and discard. Cut a thin slice from the base so it sits level. Using a small, sharp knife, cut around the inside edge of the pineapple, leaving a ½in (1cm) rim. Scoop out the center and fill it with a tropical drink.

CRUSHED & CRACKED ICE

WHITE RUSSIANS, ZOMBIES, AND FRAPPÉS ARE BEST SERVED OVER CRACKED ICE.

To crack ice, wrap the ice in a clean dish towel, and hit it carefully with a mallet or rolling pin. To crush more finely, simply hit it longer. Some food processors, but not all, can crush ice, so check the instructions first. Crack any large ice cubes before processing.

SPEND LONG DAYS PARTYING BY THE BEACH, POOL, OR LAKE,

PLAYING VOLLEYBALL AND EATING ICE CREAM, SEAFOOD, AND POPCORN.

INVITE FRIENDS TO A SUNSET PICNIC AND SERVE A FEAST FROM

WICKER BASKETS IN A DINING AREA SURROUNDED BY TINY CANDLES.

HOLD A PARTY FULL OF EASTERN PROMISE, INVITING GUESTS

OUTDOOR
PARTIES

TO RECLINE ON CUSHIONS UNDER A TENTED CANOPY

OUTDOORS. ON BALMY SUMMER EVENINGS HANG UP

LIGHTS OR HURRICANE LAMPS IN THE TREES AND ENJOY NIGHTS

FILLED WITH CAMPFIRES, SLUMBER PARTIES, AND

MIDNIGHT FEASTS. AFTER DINNER, PLAY NOISY, LIVELY

GAMES, AND END BY TELLING STORIES AND SINGING AROUND THE FIRE.

SUMMER PARTIES

SERVE CANDY COTTON, ICE POPS,
COLD BEER, AND FRUIT PUNCH,
AND FOR A DELICIOUS SUMMER
DRINK, DROP TWO RASPBERRIES IN
A CHAMPAGNE FLUTE, COVER WITH
A MEASURE OF CASSIS, AND TOP
WITH CHILLED CHAMPAGNE.
GARNISH WITH A STRAWBERRY.

SOUTH PACIFIC PARTY ▷

CREATE A BEACH IN YOUR BACKYARD, THEN HULA
HULA AND SWAY THE NIGHT AWAY TO THE STRAINS
OF A TONGAN BEAT AND THE MUSIC OF *SOUTH PACIFIC*.

Invite Attach an invitation to silk flowers threaded into
garlands (*see right*). Tell guests to come in swimwear and
grass skirts, and, if possible, to paddle to the party in boats.

Decor Create stretches of shore using sand and shells.
Hang trees with lights (*see page 39*), scatter petals in the yard,
and set up the food under a canopy (*see right*).

Table Cover tables with crêpe paper strewn
with petals. Fill terra cotta pots with orchids and
tie cutlery into bundles with raffia (*see right*).

Food Spread platters with vine leaves, and heap
with shrimp, crab claws, and barbecued fish. Serve
daquiri- and margarita-flavored ice pops (*see page 13*),
coconut ice cream, and tropical fruit salad (*see page 113*).

Drinks Offer cocktails in pineapple shells (*page 13*).

PARTY IN THE PARK

THROUGHOUT THE SUMMER, LOCAL HISTORICAL SITES AND
PARKS HOLD OUTDOOR EVENTS. ENJOY THE ENTERTAINMENT
WITH FRIENDS AND WITH SOME DELICIOUS FOOD.

Invite Ask everyone to bring an allotted dish from a menu,
a drinks ingredient, something to sit on, cutlery, and plates.

Table Bring checkered blankets to lay the food on. Tie a
helium balloon to a bottle, so friends know where you are.

Food Chips, dips, and canapés (*see pages 86–89*), rustic breads,
and summer salads (*see right*). Serve strawberries dipped in
chocolate with whipped cream. Bring a selection of cheeses,
some flasks of steaming coffee, and mints to finish.

*Scour the garden for small blooms
and pretty leaves, then tuck
them under the edge of
each place mat a few
minutes before guests arrive.*

Summer Party Menu

Chicken with Figs (*see page 99*)

Minted Potato Salad (*see page 104*)

Pesto Couscous Salad (*see page 105*)

Summer Salad

Scatter a salad with edible flowers such as nasturtiums, geraniums, borage, rose, or marigold petals. Pick fresh, unsprayed, and unblemished blooms, and check carefully for insects before washing.

•

Summer Berry Tarts (*see page 112*)

Tented Canopy

A CANOPY OR AWNING CAN BE USED AS A DELIGHTFUL SETTING FOR AN OUTDOOR MEAL, AS A CENTRAL BASE CAMP FOR A DAY OUT WITH FRIENDS, OR EVEN AS AN EXOTIC SHELTER ON A HOT SUMMER NIGHT.

Make a simple tented canopy by driving tall stakes into the ground and wrapping them with strips of wide, thick ribbon. Dye a cotton sheet and tie it to the top of the stakes, leaving the knotted ends to trail down at each corner. Decorate the corners with organza bows, swags of foliage, and ribbons.

Summer Slumber Party

CHILDREN LOVE CAMPING, SO INVITE FAMILIES TO PITCH THEIR TENTS IN YOUR BACKYARD AND ENJOY MIDNIGHT FEASTS AROUND A CAMPFIRE.

Invite Send out invitations attached to packages of marshmallows, telling children to bring along a skewer to toast them on. Remind guests also to bring a change of clothes, a sleeping bag, and a toothbrush.

Decor Pitch tents and light a campfire with adult supervision. Stand votive candles in glass jars, tie string around them as handles, and hang them from trees and shrubs. Set up folding tables and cover with paper cloths. Serve food in pots or cans, along with disposable cutlery.

Food Serve hot dogs or ribs with fried onions and cheesy baked potatoes (*see page 106*). Toast marshmallows and wash them down with creamy hot chocolate.

Games Play lots of games, and make them as loud and energetic as possible. Try tag, musical bumps, and hide and seek. Finish with telephone and campfire songs.

Making Hay Picnic

THIS IS THE BEST PARTY TO HOLD WHEN THE WEATHER IS SURE TO BE FINE. MEET IN THE COUNTRY, ERECT A TENT AS BASE CAMP (*SEE LEFT*), PUT SOFT DRINKS ON ICE, AND SPEND THE DAY PLAYING GAMES AND PICNICKING IN THE SUN – THINK *OKLAHOMA*.

Invite Call up your friends and invite them to bring along the whole family, a picnic lunch, and even the dog.

Table Use bales of hay as tables and chairs.

Food Tell people to bring their own picnic while you supply the soft drinks. Keep the drinks chilled in a trash can full of ice. Mix Mimosas (*see page 90*) in a sterilized picnic box and let people help themselves.

Games Set up nets and play volleyball, football, softball, and frisbee; take a whistle and run races; go on a nature hunt and collect butterflies and bugs in glass jars.

Must pack Bring large plastic sacks for garbage and a small first-aid kit in case of accidents.

BARBECUES

BARBECUED FOOD TASTES EVEN MORE DELICIOUS WITH FLAVORED SMOKE. DO THIS BY SPRINKLING ANY OF THE FOLLOWING ON HOT COALS: FRESH HERBS, SUCH AS ROSEMARY OR THYME; APPLE-TREE WOOD; SOAKED WOOD CHIPS FROM WHISKY, MAPLE, OR OAK BARRELS; CRACKED ALMOND OR HAZELNUT SHELLS, FIRST SOAKED IN WATER FOR 20 MINUTES.

PREPARING THE COALS

1 Lay coals on a foil-lined barbecue tray, two-deep and slightly wider than the cooking area. Make a pyramid of coals in the middle and light it.

2 Wait until the flames die down and the coals glow; this can take 45 minutes. Rake the coals evenly over the base.

3 Brush the grill rack with oil. Place food over the hottest part of the coals to seal it before moving it to a cooler part of the rack in order to cook it thoroughly.

BARBECUE EQUIPMENT

ESSENTIAL EQUIPMENT for a successful barbecue includes: long-handled tongs, basting brush, oven mitts, skewers, hinged wire rack for sausages, fish rack, long fork, lighter fuel, charcoal, and firelighters.

MONGOLIAN BARBECUE

LET GUESTS PICK AND MIX THEIR OWN FOOD BEFORE YOU COOK IT FOR THEM ON A RED-HOT GRIDDLE.

Decor Hang tin-can lights (*see page 39*) in the trees.

Table Cover a large table and surrounding area with fat candles. If you are short of seats, place a plank of wood between two flat seats, and use it as a bench.

Food Serve food in large bowls with chopsticks. Provide a wide range of fresh ingredients, such as sliced chicken, shrimp, meats, chopped vegetables, sauces, herbs and spices, all in separate bowls. To help guests decide what to eat, paste photocopied recipes around the eating area. Encourage them to try different options, and also to experiment with their own concoctions. Serve the food with bowls of salad, stir-fried rice, noodles, and a selection of breads.

BARBECUE MENU

BRUSCHETTA WITH TOPPINGS (*SEE PAGE 89*)

•

LAMB BURGERS (*SEE PAGE 101*)

MONKFISH & BACON KABOBS (*SEE PAGE 101*)

TUSCAN BEAN SALAD (*SEE PAGE 104*)

ANTIPASTO PASTA SALAD (*SEE PAGE 105*)

•

CHOCOLATE TART (*SEE PAGE 108*)

•

PITCHERS OF MIMOSAS (*SEE PAGE 90*)

PASSION FRUIT MIX (*SEE PAGE 91*)

A SELECTION OF BEERS

YAHOO PARTY

RECREATE THE DAYS OF THE GOLD RUSH AND ENJOY A RAUCOUS EVENING OF WILD WEST ACTION.

Invite Attach a label to a sheriff's badge or toy gun.

Costumes Calamity Jane, Buffalo Bill, The Lone Ranger.

Decor Surround a campfire with hay bales, hang hurricane lamps in the trees, and pitch tents for guests to sleep over in. Serve food from an improvised chuck wagon.

Music Hand out yazoos or combs and papers, and busk along to your favorite country-and-western songs.

Food Serve buckets of beans, coleslaw, grits, cornbread (*see page 88*), spicy chicken wings, and seared tuna (*see page 100*). For dessert, stuff bananas with chocolate and bake in the fire's embers (*see page 24*).

Entertainment Set up an area for line-dancing.

Games Hold a horseshoe-throwing competition, lassooing, and poker.

◁ LAZY SUMMER BARBECUE

SOME OF THE BEST PARTIES HAPPEN OUT OF THE BLUE, SO IF THE WEATHER IS BALMY ONE DAY, THROW AN IMPROMPTU BARBECUE IN THE YARD OR BY A LAKE.

Decor Make petal flares out of soda cans (*see left*). Clean a can with paint stripper and wire wool, then cut the top off using strong scissors. Cut the sides of the can into six "petals," and curl them back using a pencil. Remove a votive candle from its metal surround, place the surround in the can, and hammer a nail through both layers of metal into the end of a garden cane. Secure the nail with glue, replace the candle, and push the flare into a bucket of sand.

Table Cover the table with brown paper, and provide crayons to play word games after the meal.

Games Play blindman's bluff. Divide guests into two groups, and blindfold a player from each team. One player has to catch the other, while the second player tries to get away, both following directions shouted by their teams.

PICNICS

FOR A GREAT PICNIC, PACK FOOD
THAT IS EATEN EASILY WITH FINGERS.
PLACE ICE PACKS ON TOP; COLD AIR
WILL DROP AND KEEP FOOD COOL.
USE SMALL SCREW-TOP JARS FOR
DRESSINGS AND FREEZE ALREADY
MADE FRUIT PUNCH SO IT IS COLD
ON ARRIVAL. DON'T FORGET GARBAGE
BAGS, CONDIMENTS, HAND WIPES,
AND A CORKSCREW.

TEDDY BEARS' PICNIC

TELL PEOPLE TO BRING THEIR TEDDY BEARS TO JOIN IN
THE FUN AT THIS PICNIC. ALL BEARS MUST WEAR A
LABEL WITH THEIR OWNER'S NAME.

Invite Send on labels attached to small teddy bears.

Costumes Get a couple of guests to come as famous
bears, such as Winnie the Pooh, Paddington, or Yogi bear.

Decor Hold the party in a large field or set it in a sunny
spot in the woods. Picnic on gingham tablecloths or
make a padded mat (*see page 80*).

Food Serve savory scones with
toppings (*see page 88*), a floral summer
salad (*see page 17*), summer berry
tarts (*see page 112*), blueberry
muffins (*see page 114*), and a huge
teddy bear cake (*see page 117*).

Games Hide and seek, tag,
sing songs, frisbee.

FRUIT-PICKING PARTY

SPEND A DAY WITH FAMILY AND FRIENDS ON A FARM
WHERE YOU CAN PICK YOUR OWN FRUIT.

Food Ask everyone to bring a different course. Eat the food
together with fresh products such as butter and honey
produced at the farm. For dessert, eat some of the fresh fruit
you have picked.

Entertainment Enjoy tractor rides and visit the farm animals.

Games Challenge children to find the largest
strawberry or the longest or strangest-
looking vegetable.

PICNIC ON THE SKI TRAIL

TAKE BACKPACKS AND A PICNIC, AND ENJOY A MORNING'S
SKIING BEFORE TUCKING INTO A HEARTY LUNCH.

Table Ski to a picnic site and bury drinks and food in the
snow, wrapped in plastic bags. Also bury paper plates,
napkins, and plastic cutlery. Mark the spot.

Food Bring food already cut into portions. Pack in air tight
plastic boxes that are resilient to knocks and bumps.

Entertainment Have fun skiing all morning before finding
your picnic spot at lunch time. Sit on plastic bags to keep
dry and enjoy a meal washed down with ice-cold drinks.

Paint olives and leaves with fabric paints on napkins and tablecloths, then use a hot iron to fix the design.

PERFECT PICNIC TIPS

★ Cake-pan candles, dotted around an eating area at dusk, look enchanting. Use small, old cake pans, madeleine shells, or pastry molds. Glue the bases of two pans together to make a candleholder on a stand. Fix a candle inside each top pan, and position the candles around the picnic area.

★ Tie seashells, small stones with holes in them, or knives and forks onto string, and crisscross it along a picnic tablecloth to keep it in place when the wind blows.

★ Make a picnic place mat for each diner. Lay a paper napkin on a quilted place mat. Put a knife, fork, spoon, and disposable handy wipe on top. Roll up the mat and tie with ribbon.

FOURTH OF JULY

ENJOY THE FOURTH OF JULY WITH AN ALL–AMERICAN CELEBRATION. PLAN A DAY OF ACTIVITIES, STARTING WITH A PICNIC FOR FRIENDS AND FINISHING WITH A RED, WHITE, AND BLUE FIREWORKS DISPLAY.

Invite Attach to mini-American flags, or send out on the back of Uncle Sam postcards.

Decor Red paper plates and white napkins, blue paper cups, and plastic cutlery. Paint red and blue stripes using fabric paint on a plain white tablecloth, then spray on silver or white stars using a stencil.

Costumes Invite guests to come dressed as different states – all 52 of them.

Food Offer mini picnic pies (*see page 97*), cold, stuffed turkey (*see page 103*), minted potato salad and arugula salad (*see page 104*), mini pecan pies, and rich chocolate cheesecake (*see page 109*).

Entertainment Enjoy a game of softball or baseball and finish the day with a fireworks display.

◁ ## TUSCAN PICNIC

WHEN FLOWERS ARE IN FULL BLOOM AND CROPS ARE RIPENING, HEAD OUT FOR A DAY IN THE COUNTRY BEFORE EATING A SUNSET TUSCAN FEAST.

Invite Write your invitation directly onto a paper plate, and then decorate it with painted sunflowers.

Decor Dot tiny cake-pan candles around the picnic area (*see left*) and light them at sunset.

Table Pack traditional picnic hampers with terra cotta plates and wooden bowls. Plant fragrant herbs in terra cotta pots, and then stud the pots with colored tapers. Line the herb pots down the center of the picnic area. Roll napkins and tie a sunflower around each one.

Food Simple but delicious: focaccia bread, garlicky mixed olives (*see page 89*), salami, molasses glazed ham (*see page 102*), Tuscan bean salad (*see page 104*), antipasto pasta salad (*see page 105*), poached peaches (*see page 111*), and a selection of Italian cheeses. Serve with an Italian wine such as Chianti and Frascati.

TENNIS TEA

EVEN IF YOU CAN'T BE THERE, YOU DON'T HAVE TO MISS OUT ON THE FUN AND EXCITEMENT OF WIMBLEDON.

Invite Attach a card to a tennis ball, reminding guests to bring sun hats, visors, sunglasses, and plenty of sunblock.

Decor Set up a television outdoors with a line of director's chairs in front, then sit back and relax with a grandstand view. Serve food using daisy chain napkins (*see left and page 78*).

Food Fill bowls with strawberries and cream.

Drinks Pimm's (*see page 90*), fruit purées with sparkling water.

Games If children can't sit still, set up a game of dodge ball.

GARDEN PARTIES

ENJOY A REFINED AFTERNOON

IN A BEAUTIFUL GARDEN,

DRINKING CHAMPAGNE AND EATING

STRAWBERRIES AND CREAM.

GREEN FINGER PARTY

IN EARLY SPRING, invite friends for an afternoon swapping cuttings, trading seeds, and exchanging tips before settling down for a talk by a local nursery expert. This is a great party to hold in a greenhouse or large conservatory. Tell guests to bring problem plants for the expert's opinion.

YARD CLEAN-UP PARTY

IF YOU HAVE MOVED, or have an elderly relative who needs help tending a garden, throw a clean-up party. Send invitations on seed packages, asking guests to bring tools. Keep everyone refreshed with lemonade, and send all helpers home with small bottles of massage oil for tired limbs.

RAIN FOREST SAFARI

COME AS EXPLORERS, archaeologists, Indiana Jones, or characters from *The Jungle Book*. Play a rain forest tape for background music and rendezvous in a steamy conservatory full of plants.

CROQUET PARTY

MOW THE LAWN, tidy up the flower beds, and set up hoops for an afternoon of croquet. Transform old garden furniture with daisy prints (*see page 80*), erect parasols or awnings (*see page 17*) for guests to sit beneath, and enjoy an afternoon tea of sandwiches and petits fours (*see pages 114–15*). For the less agile, set up card tables on a terrace.

PAMPERED POOCH PARTY

ON HIS OR HER BIRTHDAY, INVITE ALL YOUR PET'S BEST DOGGY PALS TO AN AFTERNOON OF PAMPERING.

Invite Tie to a package of dog biscuits.

Decor Cushions for lounging, videos of dog shows, and *Lassie*, or cartoons of *Tom and Jerry*.

Food Nothing but the best: steak gently braised, hearts, chicken, and any other favorites, and fancy biscuits.

Entertainment Hire a dog beautician to groom and beautify your precious pooches.

PARTIES AFLOAT

TIE INVITATIONS TO POTS OF BUBBLES, TELLING GUESTS TO BRING SWIMSUITS AND PLENTY OF TOWELS, SINCE NO ONE IS GOING TO STAY DRY!

TWILIGHT SAILING

CHOOSE A SUMMER'S NIGHT with a full moon, and set sail across the harbor at dusk. Make cake-pan candles (*see page 21*) to illuminate the deck, and bring cushions and throws for guests to lounge on. If you or your friends don't have a boat, set hurricane lamps up on the pier and have the party there instead!

TUBING PARTY

IF YOU DON'T OWN A BOAT, the best option for a party afloat is to use old tire inner tubes and float down a shallow, slow-moving stream with friends. Float toward a car full of dry clothes, towels, drinks, and plenty of food.

MISSISSIPPI STEAMER

RELIVE THE DAYS OF *HUCKLEBERRY FINN*, AND CHARTER A PADDLE STEAMER ON YOUR FAVORITE STRETCH OF RIVER.

Costumes Invite guests to come dressed as saloon girls, riverboat gamblers, and characters from *Gone with the Wind*.

Music Rousing saloon-bar music played on the piano.

Food Serve smoked chicken (*see page 98*), grits, baby back ribs, cornbread (*see page 88*), and chocolate tart (*see page 108*).

Drinks Offer beer, bourbon, and Southern Comfort.

Entertainment Hire dancing saloon girls and install croupiers behind gaming tables.

SUMMER SPLASH

SHOW THE CHILDREN A SPLASHING GOOD TIME WITH A PARTY SET AROUND A POOL.

Invite Send out team swimming caps in two different colors for children to customize as they wish (*see below*).

Decor Hang tires from the trees, float a flock of rubber ducks on the pool, throw treasures to the bottom, and float as many inflatables as possible.

Games Water volleyball, swimming races, diving for treasures, water tag, and the biggest water gun fight ever. Set up wading pools or use water wings for children who can't swim. Supervise everyone at all times.

GIRLS AFLOAT

A BOAT IS THE IDEAL PLACE TO HAVE A BACHELORETTE PARTY. THERE IS NO NEED TO WATCH THE CLOCK, AND YOU CAN COME AND GO AS YOU PLEASE.

Invite Try to keep the party a surprise – the bride-to-be should not suspect what is being planned.

Drinks Champagne, of course.

Entertainment Every guest has to bring a small gift for the bride. Set the bride ten fun challenges, such as getting someone to buy her a drink, and take pictures of her completing these to mount in a signed keepsake album.

BEACH PARTIES

THINK MIAMI, MONTEGO BAY, HAWAII.
DRESS AS SEA NYMPHS OR LIFEGUARDS,
AND DANCE THE NIGHT AWAY
TO A STEEL DRUM BAND.

EATING IN STYLE ▷

★ Create a sand castle centerpiece for the dining area by filling a shallow dish or large plastic bowl with sand. Make a sand castle on the sand and decorate the centerpiece with shells and starfish (*see right*).

★ Inexpensive camping ground sheets make excellent picnic mats when faced with thick canvas. For a seaside feel, print the canvas with a pebble effect (*see page 80*).

★ For an instant canopy effect that is ideal for children's parties, spread dry towels out to form a huge picnic mat. Stand bamboo canes at the corners and link them together with streamers and balloons.

TIPS FOR A WORRY-FREE DAY

★ If you are enjoying an evening barbecue on the beach, keep looming insects at bay by lighting citronella candles and wiping exposed skin with lavender water.

★ Keep babies and young children safe from the sun by taking a small, easy-to-assemble tent to the beach. This shelters children from harmful rays, offers a sand-free area where they can play with toys, and provides somewhere for you to change them.

★ Make sure that children wear water shoes or jelly sandals to protect their feet from hot sand and from rocks that can be hidden in the water.

POTATO BAKE

MEET WITH FRIENDS WHILE IT IS STILL LIGHT, AND COLLECT KINDLING FOR A ROARING BONFIRE.

Build a fire and bury foil-wrapped potatoes in the embers. Bring plenty of toppings, along with butter, salt and pepper, paper plates, and napkins. To keep drinks cool, place cans and bottles in a large string bag, anchor it to the shore, and let the water wash over it. Finish by eating baked bananas: cut through the banana skins, stuff them with chocolate, wrap in foil, and place in the embers until the chocolate melts to a delicious goo.

TREASURE ISLAND PARTY

FLY THE JOLLY ROGER AND HEAD FOR A SANDY BEACH TO ENJOY A DAY OF SWASHBUCKLING PIRATE FUN.

Invite Attach the invite to black eye patches or pirate hats.

Costumes Dress as Long John Silver or his parrot, Captain Hook, Blackbeard, Peter Pan, or Tinkerbell.

Decor Pack "treasure-chest" picnic hampers with food tied in red and white spotted napkins. Paint sheets with a skull and crossbones, and eat on them.

Games Hide clues and treasures for children to find with maps. Set up a start and finish line for races.

BESIDE THE OCEAN CELEBRATION

HIRE A MINIBUS, PACK IT WITH KIDS, AND HEAD FOR THE BEACH FOR A BIRTHDAY PARTY WITH A DIFFERENCE.

Invite Tie a label to sunglasses, asking children to bring dry clothes, sun hat, sunblock, towel, and bathing suit.

Food Filled bagels, fresh fruit, crudités, and popcorn.

Games Give each child a party bag with a pail and shovel, a fishing net, paper flags, and a glass jar threaded with string. Look for fish and shrimp, then build a sand castle big enough to picnic in.

GAMES FOR THE BEACH

DIVIDE GUESTS INTO TEAMS, PRESENT EACH WITH PERSONALIZED TEAM T–SHIRTS, THEN BEGIN AN AFTERNOON OF BEACH OLYMPICS WITH SOME OF THE FOLLOWING GAMES:

*Softball ★ Supersoaker water guns ★ French cricket
Beach crazy golf ★ Tic-tac-toe in the sand
Tug of war ★ Volleyball ★ Diablos ★ Boules ★ Kite flying
Sand sculpting ★ Water fights ★ Hopscotch ★ Quoits
Frisbee ★ Leap-frog ★ Water relay
Touch tag ★ Inflatable races
Swimming races ★ Football*

MIDNIGHT DIP

FOR A MAGICAL NIGHTTIME DIP, time this party to take place under a full moon. Build a campfire to sit around afterward, and have flasks of hot chocolate on standby. At the stroke of twelve o'clock, throw caution to the wind and take the plunge.

NEW YEAR'S DAY DIP

CLEAR OUT CHRISTMAS cobwebs with a dip in the ocean on New Year's Day. Meet with friends on the beach, loaded up with soft drinks, bars of chocolate to replenish energy levels, and plenty of dry towels. Then take a dip, if only up to your ankles!

BEACH PARTY WINDMILLS

ARRANGE THESE BRIGHTLY COLORED WINDMILLS AROUND A PARTY AREA SO THAT GUESTS CAN FIND YOU.

Cut sheets of colorful paper into squares of the same size and glue coordinated colors together in pairs. When dry, cut diagonally from each corner almost into the center; the paper will look like four joined triangles. Punch a hole through the center of the square and through alternate outside corners of the triangles. Fold the punched corners into the center of the square, one after the other. Thread a paper fastener through the layers of paper, then thread through a hole in the top of a bamboo cane and fasten.

Anchor tablecloths with pretty sand castles or piles of rocks and seashells. Then serve a feast from colorful china plates.

GETTING MARRIED OPENS UP A WHOLE WORLD OF EXCITING PARTY

POSSIBILITIES. TAKE A CLASSIC THEME, SUCH AS SUMMER

FLORALS, AND STYLE THE DRESS, FLOWERS, INVITATIONS, AND DECOR

TO MATCH, OR BREAK WITH TRADITION AND ADOPT A MODERN MOTIF

WITH BRIGHT, TRANSLUCENT COLOR OR A

BANQUETS & WEDDINGS

GLAMOROUS COSTUME THEME. DON'T CONFINE EXTRAVAGANT

LARGE-SCALE PARTIES TO WEDDINGS - THROW A PARTY IN

A SPLENDID LOCATION TO CELEBRATE A GROUP OF FRIENDS'

BIRTHDAYS, A RETIREMENT, OR GRADUATION, OR PLAN A MAGICAL

BANQUET IN A SILK-SWATHED TENT FOR A FANTASTIC FAMILY

REUNION OR BON VOYAGE BASH. A FEAST OF IDEAS FOLLOWS.

MOORISH FEAST

SET THIS PARTY IN A TENT FILLED WITH SILK HANGINGS AND MAGIC CARPETS. LIGHT THE TENT WITH BRASS LAMPS AND SCENT IT WITH JASMINE INCENSE.

Invite Send attached to a package of incense sticks.

Costumes Belly dancers, bedouins, sultans and sultanas, Aladdin, genies, and magic carpets.

Food Serve food from platters lined with banana leaves. Tempt guests with kabobs, pesto couscous salad (*see page 105*), coconut ice cream (*see page 113*), and Turkish delight.

Drinks Sherbet, mint tea, and strong coffee.

Decor Decorate walls with hangings (*see below*), and arrange low seating so that guests can lounge. Make paper mosaic tablecloths (*see page 77*) to eat at.

Entertainment Magicians, snake charmers, and belly dancers. Paint wooden boards with people riding carpets; cut out the faces, set the boards up, and invite guests to stand behind and pose for photographs as they arrive.

Customize plain Venetian masks by painting them with poster or emulsion paint. Trim the edges with braiding, or stick on sequins, beads, organza, and tulle.

MOORISH HANGINGS

CREATE A SENSE OF OPULENCE by hanging silk saris, dyed muslin, or crushed velvet around the walls of a room. For a truly luxurious effect, embellish the cloth by adding intricate designs to the fabric with gold relief paint. The cloth can be further adorned with fake gems and the edges trimmed with gold braiding.

VENETIAN TABLECLOTHS

TO MAKE HARLEQUIN CLOTHS, fold white tablecloths into quarters, or into eighths if the tablecloths are large. Paint a black diamond in opposite quarters (or eighths) using fabric paint. When the paint is dry, iron the cloth to fix the design.

GOLD-SWIRLED GLASSES

TRANSFORM INEXPENSIVE GLASSES by adding a touch of color with a swirl or two of glass paint. Buy some cheap, plain glasses and make sure that they are clean and dry before painting. Draw a name or design on the glass using gold glass paint, then allow the design to dry.

VENETIAN MASQUERADE BALL

HOST AN EXTRAVAGANT, ELEGANT PARTY IN A GRAND VENUE WITH GUESTS DISGUISED BEHIND MASKS.

Invite Mail plain black masks, asking the guests to customize and decorate them to suit their outfits.

Costumes Pierrots, shepherdesses, 18th-century gentlemen, circus performers, and gondoliers. Dress up with white makeup, beauty spots, powdered wigs, hooped skirts, fans, and handkerchief sleeves, white tights, high buckle shoes, lace, satin, and brocade.

Decor Hang elegant mirrors and grand-looking chandeliers. Serve supper on Venetian Harlequin tablecloths (*see left*) and drink wine from gold-swirled glasses (*see left*).

Music Harpsichord and a string quartet for minuets.

Entertainment Present all female guests with a dance card to fill in for the evening. As the clock strikes midnight, insist that people join the dance floor to remove their masks and reveal their true identities.

OLDE ENGLISH BANQUET

ENJOY AN EVENING OF REVELRY IN A BARN OR OLD HALL. SET TABLES IN A LONG HORSESHOE SHAPE AND SIT THE PRINCIPAL GUESTS AT THE HEAD, AS THE LORD AND LADY.

Invite Write in old English script, then tear the edges, age by dipping in strong, cold tea, and roll and tie with red ribbon.

Costumes Anything from the era of Elizabeth I: Sir Walter Raleigh, Mary Queen of Scots, monks, friars, and peasants.

Decor Trestle tables and benches, with thrones for the lord and lady (*see below*). Serve food from wooden platters (*see below*) and drink ale from flagons. Use huge candlesticks, scatter reeds or straw on the floor, and hang garlands from the ceiling.

Food Eat by hand but allow guests knives. Serve rustic bread, molasses glazed ham (*see page 102*), roast chicken, chocolate tart (*see page 108*), platters of cheese, and bowls of fruit and nuts.

Entertainment Hire a juggler, flame thrower, and lute player.

Games Make stocks to imprison naughty guests' arms and legs, tell bawdy jokes, and dance the galliard.

MIDSUMMER NIGHT'S BALL

OPEN YOUR GARDEN FOR A MIDSUMMER NIGHT'S EVE PARTY UNDER THE STARS. DRESS CHILDREN AS FAIRIES, AND HAVE THEM HAND OUT GARLANDS OF HERBS TO WARD OFF MISCHIEVOUS SPIRITS.

Invite Send invitations attached to packages of sparklers for guests to use as fairy wands on the party night.

Costumes Dress as Titania, Oberon, or Puck, or as spirits, imps, pixies, and fairies with silver wings.

Decor Hang tiny white lights, crystals, tiny bells, and wind chimes from trees. Decorate tables with garlands of fresh herbs and flowers and seat guests on ivy heart chairs (*see below*). Fill the air with the aroma of scented candles, essential oils, and scattered petals, and create a mystical feel with dry ice or a bubble machine.

Entertainment Dress a musician as Pan and create a fairy bower in which he can play his pipes. Hire fortune-tellers and magicians and a violinist to serenade diners. End the evening with a bonfire and fireworks.

OLDE ENGLISH THRONE

CREATE REGAL SEATING by turning ordinary chairs into thrones for a lord and lady. Cut seat backs from thin plywood into the shape desired, spray them gold, and attach them to ordinary chairs. Cover the chair seats in purple and red velvet, and trim the chairs with fake ermine and jewels.

OLDE ENGLISH PLATTER

SERVE FOOD ON WOODEN BOARDS for a truly Elizabethan touch. Have a local wood merchant cut out disks about 15½in (40cm) in diameter, then seal the wood with varnish to give a washable surface.

◁ MIDSUMMER IVY HEART CHAIR

TIE EVERGREEN HEARTS to the backs of chairs for a magical, midsummer feel. Gather long lengths of ivy, and twist and secure them around heart-shaped wire templates, about 6in (15cm) in diameter. Tie each heart with a long ribbon and hang it on the back of a chair. You can attach a name place card to each heart.

WONDERLAND BALL

ENJOY A MAD, UPSIDE DOWN, BACK-TO-FRONT EVENING IN TRUE LEWIS CARROLL STYLE.

Invite Write it backward so guests have to read it in a mirror (*see below*).

Costumes The Queen of Hearts, the Mad Hatter, the White Rabbit, the Dormouse, Tweedledum and Tweedledee, the Walrus, the Caterpillar, Alice, and the Cheshire-Cat.

Decor Stand fake pink flamingoes in a pond. Hang huge playing cards on walls, and arrange flowers in upturned top hats. Cover tables with blue and white checked cloths, and tie a heart-shaped helium balloon to every chair.

Food Serve an English tea buffet (*see pages 114–15*) with food and drink labeled "eat me" and "drink me". Drink tea after the meal and serve liqueurs in fake medicine bottles.

Entertainment At the entrance of the room place distorting mirrors that make guests grow or shrink. Dance the quadrille, organize a walking poet to recite to guests, and someone to perform card tricks. Play croquet after tea.

EGYPTIAN EXTRAVAGANZA

TRAVEL BACK IN TIME TO THE 1920s, WHEN THE TREASURES OF THE TOMB OF TUTANKHAMUN WERE UNCOVERED.

Invite Written on handmade paper with a painted border of hieroglyphics around the edges.

Costumes Cleopatra, mummies, sphinxes, priestesses, scribes, khaki-dressed explorers, loincloths, loose robes, thonged sandals, heavy kohl-rimmed eyes, gold, and heavy jewelry.

Decor Create your own Egyptian tomb, straight from the Valley of the Kings. Paint huge murals depicting pyramids, dancers, musicians, scarab beetles, and the gods Isis and Osiris. Stand "ancient" vases, oil lamps, and scrolls around the room. Complete the look with archaeologists' spades, old cameras, pith helmets, maps, and binoculars. Make papier-mâché pyramids or sphinxes and put them by the front door.

Music Harp, flute, and lyre music, or groups of Egyptian or Nubian musicians.

Entertainment Spread sand on the dance floor and encourage guests to do a sand dance.

MIRROR INVITATIONS

TO MAKE REVERSE INVITATIONS, write out an invitation normally, then tape it to a window with the print side facing out. Place a sheet of colored paper against the window and over the paper, and trace the words. You will have traced an invitation that can only be read in a mirror. Complete your invitations by decorating them with playing cards from the hearts suit, or with paintings of characters from *Alice in Wonderland*. You could also attach reflective silver paper or a small mirror.

PARTY PHOTOGRAPHS

MAKE OR RENT A LARGE GILT FRAME, or paint a backdrop of Alice playing croquet with the Queen of Hearts. Set this up in the entrance to the room, and ask guests to pose for pictures as they arrive, either in front of the backdrop or behind the frame. Present the pictures to guests on leaving, or paste them in a photo album and ask guests to sign underneath.

◁ ## SHIMMY PARTY

RECREATE THE DAYS OF *THE GREAT GATSBY*, AND SPEND AN EVENING DANCING THE CHARLESTON.

Costumes Women in flapper dresses covered in sequins and bugle beads, and wearing silk stockings and garters, ostrich plumes, and swinging beads. Men in tuxedos, dress shirts and bow ties or cravats.

Decor Art Deco: trim curtains with bullion fringe and place peacock feathers and ostrich plumes in elegant vases. Fill the room with ferns placed on tall pedestals.

Table For a decadent air, make money napkin holders and coasters out of play money (*see left*). Light the table with oyster candles. Melt white candles in a tin can over low heat. When melted, remove the wicks and cut them into short lengths. Pour some wax into cleaned half oyster shells, and stand a wick in the center of each. Hold the wicks upright for 30 seconds, until the wax sets.

Entertainment Dress wait staff as famous silent movie stars such as Rudolph Valentino and Greta Garbo.

MYTHOLOGY BANQUET ▷

DRESS AS ANCIENT GODS, AND ENJOY A NIGHT OF GOOD FOOD, FINE WINE, AND MERRY-MAKING.

Invite Drawn to resemble sets of panpipes.

Costumes Dress as the Minotaur, Pluto, Zeus, Andromeda, Agamemnon, Cyclops, Hercules, Atlas, Jason, or Medusa.

Decor Hang up oil-burning lamps and stand terra cotta urns and fake grapevines around the room. Make statue heads out of papier-mâché, paint them white, and crown them with gold-sprayed laurel leaf crowns (*see right*).

Food Cover platters with vine leaves and serve garlicky olives (*see page 89*), chicken with figs (*see page 99*), festive phyllo pie (*see page 107*), honey cakes, poached peaches (*see page 111*), fresh cheeses, grapes, fruit and nuts, and baskets of breads. Serve wine from terra cotta urns or brass pitchers.

Entertainment Dress serving staff as slaves. Seat a harpist at the door to welcome guests, and hire musicians to play the lyre and the pipes for guests to dance to. Hire actors to dress as a poet, wandering philosopher, and living statues.

WINTER WEDDING

BREAK WITH TRADITION AND GIVE AN ELIZABETHAN FEEL TO A WINTER WEDDING, USING LUXURIOUS VELVETS, BROCADES, AND FAKE FURS.

Spray candlesticks gold and fit them with long tapers. Wrap trailing ivy around the candlesticks and glue individual ivy leaves to each taper.

△ INVITES & DECORATIONS

USE BERRIES, LEAVES, PINECONES, AND EVERGREENS TO DECORATE THE ROOM AND TABLES SO THAT EVERYTHING LOOKS AND SMELLS WONDERFUL.

Invite Match designs on the bride's gown, emboss in gold, and send in gold envelopes sealed with sealing wax.

Decor Scatter herbs on the floor, so when guests arrive, the air is filled with fragrance. Ideal herbs are thyme, mint, and lemon balm. Hang up wreaths of evergreens, garnet-colored roses, and cinnamon (*see above*), and hand out boutonnieres of winter berries. Secure swags of evergreen and pinecones tied with gold ribbon (*see page 42*) under windows.

THE RECEPTION ▷

Music Hire a musician to play music on the mandolin.

Table To make cinnamon candles, stretch rubber bands around the candles. Tuck cinnamon sticks of the same length under the bands, tie ribbons around the candles and remove the bands (*see right*). Enjoy the meal by candlelight.

Food Serve molasses glazed ham (*see page 102*), pommes dauphinois (*see page 106*), and roasted sweet potatoes (*see page 107*). Finish with a cheese platter, with figs and dates.

Drinks Hot toddies on arrival.

Bouquet Hand-tied roses wrapped in evergreens.

COUNTRY WEDDING

A COUNTRY THEME WORKS WELL FOR A SUMMER WEDDING. KEEP THE COLORS SOFT AND FEMININE, AND MAKE THE MOST OF THE ABUNDANCE OF FLOWERS.

THE MEANING OF FLOWERS

Bluebell – everlasting love ★ Daffodil – regard
Daisy – innocence ★ Honeysuckle – devoted affection
Ivy – fidelity ★ White rose – worthiness
Myrtle – love ★ Orchid – beauty ★ Rose – romance
Violet – faithfulness ★ Lily of the valley – happiness
Red chrysanthemum – I love you ★ Tuberose – voluptuousness
Forget-me-not – remembrance always ★ Mimosa – secret love
Camellia – perfect loveliness ★ Hyacinth – playfulness

△ INVITES & DECORATIONS ▽

HAND OUT ORGANZA POUCHES OF LOOSE WHEAT SEEDS AND PETALS FOR GUESTS TO THROW AS CONFETTI.

Invite Stamp two gold hearts on heavy cardboard. Attach two wheat ears, a sign of fertility, to each card (see above).

Decor Gather wildflowers such as chamomile, buttercups, and cornflowers and mix them with boxwood, lisianthus, and spray roses. Arrange the flowers in silver tin cans tied with coordinated ribbon and set them around the wedding venue (see below). Use wide ribbons cut from the bridesmaids' dress fabric to tie bunches of wheat, and attach them over the entrance to form an archway.

THE RECEPTION

Music Hire a Celtic ceilidh or square-dance band.

Table Cover tables in pastel-colored linen, with each laid in a different color. Tie napkins with woven wheat stems.

Food To continue the informal theme, host a country barbecue or eat in the garden, buffet style.

Drinks Mimosas (see page 90) on arrival.

Bouquet Wheat ears, lavender, wild roses and rosebuds, elderberry flowers, honeysuckle, cornflowers, or sweet peas, hand-tied with coordinated ribbons. Wear circlets of flowers and give bridesmaids small baskets of loose flowers to carry.

PETAL CONFETTI ▽

ROSE CONFETTI (*see below*) smells wonderful. Pick roses on the wedding morning. Pull off petals and put them with rose heads in silk, velvet, or organza bags. For the bags, cut out fabric twice the size of the finished bag. Fold in half, right sides facing, and stitch sides together. Turn and press flat. Cut a flap shape with zigzag edges and stitch to an inside top edge. Attach a tag. Fill with petals.

UNUSUAL WEDDING VENUES

In a park ★ Yacht ★ Train
Ski lodge★ Barge ★ Clipper
Restaurant ★ Stately home
Zoo ★ Hotel ★ On a beach
Island ★ Chapel of Love, Las Vegas
Airplane ★ Garden
Under water ★ Hot air balloon
Football stadium ★ On stage
Parachuting ★ Bungee jumping
By a lake ★ On a mountain
Movie set ★ The Empire State Building

SILK RING CUSHION

MAKE A BEAUTIFUL white silk cushion edged with lace, decorated with hearts, flowers, or doves, and embroidered with the names of the bride and groom and the date of the wedding. Stitch two ribbons to the front and tie the wedding rings to them with a bow. A ring bearer could follow the bridal party up the aisle carrying the cushion and present it to the best man when the rings are called for.

ORGANZA POUCHES

AT SUMMER WEDDINGS, instead of giving favors, make delicate pouches from organza and place wildflower seeds inside. The seeds can be planted in guests' gardens or window boxes to flower around your first wedding anniversary. To make the pouches, simply place a handful of seeds in the center of a white circle of organza, scoop up the sides to make a purse shape, and tie with a lavender-colored ribbon.

WINTER CAKE TABLE

FOR A SETTING that perfectly complements a winter wedding cake, cover a small, round table with a round cloth. Set the cake on a cake stand in the center. Swathe several feet of white tulle around the cake, covering the stand and tucking it under the cake board to resemble billowing snow. Scatter the tulle with cones, holly, mistletoe, and white roses.

AUTUMN INVITATION

COMMISSION a drawing of the church or venue and print on card. Punch two holes down the side of each, and thread with silk ribbon.

WHEAT BUNCHES

GATHER BUNCHES of oats, wheat, or corn and strip off the leaves. Take 40 stems and tie below the ears. Plant in terra cotta pots filled with florists' foam and cover each pot with moss.

ROSE PLACE SETTING

LIGHTLY SPRAY tiny terra cotta pots with gold or silver paint. Fill them with florist's foam and cover the top of each with moss. Trim the stems of dried roses to 4in (10cm) in length and stand a rose in the center of each pot. Attach a label to each, with wedding guests' names handwritten on them. Use the pots as place settings on the wedding reception tables.

WHITE WEDDING

STICK WITH TRADITION, but give your white wedding a contemporary twist. Introduce a theme such as daisies, stars, feathers, candles, fake fur, snowflakes, or cherubs to tie in with the time of year. Send out white invitations featuring your theme, such as a threaded feather or stick-on stars or daisies. Ask guests to dress from head to foot in white and men to wear a white boutonniere.

GOLDEN CHAIRS

TRANSFORM plain wooden chairs by brightening them up with a coat of paint. Sand the chairs, make sure they are completely dust-free, and then spray them with gold paint.

TULLE CHAIRS

FOR A ROMANTIC TOUCH, tie white tulle bows to each chair. Cut lengths of tulle 20 x 60in (50 x 150cm) long. Wrap one around each chair back and tie at the back with a bow.

OUTDOOR LIGHTS

GLAM UP outdoor lights by placing a white greaseproof-paper bag over each bulb and securing it with a clip. Alternatively, make small, colored paper envelopes for each light from different colored tissue paper. Punch two holes in each envelope, thread with thin wire, and use to secure the bag over each light.

MODERN WEDDING

HAVE A TAILOR-MADE wedding of your dreams. Choose a color theme and inject a riot of color into the ceremony. Specify a costume theme or dress in outfits from the 1950s or 60s, or as the characters from a favorite movie. Set the tone for the day by arriving in a convertible or an old Cadillac. Ask ushers to hand out jars of bubbles to guests so that you emerge from the wedding ceremony in a cloud of bubbles.

MODERN WEDDING RECEPTION

SPREAD TABLES with a white cloth and overlay them with another in a bright, translucent color. Wire name tags, push each one into a fresh lemon, and stand the lemon on a plate as a place setting. When guests arrive, offer them a cocktail such as a margarita or banana daiquiri (see page 90). Serve informal food that is a favorite with the bride and groom, such as pizza, pasta, sushi, or tacos.

MODERN WEDDING DECOR

WIRE BAY TREES with oranges and lemons, and place them at the entrance to the room. Give out boutonnieres made with gerberas, and decorate the venue with bunches of sunflowers or anemones set in colored glass bottles and jars. Light the outside area with flaming torches or petal flares (see page 19).

Fill shallow glass △ bowls with flowers and pebbles, and float candles around the edges.

HALLOWEEN, THANKSGIVING, CHRISTMAS, NEW YEAR'S EVE – THE FESTIVE SEASON IS THE TIME TO THROW A PARTY. STICK TO THE BARE ESSENTIALS TRADITIONAL TO THE OCCASION, OR GO ALL OUT FOR AN OVER-THE-TOP CELEBRATION WITH SHIMMERING SEASONAL DECORATIONS AND ATMOSPHERIC FOOD AND DRINK.

FESTIVE PARTIES

ON CHRISTMAS DAY SHARE THE PREPARATION AND COST OF A MEAL BY ENJOYING A HOUSE-HOPPING, MENU-SHARING CHRISTMAS DINNER WITH NEARBY FRIENDS AND FAMILY. HOLD A TREASURE HUNT FOR CHILDREN, WITH CLUES LEADING FROM ONE HOUSE TO THE NEXT. EAT A DIFFERENT COURSE AT EACH HOUSE, STARTING WITH A BRUNCH OF SMOKED SALMON AND CHAMPAGNE.

HALLOWEEN

FOR A NIGHT OF FIENDISH FUN, SEND INVITATIONS IN BLACK ENVELOPES STAMPED WITH BLOOD-RED SEALING WAX, CARVE SPOOKY FACES IN PUMPKINS, AND SERVE GUESTS BAT BISCUITS AND WORM SOUP.

WITCHES' PARTY ▽

ATTACH SCARY ORGANZA GHOST SHAPES TO THE CEILING TO BRUSH AGAINST GUESTS' FACES.

Invite Mail out jelly worms, spiders, and bats (*see below*).

Costumes Witches, black cats, warlocks, goblins, and trolls.

Decor Stand pumpkin lanterns (*see below*) at the entrance.

Food Worm soup made with thick noodles, bat-shaped gingerbread cookies (*see page 114*), toffee apples, pumpkin pie.

Games Face painting, apple bobbing, ghost stories. Hide trick-or-treat party bags outdoors under piles of raked leaves.

HORROR PARTY

USE THE HORROR MOVIES OF BORIS KARLOFF AND VINCENT PRICE AS INSPIRATION.

Costumes Dress as zombies, or whiten your face, grease back your hair, don a cape, and come as Dracula.

Decor Create a dungeon by hanging chains from the ceiling, burning red-hot coals in a fireplace, and lighting the room with candles in red-painted glass jars. Show classic black-and-white horror movies.

Music *Thriller* by Michael Jackson; demented organ playing.

Games Murder in the dark, sardines (*see page 47*), Cluedo.

CARVED PUMPKIN LIGHTING

CLEVERLY CARVED PUMPKINS make scary but fun lanterns for Halloween parties. Cut the top off a pumpkin or squash and scoop out the flesh as neatly as possible. Draw outlines of eyes, nose, and a jagged mouth on the pumpkin with a marker pen (*see right*). Using a craft knife or scalpel, carefully carve around the outlines, then cut through the skin and flesh. Remove the carved-out pieces of pumpkin, taking care not to split the skin and flesh around the cut-out shapes. Put a nightlight or candles inside.

HALLOWEEN MENU

CREAMY PUMPKIN SOUP (*SEE PAGE 92*)

•

BEEF IN BEER, SERVED FROM A BOWL INSIDE A HOLLOWED-OUT PUMPKIN (*SEE PAGE 98*)

•

CHEESY BAKED POTATOES (*SEE PAGE 106*)

•

GHOST-SHAPED MERINGUE CAKE
(*SEE PAGE 108*)

•

WITCH'S BREW (LEMONADE WITH GREEN FOOD COLORING), APPLE WHIZZ, AND MULLED WINE
(*SEE PAGE 91*)

FIREWORKS

ENJOY AN EVENING OF FURIOUS FLAMES AND FIREWORKS. HANG UP LUMINOUS STARS, PUT SPARKLERS IN POTS OF SAND, BURY POTATOES IN THE FIRE'S EMBERS, AND TOAST MOUNDS OF MARSHMALLOWS.

FIREWORKS MENU

ROASTED PEPPER & TOMATO SOUP (*SEE PAGE 92*)

•

CHILI CON CARNE

POTATOES, BAKED IN EMBERS (*SEE PAGE 24*)

•

BAKED APPLES

BONFIRE CAKES (*SEE PAGE 114*)

TRIPLE CHOC COOKIES (*SEE PAGE 116*)
SERVED IN WAXED BAGS

STARGAZER'S PARTY

THROW A NIGHTTIME PARTY OF SHOOTING STARS, PLANETS, AND CONSTELLATIONS. ASK GUESTS TO BRING TELESCOPES AND BINOCULARS, AND HAND OUT ASTRAL MAPS.

Invite Send packages of sparkling moondust and invite guests to come dressed as gods or as their sign of the zodiac.

Costumes Zeus, Thor, Eros, Libra, Capricorn, Virgo, and Aries.

Decor Hang tiny lights in trees and dot petal flares around the garden (*see page 19*). Spray chairs gold for the gods' feast.

Music The Planets by Gustav Holst.

Entertainment Finish the night with dazzling fireworks.

FIREWORKS PARTY

FOR A REALLY SPECTACULAR SHOW, ASK EACH GUEST TO DONATE TO THE FIREWORKS FUND, AND START COLLECTING FIREWOOD A FEW WEEKS IN ADVANCE.

Invite Attach labels to packs of sparklers.

Decor Illuminate the garden by punching designs in tin cans and setting candles inside (*see below and page 18*).

Food Comfort foods like mashed potatoes, bananas baked with chocolate (*see page 24*), toasted marshmallows.

Drinks Hot chocolate, mulled wine (*see page 91*), Swedish Glogg (*see page 43*), Irish coffee (*see page 13*), and spiced cider.

FIREWORKS DECOR ▷

★ Tin-can lights make decorative, safe candleholders. Clean a tin can with paint stripper and wire wool. Cut the top off the can, then cut a decorative shape around the front and back, and discard the surplus metal. Keep the design at least 1½in (3cm) high at the base. Punch a design on the can with a bradawl or hammer and nail. Set a candle inside.

★ For a lovely table setting, pick brilliantly colored red, orange, and green leaves. Press the leaves flat between blotting paper overnight. Overlay three leaves around the base of a red candle, leaving a space below for the candle to fit in the holder. Overlap leaves around the candle to resemble petals, securing with raffia.

THANKSGIVING

CELEBRATE ON THE FOURTH THURSDAY IN NOVEMBER BY GATHERING FAMILY AND FRIENDS TO GIVE THANKS FOR THE GOOD THINGS IN LIFE. TO TRANSFORM A TABLECLOTH FOR THANKSGIVING DINNER, DIP THE VEINED SIDES OF PRESSED LEAVES IN FABRIC PAINT AND STAMP ONTO THE CLOTH. IRON ON THE DRIED DESIGN.

THANKSGIVING DINNER

FOR PLACE SETTINGS, PAINT THE VEINED SIDE OF DRIED, PRESSED LEAVES WITH EMULSION OR POSTER PAINT AND STAMP ONTO RECTANGLES OF CARDBOARD. WHEN DRY, CUT AROUND HALF THE PRINT, FOLD THE CARD IN TWO, AND WRITE THE NAME (SEE ABOVE).

Food Serve roast turkey garnished with halved clementine shells filled with blueberries and cranberries.

Decor Print a leaf tablecloth and place settings (see above). Use as many different leaves as possible. Make a cornucopia centerpiece for the table by wrapping and taping cardboard around a cone-shaped piece of florist's foam. Remove the foam, and cover the cardboard with papier-mâché strips made from newspaper and wallpaper paste. Put on three coats inside and out. When dry, paint the cone and seal it with two coats of satin varnish. Place the cornucopia on a table and fill with a cascade of attractive fruits.

Entertainment Everyone play charades in the evening.

THANKSGIVING MENU

CORNBREAD (SEE PAGE 88)

CREAMY PUMPKIN SOUP (SEE PAGE 92)

•

BONED STUFFED TURKEY (SEE PAGE 103)

ROASTED SWEET POTATOES (SEE PAGE 107)

ZUCCHINI WITH GARLIC (SEE PAGE 107)

ROASTED, BUTTERED PUMPKIN

WILD RICE

•

INDIVIDUAL PECAN PIES

CHRISTMAS

DON'T LET A LACK OF SPACE STOP YOU FROM DECORATING A TREE THIS CHRISTMAS: SELECT BRANCHES OF TWISTED WILLOW AND FROST WITH SILVER SPRAY PAINT. PLACE BRANCHES IN A VASE OF FLORIST'S FOAM, AND HANG WITH ORNAMENTS. SEND OUT GINGERBREAD HEARTS, ICED AND WRAPPED IN PLASTIC WRAP, INSTEAD OF CHRISTMAS CARDS.

MIDNIGHT MASS

CHILDREN NEVER SLEEP ON CHRISTMAS EVE, SO LET THEM STAY UP AND JOIN YOU AT EVENING MASS.

Invite Send out invitations with Christmas cards, asking each child to bring a glass jar and a candle.

Food Enlist the children's help in baking triple choc cookies (*see page 116*) for Santa, using cookie cutters.

Drinks Hot chocolate and, for the adults, mulled wine (*see page 91*) and Irish coffee (*see Hot Toddies, page 13*).

Entertainment Spend the evening writing Santa letters and decorating the glass jars with glass paint and stickers. To make jar handles, loop a long piece of string into a handle, then wrap the rest of the string around the jar rim, tying the ends in a knot. Leave cookies and a drink out for Santa, then light the jar candles and walk to church singing Christmas carols. Surprise the children on their return: sneak home while everyone is at church, take a bite out of a cookie, finish the drink, make hoof-prints in the snow, and hang up a stocking for each child.

SWEDISH CHRISTMAS ▷

ENJOY A SWEDISH JULBORD, THE PERFECT MEAL TO SERVE FOR AN "OPEN HOUSE" CHRISTMAS. TELL GUESTS TO DROP IN AT THEIR LEISURE AND JOIN YOU FOR A BITE TO EAT, A GAME OR TWO, AND A GLASS OF GLOGG.

Invite Pipe onto gingerbread (*see page 114*).

Decor Stand traditional Swedish candles in every window. Decorate a tree with gingerbread cookies (*see right*). To make these, cut gingerbread dough (*see page 114*) into star, heart, and tree shapes, punch holes in the top for ribbon, bake, then ice, thread with ribbon, and hang on the tree.

Food Translated, *Julbord* simply means "Christmas table," so emulate a Swedish Christmas and offer an extensive buffet. Serve roast ham, mustard, pickled cabbage and apple sauce, rolled herrings and gravlax, meatballs, pâté, cold meats, sausages, and gingerbread cookies called *pepparkakor*.

Drinks Serve steaming cups of Glogg (*see page 43*), made from red wine, vodka, and spices.

TWIG FIR TREE

MAKE A FIR TREE shape from stiff wire. Paint a clay pot, stand the tree trunk in it, pour in plaster of Paris. When set, cover with moss. Attach bundles of twigs to the tree with wire. Thread cranberries onto string, and zigzag it up the tree, securing with wire at intervals. Attach dried orange slices (*see page 44*), rag bows, baubles, and holly as a star (*see below*).

PINECONE BUNDLES

THESE BUNDLES MAKE ATTRACTIVE SCENTED CHRISTMAS DECORATIONS.

Place pinecones on a tray and let dry out in a warm, dry place. Dot glue onto each scale, then sprinkle with glitter. Glue a long length of ribbon to the base of each cone, then gather ten cones and tie the ribbons into a bow. Attach a bundle to either end of a shelf and sprinkle the cones with a little pine oil.

Tiny Christmas cakes baked in cans make lovely gifts. Ice them and then wrap in plastic wrap.

LUMINARY

THIS LANTERN GIVES A ROOM A WONDERFUL CHRISTMAS FEEL.

Cut a rectangle of thick, colored, corrugated cardboard to measure 8 x 24in (20 x 60cm). Score a line every 6in (15cm) down the long edge of the card. Cut a Christmas shape, such as a star, angel, or holly, out of each quarter. Glue waxed paper behind each shape, then fold and stand the cardboard over a nightlight.

OAK LEAF RUNNER

FOR A QUICK decoration to run the length of a table, take a strip of corded ribbon about 2in (5cm) wide and at least 40in (1m) longer than the table. Cut "V" shapes at both ends of the ribbon. Glue a small pinecone to the ribbon at both ends of the table, then glue large, dried oak leaves along the length of the ribbon.

CHILI WREATH

THREAD RED AND GREEN chilies on lengths of string, and hang in a warm, dry place to dry out and harden. When they are dry, glue the chilies around a simple cane wreath, following the weave of the wreath. When the wreath is covered, tie with ribbon and hang up.

YULE LOG

USE A YULE LOG as a centerpiece. Find a stout, gnarled silver birch or apple tree log. Put the log on a flat surface so it sits squarely and drill seven ¾in (2cm) deep by ¾in (2cm) wide holes evenly along the top. Stand a candle in each hole and decorate with holly.

SNOWFLAKE SCENE

DRAW A SIX-POINTED snowflake shape onto a sheet of medium-weight cardboard. Cut out the shape on the card using a craft knife or scalpel. Hold the card template firmly against the inside of a clean window, and lightly spray through the shape, using fake aerosol snow. Carefully remove the stencil and repeat randomly over the windows to form a snowy scene.

CHRISTMAS MENU

SMOKED SALMON TRIANGLES
(SEE PAGE 95)

•

BONED STUFFED TURKEY
(SEE PAGE 103)

POMMES DAUPHINOIS
(SEE PAGE 106)

ROASTED PARSNIPS

•

PLUM PUDDING (SEE PAGE 110)

PAPER CHAINS

PAPER CHAINS ARE SIMPLE TO MAKE, AND CHILDREN CAN HELP.

Cut two long strips of crêpe paper, each about 2in (5cm) wide. Lay one end of each strip at right angles to the other and staple the ends in place. Fold one strip over the other at right angles, and crease the fold. Repeat, folding the strips alternately over each other until the paper is used up, then staple the ends together.

FIRE & ICE PARTY

IF HAVING CHRISTMAS IN SNOWY CLIMES, THROW A CHILDREN'S PARTY.

Ask children to bring gloves, hats, and a sled or toboggan. Hold races, then warm up with hot chocolate with marshmallows floating on top. Divide children into groups and ask each group to build the best snowman. Enjoy an ice cream birthday cake and hand out sparklers to illuminate the way home.

For a glittering Christmas tree, deck branches in white, frosted glass, and shimmering silver.

SECRET SANTA PARTY

ASK GUESTS TO BRING GIFTS OF A SET AMOUNT.

Fill a box with shredded paper and bury the gifts as guests arrive. After dinner, take turns picking a gift. If you know your guests very well, it can be more fun to buy anonymous presents for specific friends. Put guests' names in a hat, draw them out, and enclose in the invitations.

SWEDISH GLOGG

PUT A FEW PLUMP raisins and blanched almonds in the base of six glasses. Pour a bottle of red wine into a pot. Add ¼pt (150ml) vodka, 5 cloves, 2 cinnamon sticks, 8 cardamom pods, and sugar to taste. Bring almost to the boil, remove from the heat, strain, then pour into glasses. Let the glogg stand overnight in the pot for a stronger drink.

CHRISTMAS SWAGS

HANG DECORATIVE DRIED FRUIT SWAGS FROM
FIREPLACES, ALONG SHELVES, AND DOWN BANISTERS.

Thinly slice oranges and lemons into ⅕in (½cm) slices and
place them on wire racks set over baking sheets. Bake at
275°F (140°C) for 7–8 hours with the oven door ajar, until
the slices have dried and are no longer sticky. Check the
slices at intervals, since drying time can vary greatly. Remove
the fruit from the oven and let cool. Thread the slices
alternately with dried cranberries, bay leaves, small wooden
hearts, whole dried pomegranates, and ribbon bows onto
long lengths of jute string and hang them up.

For original, glittering place

settings, spell out guests' initials

using gold- and silver-colored

sugar almonds or dragées.

△ SILVER & GOLD PARTY

Costumes Whether guests dress from head to toe in
silver and gold, or simply don one item of colored
clothing or glitter makeup, this color theme is one
that even the most reluctant fancy-dress party
guest can join in with.

Decor Sand old wooden chairs, then spray
them with gold paint. Transform inexpensive glasses with
swirls of gold and silver glass paint (*see page 28*). Tie linen
napkins with thick gold braid.

Food Guild food with edible loose-leaf gold, and cover
cakes or ice cream with tiny, edible silver balls.

HOMEMADE CRACKERS

BUY CRACKER SNAPS if possible, so the crackers bang when
pulled. Cut three squares of cardboard 6 x 4½in (15 x 11cm),
and roll into three tubes, securing each with tape. Place a snap
in one tube, to hang evenly from both ends, then stuff a small
gift, a silly joke, and a party hat inside. Glue the tube halfway
down the long edge of a 13 x 10in (32 x 25cm) piece of
crêpe paper. Lay the two other tubes at both ends of
the glued tube, leaving a 1¾in (3cm) gap between
them. Wrap the crêpe paper around the tubes
and glue in place. Tie gold string into
bows in the gaps between the rolls.
Remove the end rolls and decorate.

NEW YEAR'S EVE

GATHER WITH FRIENDS TO SEE IN THE NEW YEAR. HAND OUT BELLS AND HORNS, AND MAKE AS MUCH NOISE AS POSSIBLE AT MIDNIGHT!

FIRST-FOOTING

JUST AFTER MIDNIGHT, throw open your front door and "first-foot" to your neighbor's home. Take a gift – arriving empty-handed brings bad luck. Gifts often include coal, bread, salt, or whisky. If first-footers arrive at your home, welcome them with whisky and shortbread to ensure a happy new year.

TARTAN TRIMMINGS

BRIGHTEN UP plain napkins and tablecloths by adding a tartan trim. Sew wide lengths of colorful tartan ribbon onto the edges of the fabric to form a border. Continue the tartan theme by painting a terra cotta pot with a bright tartan design, then plant it with heather or a flowering plant.

SHORTBREAD BOXES ▷

OFFER TARTAN BOXES OF SHORTBREAD TO FIRST-FOOTERS OR DEPARTING GUESTS. TRADITIONALLY, THE SHORTBREAD IS SHAPED IN TRIANGLES.

Paint a box a bright color with poster or emulsion paint. Glue a length of tartan ribbon around the edge of the box lid, gluing any excess width of ribbon inside the box. To make a rosette, loop another length of tartan ribbon eight times, gluing it in place each time it crosses the center. Add dried heather, lavender, or artificial flowers, sticking them in place between the rosette loops, and glue the rosette to the box. Line the box with tissue paper and fill with shortbread.

SCOTTISH NEW YEAR'S EVE

GREET THE NEW YEAR IN TRUE SCOTTISH STYLE.

Invite Tie invitations with a tartan ribbon and ask guests to dress in kilts and tartan.

Drinks Float aromatic clove-studded orange slices in glasses of mulled wine (*see page 91*).

Entertainment Light up the garden with flaming torches, and treat guests to a fireworks display. Dance the evening away to Scottish reels before turning up the radio and handing out horns and bells to sound in the new year. Welcome in the new year by singing "auld lang syne," then go first-footing (*see left*).

For a potentially prosperous new year, enclose a lottery ticket in new year cards.

SPANISH NEW YEAR

A SPANISH FIESTA is a great way to see in the new year. Drink cava and serve tortilla, paella, and shrimp, crabs and oysters on an ice tray (*see page 78*). Give each guest twelve grapes just before midnight. The tradition is to try to eat a grape on each chime of midnight. The number of grapes a person manages to eat is said to bring good luck for that many months of the new year.

CHINESE NEW YEAR

CELEBRATE NEW YEAR'S in Chinese style. Attach invitations to fortune cookies or Chinese good-luck calendars and sign off with "*Kung Hei Fat Choy*," which means "we hope you get rich." For a party with a splash of bright color, decorate the venue in reds, purples, and gold, and hang up delicate paper lanterns (*see right*). Serve a banquet of Chinese delicacies and set off firecrackers at midnight.

CANDLE TABLE SETTING

CREATE A DRAMATIC CENTERPIECE for a New Year's Eve dinner or buffet table. Fill a shallow glass bowl with water and float green, scented candles on the surface. Stand small fat candles and little plants set with tapers alternately around the edge of the bowl. Surround the candles with a ring of flat pebbles. Light the candles and enjoy.

NEW YEAR'S EVE MENU

ASPARAGUS AND LIME PASTA
(*SEE PAGE 94*)

•

BOEUF EN CROÛTE (*SEE PAGE 102*)

FESTIVE PHYLLO PIE (*SEE PAGE 107*)

CARROT AND ZUCCHINI MEDLEY

•

MINCEMEAT CHRISTMAS BOMBE
(*SEE PAGE 110*)

ORIENTAL LANTERNS ▷

CUT GOLD CARDBOARD 25½ x 8in (65 x 20cm) wide. Measure 1in (2.5cm) in from one of the short ends and mark with a line. Mark three more lines at 6in (15cm) intervals. Draw a ½in (1.5cm) frame in each of the four equal sections and cut out the center of each. Stick newspaper or tissue inside each panel, glue a tassel on each corner, and hang up with wire. Fold the card at the marked lines and glue the long tab to the furthest panel to make a square.

PARTY GAMES

GAMES HELP BREAK THE
ICE BETWEEN GUESTS.
DON'T FORGET TO BUY
PRIZES FOR THE WINNERS.

SARDINES

NAME SOMEONE AS "IT" and ask everyone else to count to 100 while the chosen person hides. Guests set off to find "it"; when someone does, he or she hide too in the same place. This becomes harder as more and more guests find the hiding place. The object of the game is to squeeze everyone into the same space without alerting those still looking. Warn guests not to hide in a bathtub – it is not strong enough for more than three people!

ASSOCIATIONS

INVITE A GUEST to say the first word that comes into his head. A second guest must quickly answer with a word somehow associated with the first word. The word chain continues around the group until someone breaks the chain by saying a word that isn't closely enough associated with the previous word. That guest drops out, and a new game begins, starting with a new word. Play until there is a winner.

TABOO

PICK A WORD that often comes up in conversation, such as "yes," "no," "and," or "I," and make it taboo. Choose one guest to be questioned by the others in turn, who try to make the person say the taboo word. The object of the game is for the chosen guest to last a full minute without being caught or hesitating. This is not as easy as it seems.

MUSICAL CUSHIONS

PLAY THIS GAME as you would musical chairs, but using cushions instead. Guests dance to music around a line of cushions. When the music stops, each must dive onto a cushion. Whoever does not get a cushion is out. Continue until there is a winner. The advantage of musical cushions over musical chairs is that guests cannot break or fall off a cushion.

PASS THE BOTTLE

DIVIDE GUESTS into two teams, standing in two lines. The players at the front begin with a bottle clenched between their knees. This should be passed to the knees of the next team member without being touched by any hands. If someone drops the bottle, he or she must retrieve it with the knees. The first team to pass the bottle along the whole line wins.

FOR AN EXTRA-SPECIAL BIRTHDAY, WEDDING ANNIVERSARY, OR FAMILY CELEBRATION, CHOOSE A SPECTACULAR SETTING. INVENTIVE VENUES FOR PARTIES RANGE FROM A SNOWY SKI LODGE OR SUN-BAKED VINEYARD TO AN ANCIENT CASTLE OR STATELY HOME. AN AWE-INSPIRING NATURAL WONDER SUCH AS

SPECIAL OCCASIONS

A CAVE OR WATERFALL MAKES A CREATIVE SETTING, OR OPT FOR A MODERN MINIMALIST FEEL IN AN ICE RINK, ULTRA-CHIC ART GALLERY, OR NIGHTCLUB. FOR THE ULTIMATE SPECIAL-OCCASION PARTY, PLAN AN OUT-OF-THIS-WORLD EXPERIENCE: RENT A HOT-AIR BALLOON, TAKE TO THE SKIES ON A FERRIS WHEEL AT A FAIRGROUND, OR VIEW LIFE IN THE SEA FROM A GLASS-BOTTOMED BOAT.

BIRTHDAYS

BE IT AN 8TH OR AN 80TH BIRTHDAY PARTY, A LITTLE ORGANIZING IN ADVANCE CAN TRANSFORM THE OCCASION. NOT EVERYONE LOVES HUGE PARTIES, SO MATCH NUMBERS TO THE GUEST OF HONOR'S PREFERENCE. DON'T FORGET TO PROVIDE PLENTY OF FINGER FOOD AS WELL AS A DELICIOUS BIRTHDAY CAKE (SEE PAGES 116–17).

BLACK TIE 21ST PARTY

ON A SON'S OR DAUGHTER'S 21ST BIRTHDAY, HOLD A PARTY THEY WILL ALWAYS REMEMBER AND INVITE THEIR FRIENDS TO DRESS UP FOR A BLACK-TIE EVENING.

Invite Incorporate a photograph of the host as a baby.

Food Hire caterers and treat guests to a formal three-course meal.

Decor Give the venue a sophisticated look with masses of black, white, and silver balloons and streamers.

Table Use plain white tablecloths and interweave wide strips of brightly colored crêpe paper on top to achieve a modern plaid effect. Use clashing color combinations such as orange and pink or lime green and red. Pile party poppers, streamers, and silly string in the center of each table.

Entertainment Find a stand-up comedian to perform while guests eat. After the meal, set aside a separate room for older guests to adjourn to so younger guests can enjoy themselves dancing to the beat of a dj.

OSCAR NIGHT ▷

INVITE FRIENDS TO A NIGHT AT THE OSCARS. THEME EACH TABLE TO A DIFFERENT MOVIE, AND ASK GUESTS TO DRESS AS CHARACTERS FROM A MOVIE.

Costumes Guests could dress as characters from movies such as: *The Thief of Bagdad, Barbarella, Ben Hur, La Dolce Vita, Cabaret, Some Like It Hot, The Magnificent Seven, My Fair Lady, Saturday Night Fever, Cyrano de Bergerac, Star Wars, Titanic.*

Decor Make a huge papier-mâché Oscar to stand at the entrance. Cut five-pointed star shapes from cardboard, and use them as stencils to spray cascades of gold and silver stars on tablecloths (*see right*). Hang stars and a glitter ball from the ceiling, and set up moving spotlights.

Drinks Build a champagne fountain to greet guests on arrival. Have a bartender mixing cocktails to order.

Entertainment Take each guest's photograph next to the Oscar. Place silver-sprayed disposable cameras on tables (*see right*). Hire a band to play movie scores or Fred Astaire and Ginger Rogers look-alikes to start the dancing.

Enjoy a day of mystery and suspense with a murder-mystery party on a train. Ask guests to dress in 1920s-style clothing, and book a jazz band to go along on the trip.

ORIENT EXPRESS BIRTHDAY

HIRE A RESTORED STEAM TRAIN FOR A SPECIAL BIRTHDAY CELEBRATION, AND RELIVE THE HEYDAY OF THE 1920s AND AGATHA CHRISTIE.

Invite Print invitations to look like railroad tickets.

Costumes Adopt period costume, with women in flapper dresses and feather boas, and men in suits. Dress catering staff in Twenties-style butler and maid costumes.

Music Hire a jazz band to welcome guests aboard.

Food Serve delicious canapés such as salmon pinwheels (*see page 86*), cheese twists (*see page 88*), and blini with quail eggs and smoked fish (*see page 89*).

Entertainment Host a murder-mystery game, with friends playing different roles, and spend an afternoon in delicious suspense as you discover whodunit.

LIFE BEGINS AT 40, 50, OR 60

WHEN A FRIEND OR FAMILY MEMBER HAS A MILESTONE BIRTHDAY, BE SURE TO CELEBRATE IN STYLE.

Invite Secretly borrow the address book of your friend or relative, and list everyone who should be invited. Emphasize the need for secrecy on the invitations.

Decor Ask friends to help decorate the venue while others take the unsuspecting guest of honor out for the day. Collect a selection of photographs of the birthday guest from childhood onward. Enlarge them on a photocopier, paste to boards with captions, and arrange around the venue.

Food Serve the guest of honor's favorite meal, whether pizza, hot dogs, or loads of pastries and cakes.

Entertainment Invite guests to buy presents to help the guest of honor through the next ten years. Gifts could include a massage, golf lessons, a spa treatment, or a pedicure. Alternatively, several friends could buy a significant joint gift, such as a cruise, flying lessons, or a flight to a destination the birthday guest has always wanted to visit.

BACK TO SCHOOL PARTY

ENJOY AN EVENING OF TEENAGE NOSTALGIA, AS YOU AND YOUR FRIENDS GO BACK TO SCHOOL FOR THE NIGHT.

Costumes Dress as you did at school, complete with ponytail and bobby socks, saddle shoes and poodle skirts.

Decor Ask guests to provide school-age photos of themselves in advance. Hang them on the wall and try to guess who is who.

Music Play the soundtrack to the movie *Grease*.

Table Cover table tops with sheets of plywood painted with blackboard paint. Write the dinner menu in chalk on the tables and hand out chalk for guests to write messages and play word games.

Food Serve dishes that are favorites with children. For dessert, bake a huge birthday cake (*see page 117*).

Games Play games such as musical cushions, associations, and sardines (*see page 47*).

ASIAN BANQUET

WHETHER YOU COOK YOUR OWN DISHES OR BUY THEM FROM A LOCAL RESTAURANT, A BANQUET OF THAI OR CHINESE FOOD ALWAYS LOOKS STUNNING.

Invite Attach to a pair of wooden chopsticks.

Decor Arrange twisted willow, single stems of orchid, or bamboo in tall, elegant vases and set around the room. Gather a collection of smooth pebbles and arrange in piles on empty surfaces.

Table Spread comfortable cushions on the floor around a low table. Cover the table with sheets from an Asian newspaper and place Bamboo Candles (*see right*) on top as a centerpiece. Lay out Orchid Napkins (*see right and below*) and serve food from bamboo steamers.

Food Complement the menu (*see right*) with rice bowls filled with shrimp toast and dishes of dipping sauces.

Drinks Serve jasmine tea, warm sake, or plum wine in delicate Chinese teacups.

BAMBOO CANDLES

A square glass vase makes an attractive vessel for this candle display. Cut lengths of green bamboo to the same height as the vase is deep. Secure the bamboo lengths to the outside of the vase with raffia and fill the center with tightly packed long white tapers.

ORCHID NAPKINS

Roll up neatly a white fabric napkin, then flatten it slightly. Fold an 8 x 12in (20 x 30cm) strip of newspaper in half lengthwise, and wrap around the napkin, securing it with tape. Tuck a pair of chopsticks under the paper strip, and place an orchid, jasmine flower, or fortune cookie on top.

BANQUET MENU

SWEET & SOUR SHRIMP (*SEE PAGE 94*)

•

THAI GREEN CURRY (*SEE PAGE 103*)

STIR–FRIED GREEN VEGETABLES (*SEE PAGE 105*)

NOODLES

PLAIN BOILED THAI FRAGRANT RICE

•

COCONUT ICE CREAM (*SEE PAGE 113*)

MONEY-NO-OBJECT PRESENTS

Swimming with dolphins ★ African safari ★ Balloon flight
Flying lesson ★ Gliding lesson ★ Off-road driving
Skiing lessons ★ Vintage car racing ★ Trip to San Fransisco
Flight on Concorde ★ Riding lessons
White-water rafting ★ Health-club membership
Waterskiing lessons ★ Power boat racing ★ Record a song
Lunch at the Eiffel Tower ★ Scuba-diving lessons
Golf lessons ★ London tour ★ Whale watching
Trip to New York ★ Jet skiing ★ Salsa-dancing lessons
Nile cruise ★ Parachute jump

ANNIVERSARIES

A PHOTOGRAPH ALBUM SHOWING A COUPLE'S YEARS TOGETHER MAKES A LOVELY GIFT. INTERVIEW FAMILY AND FRIENDS, AND ASK THEM TO SHARE THEIR MEMORIES BY DONATING A PHOTO FOR THE ALBUM.

To make a personalized plate ▷ for an anniversary couple, ask guests to sign their name on a white platter using quick-drying ceramic paint.

WEDDING ANNIVERSARY THEMES

1st – paper ★ 2nd – cotton ★ 3rd – leather
4th – fruit and flowers ★ 5th – wood ★ 6th – sugar
7th – woolen ★ 8th – bronze ★ 9th – pottery
10th – tin ★ 12th – silk, fine linen ★ 15th – crystal
20th – china ★ 25th – silver ★ 30th – pearl
35th – coral ★ 40th – ruby ★ 50th – golden
55th – emerald ★ 60th – diamond
65th – blue sapphire ★ 70th – platinum

NIGHT OF NOSTALGIA

INVITE GUESTS to dress in clothing from the era you married in: 1940s' clothing; postwar New Look, or military dress; wide, flared skirts and leather jackets for the 1950s; hippy kaftans, beads, and beards for the 1960s; disco sequins for the 1970s; and power dressing shoulder pads for the 1980s. Hire a dj or band to play the music that was popular in the year you married.

ANNIVERSARY AT THE RACES

RENT A VINTAGE CAR and spend an anniversary at the races. Meet with friends, and picnic on champagne before making your way to the racetrack and occupying a section for the day. Set up a betting pool between guests by asking them to place a set amount in a hat. Ask everyone to pick winners for each race: award ten points for a winner, five points for second place, and three points for third place. Whoever has the highest number of points at the end of the day takes the winnings.

THEME PARTIES

THROW A THEME PARTY TO MARK

ANY OCCASION: A REUNION,

RETIREMENT, GRADUATION – OR JUST

BECAUSE YOU WANT TO PARTY.

IDEAS FOR THEME PARTIES

The circus ★ *Antarctica* ★ *Tintin*
Robbers and outlaws ★ *Angels*
Victorian days ★ The Addams Family
Sumo wrestlers and geisha girls ★ *Carmen Miranda*
Dracula ★ *Cartoons* ★ Batman and Robin
Shakespeare's plays ★ *Aladdin* ★ *Dracula*
Jaws ★ *Imps and goblins* ★ *World leaders*
Superman ★ *Julius Caesar* ★ Beauty and the Beast
Elvis ★ The Three Musketeers★ *Matadors*
The Godfather ★ Mary Poppins

BEAUJOLAIS NOUVEAU PARTY

CELEBRATE WHEN THE LATEST BEAUJOLAIS WINE
REACHES THE STORES EACH NOVEMBER.

Invite Send invitations out on mini French flags. Ask
one third of the guests to dress in blue, one third to dress
in white, and one third to dress in red.

Music Play Edith Piaf or Django Reinhardt's hot jazz.

Food Ask guests to bring a portion of their favorite
French cheese, while you supply bread, wine, and grapes.

Entertainment Pit teams in different colors against
each other in a series of races and games (*see page 47*).

COSTUME IDEAS FOR A GANGSTERS PARTY

TAKE INSPIRATION FROM *BONNIE AND CLYDE*,
BUGSY MALONE, AND JAMES CAGNEY FILMS.

Fedoras ★ *Cigarette holders* ★ *Sharp suits*
Tommy guns ★ *Kohl-rimmed eyes* ★ *Spats*
Black tie ★ *Patent leather shoes* ★ *Large overcoats*
Cloche hats ★ *Dancer's feather costumes*
Bobbed hair ★ *Fake-fur wraps* ★ *Cupid-bow lips*
Feather boas ★ *Silk stockings* ★ *Sequins*

PROHIBITION PARTY

RECREATE THE CHICAGO OF AL CAPONE AND THE
PROHIBITION, WHEN GANGSTERS AND THEIR GIRLFRIENDS
HAUNTED NOTORIOUS SPEAKEASIES.

Costumes Dress in flapper dresses, or as dancing girls in
exotic costumes. Wear sharp suits and bring toy Tommy
guns (*see left*) to complete the outfit.

Decor Keep the lighting low and intimate and black out the
windows. Set up a bar with a bartender in suspenders.

Drinks Serve "bootleg" bourbon. Ask the bartender to make
champagne cocktails (*see page 90*) and pink gins (*see page 91*).

For a 1950s table, use a pastel ▽ tablecloth. Lay a runner over the cloth, place old 45s on top, and cover with clear plastic.

50S & 60S COFFEEHOUSE PARTY

EVOKE THE ERA OF SWINGING COFFEEHOUSES, WHEN THE BEACH BOYS SURFED THE SUMMER AWAY.

Costumes Bomber jackets, white T-shirts and jeans, hooped petticoats, pedal pushers, and twin sets.

Decor Deck the room in pastel blues and pinks. Rent a jukebox and clear space for jiving.

Music Elvis, Frankie Avalon, and The Beach Boys.

Food Burgers, fries, and ice cream sundaes.

Drinks Cappuccino, milkshakes, and ice cream sodas.

INFORMAL PARTY MENU

CHEESE TWISTS (*SEE PAGE 88*)
BRUSCHETTA WITH TOPPINGS (*SEE PAGE 89*)

•

ASPARAGUS & LIME PASTA (*SEE PAGE 94*)

•

CHICKEN WITH FIGS (*SEE PAGE 99*)
MINTED POTATO SALAD (*SEE PAGE 104*)
PESTO COUSCOUS SALAD (*SEE PAGE 105*)

•

CHOCOLATE TART (*SEE PAGE 108*)

CREPE PARTY

SERVE A VARIETY OF SWEET AND SAVORY FILLINGS FOR GUESTS TO EAT WITH CREPES.

Invite Write the invitation on a baggage label, then attach to a fresh lemon with a length of raffia.

Food Offer a selection of delicious fillings. These could include grated cheeses, creamed mushrooms and asparagus, ice cream and nuts, maple syrup, chocolate, lemon, and sugar.

Entertainment Ask guests to help you flip the crepes in the pan. See who can toss the crepe highest and still catch it in the pan.

COSTUME IDEAS FOR A 1970S NOSTALGIA PARTY

*Platform shoes ★ Crocheted outfits ★ Mini and maxi skirts
Hot pants ★ Jeans ★ Kaftans ★ Glitter and gold lamé
Blue eyeshadow ★ Capes and long scarves ★ Denim jackets
Bell-bottom jeans ★ Culottes ★ Safety Pins ★ Long hair
Beards ★ Wooden beads ★ Sandals ★ Mohawk hairstyles
Torn clothes ★ Leather jackets*

GREAT COMPANY IS THE ESSENCE OF AN ENJOYABLE EVENT, AND A PARTY WITH CLOSE FRIENDS CAN BE AS FORMAL OR INFORMAL AS YOU CHOOSE. WHETHER PLANNING A VALENTINE'S DAY SURPRISE, A LUNCH, BRUNCH, OR DINNER PARTY, MAKE GUESTS FEEL SPECIAL BY HAVING THE ROOM AND FOOD LOOK SPECTACULAR.

INTIMATE PARTIES

GIVE A DINNER CELEBRATION AN INTIMATE RESTAURANT FEEL BY SERVING FOOD ON OVERSIZED WHITE PLATES OR ON COORDINATED PLATTERS. OIL LAMPS OR CANDLELIGHT CREATE INSTANT ATMOSPHERE. MAXIMIZE LIGHTING BY SURROUNDING AN AREA WITH PLENTY OF MIRRORS OR ARRANGE TINY WHITE LIGHTS AROUND A ROOM OR YARD.

VALENTINE'S DAY

FOR BREAKFAST, FILL THE ROOM WITH FRESH BLOOMS, THEN COOK SMOKED SALMON AND SCRAMBLED EGGS, AND SERVE ON HEART-SHAPED TOAST.

VALENTINE'S DINNER

SURPRISE YOUR VALENTINE BY TRANSFORMING A ROOM AT HOME INTO A BISTRO FOR THE NIGHT.

Invite Request your Valentine's presence by sending a menu in a Valentine's Day card.

Decor Set the table with a white cloth and scatter red rose petals around it. Light the room with scented candles.

Food Serve a gourmet meal for two, preparing as much as possible in advance. Begin with garlicky mixed olives (*see page 89*), crudités, and champagne. Follow with oysters, seared tuna (*see page 100*), and, for dessert, passion fruit sorbet.

ROMANTIC SURPRISES

SHOW HOW MUCH YOU CARE BY TREATING YOUR PARTNER TO A VALENTINE'S DAY TO REMEMBER.

Pick up your partner in a chauffeur-driven limousine
Rent a house in the country ★ Take your partner to Paris, Venice, New York, Fiji, or Honolulu ★ Send a red rose every hour
Declare your love in a newspaper ad
Book orchestra seats at the theater ★ Enjoy lunch on a boat
Treat your partner to a massage or spa trip

APHRODISIACS

THE FOLLOWING FOODS ARE REPUTED TO HAVE APHRODISIAC PROPERTIES:

Asparagus ★ Caviar ★ Oysters
Pomegranates ★ Lobster
Bird's nest soup ★ Cockles ★ Eels
Ginseng ★ Saffron ★ Truffles ★ Mussels
Anchovies ★ Scallops ★ Steaks
Figs ★ Clams ★ Chocolate

△ VALENTINE'S DAY TREATS

★ FOR A MESSY SURPRISE, fill a Valentine's Day card with tiny heart-shaped confetti cut from red tissue paper (*see above*). Send the confetti with a card made by sewing two red felt heart shapes together. Stuff, scent with lavender oil, stick onto a plain, handmade card, and fill with the confetti.

★ SERVE A VALENTINE'S DAY MEAL from hand-decorated plates. Paint white china with hearts, cupids, arrows, and roses, using quick-drying paint.

★ A VALENTINE'S DAY PIZZA indulges those who prefer the simpler things in life. Cut a large heart shape out of pizza dough and top with your partner's favorite fillings.

PARTIES FOR FRIENDS

SOME OF THE BEST PARTIES BEGIN AS A QUIET NIGHT WITH FRIENDS, SO WHEN THROWING AN INFORMAL, INTIMATE PARTY, TRY NOT TO OVERPLAN.

THE DESSERT CLUB

DESSERTS ARE OFTEN THE BEST PART OF A MEAL, SO INVITE FRIENDS FOR AN EVENING CONSISTING ONLY OF THEIR FAVORITE DESSERTS.

Invite Attach invitations to miniature boxes of truffles or chocolates.

Food Serve tiny portions of each dessert so that each guest can try a few. Offer hazelnut meringue cake (*see page 108*), tiramisu (*see page 109*), peach melba trifle (*see page 111*), tarte au citron (*see page 112*), and any other favorite desserts.

Drinks Serve dessert wines. After, offer coffee flavored with cardamom or cinnamon.

LADIES' PAMPERING NIGHT

ASK FRIENDS TO CONTRIBUTE A SET AMOUNT OF MONEY AND HIRE A BEAUTICIAN, HAIRDRESSER, AND MASSEUR TO COME TO YOUR HOME FOR THE EVENING.

Spend the evening with a small group of close friends, catching up on news while enjoying treatments and swapping beauty tips. Buy ready-made snacks, or make canapés in advance and refrigerate or freeze them for later.

△ NAPKIN ROSES

WHEN BEST FRIENDS PARTY TOGETHER, it's good to put extra thought into details – even the napkins. To make a napkin rose, spread out a red or pink two-ply paper napkin, and make a 4in (10cm) fold down the left-hand side. Loosely roll the napkin up from the bottom edge around the index finger of your left hand. Wrap the layers loosely enough for there to be a small gap between each. Tightly pinch the napkin at the end of your index finger, and remove your finger. Hold the napkin beneath the flower and form a stem by twisting each hand in opposite directions. Repeat with several napkins and place the napkin roses in a vase or basket.

Throw a party at which people dress as and impersonate one of their closest friends for the evening.

BACKWARD BASH

INVITE FRIENDS TO JOIN YOU FOR A DINNER PARTY IN REVERSE.

Invite Send out invitations written back-to-front (*see page 30*).

Food Serve the entire meal backward, starting with coffee and mints, and ending with olives and canapés.

Drinks Meet guests at the door with a glass of port and finish the evening with aperitifs.

QUIZ NIGHT

PIT YOUR GUESTS' WITS against each other by holding a quiz night at home. Ask questions on categories such as general knowledge, history, sports, and movies. Hold a music contest, where you play a few notes from well-known cassettes or CDs on a piano or keyboard and ask guests to guess the artist, song title, and year of release. Award prizes to the winners.

ARMCHAIR SPORTS

ARRANGE AN AFTERNOON WITH FRIENDS, WATCHING A TELEVISED SPORTS EVENT.

Invite friends to join you on the day of a televised football game, auto racing event, or baseball game. Serve chips, pizza, and beer, and encourage friends to dress in their team's colors and to bring whistles and horns to cheer them on.

GAMES EVENING

ASK EVERYONE to arrive with a couple of favorite board games. Separate guests into different teams and hold a contest to see which team is the outright winner. For a livelier evening, intersperse board games with more active ones, such as blindman's bluff (*see page 19*) and pass the bottle (*see page 47*).

Hold a hat party, where guests must wear their silliest hat all evening.

ICEBREAKERS

★ SEAT PEOPLE around the dinner table before serving the meal. Ask them each in turn to tell a secret about themselves – the funnier the secret, the better.

★ ASK THE FIRST PERSON at a party to open the door for the next guest. They can chat together until the second guest has to answer the door for the next person. Continue until everyone has arrived.

PERSONALIZED CHAIRS

SURPRISE CLOSE FRIENDS who often come for dinner by personalizing chairs with their names. To do this, make spare covers out of canvas to fit over chair backs. Stencil friends' names on the canvas (*see personalized napkins, page 78*) and put the chair backs in place before your guests arrive.

HOUSEWARMING

INVITE FRIENDS TO EARN THEIR DINNER BY HELPING YOU PAINT YOUR HOME.

When you move into a new house, persuade friends to help with the decorating. Ask guests to bring paint-brushes and rollers, and then get everyone to work for an hour or two, stripping wallpaper and painting. Reward your helpers by cooking a meal after all the hard work.

DINNER PARTY MENU

SMOKED SALMON TRIANGLES
(SEE PAGE 95)

•

MONKFISH & BACON KABOBS
(SEE PAGE 101)

TUSCAN BEAN SALAD (SEE PAGE 104)

ROASTED SWEET POTATOES
(SEE PAGE 107)

•

CHOCOLATE ROULADE
(SEE PAGE 109)

GREEK DANCING PARTY

ENJOY A FUN, NOISY EVENING EATING DELICIOUS *MEZE* AND DRINKING RUSTIC WINE.

Offer simple *meze*-style food such as tzatziki, stuffed vine leaves, feta salad and garlicky mixed olives (*see page 89*). Drink wine, retsina, or ouzo, then link arms in a circle and dance to Greek folk music.

◁ *Make origami table decorations using colored paper and use them as place settings.*

OYSTERS & GUINNESS

CELEBRATE THE DAY OF IRELAND'S PATRON SAINT, ST. PATRICK, ON MARCH 17TH.

Drink glasses of Guinness, eat oysters, and serve a traditional Irish stew. Light the room with oyster candles (*see page 31*), and dance the night away to the sound of fiddles and pipes.

MORE ICEBREAKERS

★ AS GUESTS ARRIVE, pin the name of someone famous to their backs. Guests must discover who they are by asking questions to which others can only answer "yes" or "no."

★ INVITE EACH GUEST at a dinner party to talk to the stranger on the right. After some time, ask people to introduce their partner, revealing three, newly discovered, interesting facts about the person.

WINE-TASTING PARTY

ASK FRIENDS TO BRING BOTTLES OF WINE OF DIFFERENT VALUES AND COUNTRIES OF ORIGIN.

Buy a selection of bread, crackers, cheese, and fruit, and provide paper, pens, and glasses. Cover the wine labels and taste the wines. Invite guests to award marks of one to ten. End the evening by revealing the country and cost of the wine, and who bought which bottle.

A TEA PARTY IS A CHARMING SETTING FOR A GATHERING OF FRIENDS. USE IT TO CELEBRATE SUMMER SPORTS DAYS, AUTUMNAL AFTERNOONS, OR COZY WINTER DAYS IN FRONT OF A FIRE. THERE IS A HUGE VARIETY OF TEAS TO CHOOSE FROM. SELECT A BLACK OR GREEN TEA FROM INDIA, AFRICA, OR CHINA, AND SERVE IT

TEA PARTIES

WITH MILK OR FRESH LEMON SLICES, OR CHILL AND SERVE IN TALL GLASSES OVER CRUSHED ICE. IDEAL ACCOMPANIMENTS FOR TEA ARE INDIVIDUAL CAKES, PASTRIES, AND SANDWICHES. THE PERFECT CUCUMBER SANDWICH IS MADE WITH BUTTERED, WAFER-THIN SLICED BREAD, FILLED WITH DELICATE SLICES OF CUCUMBER, AND CUT INTO DAINTY TRIANGLES.

SUMMER TEA DANCE

TRANSFORM A ROOM INTO A PALM COURT TO RECREATE THE HEYDAY OF THE TEA DANCE CIRCA 1910. HIRE A STRING QUARTET AND SPEND THE AFTERNOON DANCING THE WALTZ AND FOXTROT.

Invite Use gold calligraphy on embossed white cardboard. Enclose a dance card for each female guest.

Decor Fill the room with potted plants. Clear an area for dancing and hang a glitter ball above the dance floor.

Table Cover a large table with a crisp white linen cloth, and use silverware and china to display sumptuous sweet treats.

Food Salmon pinwheels (*see page 86*), cheese twists (*see page 88*), mini meringues (*see below and page 115*), and Madeira cake (*see page 117*), all served from a tea cart.

Drinks Age an inexpensive plastic urn with a verdigris or pewter paint kit and use it as a bowl for fruity summer punch or iced tea.

For iced tea, pour 1¾pt (1l) of cold lemonade over 3 tbsp Ceylon tea leaves. Cover, stir, and chill overnight. Strain, add sugar to taste and slices of lemon. Serve over crushed ice.

SPORTS PICNIC

ENJOY A SUMMER AFTERNOON OF SOFTBALL OR TENNIS. BRING ALONG PLENTY OF FANS AND ENJOY A DELICIOUS PICNIC.

Invite Send attached to scorecards.

Decor Picnic on linen tablecloths or padded beach mats (*see page 80*). Make the meal as elegant or relaxed as you wish. For a formal afternoon, use linen napkins and silverware, and for a more informal picnic, pack large bowls of popcorn and finger food treats, and pitchers for cold drinks.

Food Quiches (*see page 86*), mini picnic pies (*see page 97*), salads, bread, cheeses, fruit, and a selection of home-baked cakes (*see menu, right*).

Games Play frisbee after the meal.

TEA PARTY DECOR ▷

★ Cheer up plain white dishes by decorating with quick-drying water-based ceramic paints. Try freehand painting (*see right*), or make a simple stamp to print with by carving a design into an eraser or potato (*see page 79*).

★ Old cups, saucers, and other matching pottery make lovely vessels for candles to sit in. Drip a little wax into the base of a teacup and stand a candle in the base. Or place each candle in a small foil dish first, so that the teacup remains free of wax.

★ Easy to construct, a simple, tiered cake stand is ideal for displaying larger cakes and smaller, individual treats. Make the stand by selecting three attractive china plates of different sizes. Place two upturned glass bowls between the plates, stacking them with the smallest plate on top. Alternatively, replace each bowl with four plaster pillars set in a square.

HIGH TEA MENU

CUCUMBER SANDWICHES

SAVORY SCONES (*SEE PAGE 88*)

•

HONEY SANDWICHES

PETITS FOURS (*SEE PAGE 115*)

MINI MERINGUES (*SEE PAGE 115*)

TRIPLE CHOC COOKIES (*SEE PAGE 116*)

LUXURY FRUIT CAKE (*SEE PAGE 116*)

•

DARJEELING, CEYLON, AND CHINA TEAS

ICED TEA (*SEE OPPOSITE*)

MAD HATTER'S TEA PARTY

THRILL GUESTS WITH AN AFTERNOON PARTY AT WHICH EVERYTHING IS LARGER OR SMALLER THAN LIFE. SET UP SMALL TABLES AND CHAIRS FOR CHILDREN AND DECORATE THE AREA WITH GIANT PAINTED TEACUPS.

Invite Cut cardboard into the shape of a top hat and write the details along the brim.

Costumes Guests should arrive wearing hats and dressed in clothes that are either too large or too small.

Decor Stamp napkins and tablecloths with heart shapes (*see page 79*) and tie helium balloons around the venue.

Food Offer summer berry tarts (*see page 112*), gingerbread (*see page 114*), and petits fours (*see page 115*).

Games Play musical cushions (*see page 47*) and pass the hat: guests pass a hat from head to head to music and whoever is left wearing the hat when the music stops is out. The game continues until there is a winner.

ICE BOWL ▷

A DELICATE ICE BOWL MAKES THE PERFECT
CENTERPIECE FOR A SUMMER TABLE AND IS
DECEPTIVELY SIMPLE TO MAKE.

1 Stand a large glass bowl in a sink and tape a smaller
plastic bowl inside, so that the top of both bowls will
be level when water is poured between them.

2 Pour bottled or filtered water to fill the gap between
the bowls. Either leave the water clear or arrange flower
petals or fruit slices between the bowls. Place a couple
of small weights inside the small bowl and freeze.

3 When the water has frozen, fill a sink with hot water
and immerse the bowls for 10 seconds. Take the bowls
out and twist the larger bowl away from the ice.

4 Fill the small bowl with hot water, leave for 10 seconds,
and carefully lift it away from the ice bowl. Freeze the ice
bowl until it is needed.

To make a hot toddy to drink

in colder weather, mix one part

Cointreau with five parts hot tea.

Pour into glasses and garnish

with orange slices studded

with cloves.

FLOWER CENTERPIECE

TRY MIXING FLOWERS with fruits and vegetables to make
a contemporary, colorful table decoration. Stand a small
square glass vase inside a larger square glass vase, then push
whole red chilies, slices of orange, lemon, or lime, or even
small pebbles and seashells in the gap between the vases.
Finally, fill the inner vase with water and add a bouquet of
tulips or narcissi.

COLORED GLASS VASES

KEEP EMPTY MINERAL WATER BOTTLES: blue or green
colored glass bottles in interesting shapes make ideal vases
for single stems or branches of willow. To make a table
centerpiece, stand several differently sized bottles in a group,
fill with water, and arrange with branches of willow or
tulips, irises, and long grasses.

EASTER

EVERYONE LOVES RECEIVING FLOWERS AT EASTER, AND A BOUQUET IS EASY TO MAKE. TAKE A BUNCH OF NARCISSI, TULIPS, OR OTHER LONG-STEMMED FLOWERS, HOLD THEM TIGHTLY IN ONE HAND, AND ARRANGE LARGE ORNAMENTAL OR SAVOY CABBAGE LEAVES BENEATH THE FLOWERS. SURROUND THE BOUQUET WITH TISSUE PAPER AND TIE WITH RIBBON.

EASTER TEA

CELEBRATE EASTER BY THROWING A PARTY IN YOUR HOME FOR FRIENDS AND FAMILY.

Invite Write on lengths of wide yellow ribbon, then tie them around small bouquets (*see below*).

Decor Fill the room with vases of fresh flowers and hang blown eggs from tree branches.

Food Offer hot-cross buns, and bake tarte au citron (*see page 112*), blueberry muffins (*see page 114*), and a luxury fruit cake (*see page 116*).

Entertainment Spend the afternoon painting and staining blown eggs (*see below*). Hide tiny foil-wrapped chocolate eggs around the yard and send the children on an Easter egg hunt.

◁ STAINED EASTER EGGS

BLOWING EGGS IS A TRADITIONAL EASTER PASTIME THAT CHILDREN LOVE. THIS IS A BEAUTIFULLY DELICATE VARIATION ON PAINTING BLOWN EGGS.

1 Hold an egg over a bowl and prick a hole in either end with a needle. Use a cocktail stick to enlarge the holes, then push it inside the egg to pierce the yolk. Blow into the rounded end of the egg, catching the contents in the bowl. Rinse the egg with cold water and let dry.

2 Wet a selection of tiny flowers and lay them, good-side down, on the eggshell, smoothing the petals flat. Carefully cover the flowers with onionskin before slipping the egg inside an old stocking and tying it tightly to keep the onionskins in place.

3 Put the wrapped egg in a pan of cold water, bring to a boil, and boil for 10 minutes. Remove from the water and let the egg cool before cutting away the stocking. Peel away the onionskin and discard the flowers to reveal the flower-printed egg.

KEEP CHILDREN'S PARTIES SHORT AND FUN. CHILDREN ARE EASILY TIRED, SO LIMIT A PARTY TO A COUPLE OF HOURS BUT PACK IT FULL OF EXCITING ACTIVITIES, WHETHER BOWLING, SWIMMING, OR ICE SKATING. DECIDE WELL IN ADVANCE ON THE THEME, VENUE, NUMBERS, FOOD, AND PARTY BAGS, AND

CHILDREN'S PARTIES

ORGANIZE GAMES, WITH PRIZES FOR EVERY CHILD. ALLOW CHILDREN TO DRAW UP THE GUEST LIST AND TO DECIDE WHAT FOOD TO SERVE. MAKE SURE THAT THE AFTERNOON IS FILLED BY DRAWING UP A PARTY TIMETABLE. ENLIST AS MUCH HELP AS POSSIBLE FROM FRIENDS, AND CONSIDER HIRING A CHILDREN'S ENTERTAINER SUCH AS A MAGICIAN, PUPPETEER, OR CLOWN.

FANCY DRESS IDEAS

Cowboys ★ Astronauts and space invaders
Clowns ★ Pirates ★ Animals
Cops and robbers ★ Monsters ★ Homemade hats
Nursery rhymes ★ Teddy bears' picnic
Halloween ★ Fairy tales ★ Sports heroes
Caribbean island ★ 1970s disco
National dress ★ Kings and queens
Explorers ★ The future

PLACES FOR A CHILDREN'S PARTY

Circus ★ Zoo ★ Carnival
Swimming pool ★ Children's zoo ★ Sports event
Theme park ★ Movies ★ Bowling alley
Ice rink ★ Arts and crafts center ★ Beach
Game room ★ Water park ★ Go-kart course
Double-decker bus ★ Picnic site
Puppet show ★ Restaurant

MEXICAN PIÑATA ▷

HANG A PIÑATA DONKEY FROM A TREE AND ALLOW
EACH CHILD TO TRY, BLINDFOLDED, TO HIT IT WITH A
STICK, RELEASING THE TREATS INSIDE.

1 Blow up a large balloon. Fold a sheet of newspaper
into a strip 4in (10cm) wide and tape it around the center
of the balloon. Using wallpaper paste, stick five layers of
torn newspaper onto the balloon, avoiding the knot.

2 When the newspaper is dry and hard, glue on legs made
from cardboard rolls, and a head and neck shaped from
cardboard. Cut a hole in the top of the body and take out
the balloon. Fill the belly with candy and small gifts.

3 Cut about 30 long strips of colored crêpe paper
4in (10cm) wide. Lay two strips on top of each other and
machine-sew down the center. Fold the strips in half along
the stitched line and cut a fringe, taking care not to cut the
stitching. Cover the donkey in glue and wind crêpe paper
strips around to cover it completely. Add ears, eyes, and
a saddle. Thread wire through the piñata and hang up.

CHILDREN'S NAPKIN IDEAS

MAKE A CHILDREN'S PARTY TABLE A RIOT OF COLOR
BY USING PAPER NAPKINS TO THEIR FULL POTENTIAL.

★ Make cookie beds as place settings. Lay a folded napkin
on a table and lift one of the loose corners toward you,
pressing it down in place. Write a child's name on a parcel
label, tie it around the neck of a gingerbread man, and slip
him under the napkin flap so he looks as if he is in bed.

★ Make pretty wrappings for small table gifts. Lay a colored
paper napkin, good side down, on a table and place a small
present in the center. Draw up the corners of the napkin and
secure the gift with a tied ribbon.

★ To make candy-cane napkins, lay two coordinating
napkins on top of each other, one corner pointing toward
you. Slide the top napkin 1in (2.5cm) away from you, so you
can see two edges of the napkin beneath. Starting at the
nearest corner, roll the napkins away from you. When you
reach the top corner, fold in half and stand in a beaker.

PARTY BAG GIFTS

DON'T FORGET TO PACK PARTY BAGS FOR CHILDREN TO TAKE HOME. FILL THE BAGS WITH FAVORITE CANDIES, TOYS, GAMES, AND MAGIC TRICKS.

Slice of birthday cake ★ *Balloons*

Yo-yo ★ *Water gun* ★ *Colored chalk*

Mini toy animal ★ *Deck of cards*

Face-painting crayons ★ *Chocolate coins*

Connect the dots book ★ *Dice*

Bubbles ★ *Toy handcuffs* ★ *Joke book*

Whoopie cushion ★ *Poster paints and brushes*

Coloring book ★ *Novelty-shaped eraser*

Plastic vampire teeth ★ *Magic tricks*

Marbles ★ *Lollipops*

COOKIE-BAKING PARTY

CHILDREN LOVE TO BAKE. HOLD A PARTY WHERE THEY MAKE, BAKE, AND DECORATE THEIR OWN COOKIES.

Invite Attach invitations to gingerbread men (*see page 114*) wrapped in plastic wrap.

Costumes Sew chef's hats and aprons for everyone to wear when baking. Allow children to take these home at the end of the afternoon.

Entertainment Buy a selection of animal-shaped cookie cutters, shaped as cats, cows, pigs, and ducks, and gingerbread people. Let everyone join in making and rolling out the dough and stamping out the shapes. When the cookies have been baked, give each child his or her own farmyard of cookies to decorate with small candies, sugar strands, and tubes of colored icing. Award prizes for the best-decorated cookies, and let children take their creations home in party bags. Give the cookie cutters as gifts in the bags.

PARTY FOOD

KEEP FOOD SIMPLE: CHILDREN LIKE TO GRAZE AND EAT WITH THEIR FINGERS. GIVE FOOD APPEAL BY OFFERING MINI-VERSIONS FOR SMALL MOUTHS.

★ To make children's ice pops, fill small plastic or paper molds with fruit juice and freeze until slushy. Stand a crafts stick in the center of each mold and freeze. When solid, carefully squeeze out the pops.

★ To make Jell-O® sailboats, scoop out the fruit from orange halves. Fill the halves with Jell-O® and fruit. When set, quarter the oranges and add a cocktail stick mast.

GAMES

FILL A CHILDREN'S PARTY WITH PLENTY OF GAMES, AND BE SURE THAT EVERY CHILD WINS A PRIZE BY THE END OF THE DAY.

TELEPHONE

SIT CHILDREN in a circle and whisper a message into one child's ear. The child whispers it into the ear of the next child, and so the message is passed around the circle. The last child to receive the message says it out loud, and it is compared to the message the first child was given.

SQUEAK, PIGGY, SQUEAK

A CHILD stands in the center of a seated circle of children and is blindfolded and spun around. The child must then find a seated child and identify him by sitting on his lap and asking him to "squeak, piggy, squeak." The chosen child should squeak, disguising his voice. A child correctly named goes into the center; if not, the first child starts again.

BEACH GAMES

ENJOY A DAY at the beach, playing beach Olympics. Mark a start and finish line, then divide children into teams and play three-legged, piggy-back, wheelbarrow, and sack races. Ask children to bring hats and bathing suits, and don't forget pails, shovels, water guns, sunblock, and a first-aid kit.

Award children medals made of chocolate disks wrapped in foil and tied with ribbon.

WHO AM I?

MAKE PAPER HATS and write the name of a famous person or fictional character on each. Sit children in a circle and place a hat on each head, without letting the child see the name on it. Children ask each other questions that require a yes or no answer. Each child continues questioning until he or she guesses something incorrectly. The next child in the circle then starts asking questions.

LEMON RELAY

DIVIDE CHILDREN into two teams and mark a start and finish line. The first child in each team has to roll a lemon up the room and back, using only a pencil. When they finish, they pass the pencil and lemon to the next child, who continues the race. The lemon and pencil should be passed in relay down the whole team. The first team to roll the lemon home wins the race.

FIRE! FIRE!

LINE UP two teams. Put a full bucket of water in front of each line and an empty bucket at the back. When a whistle is blown, the first child in each line scoops up water from the bucket into a container and passes it to the back of the line, where the water is poured into the bucket. The empty container is then passed back to the front. The first team to empty the bucket of water is the winner. This game is best played outdoors!

DOODLING GAMES

COVER A DINING TABLE with brown paper. Trace around plates, cutlery, and glasses using wax crayons, and add children's names as place settings. Stand the crayons in plastic cups, and place around the table for children to doodle with over lunch.

BABY PARTIES

DECORATE BABIES' FIRST PARTY INVITATIONS WITH PRINTS OF THEIR HANDS AND FEET.

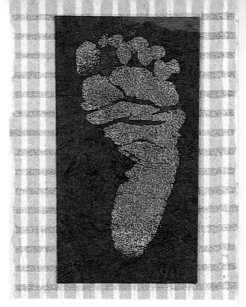

SENSORY PARTY

CRAWLING BABIES AND TODDLERS LEARN BY TOUCH AND FEEL, SO THROW A PARTY THEY'LL LOVE.

Create a sensory room by arranging cardboard boxes, cardboard tubes, pages from old magazines, tissue paper, and foil trays on the floor. Thread scrunched foil balls and bells onto string and hang from a door frame. Blow bubbles and lay out wooden spoons for children to have fun making a racket with.

Let babies scribble on their own cardboard party invitations using colored, chunky pens.

◁ BABY FOOTPRINT

IMMORTALIZE A NEW BABY BY TAKING A FOOTPRINT.

Paint the baby's foot with embossing ink. Print by pressing the foot onto a sheet of paper, making sure the toes are as flat as possible. Sprinkle embossing dust on the wet print, tap off the excess, and heat the dust with an electric paint stripper or hair dryer so it melts and looks embossed. Repeat with your baby's hands, if desired.

NAMING CEREMONY PRESENT IDEAS

Adopt a baby animal
Silver box for milk teeth
Name a star ★ Silver bookmark
Cross-stitched sampler of the
baby's name and birthday
Minted coin set ★ Bank account
Stenciled child's stool (*see page 81*)
Silver jewelry

WATERBABY PARTY

OLDER BABIES ARE FASCINATED BY EACH OTHER, SO MEET WITH OTHER PARENTS AND LET YOUR CHILDREN GET TO KNOW EACH OTHER.

Appoint a meeting time at a local swimming pool. Bring water wings and rubber ducks, and encourage babies to splash and swim under your close supervision. Invite the other parents back to your house afterward for coffee and cake.

BABY SHOWER PARTY

CELEBRATE AN IMPENDING BIRTH BY ORGANIZING A BABY SHOWER.

Invite Send with a photo of the very pregnant mother-to-be.

Food Ask everyone to bring a different dinner course.

Entertainment Bring gifts for the new baby or pampering treats for the expectant mother. Friends could join together to buy a carseat or crib.

TREE-PLANTING PARTY

MARK THE BIRTH OF A BABY BY PLANTING A TREE IN HIS OR HER HONOR.

When the baby is one month old, invite grandparents and friends to join you in planting a sapling. Take a picture of everyone with the new baby in front of the tree.

INDIVIDUAL DECORATIVE TOUCHES SUCH AS STYLED NAPKINS, TABLECLOTHS, AND TABLE PLACE SETTINGS MAKE A PARTY SPACE LOOK REALLY SPECIAL. PAY AS MUCH ATTENTION TO DECORATING TABLE LEGS OR REVAMPING GARDEN FURNITURE AS YOU DO TO PARTY FOOD, AND YOU WILL CREATE AN OCCASION TO REMEMBER.

FINISHING TOUCHES

USE COLORS AND DECOR TO REFLECT A PARTY THEME, WITH BRIGHT OCHERS AT A FIREWORKS PARTY, OR DELICATE FLORAL FABRICS AT A SUMMER BABY SHOWER. DON'T NEGLECT LIGHTING IN A ROOM. CREATE THE RIGHT AMBIENCE WITH CANDLES AND SPOTLIGHTS. CUSTOMIZE FABRIC, PLATES, AND GLASSES WITH YOUR OWN HAND-CRAFTED DESIGNS TO COMPLETE THE SETTING.

INVITATIONS

CREATE AND SEND OUT HAND-YOUR PARTY A UNIQUE, PERSONAL CRAFTED INVITATIONS TO GIVE TOUCH THAT GUESTS WILL LOVE.

BUTTON INVITATIONS

Print invitations on small rectangles of white cardboard. Cut white tulle fabric or tracing paper to the same size as each card. Attach the fabric to the top of the front of the card with a mother-of-pearl button and white thread.

COORDINATED INVITATIONS

Decorate stationery with a handmade stencil. Choose an idea from the party theme, taking inspiration from a swatch of fabric, fruit, or flower, and draw the design on clear acetate. Cut out the design using a scalpel, and transfer to good-quality writing paper using a stencil brush and acrylic paint. Cut the printed paper to size for use as invitations, menus, and place cards.

PICTURE PERFECT INVITES

Use a passport photo booth to take pictures of the party hosts. Take as many photos as there are guests. If you are sending out wedding invitations, take photos of the bride and groom wearing a tiara and top hat. Print the text on coordinating paper and mount on cardboard below the photo.

PLATE INVITATIONS

For an outdoor party, write directly on paper plates using colored markers. Mail the plates to guests.

RIBBON INVITATIONS

Fold a rectangle of white cardboard in half and punch two holes on the folded side. Thread with colored ribbon, tie in a bow.

PAPER CRAFTS

GO TO TOWN DECORATING PAPER, WHETHER FOR USE AS WRAPPING OR TO COMPLEMENT DINNER TABLE DECOR.

LEAF PRINTS

Press leaves overnight between the pages of a book. To decorate glasses, thinly brush the veined side of a leaf with emulsion paint and print on a cardboard rectangle. When the prints are dry, cut out the leaf shape, leaving a rectangle of card at the bottom of the leaf. Make two cuts in the bottom of the card, and use these to attach the print to a wine glass or tumbler. To make leaf wrapping paper, print leaves on tissue paper.

DECORATED NAME TAGS

For a large-scale party where few guests know each other, mail out attractive name tags with the invitations, stamping the tags with rubber stamps (*see Customized Paper, right*).

PAPER PHOTOGRAPH ALBUM

Customize the front of a photo album using photosensitive paper. Gather a selection of shells, pressed flowers, and leaves, and lay them on the light-sensitive paper. Leave the paper exposed to direct sunlight or a strong lamp for five minutes, then remove the objects and wash the paper to remove the light-sensitive coating. Glue three rows of three clear plastic cases to the front of a photo album. Cut out the paper to fit the cases and slip an image into each pouch.

CUSTOMIZED PAPER

Cut an image out of an eraser and use to stamp cards, paper, and gift tags, using colored or embossing ink.

CHERUB INVITATIONS ▷

1 Mix together 3 cups sifted flour, 1 cup salt, and 1 cup water to form a soft and pliable, but not sticky, dough. Knead the dough for five minutes until smooth and roll out.

2 Shape the dough into cherubs 4in (10cm) long (*see right*). Arrange the cherubs on greased baking sheets and bake for 8 hours, or overnight, at 225°F/110°C.

3 Let the dough cool on the baking sheets, then paint and varnish the cherubs and stick on invitation cards.

◁ MUSICAL GIFT WRAP

1 Paint a plain cardboard gift box with gold emulsion paint. Allow to dry.

2 Cut out strips of music from an old musical score and glue the strips randomly to the box.

3 When the glue is dry, complete the gift wrap by placing a present inside the box and tying it with a long length of shimmering ribbon.

PAPER MOSAIC TABLE ▷

1 Draw a mosaic pattern on paper, making it large enough to cover a table top.

2 Cut strips of thin, colored cardboard or paper ¾in (2cm) wide, then cut the strips into ¾in (2cm) squares. Paste the squares onto the design, trimming to fit as necessary.

3 Give the finished mosaic a coat of clear varnish to seal and protect it, then place on the table.

NAPKINS

USE FLOWERS OR FOLD NAPKINS TO MATCH A PARTY THEME AND, FOR AN EXTRA-SPECIAL FINISH, STENCIL ON GUESTS' INITIALS.

WATER LILY NAPKINS

Fold each corner of an open napkin in to meet the center, then repeat twice. Turn the napkin over and fold the four corners into the center. Hold the center flat and bend one corner toward the center, until a point from the layer beneath is free. Tug the freed point upward, until it softly wraps around. Repeat to create four petals, then pull the points up from beneath these to make eight petals.

FLORAL NAPKINS

Iron fabric napkins, fold them in half, then roll into sausage shapes. Tie each napkin with wide ribbon and tuck a flower beneath the ribbon. Use flowers that do not wilt, such as gerberas, carnations, and chrysanthemums.

DAISY-CHAIN NAPKINS

Draw a six-petal daisy with a stem and two leaves on a plain linen napkin. Stitch around the design using yellow and green silk in chain-stitch, then iron the napkin.

PERSONALIZED NAPKINS

Draw a guest's initials in italic script on white paper. Lay a sheet of clear acetate on the paper, and trace the initials with indelible pen. Cut out the traced initials using a craft knife, then lightly spray the back of the acetate stencil with spray mount and stick it to a fabric napkin. Paint through the stencil using fabric paint, applying it with a small sponge or brush. Remove the stencil. When the fabric paint is dry, use a hot iron to fix it.

PLATES & GLASSES

GIVE GLASSES ADDED GLAMOR BY EMBELLISHING THEM WITH FROSTED PATTERNS, GOLD PAINT, OR GLASS GEMS.

PLATTERS

For a stylish occasion, serve dinner plates on top of coordinated platters, or spray inexpensive larger plates with silver or gold paint to create opulent platters.

FLOWER PLATTERS

Sit a dinner plate on a large platter, and tuck flowers, herbs, and leaves between the edges of the two plates.

ICE TRAY

Fill a plain, shallow metal tray with mineral water or filtered water. Put slices of lemon, lime, and parsley in the water and place the tray in the freezer until the water is frozen solid. Arrange *fruits de mer* on the ice and serve.

BANANA-LEAF PLATTERS

To serve canapés or a Moorish or Roman banquet, dispense with plates and serve food on trays of banana or vine leaves.

RIBBON-THREADED PAPER PLATES

Using a hole punch, make 16 evenly spaced holes around the edge of each plate. Thread with ribbon and tie in a bow.

BREAD BOWLS

Serve soup from hollowed-out round bread loaves. Cut the top off individual loaves and scoop out the bread to leave a ½in (1cm) crust. Brush the entire loaf and lid, inside and out, with egg white and bake at 325˚F/160˚C until crisp. You can eat the bowls after eating the soup.

Sweetheart Napkins ▷

1 Use a small, sharp knife to score a heart shape on the cut edge of one half of a potato.

2 Cut away the potato surrounding the heart shape to leave a raised image. Blot the shape on paper towel to rid it of moisture.

3 Print on a napkin by dipping the potato in fabric paint. Add a checked border by dipping a square of potato in another color. When the design is dry, iron. Roll up and tie with a wooden heart threaded on raffia.

◁ Etched Glasses

1 Wrap a clean glass with strips of fine masking tape to create the outline of the desired pattern. To make a spotted glass, use thicker masking tape with circles cut in it.

2 Spray the glass with etching spray, available from crafts stores. The spray will turn the unmasked areas of the glass opaque.

3 Let the glass dry, then peel away the masking tape to reveal the design. Wash the etching spray off before using the glass.

Jeweled Goblets ▷

1 To make a luxurious gem-encrusted goblet, first spray a plain glass with gold paint.

2 When the paint is dry, use gold paint to cover the glass with a swirled pattern.

3 Glue fake glass or plastic gems to the glass to resemble precious stones. Use the goblets with a matching tablecloth (*see Opulent Tablecloth, page 81*).

FABRIC IDEAS

SWATHE A DINNER TABLE IN FABRIC DESIGNED FOR THE OCCASION

TO GIVE THE PERFECT BACKDROP FOR A PARTY BANQUET OR FEAST.

WEIGHTED TABLECLOTH

To ensure a tablecoth does not blow away during an outdoor party, sew attractive objects to the hem to weigh it down. Attach items such as seashells, glass beads, and small weights, sewn on with colored silk or thread.

TABLE RUNNER

Rectangular tables look great dressed with a table runner. Cover a table with an ironed white cloth. Cut a long strip of fabric at least 19½in (50cm) wide and 40in (1m) longer than the table. Hem the fabric, iron, and lay down the center of the table. Coordinate napkins and flowers with the runner, or arrange individual flowers in colored mineral water bottles down the length of the runner.

RAFFIA BEACH MAT

Raffia beach mats make excellent tablecloths for outdoor parties, and can be laid on the floor at picnics. Paint pebbles with bright emulsion paint and use to hold the mat in place.

PEBBLE-PRINT BEACH MAT

Iron a large square of canvas or heavy-duty cream fabric. Halve a selection of different-sized potatoes and blot them with paper towel. Prepare gray, pale blue, pale red, brown, and orange fabric paints in separate shallow bowls. Dip the potatoes in the paints and print pebble shapes on the fabric, overlapping the prints, so that little fabric is visible. When dry, iron. Back the mat with wadding and a layer of water-resistant fabric or an old sheet, then sew the three layers together.

TABLES & CHAIRS

BRING FURNITURE TO LIFE BY PAINTING  IT IN BOLD COLORS OR DECKING

IT WITH SWAGS OF SCENTED FLOWERS OR EVERGREENS.

FLORAL TABLE SWAG

Cut chicken wire 29in (75cm) wide and slightly longer than the table. Lay blocks of 4in (10cm) thick florist's foam along one long edge of the wire. Roll the wire around the foam to make a sausage shape. Bend the wire in the center to give a swag shape. Arrange cut flowers in the holes in the wire, pushing the stems into the foam. Use larger blooms in the center of the swag. Tie the ends with ribbon and hang along a table.

BEAUTIFUL TABLE LEGS

Dress up a table by wrapping wide strips of coordinating ribbon, crêpe paper, or long lengths of trailing ivy up the legs. Tie with bows of colored ribbon.

WINTER LIGHTED TABLE

Make a table swag (see left) from evergreens, holly, and ivy, and loop it along the length of a table. Lightly spray the swag with fake snow, then weave tiny white lights along its length, tying them with ribbon bows. Sprinkle the swag with orange or pine oil so the heat from the lights scents the room.

PAINTED GARDEN FURNITURE

Brighten plastic garden furniture with flower, spot, or leaf patterns. Wash furniture in hot, soapy water, then spray with heavy-duty aerosol paint. Cut a pattern into a sponge to form a stamp (see Daisy-stamped Tablecloth, right), dip into a contrasting paint color, and stamp on the design.

OPULENT TABLECLOTH ▷

1 Select a length of silk, crushed velvet, or brocade in purple, deep blue, red, or dark green.

2 Add intricate designs using gold or silver paint in a swirled pattern, leaving the center empty and including small shapes to decorate with fake gems. When dry, iron. Glue glass or plastic gems to the small shapes.

3 Embellish the tablecloth further by trimming it with gold or silver braiding. Use the tablecloth with matching glasses (*see Jeweled Goblets, page 79*).

◁ DAISY-STAMPED TABLECLOTH

1 Cut the shape of a daisy petal from a sponge-backed scouring pad using a sharp pair of scissors.

2 Dampen the sponge in water, squeeze dry, and brush with as thin a layer of white fabric paint as possible. Stamp circles of petals on a plain cloth. Recoat the stamp every 3–4 prints.

3 Stamp the center of the daisies with a cotton bud dipped in yellow fabric paint. Iron the dry design.

CHILD'S STOOL ▷

1 Little stools make memorable gifts for children at a party. Buy one unvarnished wooden stool per child and paint brightly with emulsion paint.

2 Make a stencil (*see Personalized Napkins, page 78*) and stencil a design or name on each stool.

3 Seal the stools with three coats of clear varnish. Use the stools for musical chairs at a children's party, then present them to children when they leave.

FLOWERS & FRUIT

TO COMPLETE A DINNER PARTY AND TABLE LINEN WITH SETTING, ADORN THE ROOM FLOWERS AND FRUIT.

GILDED TREES

Hang bay trees with gilded pears, lemons, or limes to create a delightful room decoration. If using citrus fruit, wash it first in hot soapy water to remove any wax, then dry well. Spray the fruit with gold aerosol paint and attach to the bay tree by threading with 10in (25cm) lengths of flexible wire, twisting the wire around tree branches and cutting off the excess. Lightly spray the bay tree with gold paint and let dry.

FLOATING FRUIT BOWL

Fill a shallow, attractive glass bowl with an assortment of fruit such as lemons, clementines, and kumquats. Fill the bowl with water and dot with floating candles in coordinating colors. Scatter gerbera petals in the water.

FRUIT-STAMPED LINEN

Stamp linen with fruit for a harvest party or wedding. Use white paint on calico or beige fabric for a stunning effect. Iron the cloth and lay flat. Cut apples and pears in half lengthwise, wipe the cut side with paper towel, and coat with fabric paint. Press the fruit firmly and evenly onto the fabric, then carefully repeat to form a pattern. When dry, iron the design with a hot iron.

LAVENDER CANDLE COLLARS

Tie together with wire 10 stems of lavender just under the flowers, and trim the stems short. Repeat to make seven bundles. Bend wire loosely around a candle and remove the candle. Wire the lavender to the wire circle. Put a candle in a candleholder and place the lavender over the candle, resting on the holder.

LIGHTING

STORE CANDLES FOR A LARGE PARTY COOLER CANDLES LAST LONGER AND IN A REFRIGERATOR OR COLD ROOM – THEY WILL GLOW INTO THE NIGHT.

LACY CANDLES

Embellish plain white candles with a pattern of gold or silver spray paint. Cut a length of paper doily to fit around a candle. Fix in place with masking tape and spray with gold or silver aerosol paint. Let the paint dry before removing the doily.

SUMMER LANTERNS

Light up a garden party in summer by painting plain glass jars. Decorate the jars with translucent glass paint in a variety of bright colors, then allow to dry. Loop a long piece of string to make a handle, then wrap the rest of the string around the jar rim and tie the ends in a knot. Hang the jar from a tree.

VEGETABLE CANDLES

To make unusual outdoor table decorations, tie baby vegetables, such as carrots or zucchini, around fat candles. Keep the vegetables in place as you work with a rubber band wrapped around the candle. When complete, tie raffia around the vegetables and remove the rubber band.

ORANGE CANDLES

Cut a thin slice from the top of an orange, stand a votive candle on the cut end and score around its shape using a serrated knife. Remove the candle and scoop the flesh out from inside the scored circle, using the knife and a teaspoon. Stud the orange with cloves and set a candle inside.

FLOWER DECOUPAGE ▷

1 Press delicate flowers such as pansies and daisies in blotting paper between the pages of a heavy book. Let dry out for one week.

2 Put a thin layer of glue on the back of the flowers. Position the flowers on the outside of a terra cotta pot painted white, then press firmly in place.

3 When the glue is dry, give the flowers a light coat of thinned glue to protect them.

◁ DRIED APPLE WREATH

1 Cut apples into ⅛in (3mm) thick slices. Soak the slices for 10 minutes in a bowl with 1 small cup of lemon juice, 1½ tbsp salt, and enough water to cover.

2 Dry the slices on paper towel and bake on wire racks at 275˚F/140˚C for 5–6 hours, checking them regularly. Remove when the slices are leathery but not browned. Let cool.

3 Thread the slices with bows onto 18in (45cm) wire. Join the ends to form a wreath.

FLOATING CANDLE CENTERPIECE ▷

1 Wine glasses make ideal containers for floating candles. Stand some wine glasses, or a selection of different-sized glasses, on a circular mirror.

2 Dye some water with food coloring, then fill each wine glass with the water.

3 Float a small candle in a coordinating color in the water. Complete the centerpiece by arranging glass beads on the mirror.

THERE ARE OVER 100 DELICIOUS RECIPES IN THIS SECTION THAT CAN BE USED FOR ANY OCCASION, FROM PICNICS AND TEA PARTIES TO BANQUETS & BALLS. AS WELL AS TRADITIONAL AND SEASONAL PARTY FAVORITES, THERE ARE SOME TWISTS ON CLASSIC DISHES AND A NUMBER OF NEW RECIPES SO

FOOD & DRINK

THAT YOU CAN CHOOSE FOOD & DRINK FRIENDS AND FAMILY WILL LOVE. ENTERTAINING SHOULD BE FUN, SO THE RECIPES AND DRINKS FEATURED ARE ALL QUICK TO PREPARE YET GIVE IMPRESSIVE RESULTS. THIS WILL GUARANTEE THAT YOU WON'T BE STUCK IN THE KITCHEN AT YOUR OWN PARTY, BUT CAN CIRCULATE AND HAVE AS GOOD A TIME AS YOUR GUESTS.

CANAPÉS & DRINKS

CANAPÉS AND FINGER FOODS ARE IDEAL FOR SERVING AT COCKTAIL PARTIES, WITH INFORMAL DRINKS, AND ON PICNICS. MANY CAN BE PREPARED IN ADVANCE, GIVING YOU TIME TO CHECK ON EVERYONE'S DRINKS AND JOIN IN THE FUN.

SALMON PINWHEELS

A MODERN VERSION OF A CLASSIC. THESE SALMON ROLLS (TROUT WORKS JUST AS WELL) CAN BE MADE AND CHILLED UP TO 24 HOURS IN ADVANCE. SLICE JUST BEFORE SERVING.

MAKES 30

8oz (250g) cream cheese • grated zest of 1 lemon
freshly ground black pepper • 2 tbsp snipped fresh chives
½lb (250g) smoked salmon or smoked trout

1 Beat together the cream cheese, lemon zest, black pepper, and fresh chives until smooth.

2 Lay the strips of salmon or trout on a work surface. Spread the cheese mixture on the salmon and roll up, as if making mini jelly rolls. Thinly slice into pinwheels.

MUSHROOM BUNDLES

THESE ARE VERY QUICK AND SIMPLE TO MAKE. THEY CAN BE ASSEMBLED IN ADVANCE AND CHILLED OVERNIGHT, OR FROZEN FOR UP TO A WEEK. COOK JUST BEFORE SERVING.

MAKES 24

24 small mushrooms • ⅓ cup (90g) cream cheese with herbs
12 sheets of phyllo pastry • 2 tbsp olive oil

1 Preheat the oven to 400°F (200°C). Remove the stems from the mushrooms. Place a teaspoonful of cream cheese in the center of each mushroom.

2 Cut each phyllo sheet in half, brush with oil, and place a mushroom in the center. Draw the pastry corners over the mushroom to make a bundle, pinching to seal. Bake for about 5 minutes, or until golden.

CARAMELIZED ONION QUICHES

USE THE CHOCOLATE TART PASTRY ON PAGE 108, REPLACING THE SUGAR AND EGG WHITE (USE THE YOLK) WITH A PINCH OF SALT AND A LITTLE WATER TO BIND IT.

MAKES 20

1 batch shortcrust pastry • 3 onions • 3 tbsp olive oil
1 tsp superfine sugar • 2 medium eggs • ⅔ cup (150ml) light cream
salt and freshly ground black pepper • 2 tbsp chopped fresh thyme

1 Preheat the oven to 400°F (200°C). Roll out the pastry on a lightly floured surface. Using a 3in (7.5cm) fluted cutter, cut out 20 rounds and use to line a muffin pan. Chill in the refrigerator for 10 minutes. Line the pastry shells with scrunched foil and bake blind for 5 minutes.

2 Finely chop the onions and cook with the oil and sugar for about 15 minutes in a covered pan over low heat, until golden. Stir frequently to prevent sticking. Spoon the onion mixture into the pastry shells.

3 Beat together the eggs, cream, and seasoning. Divide among the onion quiches and sprinkle with thyme. Bake for 15–20 minutes or until puffy and set.

VARIATIONS

SUN-DRIED TOMATO: Use only 1 onion, together with 5 chopped sun-dried tomatoes, and continue as directed.

ASPARAGUS & FRESH PEA: Blanch ½lb (200g) asparagus, trimmed and halved, with 1½ cups (175g) peas. Arrange in the pastry shells. Combine 3 tablespoons snipped chives, 3 medium eggs, 1¼ cups (300ml) heavy cream, and season. Pour over the vegetables and bake for 25–30 minutes.

SALMON PINWHEELS

MUSHROOM BUNDLES

SAVORY
SCONES,
TOPPED WITH
SALAMI,
PROSCIUTTO,
AND SMOKED
SALMON

CARAMELIZED
ONION QUICHES

SALMON PINWHEELS

SAVORY SCONES

TO MAKE SWEET SCONES, OMIT THE CHEESE AND ADD
2 TBSP EACH OF SUGAR AND MIXED DRIED FRUIT.
TOP WITH JAM, CREAM, AND BERRIES.

MAKES 18

2½ cups (300g) self-rising flour • ½ cup (100g) butter, diced
3½oz (100g) fontina cheese • 1 medium egg • ½ cup (150ml) milk
FOR THE TOPPINGS
1 cup (200ml) crème fraîche • 6 slices smoked salmon
6 slices salami • 6 slices prosciutto
fresh herbs, such as dill, marjoram, and thyme, to garnish

1 Preheat the oven to 425°F (220°C). Sift the flour into a
bowl and rub in the butter. Finely grate the cheese and
add it to the bowl with the egg and milk. Mix to a soft, but
not sticky, dough. Roll on a floured surface to 1in (2.5cm)
thick, and cut out 18 rounds. Put on a greased baking sheet
and bake for 12–15 minutes or until golden. Let them cool.
2 Halve the scones and add a little crème fraîche and
half a slice of topping to each. Garnish with herbs.

CORNBREAD

SERVE THIS SLICED, TOASTED, AND CUT INTO TRIANGLES,
DRIZZLED WITH CHILI SAUCE OR EXTRA–VIRGIN OLIVE OIL.

MAKES ONE 1LB (500G) LOAF

1 medium egg • ½ tsp saffron strands • 1½ cups (350ml) buttermilk
6 tbsp (90g) butter, melted • 1½ cups (75g) all-purpose flour
1 cup (125g) fine cornmeal (polenta) • 1 tbsp baking powder
2 tsp superfine sugar • 1 tsp fine salt • 3 tbsp poppy seeds

1 Preheat the oven to 400°F (200°C). Butter a 1lb (500g)
loaf pan, and line the base with waxed paper.
2 Beat together the egg, saffron, buttermilk, and melted
butter. Sift the flour, cornmeal, baking powder, sugar,
and salt into a bowl. Make a well in the center and stir
in the egg mixture and the poppy seeds.
3 Spoon the mixture into the prepared pan and bake for
about 30 minutes, or until risen and cooked through.
4 Let it cool in the pan for 5 minutes before
transferring to a wire rack to cool completely.

PUFF PASTRY PIZZAS

YOU CAN FREEZE THE PASTRY CIRCLES IN ADVANCE,
THEN TOP AND BAKE THEM LATER.

MAKES 20 SMALL PIZZAS

13oz (400g) puff pastry • 8 medium tomatoes, sliced
3 cloves garlic, sliced • 2 tsp sea salt
¼ cup (60ml) olive oil • fresh basil leaves, to garnish
2oz (60g) Parmesan • 20 pitted black olives, halved

1 Preheat the oven to 425°F (220°C). Roll out the pastry
thinly on a floured surface. Using a 3in (7.5cm) fluted
cutter, cut 20 circles from the pastry and place on a
baking sheet. Arrange the tomatoes and garlic on top.
Sprinkle with the sea salt and olive oil, and bake for
10–12 minutes or until golden.
2 Garnish with basil leaves. Use a vegetable peeler to
shave pieces of Parmesan onto the pizzas. Scatter the
black olives and serve warm.

CHEESE TWISTS

ANOTHER GREAT PARTY STANDBY. USE PESTO, RED
PEPPER, OR SUN–DRIED TOMATO PASTE AS AN
ALTERNATIVE TO CHEESE.

MAKES 40

13oz (400g) puff pastry • 1 medium egg, beaten
½ cup (100g) aged Cheddar or Parmesan, finely grated
2 tbsp sesame seeds • 2 tbsp poppy seeds

1 Preheat the oven to 425°F (220°C). On a lightly floured
work surface, roll out the pastry thinly into a large
rectangle. Brush with the beaten egg to within ½in (1cm)
of the edge. Sprinkle with the cheese.
2 Fold the pastry in half and roll gently with a rolling
pin. Sprinkle half the pastry with sesame seeds and the
other half with poppy seeds. Cut the pastry into thin strips
using a sharp knife and twist each strip at both ends.
3 Arrange on a baking sheet and bake for about
12–15 minutes or until golden. You can make and
chill these up to 24 hours in advance, or freeze them
for up to a month before baking.

GARLICKY MIXED OLIVES

7½oz (225g) black olives • 7½oz (225g) pimento-stuffed green olives
3 cloves garlic, sliced • 1 cup (250ml) extra-virgin olive oil
half a lime, sliced • a few sprigs of fresh thyme
freshly ground black pepper

Mix all the olives in a bowl, then add all the other ingredients, seasoning with black pepper. Mix well, cover with plastic wrap, and chill for at least 48 hours.

BRUSCHETTA

SERVES 6

1 baguette, sliced • 3 tbsp extra-virgin olive oil
2 cloves garlic, minced • freshly ground black pepper
FOR THE TOPPINGS
4 cups (300g) mushrooms in jars • 3 tbsp snipped chives
3 tbsp black olive tapenade • 1 cup (200g) canned cannellini beans
10oz (300g) mixed peppers and sun-dried tomatoes in olive oil
2 tbsp chopped fresh oregano • 6 slices salami
12 black olives • 4 tbsp mascarpone cheese
3½oz (100g) mozzarella, sliced • grated zest of 1 lemon
fresh marjoram, to garnish • 2 tbsp olive oil

1 Brush one side of each bread slice with olive oil, sprinkle with garlic, season with black pepper, and then broil until lightly browned. Turn the slices over, prepare the other side in the same way, and broil.

2 To serve, either put a selection of toppings in small bowls and let guests help themselves, or make a platter of ready-topped bruschetta as follows:

★ Drain the mushrooms and arrange on the bruschetta. Season with black pepper and garnish with minced chives.

★ Spread the tapenade over the bruschetta and top with drained cannellini beans.

★ Drain the peppers and sun-dried tomatoes and arrange on the bruschetta. Season and sprinkle with the oregano.

★ Curl each slice of salami and arrange on the bruschetta, garnish with black olives, mascarpone, and oregano.

★ Arrange the mozzarella on the bruschetta, sprinkle with lemon zest and marjoram, and drizzle with olive oil.

BLINI WITH QUAIL EGGS & SMOKED FISH

THESE SMALL RUSSIAN PANCAKES ARE
TRADITIONALLY MADE USING BUCKWHEAT FLOUR.
THIS RECIPE IS A DELICIOUS, LIGHTER VERSION
MADE WITH REGULAR FLOUR.

SERVES 6

FOR THE BLINI
1½ cups (175g) all-purpose flour • 1 tsp salt • ½ pkg instant yeast
1 medium egg, separated • scant cup (200ml) tepid water
⅔ cup (200ml) milk • 2 tbsp sunflower oil
TO COMPLETE
12 quail eggs • 7½oz (225g) smoked salmon
1 cup (200ml) crème fraîche • 3½oz (100g) caviar
sprigs of fresh chervil • 1 lemon, cut into wedges
ground cayenne pepper

1 Sift the flour into a bowl, add the salt, then stir in the yeast. Beat the egg yolk with the water and stir into the flour. Beat the egg white until it is stiff but not dry, and fold into the flour mixture. Cover the bowl and let stand for 30 minutes.

2 Heat the milk until it just begins to boil, then beat it into the flour mixture to form a batter. Cover the bowl again and leave the batter for a further 30 minutes or until it is well risen and bubbly.

3 Meanwhile, to cook the quail eggs, place them in a pot of lightly salted water, bring to a boil, and simmer for about 4 minutes, then shell and cut in half.

4 To cook the blini, heat a skillet and wipe it with a piece of paper towel dipped in a little of the oil. Drop spoonfuls of the batter to make pancakes measuring about 3in (7.5cm) in diameter.

5 Cook for 1–2 minutes on each side, until golden and cooked through. Keep warm while cooking the remaining blini, wiping the pan with a little more oil as necessary.

6 Serve the warm pancakes topped with the quail eggs, smoked salmon, crème fraîche, caviar, fresh chervil, lemon wedges, and a sprinkling of cayenne pepper.

DRINKS WITH A KICK

◁ **MIMOSA:** Squeeze the juice of 6 large oranges into a pitcher. Pour a little of the fresh orange juice into each glass and top off with champagne. To take this drink to picnics, squeeze the orange juice into a rigid plastic container, and surround a bottle of champagne or sparkling white wine with plenty of ice packs. Serves 10.

◁ **PIMM'S:** To prepare the flavorings, wash and halve 1 quart (300g) strawberries; thinly pare the zest from 2 lemons; thinly slice 2in (5cm) cucumber (having discarded the seeds); segment 2 clementines (skin and pith removed). Stir these into a pitcher containing 1¼ cups (300ml) Pimm's. Cover and leave for up to 1 hour before topping off with 3¾ cups (900ml) chilled sparkling white wine or lemonade, and borage ice cubes (*see below*). Serves 10.

BORAGE ICE CUBES: Quarter fill an ice-cube tray with cold water, set a borage flower in each cube, and freeze for 1 hour. Top with ice water and freeze until solid.

CHAMPAGNE COCKTAILS: Pour ¼ cup (60ml) of either crème de cassis, brandy, or sloe gin into each glass and top off with champagne.

BANANA DAIQUIRI: Blend together ¼ cup (60ml) white rum, 2 tbsp (30ml) crème de banane, 2 tbsp (30ml) orange juice, 1 tbsp (15ml) lime juice, a quarter of a fresh, mashed banana, 1 tsp (5ml) whipping cream, and 1 tsp superfine sugar. When thoroughly blended, add a glass of crushed ice and briefly blend again. Garnish with banana slices and serve with a wide straw. Serves 1.

MARGARITA: Decorating the glass is a key part of serving margaritas. Dip the rim of a long-stemmed, wide-brimmed cocktail glass in a dish of lime juice and then into fine salt. Attach a thin half slice of lime to the rim. Then, in a cocktail shaker packed with ice, shake together ¼ cup (60ml) tequila, 3 tbsp (45ml) triple sec, and 1 tbsp (15ml) lemon or lime juice. Strain, leaving the ice behind, and serve. Serves 1.

SEA BREEZE: Combine 3 tbsp (45ml) vodka, ¼ cup (60ml) grapefruit juice, and 6 tbsp (90ml) cranberry juice. Shake in a cocktail shaker with a glassful of crushed ice. Pour into a glass and garnish with slices of lime. Serves 1.

Apple Whizz: Mix together equal quantities of well-chilled apple juice and cider. Serve each glass decorated with slices of apple.

Mulled Wine: The secret to making good mulled wine is not to overheat it. It is ready to serve just as the steam rises and before the liquid bubbles. Traditional mulled wine is made by heating a bottle of red wine in a saucepan together with a sliced orange, a stick of cinnamon, and 3–4 cloves. Some people add sugar or sliced clementines for extra sweetness, while juniper berries give a bit more fruitiness. If you want a really warming drink, add a glass of brandy to the pan just before serving. Serves 6.

Pink Gin: Coat the bottom half of a frosted glass with 4 dashes of angostura bitters and discard the excess. Add ¼ cup (60ml) gin and stir in a little ice water. Serves 1.

Sangria: Half fill a large pitcher with ice cubes. Pour in a bottle of Spanish red wine, then add ¼ cup (60ml) brandy and stir well. If desired, top off with carbonated water. Decorate with sliced apricots and strawberries. Serves 6.

ALCOHOL-FREE DRINKS

Cranberry Cocktail: Squeeze the juice of 2 oranges and 1 lime. Put ice cubes into a plastic bag and crush with a rolling pin. Put the ice in a pitcher and pour over the fruit juice and 2 tbsp honey. Pour into glasses and top off with cranberry juice. Decorate the glasses with wedges of orange or lime. You can make this drink in a thermos for picnics. Serves 6.

Passion Fruit Mix: Scoop out the flesh of a honeydew melon and place in a food processor. Halve 3 passion fruits and strain the juice into the processor. Blend the fruit mixture until smooth. Pour into a pitcher and top with chilled sparkling mineral water or lemonade. If taking this drink to a picnic, add the sparkling water or lemonade on arrival. Serves 6.

Apricot Fruit Cup: Mix together equal quantities of apricot juice and sparkling grape juice. Pour this mixture into glasses filled with slices of fresh apricot, strawberries cut in half, a sprig of fresh mint, and plenty of ice.

FIRST COURSES

WHETHER A SOUP THAT SUITS AN OCCASION SUCH AS HALLOWEEN, OR A LIGHT SUMMER TAPAS SELECTION FOR FRIENDS AND FAMILY, FIRST COURSES SHOULD ALWAYS MAKE AN IMPRESSION AND LEAVE YOUR GUESTS WANTING MORE.

ROASTED PEPPER & TOMATO SOUP

TRY SERVING THIS SOUP AT JULY 4TH PARTIES.

SERVES 4

2 large red peppers, halved, seeded, and cut into chunks
2lb (1kg) ripe plum tomatoes, quartered • 2 cloves garlic, halved
¼ cup (60ml) olive oil • sea salt, for sprinkling
1¼ cups (300ml) vegetable stock • freshly ground black pepper
FOR THE CROUTONS
2 tbsp olive oil • 1 clove garlic, halved
4 thick bread slices, crusts removed
2 sprigs rosemary, broken into pieces

1 Preheat the oven to 500°F (260°C). Put the peppers, tomatoes, garlic, and olive oil in a roasting pan and sprinkle with sea salt. Mix and then roast for about 15 minutes, stirring occasionally to ensure even cooking.

2 Transfer this mixture to a food processor and blend, gradually adding the vegetable stock, until smooth. Pour into a pan, heat gently, and season to taste.

3 Meanwhile, heat the oil for the croutons in a skillet and add the garlic. Cut the bread into cubes, add them to the pan, and stir until golden. Drain the croutons, discarding the garlic, and sprinkle with the pieces of rosemary. Divide the soup among warmed bowls and scatter the croutons and rosemary over the top.

CREAMY PUMPKIN SOUP

SERVES 6

2 tbsp olive oil • 1 onion, chopped • 2 tsp ground ginger
2½lb (1.25kg) pumpkin, peeled, seeded, and chopped
1 large potato, peeled and chopped • 5 cups (1.25 liters) vegetable stock
1¼ cups (300ml) heavy cream • salt and freshly ground black pepper
2 tbsp chopped fresh cilantro, to garnish

1 Heat the oil in a heavy-bottomed pan and cook the onion until softened but not browned. Add the ginger and stir well. Add the pumpkin and potato and stir-fry over high heat for 5 minutes. Add the stock and bring to a boil. Simmer for 25 minutes, until the pumpkin is tender.

2 Blend in a food processor, then pour the smooth soup back into a pan and stir in the cream. Season with salt and pepper to taste and serve garnished with the chopped cilantro.

COCK-A-LEEKIE SOUP

SERVES 4

2 tbsp sunflower oil • 2 leeks, sliced
1 tsp granulated sugar • 2 chicken breasts, cooked and shredded
½ cup (125g) pitted prunes • 2½ cups (600ml) chicken stock
salt and freshly ground black pepper

1 Heat the oil in a pan, stir in the leeks and sugar, and cook gently for 5 minutes, until the leeks have softened.

2 Stir in the chicken, prunes, and stock. Bring to a boil, then reduce the heat and simmer for 10 minutes. Season with salt and freshly ground black pepper to taste.

TAPAS SELECTION

SERVES 8

CALAMARI

½lb (250g) baby squid • 1 medium egg, beaten
salt and freshly ground black pepper • 1 tbsp flour
1¼ cups (300ml) sunflower oil • lime wedges

1 Cut the squid into rings, leaving the tentacles whole. Dip in a little beaten egg, then coat in seasoned flour. Heat the oil in a large, deep pan.

2 Cook the squid in batches for 1–2 minutes. Drain on paper towels and serve with lime wedges.

POTATOES WITH CHORIZO & AÏOLI

1 cup (200ml) olive oil • ¼lb (125g) chorizo, sliced
1lb (450g) small new potatoes • 1 tsp coarse sea salt
2 large sprigs rosemary • 3 cloves garlic • 1 medium egg
2 tbsp lemon juice • 1 tsp mustard • 4 tbsp sunflower oil

1 Heat 4 tablespoons of the olive oil in a pan. Stir in the chorizo and potatoes, cover, and heat until the oil sizzles. Simmer gently for about 10 minutes, shaking the pan frequently. Add the salt and rosemary and cook for 5 minutes longer, until the potatoes are very tender.

2 To make the aïoli, blend the garlic, egg, lemon juice, and mustard in a food processor, gradually adding the remaining olive oil and the sunflower oil. Season to taste. Skewer the potatoes and chorizo with toothpicks and serve with the aïoli.

MEATBALLS WITH RED SAUCE

2 scallions, chopped • 2 cloves garlic, crushed
1lb (450g) lean ground lamb • ½ cup (30g) fresh white bread crumbs
1 egg yolk • 2 roasted, seeded red peppers • 1 red chili
1¼ cups (150ml) vegetable stock • 1¼ cups (150ml) heavy cream

1 Combine the scallions, garlic, lamb, bread crumbs, and egg yolk in a bowl. Shape into small balls.

2 Blend the peppers, chili, stock, and heavy cream in a processor. Heat in a pan until hot, then simmer.

3 Cook the meatballs in a nonstick pan for 10 minutes, until browned. Put them in the sauce and simmer for 5 minutes. Serve with toothpicks.

ASPARAGUS & LIME PASTA

SERVES 4

8oz (225g) fresh angel hair pasta • salt
½lb (250g) asparagus spears, halved • 2 cups (450ml) heavy cream
juice and zest of 1 lime • 2 tbsp chopped fresh parsley
shavings of Parmesan, to garnish • freshly ground black pepper

1 Cook the pasta in a large pot of boiling salted water for 2 minutes, or until al dente. Blanch the asparagus in boiling salted water for 2 minutes, then drain.

2 Meanwhile, heat the cream with the lime juice and zest. Add the pasta and the asparagus to the hot cream. Spoon onto serving plates and garnish with the parsley and shavings of Parmesan. Season with freshly ground black pepper to taste.

SWEET & SOUR SHRIMP

THIS DELICIOUS RECIPE ALSO WORKS WELL WITH DICED CHICKEN AND PORK.

SERVES 6

18 whole raw jumbo shrimp • 1 tbsp sunflower oil
2 shallots, finely chopped • 1 clove garlic, finely chopped
1 red chili, seeded and finely chopped • 2 tbsp tomato paste
1 tbsp superfine sugar • juice and zest of 1 orange • 1 tbsp cornstarch
salt and freshly ground black pepper • 4oz (125g) crispy seaweed

1 Carefully peel the shells from the shrimp, leaving the tails intact. Remove the black veins that run down the back of the shrimp.

2 Heat the oil in a skillet and cook the shallots, garlic, and chili for 3 minutes. Add the tomato paste, sugar, and orange zest. Combine the orange juice with the cornstarch, add to the pan, and season. Heat until the mixture bubbles.

3 Add the shrimp to the pan and cook until they have turned pink and are cooked through.

4 Cook the seaweed according to package directions. Serve some on each plate with the shrimp on top. Spoon the sauce over it, if desired.

SMOKED SALMON TRIANGLES

SERVES 6

FOR THE TRIANGLES

⅓ cup (90g) herb-flavored cream cheese • ½lb (200g) cooked shrimp
grated zest of 1 small lime • salt and freshly ground black pepper
12 slices of smoked salmon, each 8in x 3in (20cm x 7.5cm)

FOR THE SALAD

¼ cup (90ml) olive oil • juice of 1 small lime
2 tsp Dijon mustard • small bunch basil leaves
mixed salad greens

1 Beat the cheese until smooth, then chop the shrimp and fold in with the lime zest. Season to taste.

2 Lay the slices of smoked salmon on a work surface. Put a small spoonful of the cheese mixture on one corner of each strip and shape roughly into a triangle. Fold the salmon around the cheese, rolling it up to make neat triangles. Arrange on a tray, then cover and chill until ready to serve.

3 For the dressing, put the oil, lime juice, mustard, and basil in a blender or food processor and blend until the basil is very finely chopped. Season with salt and freshly ground black pepper to taste. Strain through a fine strainer into a pitcher.

4 To serve, place one salmon triangle on each plate and divide the mixed salad greens among the plates. Set a second triangle to the side and drizzle with a little dressing. Serve the remaining dressing separately.

PROSCIUTTO & EGG MOUSSES

THESE TASTY LITTLE MOUSSES ARE QUICK TO MAKE AND CAN BE PREPARED 24 HOURS BEFORE A PARTY.

SERVES 8

8oz (250g) chive-flavored cream cheese • 1¼ cups (300ml) crème fraîche
12 hard-boiled eggs, chopped • salt and freshly ground black pepper
7oz (200g) prosciutto • 8 tbsp snipped chives • arugula

1 Beat together the cream cheese and crème fraîche. Fold in the eggs and season with salt and pepper.

2 Line 8 small ramekins with plastic wrap, then with the prosciutto, leaving some overlapping the sides. Divide the egg mixture among the ramekins and cover with the overlapping prosciutto. Chill for at least 3 hours.

3 Turn the molds out onto chilled plates. Sprinkle with chives and serve garnished with arugula.

KOFTA MEATBALLS

SERVE WITH A TOMATO SALAD OR WITH TOMATO SAUCE AND RICE AS A MORE SUBSTANTIAL DISH.

SERVES 6

2 cloves garlic, finely chopped • 1 onion, finely chopped
2 tsp garam masala • 1 tsp ground coriander
1 tsp ground turmeric • 1 tbsp tomato paste
⅞lb (400g) lean ground lamb
salt and freshly ground black pepper • 2 tbsp olive oil

TO SERVE

tomato and avocado salsa • cucumber raita
6 mini pita breads

1 In a bowl, lightly work the garlic, onion, garam masala, coriander, turmeric, and tomato paste into the ground lamb. Season with a little salt and pepper.

2 With damp hands, shape the mixture into about 24 balls. Heat the oil in a skillet and cook the meatballs for about 10 minutes, turning frequently.

3 Serve hot with tomato and avocado salsa, raita, and warmed, sliced pita bread.

MAIN COURSES

WHEN ENTERTAINING, SIMPLE DISHES, DONE WELL, ALWAYS IMPRESS. WHETHER SERVED AT A BLACK TIE PARTY OR AN IMPROMPTU BARBECUE, A PIZZA MADE WITH PIZZAZZ IS BETTER THAN SOMETHING MORE SOPHISTICATED THAT FALLS FLAT.

SCRAMBLED EGGS IN BRIOCHE

A MARVELOUS LAST–MINUTE BRUNCH DISH THAT IS ALSO WONDERFUL WHEN FRIENDS ARRIVE UNEXPECTEDLY. STORE–BOUGHT BRIOCHES ARE EXCELLENT – IT'S WORTH KEEPING PLENTY IN THE FREEZER.

SERVES 4

4 brioches
2 tbsp butter • 4 medium eggs • ½ cup (150ml) heavy cream
2 tbsp snipped fresh chives • 4 tbsp caviar
freshly ground black pepper

1 Cut the top off each brioche and scoop out the center. Place the brioches on a baking sheet and warm them in a low oven while making the scrambled eggs.

2 Melt the butter in a heavy-bottomed pan over low heat. Beat together the eggs and cream. Pour the egg mixture into the pan with the melted butter and cook over low heat until the eggs start to scramble. The secret of good scrambled eggs is to keep the heat low and to stir the eggs frequently. Don't hurry or the mixture will become rubbery.

3 Remove the scrambled eggs from the heat and mix in the snipped chives. Fill each warmed brioche with scrambled eggs and garnish with caviar and freshly ground black pepper.

SIMPLE KEDGEREE

THIS DISH IS GREAT PREPARED AHEAD. IT CAN BE MADE THE NIGHT BEFORE AND REFRIGERATED UNTIL READY TO HEAT AS GUESTS ARRIVE FOR BRUNCH. IT ALSO MAKES A GREAT SUPPER PARTY DISH.

SERVES 4

2 cups (375g) long-grain white rice • ¼ cup (60g) butter
1 onion, finely chopped • 2 cups (450ml) heavy cream
3 tbsp chopped fresh dill • salt and freshly ground black pepper
6 hard-boiled eggs, chopped • 10oz (300g) smoked salmon slices
2 tbsp chopped fresh cilantro • 2 tbsp mild curry paste

1 Cook the rice in a large pot of salted boiling water for 10 minutes or according to package directions.

2 Meanwhile, melt the butter in a large pan and cook the onion for about 5 minutes or until softened but not browned. Drain the rice and stir into the onion, with 1¼ cups (300ml) of the cream and the dill. Season with salt and black pepper, to taste.

3 Quickly fold the hard-boiled eggs and smoked salmon into the hot rice mixture and spoon into a serving dish. Garnish with the cilantro and keep warm. Heat the remaining cream, stir in the curry paste, and serve with the smoked salmon. (Curry sauce is the traditional accompaniment to this dish.)

VARIATION

LUXURY EGG & SMOKED SALMON FIRST COURSE: Omit the curry paste and substitute a mixture of white and wild rice for the white rice. Replace the chopped cilantro with chervil and serve each portion topped with a poached egg to make an elegant appetizer for eight people.

PIZZA

EACH TOPPING IS ENOUGH FOR TWO PIZZAS. AS YOU
GET MORE CONFIDENT, MAKE YOUR OWN TOPPINGS WITH
SLICES OF SALAMI AND COMBINATIONS OF VEGETABLES.

MAKES FOUR 8IN (20CM) PIZZAS

4 cups (450g) all-purpose flour • 1 tsp salt • 1 tsp yeast
about 1¼ cups (300ml) lukewarm water
FOR THE TOPPINGS
2 tbsp olive oil • 1 onion, chopped • 2 cloves garlic, minced
24oz (750g) chopped canned tomatoes
fresh basil leaves, to garnish • salt and freshly ground black pepper
THREE-CHEESE TOPPING
5oz (150g) mozzarella, sliced • 5oz (150g) goat cheese, sliced
2oz (60g) pecorino cheese, coarsely grated
HAM & MUSHROOM TOPPING
1½ cups (125g) mixed mushrooms, thinly sliced
3½oz (100g) prosciutto, cut into strips
3½oz (100g) mozzarella, grated

1 To make the pizza crust, first sift the flour and salt into
a large bowl. Stir in the yeast and enough lukewarm
water to make a soft but not sticky dough. Turn the dough
out onto a lightly floured work surface and knead for
10 minutes, until smooth and elastic. Place in a greased
bowl and cover with plastic wrap. Let rise for about
1 hour in a warm place or until doubled in size.

2 Meanwhile, to make the topping, heat the oil in
a large skillet. Cook the onion and garlic in the oil
until softened but not browned. Add the tomatoes and
boil rapidly for about 15 minutes, stirring occasionally,
until the tomatoes are reduced and very thick. Remove
from the heat and allow to cool.

3 Punch down the dough and shape into four rounds,
each 8in (20cm) across. Preheat the oven to 450°F
(230°C). Spread the tomato mixture over the pizzas.
Scatter the three cheeses on two of the pizzas and the
mushrooms, prosciutto, and mozzarella on the other two.

4 Bake the pizzas in the preheated oven for
12–15 minutes, until the toppings are golden and the
pizzas are cooked through. Garnish each pizza with fresh
basil leaves and season, then serve.

MINI PICNIC PIES

MAKES 12

2 tbsp sunflower oil • 1 onion, chopped • ½ tsp ground cinnamon
½ tsp grated nutmeg • ½lb (250g) ground turkey
salt and freshly ground black pepper
12oz (375g) puff pastry • 2oz (60g) ham, cut into 12 cubes
beaten egg, to glaze

1 Preheat the oven to 425°F (220°C). Heat the oil in a
skillet, add the onion, and cook for about 5 minutes,
until softened. Add the cinnamon, nutmeg, and ground
turkey. Cook, stirring occasionally, until the turkey is lightly
browned, about 10 minutes. Remove the pan from the heat
and let cool. Season with salt and pepper to taste.

2 Using plain or fluted cookie cutters, cut out 12
rounds of pastry, each 3in (7.5cm) across, and use to
line tart pans. Cut 12 smaller rounds to make tops. Using
a teaspoon, divide half the turkey mixture among the
pastry-lined pans. Place a ham cube in each and spoon
the remaining turkey mixture over it.

3 Dampen the pastry rims with a little water and press
on the tops to seal. Brush the pies with a little egg and
make a small slit in the top of each. Bake in the preheated
oven for about 25 minutes or until puffy and golden.

VENISON & SAUSAGE HOTPOT

SERVE WITH CREAMY MASHED POTATOES AT WINTER PARTIES, WHERE COMFORT FOOD IS CALLED FOR.

SERVES 6

2 tbsp sunflower oil • 12 shallots, peeled and halved
2 celery stalks, sliced • ¼lb (100g) baby carrots, trimmed
1lb (450g) pork sausage links • 2 tsp ground allspice
1 tbsp flour • 1½lb (750g) venison, cubed
juice and zest of 1 orange • 3¾ cups (900ml) beef or venison stock
salt and freshly ground black pepper • 2 tbsp chopped fresh parsley

1 Heat the oil in a large casserole, add the shallots, celery, and carrots and cook for about 10 minutes, until softened but not browned. Remove the vegetables from the casserole. Add the sausages and cook for about 5 minutes, turning frequently, until they have browned. Remove the sausages from the casserole.

2 Mix the allspice with the flour. Toss the venison cubes in the seasoned flour to coat. Add the venison to the pan and cook until sealed and browned on all sides.

3 Return the vegetables and sausages to the pan with the orange juice, zest, and stock. Mix well, then cover and cook until the venison is tender, about 45 minutes. Season to taste, then stir in the chopped parsley and serve with creamy mashed potatoes.

VARIATION

BEEF IN BEER: Replace the venison and sausage with 2lb (1kg) lean cubed beef and substitute beer for the stock, following the directions above.

QUICK CASSOULET

SERVES 8

8 duck breasts, halved • 8 chicken drumsticks
2 onions, chopped • 3 cloves garlic, crushed
½lb (225g) bacon, chopped
24oz (750g) canned cannellini beans, drained
3 cups (750g) chopped canned tomatoes • 1¼ cups (300ml) chicken stock
3 tbsp chopped fresh marjoram and oregano
⅓lb (175g) salami, thickly sliced
salt and freshly ground black pepper • fresh oregano, to garnish

1 Put the duck breasts in a large casserole and cook on each side until browned, about 8 minutes. Remove the duck from the casserole and pour off all but 1 tablespoon of the duck fat. Add the chicken drumsticks to the pan and cook for 10 minutes, or until golden on all sides. Remove from the casserole.

2 Add the onions, garlic, and bacon to the casserole and stir for 5 minutes or until the onion has softened. Return the duck and chicken to the casserole and stir in the beans, tomatoes, chicken stock, chopped herbs, and salami. Bring to a boil, then simmer for about 1 hour or until the meat is tender.

3 Season with salt and freshly ground black pepper and garnish with oregano. Serve with mashed root vegetables or potatoes, or crusty bread and a salad.

SMOKED CHICKEN

SERVES 4

2 tbsp lapsang souchong tea leaves • 4½ cups (1 liter) boiling water
1 medium-sized chicken • 1 lemon, sliced • 2 star anise
1 cinnamon stick, broken

1 Put the tea leaves in the boiling water and mix well. Place a wire rack over a large skillet or wok. Lay the chicken on the rack and pour the tea over it. Scatter the lemon slices, star anise, and cinnamon stick over the chicken, then bring the tea back to a boil.

2 Cover the skillet and simmer for about 1 hour, or until the chicken is cooked through. Serve with rice and stir-fried vegetables.

CHICKEN WITH FIGS

THIS DISH IS BEST SERVED WITH A GREEN SALAD, MINTED POTATO SALAD, AND PESTO ON THE SIDE.

SERVES 6

6 chicken breasts, with skin • 6 tbsp red currant jelly
2 tbsp light soy sauce • 2 tbsp coarsely chopped fresh rosemary
2 cloves garlic, finely chopped • salt and freshly ground black pepper
3 tbsp olive oil • 9 baby eggplants, sliced lengthwise
9 fresh figs, halved

1 Make slits through the skin and flesh of the chicken and place in a shallow dish. Beat together the red currant jelly, soy sauce, rosemary, garlic, seasoning, and 1 tablespoon olive oil. Pour the mixture over the chicken, cover, and chill for at least half an hour, but preferably overnight, turning the chicken once.

2 Heat half the remaining oil in a skillet and cook the chicken until well browned on each side. Set aside. Heat the remaining oil in the pan and cook the eggplant slices on both sides until lightly browned.

3 Return the chicken to the skillet and continue cooking until cooked through and tender. Quickly heat the fig halves in the pan and serve the dish with potato salad, pesto, and a green salad.

CHICKEN TIKKA

COOKING INDIAN FOOD IS VERY EASY WITH SO MANY EXCELLENT CURRY PASTES AVAILABLE IN SUPERMARKETS.

SERVES 6

6 chicken cutlets, boned and skinned
10oz (300g) chicken tikka paste • ⅔ cup (150ml) plain yogurt
1 tbsp olive oil • 1 onion, chopped • 2 cloves garlic, chopped
TO SERVE
1in (2.5cm) piece of cucumber, finely diced • juice of ½ lime
2 tbsp chopped fresh mint • naan bread

1 Cut the chicken breasts into bite-sized pieces. Mix together the paste and half of the yogurt and use to coat the chicken. Cover and chill for at least 30 minutes, or overnight, if possible.

2 Heat the oil in a pan and cook the onion and garlic until softened and lightly browned. Add the marinated chicken and cook for about 15 minutes, until the chicken is tender and cooked through.

3 Mix the remaining yogurt with the cucumber, lime juice, and chopped mint. Serve with the chicken, accompanied by Chickpea Dal (*see page 106*), rice, and the warmed naan bread.

Poached Salmon in Aspic

THE PERFECT DISH FOR SUMMER BUFFET CELEBRATIONS, THIS IS ONE OF THE FEW CLASSIC RECIPES THAT IS MUCH EASIER TO MAKE THAN IT LOOKS.

SERVES 8

1 fresh salmon weighing about 5lb (2.5kg)
1 bottle white wine • 1 shallot, sliced
1 lemon, cut into 4 segments • 1 bay leaf • 2 celery stalks,
cut into large chunks • 8 white peppercorns • 2 tbsp parsley stems

FOR THE LIME MAYONNAISE

⅔ cup (150ml) mayonnaise • grated zest and juice of 1 lime
4 tbsp chopped fresh mixed herbs, such as parsley,
tarragon, chervil, and dill

TO COMPLETE

¾oz (20g) package gelatin • 1 cucumber, halved and thinly sliced
flat-leaf parsley, to garnish

1 Cut the fish in half just in front of the large fin on the top of its back. Put both halves in a large roasting pan. Add the white wine and enough water just to cover the salmon. Scatter the shallot slices, lemon segments, bay leaf, celery, peppercorns, and parsley over the fish. Cover the fish tightly with a large sheet of foil.

2 Put the roasting pan on the stove and slowly bring the liquid to a boil, about 10 minutes. Simmer for 5 minutes, then remove from the heat. The salmon will continue to cook as it cools in the liquid.

3 Carefully remove the salmon from the pan. Strain and reserve the liquid. Peel away the skin from the sides of the fish. Carefully remove the fillets from the bone and set aside. (Don't worry if the fillets fall apart–the fish will be stuck together with the mayonnaise.)

4 Beat together all the ingredients for the mayonnaise. Use it to put the boned fish back together again, then chill. Use the reserved liquid to make the gelatin according to package directions. Chill until it just starts to set.

5 Brush the salmon with a layer of gelatin. Arrange the cucumber slices down the sides of the fish to look like scales. Brush with more layers of gelatin, then chill for up to 6 hours. Garnish with flat-leaf parsley just before serving.

VARIATION

COULIBIAC: Another summer celebration salmon dish that is very easy to serve and popular at buffets.

★ Cook a 1lb (500g) salmon fillet as described above. Divide 1lb (500g) puff pastry in half. Roll one portion 1in (2.5cm) larger than the salmon fillet and the other 2in (5cm) larger than the fillet. Put the salmon on the smaller piece of pastry.

★ Sprinkle the salmon with ⅓ cup (75g) cooked long grain rice, ⅓ cup (75g) finely chopped spinach, and 4 sliced hard-boiled eggs.

★ Brush the rim of the pastry with a little beaten egg yolk and place the remaining piece on top, pressing the edges together to seal. Use any pastry trimmings to make scales.

★ Bake in a 425°F (220°C) preheated oven for 30 minutes. Serve with the lime mayonnaise.

Seared Tuna

QUICK AND EASY TO PREPARE, THIS DISH IS A TASTY OPTION FOR AN IMPROMPTU GATHERING.

2 medium-sized tuna steaks • 2 sprigs rosemary
1 tbsp olive oil • salt and freshly ground black pepper

1 Preheat a skillet. Rinse the tuna steaks, pat dry, then make tiny slits in the flesh. Break off small pieces of rosemary and gently press them into the slits. Brush the steaks on both sides with the oil and season with salt and black pepper.

2 Cook the tuna steaks for about 3 minutes on each side, or according to taste. The tuna should be sealed on the outside but still pink on the inside. Serve with steamed vegetables.

LAMB BURGERS

THESE ARE VERY EASY TO MAKE. REPLACE THE LAMB
WITH TOFU FOR A VEGETARIAN ALTERNATIVE.

SERVES 8

2lb (1kg) ground lamb • 1 tbsp mint jelly • 1 clove garlic, crushed
1 shallot, finely chopped • salt and freshly ground black pepper
FOR THE SAUCES
1 large red onion, chopped • 2 tbsp olive oil
¾lb (375g) mushrooms, chopped
1¼ cups (300ml) heavy cream • 1 tbsp flour
TO SERVE
8 sesame seed rolls • 8 tbsp relish • salad greens

1 Mix together the ground lamb, mint jelly, garlic, and
shallot and season with salt and pepper. Divide the
mixture into 8 pieces and pat into rounds. Cook under
a hot broiler or on a grill for 5 minutes on each side.

2 To make the sauce, cook the onion in the oil until
softened, then add the mushrooms and simmer until
all the liquid from the mushrooms has evaporated. Blend
the cream with the flour, add to the pan, and mix well.
Simmer the sauce for 5 minutes or until thickened.

3 Split the rolls. Put 1 tablespoon relish on the bottom
half of each roll and add greens. Top with the burger,
spoon the sauce over it, then add the top half of the roll.

MONKFISH &
BACON KABOBS

MONKFISH HAS WONDERFULLY FIRM FLESH, MAKING
IT IDEAL FOR THREADING ON KABOB SKEWERS. WRAP
THE FISH IN BACON TO KEEP IT MOIST AND FULL OF
FLAVOR. YOU WILL NEED 12 SKEWERS.

SERVES 6

½lb (250g) bacon • 3 tbsp sun-dried tomato paste
1½lb (750g) monkfish fillets, cubed • 6 large shallots, quartered
12 black olives • 2 tbsp olive oil • a few sprigs of thyme
salt and freshly ground black pepper

1 If using wooden skewers, soak them in water for
15 minutes. Preheat the broiler. Lay the bacon slices
on a board and spread thin with the tomato paste.
Wrap each monkfish cube in a bacon slice and thread
onto the skewers, alternating with the pieces of shallot.
Thread a black olive on the end of each skewer.

2 Mix the oil and thyme together and season with
salt and freshly ground black pepper. Brush over the
kabobs and broil for 2–3 minutes on each side, brushing
with more of the flavored oil as necessary.

Molasses Glazed Ham

SERVE WITH ZUCCHINI WITH GARLIC (PAGE 107) OR
POMMES DAUPHINOIS (PAGE 106).

SERVES 8

4lb (2kg) unsmoked country ham • 2 onions, halved
about 35 whole cloves • 3 bay leaves
10 peppercorns • 2½ cups (600ml) apple cider

FOR THE GLAZE

4 tbsp butter • 4 tbsp molasses • a few whole cloves

FOR THE CRANBERRY SAUCE

3 cups (350g) fresh or frozen cranberries
¾ cup (175g) superfine sugar • grated zest and juice of 2 clementines
2 tbsp Cointreau or orange liqueur • 1 tbsp red currant jelly

1 Soak the ham in cold water for about 6 hours, then drain.
Place it in a large pan with the onions, 5 cloves, the bay
leaves, and the peppercorns. Add the cider and enough
water to cover the ham. Slowly bring to a boil. Cover and
simmer for 2 hours. Preheat the oven to 425°F (220°C).

2 For the glaze, melt the butter and molasses in a pan.
Drain the ham, peel off the skin, and score the fat
in a criss-cross pattern with a sharp knife. Place in a
roasting pan and stud with the cloves. Brush with the
glaze and bake for 25–30 minutes, or until crisp.

3 Meanwhile, bring all the ingredients for the cranberry
sauce to a boil and simmer for 20 minutes, stirring
occasionally. Serve the ham with the cranberry sauce.

Boeuf en Croûte

THIS IS THE PERFECT DISH TO SERVE ON NEW YEAR'S
EVE. IT CAN BE MADE IN ADVANCE, IT LOOKS
SPECTACULAR, AND IT TASTES DIVINE.

SERVES 8

2 tbsp olive oil • 3lb (1.5kg) fillet of beef
13oz (400g) store-bought puff pastry • beaten egg yolk, to glaze
flat-leaf parsley, to garnish

FOR THE STUFFING

2 tbsp butter • ¼lb (100g) mushrooms, finely chopped
2 cloves garlic, crushed • 2 tbsp chopped fresh parsley
salt and freshly ground black pepper

1 Preheat the oven to 425°F (220°C). Heat the oil in a large skillet. Add the meat and brown on all sides for about 10 minutes. Transfer to a roasting pan and bake for 20 minutes. Let cool.

2 For the stuffing, add the butter to the skillet and heat until foaming. Add the mushrooms and garlic and cook for 5 minutes or until the mushrooms are soft. Remove from the heat and stir in the parsley and seasoning.

3 Roll the pastry into a rectangle large enough to wrap around the beef. Spread the mushroom mixture down the center of the pastry and put the beef on top.

4 Brush the edges of the pastry with the beaten egg yolk. Fold the long pastry edges over the beef. Turn the beef over, transfer to a baking sheet, and tuck under the ends of the pastry. Brush liberally with beaten egg to glaze.

5 Bake in the hot oven for 30–40 minutes. Remove from the oven and let stand for 10 minutes. Garnish with flat-leaf parsley before serving.

THAI GREEN CURRY

SERVES 8

FOR THE CURRY PASTE

4 green chilies, halved and seeded • 2 stalks lemongrass, sliced
3 shallots, peeled and halved • 4 cloves garlic
½in (1cm) piece of galangal (Thai ginger) or fresh ginger, peeled
grated zest of 1 lemon • 1 tsp coriander
1 tsp ground cumin • 1 tsp shrimp paste

TO COMPLETE

1¾ cups (400ml) coconut milk • 8 chicken cutlets, skinned
8oz (225g) canned bamboo shoots • 2 tbsp Thai fish sauce
2 tbsp dark brown sugar • 1 red and 1 green chili, seeded
and cut into strips • 2 tbsp chopped fresh cilantro

1 Blend all the paste ingredients together in a food processor until smooth. In a large pan, bring half the coconut milk to a boil, then simmer until reduced by half. Add the paste and simmer for 5 minutes longer.

2 Slice the chicken and add to the skillet with the remaining coconut milk, bamboo shoots, fish sauce, and dark brown sugar. Stir well and simmer for 10 minutes or until the chicken is tender. Garnish with strips of red and green chili and the cilantro. Serve with Turmeric Pilaf (page 106).

BONED STUFFED TURKEY

DON'T SERVE TURKEY JUST ON HOLIDAYS–IT MAKES GOOD PARTY FARE ALL YEAR. TO MAKE CARVING EASY, ASK YOUR BUTCHER TO BONE THE TURKEY.

SERVES 8

11lb (5kg) turkey, breast bones removed, legs intact
salt and freshly ground black pepper • 2 tbsp butter

FOR THE STUFFING

1 large onion, chopped • 2 tbsp olive oil
½lb (250g) bacon, chopped • 2½ cups (250g) fresh white bread crumbs
2 tbsp chopped fresh thyme • 2 tbsp chopped fresh parsley
grated zest of 2 lemons • 1 medium egg, beaten

1 Preheat the oven to 375°F (190°C). Spread the turkey out on a work surface and season liberally with salt and freshly ground black pepper.

2 For the stuffing, cook the onion in the oil until softened but not browned. Mix with all the remaining stuffing ingredients and pack neatly into the center cavity of the bird. Using skewers and, if you have one, a trussing needle, carefully reshape the bird and tie securely.

3 Place the turkey in a large roasting pan. Smear with the butter and season with plenty of salt and freshly ground black pepper. Cover with a sheet of buttered foil. Roast the turkey for 4½ hours–allowing 25 minutes per pound plus 25 minutes, or until the juices from the thickest part of the thigh run clear when pierced with a fork. Remove the foil for the last 25 minutes of the cooking time to allow the turkey to brown.

4 Remove the bird from the oven, cover tightly with foil, and let stand for 15 minutes to make carving easier or, if serving cold, let cool.

VARIATION

If you would rather not bone and stuff the turkey, fill its cavity with onions, halved lemons, and a small bunch of thyme. Cook as above. Shape the stuffing into small balls and cook around the turkey for the last 25 minutes of the cooking time.

VEGETABLES & SALADS

ATTRACTIVE, NUTRITIOUS, AND DELICIOUS, VEGETABLES LIE AT THE HEART OF ANY SUCCESSFUL PARTY MEAL. ENRICH YOUR MENUS WITH AN EXCITING MIX OF THESE TASTY MAIN COURSE VEGETABLE DISHES AND ACCOMPANIMENTS.

TUSCAN BEAN SALAD

TO SAVE TIME SOAKING AND COOKING DRIED BEANS, BUY THE CANNED VARIETIES. THIS SALAD CAN ALSO BE SERVED WARM WITH SMOKED SAUSAGE AS A QUICK SUPPER-PARTY DISH.

SERVES 8

15oz (475g) canned cannellini beans, rinsed and drained
15oz (475g) canned flageolet beans, rinsed and drained
15oz (475g) canned black-eyed peas, rinsed and drained
1 cup (150g) black olives • basil leaves, to garnish

FOR THE DRESSING

1 tbsp red wine vinegar • 6 tbsp (90ml) extra-virgin olive oil
2 tbsp Parmesan, grated • small bunch basil
salt and freshly ground black pepper

1 In one large serving bowl or several smaller ones – depending on table size and location–mix together the drained beans and olives.

2 Blend the vinegar, oil, and Parmesan in a food processor. Add the leaves from the basil and process again. Season with salt and black pepper to taste.

3 Drizzle the dressing over the beans and olives and toss to coat. Scatter small basil leaves over the dish just before serving.

MINTED POTATO SALAD

THIS CAN BE SERVED HOT OR COLD AND IS AN IDEAL ACCOMPANIMENT TO LAMB AND CHICKEN DISHES.

SERVES 8

2lb (1kg) small new potatoes • 2 sprigs mint

FOR THE DRESSING

4 tbsp mayonnaise • 4 tbsp plain yogurt
3 tbsp chopped fresh mint leaves • 2 tbsp capers, rinsed and drained
salt and freshly ground black pepper

1 Put the potatoes in a saucepan and cover with cold water. Add a little salt and the sprigs of mint. Bring to a boil, then simmer for 12–15 minutes or until the potatoes are cooked. Drain and discard the mint.

2 Meanwhile blend the dressing ingredients in a food processor. Once smooth, season with salt and pepper.

3 Toss the warm potatoes in the dressing. Serve warm or let cool.

ARUGULA SALAD

SERVES 6

8oz (250g) arugula • 3 tbsp walnut oil
2 tbsp olive oil • 2 tbsp red wine vinegar
2 tsp grainy mustard • ½ tsp superfine sugar
1 cup (125g) walnut halves

Place the arugula in a bowl. Whisk the oils, vinegar, mustard, and sugar together to make a dressing, then toss with the greens. Serve sprinkled with the walnut halves.

ANTIPASTO PASTA SALAD

SERVES 4

8oz (250g) fusilli • ½lb (275g) roasted peppers in oil, drained
1 cup (100g) pitted black olives • 4 sun-dried tomatoes, quartered
¼lb (100g) Roquefort cheese, crumbled • 10 slices salami
mixed salad greens

FOR THE DRESSING

4 tbsp oil from the peppers • 4 tbsp white wine vinegar
2 tbsp chopped fresh oregano • 2 cloves garlic, crushed
salt and freshly ground black pepper

1 Cook the pasta in a large pot of boiling water, according to the package directions. Drain, then rinse with cold water.

2 Cut the peppers into long, fine strips. Mix together the peppers, olives, tomatoes, and cheese. Stir in the pasta and salami and mix well.

3 Divide the salad greens among four glass bowls and spoon the pasta salad over them. Whisk together all the ingredients for the dressing and divide among the bowls. Serve at once.

PESTO COUSCOUS SALAD

THIS SALAD CAN BE MADE QUICKLY USING MOSTLY PANTRY INGREDIENTS.

SERVES 8

2½ cups (450g) instant couscous • ½ cup (125g) fresh pesto
4oz (125g) sun-dried peppers in oil, drained and sliced
4oz (125g) grilled eggplant, drained and sliced
salt and freshly ground black pepper • basil leaves, to garnish

1 Put the couscous in a heatproof bowl. Cover with boiling water and let stand for 5 minutes, or until the liquid has been absorbed and the couscous is tender.

2 Stir the pesto into the couscous to color it evenly. Fold in the peppers and eggplant, then season with salt and black pepper to taste. Spoon into a serving dish and garnish with basil leaves just before serving.

STIR-FRIED GREEN VEGETABLES

SERVES 6

2 tbsp peanut oil • 3 scallions, trimmed and quartered
1 green pepper, seeded and thinly sliced • ¼lb (125g) savoy cabbage, thinly shredded • ¼lb (125g) snow peas, trimmed and halved
½ cup (60g) bean sprouts • 1 tbsp Thai green curry paste

1 Heat the peanut oil in a wok or large skillet until very hot. Add the scallions and green pepper and cook for about 3 minutes. Add the cabbage and snow peas and stir for another 2 minutes.

2 Stir in the bean sprouts, then add the Thai green curry paste. Continue to stir until the sauce starts to bubble and the vegetables are well flavored. Serve immediately.

CHICKPEA DAL

SERVE THIS DISH WITH CURRIES AND OTHER SPICY
FOOD. AS AN ALTERNATIVE TO CHICKPEAS, USE YELLOW
OR ORANGE SPLIT PEAS, COOKED ACCORDING TO
PACKAGE DIRECTIONS.

SERVES 8

2 tbsp sunflower oil or ghee • 1 medium onion, finely chopped
1 tsp coriander • 1 tsp garam masala • 1 tsp turmeric
large pinch of hot chili powder • large pinch of salt
3 cups (800g) cooked chickpeas • 2 tbsp chopped fresh cilantro

1 Heat the oil or ghee in a large pan, add the onion,
and cook for about 3 minutes. Add the spices and salt
to the pan and cook, stirring constantly, for 1–2 minutes,
until the spices begin to release their aromas.

2 Stir the chickpeas into the pan and cook for
5 minutes longer. Garnish with the chopped
fresh cilantro before serving.

TURMERIC PILAF

LONG–GRAIN RICE COOKED IN A FLAVORED STOCK
IS FIT FOR THE FINEST BANQUET. TURMERIC TURNS THE
RICE A WARM, DELICATE YELLOW.

SERVES 8

2 tbsp sunflower oil • 1 medium onion, finely chopped
2 cloves garlic, finely chopped • 2 tsp turmeric • 1 tsp ground ginger
1 tsp ground coriander • ½ tsp salt • 3¼ cups (750ml) vegetable stock
2½ cups (500g) long-grain rice • cilantro, to garnish

1 Heat the oil in a large saucepan, add the onion and
garlic, and cook for 2 minutes. Add the turmeric,
ginger, coriander, and salt and cook for 2 minutes
longer, stirring constantly. Pour the stock into the pan
and bring to a boil.

2 Add the rice to the pan. Cover and simmer for
15 minutes, or until the rice is tender and the
liquid has been absorbed. Serve in a warm dish,
garnished with cilantro.

POMMES DAUPHINOIS

SERVES 8

melted butter, to grease dish
2lb (1kg) waxy potatoes, peeled and thinly sliced
2 medium onions, thinly sliced • 4 tbsp butter, cubed
salt and freshly ground black pepper • 1¼ cups (300ml) heavy cream
2 cloves garlic, peeled • ½ cup (60g) Parmesan, grated
1 tbsp snipped fresh chives, to garnish

1 Preheat the oven to 350°F (180°C). Brush a large,
shallow, ovenproof dish with a little melted butter.

2 Put the potatoes in a saucepan, cover with water, and
bring to a boil. Simmer for 3 minutes, then drain.

3 When the potatoes have cooled, arrange a layer in
the bottom of the dish. Cover with a layer of onions,
then top with some butter cubes and seasoning. Repeat
this sequence until all the ingredients have been used.

4 Meanwhile, heat the cream with the garlic. When
boiling, remove it from the heat and strain over the
potatoes. Sprinkle with Parmesan. Bake for 1¼ hours, until
lightly browned. Serve garnished with the snipped chives.

CHEESY BAKED POTATOES

MAKES 6

6 medium baking potatoes • 3 tbsp extra-virgin olive oil
coarse sea salt, for sprinkling • a few sprigs of thyme
FOR THE TOPPING
3oz (90g) Gruyère cheese, grated • 3oz (90g) Red Leicester cheese, grated
salt and freshly ground black pepper • 2 tsp dry mustard

1 Preheat the oven to 350°F (180°C). Lightly prick the
skins of the potatoes, then arrange in a roasting pan.
Drizzle with the olive oil, sprinkle with sea salt, and
scatter the thyme sprigs. Bake for 1 hour or until the
potatoes are soft on the inside.

2 Remove from the oven, halve, and scoop out the flesh.
Mix the flesh with the grated cheese, season with salt,
pepper, and the dry mustard, to taste. Return the potato
to the skins and, if necessary, reheat before serving.

Roasted Sweet Potatoes

THESE BRIGHT ORANGE POTATOES MAKE A
DELICIOUS ALTERNATIVE TO ORDINARY ROASTED POTATOES.
SERVE WITH ANY ROASTED MEAT.

SERVES 8

1lb (500g) sweet potatoes • 1 tsp salt
½ cup (90g) vegetable shortening • a few sprigs rosemary

1 Preheat the oven to 425°F (220°C). Peel the potatoes
and cut into even-sized pieces. Place them in a
saucepan, cover with water, and add the salt. Bring to
a boil and cook for about 5 minutes. Drain the water
from the pan, then use a fork to score the surfaces of
the potatoes on all sides.

2 Put the shortening in a roasting pan and heat in
the oven or on the stove until it melts and begins to
bubble. Carefully add the potatoes and roast in the oven
for about 50 minutes. Turn the potatoes occasionally
to make sure they brown and crisp evenly. After
40 minutes, add the rosemary sprigs.

Zucchini with Garlic

YOU CAN ALSO TRY THIS RECIPE USING CARROTS, BRUSSELS
SPROUTS, TURNIPS, OR RUTABAGA INSTEAD OF ZUCCHINI,
OR USE A SELECTION TO MAKE A TASTY VEGETABLE MEDLEY.

SERVES 8

6 tbsp (90g) butter • 1–2 cloves garlic, very thinly sliced
juice and zest of 1 small lime
1½lb (750g) small zucchini, halved and trimmed into barrel shapes
salt and freshly ground black pepper • 2 tbsp chopped fresh parsley

1 Melt the butter in a pan, add the garlic, and cook for
2 minutes. Add the lime zest and juice and, when
bubbling, add the zucchini and cook for 3–4 minutes,
or until tender.

2 Season with salt and freshly ground black pepper to
taste and serve sprinkled with the chopped parsley.

Festive Phyllo Pie

THIS RICHLY FLAVORED DISH MAKES HEARTY HOLIDAY
FARE, EITHER SERVED COLD AT A BUFFET LUNCH OR
PIPING HOT AT A FESTIVE DINNER.

SERVES 8

FOR THE FILLING
2 yellow peppers • 2 green peppers • 2 red peppers
2 tbsp butter • 2 medium leeks, trimmed and sliced
10oz (300g) mushrooms, trimmed and sliced
2 cloves garlic, chopped • ½lb (250g) Gruyère cheese, thinly sliced
2 tbsp chopped fresh parsley • salt and freshly ground black pepper
FOR THE PASTRY
10oz (300g) phyllo pastry, thawed if frozen • 2 tbsp butter, melted
TO GARNISH
½ each yellow, green, and red pepper

1 Preheat the oven to 400°F (200°C). Arrange all the
peppers on the rack of a broiler pan and cook under
a hot broiler, turning occasionally until the skins blacken
on all sides. Carefully transfer the peppers to paper bags
and let cool. Take the peppers from the bags and peel,
core, seed, and quarter them.

2 Melt the butter in a pan and cook the leeks for about
5 minutes, until softened. Remove from the pan and
set aside. Add the sliced mushrooms and garlic and cook
for 5 minutes longer, or until the liquid has evaporated.

3 Use two thirds of the phyllo pastry to line a 10in
(25cm) round springform pan. Brush the pastry
with melted butter.

4 Layer the peppers, leeks, mushrooms, and cheese
in the pastry shell, sprinkling each layer with the
parsley, salt, and pepper.

5 Cover the top of the pie with strips of the remaining
phyllo and brush with a little more melted butter.
Bake the pie for about 20 minutes or until golden.
Remove the sides of the pan and return the pie to the
oven briefly to brown the sides lightly.

6 Meanwhile, prepare the pepper halves for the garnish
as in step 1. Cut holly leaf shapes from the peppers
and use to garnish the pie before serving.

DESSERTS & CAKES

THESE DELICIOUS CONFECTIONS DO TAKE MORE TIME TO CREATE THAN
OTHER RECIPES IN THE BOOK, BUT NO PARTY IS COMPLETE WITHOUT THEM.
THE TRICK IS TO MAKE THEM A DAY, A WEEK, OR EVEN A MONTH IN ADVANCE.

HAZELNUT MERINGUE CAKE

THIS CAKE CAN BE MADE SHAPED LIKE A GHOST FOR
A HALLOWEEN PARTY. CREATE THE GHOST'S EYES AND
MOUTH FROM LICORICE OR BLACK–TINTED ICING.

MAKES ONE 8IN (20CM) CAKE

4 medium egg whites • 1 cup (250g) superfine sugar
1 cup (125g) hazelnuts, toasted and chopped

TO COMPLETE

3 tbsp sugar • 12 hazelnuts • 1¼ cups (300ml) heavy cream
2 tbsp confectioner's sugar • 2 tbsp strong black coffee
sifted confectioner's sugar • sifted cocoa powder

1 Preheat the oven to 225°F (110°C). Line three baking
sheets with baking parchment, each marked with an
8in (20cm) circle, or ghost shape.

2 Beat the egg whites with an electric mixer until stiff
but not dry. With the mixer running, add the sugar
1 tablespoon at a time, making sure the mixture is stiff
before adding more sugar. When all the sugar has been
added, the mixture will be stiff and shiny. Fold in the nuts.

3 Divide the mixture among the marked shapes
and spread flat. Bake for about 3 hours, or until the
meringues are crisp and dry. Let cool.

4 Heat the granulated sugar in a pan with 1 tablespoon
water until it has dissolved and browned. Add the
hazelnuts and stir to coat evenly. Transfer the coated
hazelnuts to a lightly oiled surface and let cool.

5 Lightly whip the cream with the confectioner's sugar
and coffee. Use the flavored cream to sandwich the
meringues together. Arrange the caramel-coated hazelnuts
on top. Serve dusted with confectioner's sugar and cocoa.

CHOCOLATE TART

SERVES 8

FOR THE PASTRY

2 cups (250g) all-purpose flour • 1 stick (125g) butter, diced
½ cup (60g) confectioner's sugar, sifted • 1 medium egg, beaten

FOR THE FILLING

10oz (300g) semisweet chocolate, chopped
½ cup plus 1 tbsp (150g) unsalted butter • ½ cup (80ml) heavy cream

TO SERVE

sifted confectioner's sugar • sifted cocoa powder
¾ cup (150ml) heavy cream, lightly whipped

1 Sift the flour into a bowl, then rub in the butter until
the flour has the texture of coarse bread crumbs. Mix
in the confectioner's sugar, then stir in the egg. Add a little
ice water, if necessary, to form a soft but not sticky pastry.
Cover and chill for about 15 minutes.

2 Preheat the oven to 375°F (190°C). Roll out the pastry
on a lightly floured surface and use it to line
a 10in (25cm) tart pan. Prick the base and chill for
15 minutes. Line the pastry crust with scrunched foil and
bake for 10 minutes. Discard the foil and return the
pastry to the oven for 5 minutes longer.

3 Meanwhile, put the chopped chocolate, butter, and
cream in a heatproof bowl. Set the bowl over a pan
of simmering water. Heat the mixture until the chocolate
melts, stirring frequently to make sure the ingredients
blend together.

4 Remove the bowl from the heat and stir the mixture
until it begins to cool and thicken. Pour the mixture
into the baked pastry crust and let set. Serve sprinkled
with sifted confectioner's sugar and cocoa powder.
Accompany each slice of tart with a little whipped cream.

CHOCOLATE ROULADE

THE MARVELOUS THING ABOUT THIS RICH DESSERT IS THAT IT CAN BE MADE, FILLED, AND FROZEN FOR UP TO A MONTH BEFORE SERVING.

SERVES 8

FOR THE SPONGE CAKE

4 medium eggs, separated • ⅔ cup (150g) superfine sugar
2 tbsp all-purpose flour, sifted • 2 tbsp cocoa powder, sifted
2½oz (75g) semisweet chocolate, melted
sifted confectioner's sugar

FOR THE FILLING

1¾ cups (450ml) heavy cream • 2½oz (75g) semisweet chocolate, melted

1 Preheat the oven to 350°F (180°C). Grease and line a jelly roll pan measuring 8in x 12in (20cm x 30cm). Beat the egg yolks and half the sugar with an electric mixer until pale and thick, about 5 minutes. Fold in the flour, cocoa powder, and melted chocolate.

2 Beat the egg whites until stiff, gradually adding the remaining sugar. Fold the egg whites into the chocolate mixture. Spread the cake mixture into the prepared pan and bake for 20 minutes or until well risen and springy to the touch. Cover with a damp dish towel, then let cool.

3 Turn the sponge cake out onto a sheet of waxed paper dusted with confectioner's sugar. Stir ½ cup (150ml) of the heavy cream into the melted chocolate and whisk until thick. Spread the chocolate mixture over the roulade. Whip the remaining cream and spread it over the chocolate mixture.

4 Use the waxed paper to help you roll up the roulade. The roulade will crack as it rolls. Cover and chill for up to 12 hours before serving, or freeze for up to one month.

RICH CHOCOLATE CHEESECAKE

SERVES 8

13oz (400g) chocolate wafers • ½ cup (100g) butter
sifted confectioner's sugar

FOR THE FILLING

8oz (250g) semisweet chocolate • ½ cup (150ml) sour cream
3 medium eggs • ½ cup (125g) superfine sugar
1¼lb (625g) cream cheese, softened

1 Preheat the oven to 350°F (180°C). Finely crush the chocolate wafers in a food processor. Melt the butter in a pan and stir in the crushed cookies. Spoon into a 9in (23cm) springform pan and press down on the bottom of the pan. Chill while preparing the filling.

2 Break the chocolate into pieces and melt in a bowl placed over a pan of simmering water. Remove from the heat and stir in the sour cream. Beat the eggs and sugar until pale and thick. Blend in the softened cream cheese, then fold in the chocolate mixture.

3 Pour the mixture over the cookie layer and bake for 1½ hours or until firm to the touch. Let cool in the pan. Remove the sides of the pan and transfer the cheesecake to a flat serving plate. Sprinkle liberally with sifted confectioner's sugar.

TIRAMISU

SERVES 4

4oz (125g) vanilla wafers • 4 tbsp strong black coffee
4 tbsp coffee liqueur • 1¼ cups (300ml) crème Anglaise
8oz (250g) mascarpone cheese
1¼ cups (300ml) heavy cream, lightly whipped • sifted cocoa powder

1 Divide the cookies among four glass dishes. Pour the black coffee and coffee liqueur over the cookies.

2 Pour a layer of crème Anglaise over the cookies. Beat together the mascarpone and cream and smooth it down over the mixture. Chill for at least one hour. Serve dusted with cocoa powder.

MINI BAKED ALASKA

THIS GREAT DESSERT CAN BE PREPARED WELL IN ADVANCE.
ADD THE MERINGUE AND BAKE JUST BEFORE SERVING.

SERVES 8

FOR THE BASE

3 medium eggs • ¼ cup (75g) superfine sugar
4 tbsp all-purpose flour, sifted • 1 tbsp cocoa powder, sifted

FOR THE ICE CREAM

⅓ cup (60g) golden raisins • 6 tbsp (90ml) brandy
14fl oz (400ml) crème Anglaise • 1½ cups (600ml) heavy cream

FOR THE MERINGUE

6 medium egg whites • 1¼ cups (350g) superfine sugar

1 To make the sponge cake base, first preheat the
oven to 375°F (190°C). Grease and line a jelly roll pan
measuring 8in x 12in (20cm x 30cm). Use an electric
mixer to beat the eggs with the sugar until thick and
pale, about 5 minutes.

2 Sift the flour and cocoa powder together and
carefully fold into the egg mixture. Pour into the
prepared pan and bake for about 12 minutes or until
risen. Turn out onto a wire rack and cool. Cut out
8 rounds using a 3in (7.5cm) diameter ramekin.

3 Put the raisins into a small bowl and pour the brandy
over them. Let stand for about 1 hour. Meanwhile,
stir the crème Anglaise and heavy cream together, then
freeze until firm. Fold the raisins and brandy into the
custard mixture and freeze until solid, about 2 hours.

4 Preheat the oven to 425°F (220°C). Place the sponge
rounds on a large baking tray and put a large scoop
of the ice cream on top of each one. Put the tray in the
freezer while preparing the meringue.

5 Beat the egg whites until stiff. Gradually beat in the
superfine sugar. Swirl or pipe the meringue onto the
ice cream and sponge cake, covering them completely.
Bake for 5–7 minutes, then serve immediately.

VARIATION

MINCEMEAT CHRISTMAS BOMBE: In step 3, stir 4oz (125g)
vegetarian mincemeat and 2 tablespoons of brandy into
the ice cream mixture and freeze in a 1 quart (1 liter) mold
lined with plastic wrap. Follow the recipe as instructed.

PLUM PUDDING

SERVES 8

½lb (250g) pitted prunes, chopped • ½lb (250g) raisins
½lb (250g) golden raisins • 1 cup (275ml) brown ale • 2 tbsp molasses
9 tbsp (75g) all-purpose flour • 1 tsp ground mixed spice
6oz (175g) shredded vegetarian suet • 3 cups (175g) bread crumbs
1 cup (250g) dark brown sugar • ½ cup (60g) slivered almonds
1 apple, peeled, cored, and grated • grated zest and juice of 1 orange
2 medium eggs, beaten

TO COMPLETE

4 tbsp brandy • sifted confectioner's sugar
brandy butter and cream, to serve

1 Put the dried fruit in a bowl, pour the brown ale over
it, then stir in the molasses. Cover the bowl with
plastic wrap and let stand overnight.

2 Mix the flour, mixed spice, suet, bread crumbs, sugar,
almonds, and apple. Fold the fruit mixture into the flour.
Add the orange zest and juice and eggs and mix well.

3 Spoon the mixture into a greased 2 quart (2 liter)
pudding mold. Cover with greased waxed paper and
foil, then tie securely with string.

4 Place the pudding in a covered pan containing
1in (2.5cm) of boiling water and steam for 6 hours,
adding more boiling water as necessary. Allow to cool,
then wrap in fresh waxed paper.

5 Before serving, steam for a further 4 hours before
turning out onto a warmed serving plate.

6 To flame the pudding, pour a little warmed brandy
around the base of the pudding, dust with
confectioner's sugar, and light with a match. Serve with
brandy butter (below) and cream.

BRANDY BUTTER

¾ cup (175g) butter, softened • 1½ cups (175g) confectioner's sugar
2 tbsp brandy

Beat together the softened butter and the sugar until pale
and light. Gradually blend in the brandy. Spoon into a
serving dish, cover, and chill until ready to serve.

POACHED PEACHES

Stored in airtight jars, poached peaches make an ideal dessert for picnics.

MAKES ONE JAR

1 bottle dessert wine • ¼ cup (60g) superfine sugar
thinly grated zest of 1 orange • 3 whole cloves
1 cinnamon stick, halved • 8 ripe but firm peaches

1 Pour the wine into a shallow pan, then add the sugar, orange zest, cloves, and cinnamon. Heat gently until the sugar has dissolved, then add ¾ cup (150ml) water.

2 Add the peaches to the pan and cover with a circle of baking parchment. Cook gently for about 30 minutes, or until the peaches are tender.

3 Carefully transfer the peaches to a sterilized, sealable jar and cover with the liquid. Seal and allow to cool.

PEACH MELBA TRIFLE

SERVES 8

½lb (250g) ladyfingers • 6 peaches, peeled, pitted, and sliced
1 cup (250g) raspberries • ½ cup (150ml) medium dry sherry
14fl oz (400ml) crème Anglaise

FOR THE TOPPING

2½ cups (600ml) heavy cream • grated zest of 1 orange
6 tbsp (90ml) brandy • 2 tbsp superfine sugar
2 tbsp sliced almonds, toasted

1 Line the bottom of a large glass bowl with the ladyfingers. Arrange the sliced peaches on top. Sprinkle the raspberries over the peaches and add the sherry. Cover and set aside for at least 3 hours.

2 Put the crème Anglaise over the fruit. Beat the cream, orange zest, brandy, and sugar until stiff. Spoon it over the crème Anglaise. Cover and chill for up to 12 hours. Sprinkle with the almonds just before serving.

VARIATION

WINTER TRIFLE: Replace the peaches with ½lb (250g) dried apricots soaked in ½ cup (150ml) brandy. Omit the sherry and raspberries. Melt ⅓ cup (100g) strawberry jam and pour it over the apricots. Continue as instructed.

RICOTTA TART WITH SEASONAL FRUIT

THIS CLASSIC ITALIAN TART IS IDEAL TO SERVE AT PICNICS OR BUFFET PARTIES WITH FRESH FIGS OR SEASONAL FRUIT.

SERVES 8

1 batch pastry (see Chocolate Tart, page 108)
3 fresh figs, quartered, or seasonal fruit, to decorate

FOR THE FILLING

1lb (500g) ricotta cheese • 4 medium eggs, separated
½ cup (100g) superfine sugar • grated zest of 1 lemon
¾ cup (175g) dried fruits such as cranberries,
mangoes, or peaches, chopped • 2 tbsp all-purpose flour

1 Preheat the oven to 375°F (190°C). Roll out the pastry on a lightly floured work surface and use it to line an 8in (20cm), deep fluted tart pan. Line with scrunched foil and bake blind for 10 minutes. Remove the foil and return to the oven for 10 minutes longer.

2 Meanwhile, beat together the ricotta, egg yolks, sugar, lemon zest, dried fruits, and flour. Whip the egg whites until stiff, then fold them in using a large metal spoon. Spoon the mixture into the pastry shell and bake for 1 hour or until golden and set. Let cool before serving.

VARIATIONS

TARTE AU CITRON: Prepare and bake the pastry shell as above. Stir together 1 cup (250g) sugar and 2 tablespoons cornstarch in a heatproof bowl. Gradually mix in the grated zest and juice of 2 lemons and 7 tablespoons (100g) butter.

★ Set the bowl over a pan of simmering water and stir until the butter and sugar have melted. When the mixture begins to thicken, remove it from the heat.

★ Beat 3 medium eggs into the mixture and return it to the heat for 3 minutes. Pour the lemon mixture into the pastry shell. Bake at 375°F (190°C) for 20 minutes or until the lemon custard has almost set.

★ Let cool in the pan for about 10 minutes before transferring to a serving plate. Serve dusted with confectioner's sugar and decorated with a few raspberries.

PECAN PIES: Line the 8in (20cm) tart pan or six individual 4in (10cm) tartlet pans and bake blind as instructed above.

★ Divide 3 cups (400g) pecans between the pastry shells.

★ Mix together 2 tablespoons melted butter, 1 cup (175g) light brown sugar, 4 medium eggs, ¾ cup (175ml) golden syrup, and ½ cup (30g) all-purpose flour. Pour into the pans and bake for 45 or 30 minutes, respectively.

SUMMER BERRY TARTS

MAKES 16

1 batch pastry (see Chocolate Tart, page 108)

CRÈME PATISSIÈRE

3 medium egg yolks • ½ cup (100g) superfine sugar
2 tbsp cornstarch • 1¼ cups (300ml) milk

FOR THE TOPPING

4 cups (450g) mixed summer berries, such as strawberries, blueberries,
and raspberries • 4 tbsp red currant jelly

1 Preheat the oven to 375°F (190°C). Divide the pastry into 16 pieces. Roll out the pieces on a lightly floured surface and use them to line 3in (7.5cm) tart pans. Prick the bottoms and chill for 10 minutes. Line each with foil and bake blind for 5 minutes. Remove the foil and return to the oven for 5 minutes longer.

2 Whisk together the egg yolks, superfine sugar, and cornstarch with 2 tablespoons milk. Heat the remaining milk until it begins to bubble, then pour it into the egg mixture, whisking constantly.

3 Rinse out the pan and return the mixture to it. Reheat, stirring occasionally, until the mixture boils and thickens. Whisk until thick and smooth. Let cool, covered with dampened waxed paper.

4 Spoon the mixture into the cooled pastry shells. Just before serving, top the tartlets with the berries and brush with warmed red currant jelly to glaze.

TROPICAL FRUIT SALAD

SERVES 8

3 small pineapples • 2 mangoes • 2 kiwis • 2 papayas
zest and juice of 2 oranges and 1 lime • ⅔ cup (150g) superfine sugar

1 Trim and peel the pineapples and cut the flesh into wedges. Peel, pit, and slice the mangoes, and peel and slice the kiwis. Peel the papayas, discard the seeds, and then cut into slices. Mix all the fruit in a bowl.

2 Heat the juice of the oranges and the lime with the sugar. Once the sugar has dissolved, bring the mixture to a boil, then simmer for 5 minutes. Stir in the zest of one of the oranges and half the lime. Pour the syrup over the fruit and mix well. Chill, then serve.

COCONUT ICE CREAM

SERVED WITH A TROPICAL FRUIT SALAD, THIS DELICATELY
FLAVORED COCONUT ICE CREAM IS THE PERFECT DESSERT
TO COMPLEMENT SPICY FOOD.

SERVES 8

1¼ cups (300ml) milk • ⅔ cup (150ml) coconut milk
4 green cardamom pods, crushed • 2 strips lemon zest
4 medium egg yolks • ½ cup (125g) superfine sugar
1 tbsp cornstarch • 1 cup (200ml) heavy cream, lightly whipped

1 Heat the milk with the coconut milk, cardamom pods, and lemon zest until it just begins to boil. Meanwhile, whisk the egg yolks with the sugar and cornstarch until pale and light.

2 Pour the warm milk into the egg mixture and whisk together to form a custard. Rinse the pot, add the custard, and continue heating until it begins to thicken and bubble. Remove from the heat and allow to cool.

3 Strain the custard and fold in the heavy cream. Freeze in a container for 2 hours or until slushy. Whisk until smooth and return to the freezer for 2 hours longer. Whisk again, then freeze until solid.

4 Let the ice cream stand for about 10 minutes at room temperature before serving with the Tropical Fruit Salad (*see above*).

BLUEBERRY MUFFINS

MAKES 12 LARGE OR 24 SMALL MUFFINS

1½ cups (175g) all-purpose flour • ¼ cup (75g) brown sugar
1 tbsp baking powder • 1 tsp ground cinnamon • ½ tsp salt
1¼ cups (150g) fresh blueberries • ¾ cup (175ml) buttermilk
1 medium egg, beaten • ½ cup (25g) butter, melted

1 Preheat the oven to 425°F (220°C). Line a muffin pan with paper baking cups.

2 Sift together the flour, sugar, baking powder, cinnamon, and salt. Stir in the blueberries.

3 Whisk together the buttermilk, egg, and melted butter. Gradually work the liquid into the flour mixture. Spoon into the paper cups and bake for about 8–15 minutes, depending on size, or until well risen.

BONFIRE CAKES

MAKES 16

¾ cup (175g) butter, softened • 1 cup (175g) brown sugar
3 medium eggs, beaten • 1½ cups (175g) self-rising flour
½ cup (125g) raspberry jam

TO DECORATE

½ cup (125g) unsalted butter, softened • ¾ cup (200g) confectioner's
sugar, sifted • 4oz (125g) semisweet chocolate, melted

1 Preheat the oven to 375°F (190°C). Line a muffin pan with paper baking cups.

2 Cream the butter and sugar until pale and light. Gradually beat in the eggs, then sift the flour over the creamed mixture and fold in.

3 Half fill the paper cups with the cake batter. Put a little raspberry jam on top before adding the remaining cake mixture. Bake for 15–20 minutes or until risen. Let cool, then remove the paper cups.

4 To decorate, beat the butter with the confectioner's sugar and half the melted chocolate. Spread the remaining chocolate onto a clean flat surface and leave until just set. Use a knife to make chocolate curls.

5 Turn the cakes upside down and spread the chocolate icing over them. Arrange the chocolate curls on the top and sides to resemble twigs and branches on a bonfire.

GINGERBREAD

CUT OUT BEAR SHAPES FOR CHILDREN'S PARTIES AND
DECORATE WITH FACES OR USE CHRISTMAS–SHAPED
COOKIE CUTTERS TO MAKE TREE DECORATIONS.

MAKES 16

¼ cup (60g) butter, softened • ⅓ cup (125g) brown sugar
3 tbsp molasses • 1 tbsp corn syrup
½in (1cm) piece of ginger, chopped • ¼ cup (60ml) warm water
2 cups (350g) self-raising flour • 2 tsp ground ginger
½ tsp ground cinnamon

TO DECORATE

sifted confectioner's sugar • food coloring (optional)

1 Preheat the oven to 350°F (180°C). Grease 2 baking sheets with a little butter.

2 Cream the butter and sugar until pale and light. Beat in the molasses, corn syrup, and chopped ginger, then stir in the warm water.

3 Sift the flour, ground ginger, and cinnamon into the creamed mixture, then mix to form a soft dough.

4 Knead on a floured surface and roll out thinly. Cut out 16 shapes and arrange on the baking sheets. Use a skewer to make small holes for stringing, if desired. Bake for 8–10 minutes, until golden. Let cool for 3 minutes before transferring to a wire rack to cool completely.

5 Sift some confectioner's sugar into a small bowl. Add a few drops of water, and food coloring, if using, to give a smooth consistency. Use a pastry bag to pipe decorations. Let set.

PETITS FOURS

DECORATE THESE DELICIOUSLY LIGHT CAKES WITH EDIBLE
FLOWERS OR CANDIED FRUIT PEEL.

MAKES 16

1 cup (250g) butter, softened • ¼ cup (300g) superfine sugar
grated peel of 1 lemon and 1 small orange • 4 medium eggs, beaten
3 cups (300g) self-rising flour • ¼ cup (60g) cornstarch
3 tbsp milk
TO DECORATE
6 tbsp apricot jam, strained and warmed • 1½lb (750g) white marzipan
2lb (1kg) fondant icing • food coloring (optional)
crystalized flowers • candied fruit peel

1 Preheat the oven to 350°F (180°C). Butter and
line a 8in x 12in (20cm x 30cm) cake pan.

2 Cream the butter with the sugar and grated peel until
pale and light. Gradually beat in the eggs. Sift the
flour and cornstarch over the batter and fold in until just
mixed. Add the milk and stir until smooth.

3 Spoon the batter into the cake pan and bake for
about 45 minutes or until well risen and golden.
Turn out onto a wire rack and let cool.

4 Cut the cake into 16 shapes (circles, ovals, squares, or
triangles). Brush the sides and tops of the petits fours
with the warmed apricot jam. Roll out the marzipan and
use it to cover the cakes. Let dry for about 1 hour. Color
the fondant, if desired, roll it out, and use to cover the
cakes. Decorate with the crystalized flowers and fruit peel.

MINI MERINGUES

MERINGUES CAN BE MADE IN A VARIETY OF SHAPES
FOR THEMED PARTIES, SUCH AS SNOWMEN AT
CHRISTMAS OR GHOSTS FOR HALLOWEEN. THE
MERINGUES CAN BE MADE UP TO TWO WEEKS AHEAD
AND FILLED AN HOUR BEFORE SERVING.

MAKES ABOUT 20

3 medium egg whites • ¾ cup (175g) superfine sugar
FOR THE FILLING
½ cup (150ml) heavy cream • 1 tbsp superfine sugar
½ tsp vanilla extract

1 Preheat the oven to 225°F (110°C). Line 2 baking sheets
with baking parchment. If making snowmen or ghosts,
draw the shapes on the underside of the parchment.

2 Using an electric mixer, beat the egg whites until stiff.
With the mixer running, add the sugar, 1 tablespoon
at a time, making sure the mixture has thickened before
adding more. The mixture should be stiff and glossy.

3 Spoon the mixture into a pastry bag fitted with a star
or plain nozzle. Pipe the mixture into the desired
shapes. Bake for 2 hours or until the meringues are crisp
and dry. Let cool.

4 Lightly whip the cream with the sugar and vanilla
extract. Use the flavored cream to sandwich the
meringues together.

SIMPLE CUPCAKES

MAKES 16

¼ cup (100g) butter, softened • ½ cup (100g) sugar
2 medium eggs • 1 cup (100g) self-rising flour

1 Preheat the oven to 375°F (190°C). Cream the butter
and sugar together until pale and light. Beat
in the eggs, then sift in the flour and mix together.

2 Fill a muffin pan lined with paper baking cups with
the batter. Bake for 15 minutes or until golden and
risen. Let cool, then remove the paper cups, and ice with
glacé icing (*see Gingerbread, opposite*) if desired.

TRIPLE CHOC COOKIES

MAKES 20

3½oz (100g) each white, semisweet, and milk chocolate
½ cup (60g) pecans, roughly chopped • 7 tbsp (100g) butter, softened
½ cup (100g) light brown sugar • 1 medium egg, beaten
1¾ cups (225g) all-purpose flour • ½ tsp baking powder

1 Preheat the oven to 350°F (180°C). Chop the chocolate into chunks. Mix with the chopped pecans.

2 Beat the butter and sugar until light and fluffy, then gradually beat in the egg. Sift the flour and baking powder and fold into the creamed mixture. Stir in the chocolate and nuts.

3 Drop large teaspoons of the batter onto a greased baking sheet and bake for 12–15 minutes. Let cool for about a minute before transferring to a wire rack.

CHOCOLATE CAKE

MAKES ONE 8IN (20CM) ROUND CAKE

FOR THE CAKE

6 medium eggs, separated • ¾ cup (175g) superfine sugar
8oz (250g) semisweet chocolate, melted • 2 tbsp (30g) cornstarch
1 tbsp cocoa powder

TO COMPLETE

5½oz (160g) semisweet chocolate • ½ cup (100ml) crème fraîche

1 Preheat the oven to 350°F (180°C). Grease a deep 8in (20cm) round cake pan and line the bottom with waxed paper. Beat the egg yolks and half the sugar until pale and thick. Fold in the melted chocolate.

2 Beat the egg whites until stiff, gradually adding the remaining sugar. Fold the egg whites into the chocolate mixture using a large spatula. Sift together the cornstarch and cocoa powder and fold into the batter. Spoon into the prepared pan and bake for 35 minutes or until risen. Let stand for 5 minutes before turning out onto a wire rack to cool completely.

3 Melt 3½oz (100g) of the chocolate and stir in the crème fraîche. Swirl over the cooled cake. Using a vegetable peeler, make curls from the remaining chocolate and sprinkle on top of the cake. Tie a ribbon around the cake.

LUXURY FRUITCAKE

MAKES ONE 9IN (23CM) ROUND CAKE

½ cup (100ml) dark rum • ½ cup (100ml) medium-dry sherry
⅓ cup (90ml) water • 2lb (1kg) mixed dried fruit
2 tbsp ground mixed spice • 1 tbsp unrefined molasses
1 cup (225g) butter • 1½ cups (350g) light brown sugar
5 medium eggs, beaten • 2 cups (225g) self-rising flour
3½oz (100g) mixed nuts, chopped

TO COMPLETE

4 tbsp strained apricot jam, warmed • 2lb (1kg) white marzipan
1 tbsp vodka or gin • 2lb (1kg) white fondant

1 Pour the rum, sherry, and water into a pan and stir in the dried fruit, mixed spice, and molasses. Bring to a boil, then simmer for 15 minutes, stirring occasionally. Let cool.

2 Preheat the oven to 325°F (160°C), then grease and line a deep 9in (23cm) round cake pan. Cream the butter and sugar until pale and light, then gradually beat in the eggs. Sift the flour and fold it into the batter using a large spatula. Stir in the nuts, then the cooled fruit mixture and liquid.

3 Spoon the mixture into the prepared cake pan. Level the surface and make a shallow well in the center to ensure a level top once the cake is baked. Bake for 3 hours or until a skewer inserted into the center comes out clean. Let cool in the pan. Remove the lining paper and wrap in fresh waxed paper and foil. Store in a cool, dry place for up to one month. The cake can be iced up to two weeks before serving.

4 To cover the cake with marzipan, first brush the cake with the warmed apricot jam. Roll the marzipan into a round large enough to cover the top and sides of the cake. Once in position, smooth the marzipan using your hands or a spatula. Let it set for at least 1 hour.

5 Brush the marzipan with the vodka or gin. Roll the fondant into a round large enough to cover the top and sides of the cake. Carefully position it over the cake and smooth.

Madeira Cake

THE VARIATIONS THAT FOLLOW THIS CAKE RECIPE MAKE
IT PERFECT FOR SPECIAL OCCASIONS.

*1¼ cups (300g) unsalted butter • 1¼ cups (300g) brown sugar
6 medium eggs, beaten • 1½ cups (175g) self-rising flour
1½ cups (175g) all-purpose flour • ¾ cup (90g) ground almonds
grated zest and juice of 2 medium oranges*

1 Preheat the oven to 350°F (180°C). Butter and line
a deep 9in (23cm) round cake pan.

2 Cream the butter and sugar until pale and fluffy.
Gradually beat in the eggs, adding a little sifted flour
to prevent the mixture from curdling.

3 Sift the remaining flours together and add the
almonds. Fold the flour and almond mixture into
the creamed mixture with the orange zest and juice.

4 Spoon into the prepared pan and bake for 35 minutes.
Reduce the temperature to 325°F (160°C) and bake for
45 minutes longer or until a skewer inserted in the center
comes out clean. Turn out onto a wire rack to cool.

Teddy Bear

1 Cut the cake into a teddy-bear shape and use the
trimmings to make a slightly raised tummy and cheeks.
Brush the cake with a little warmed, strained apricot jam.

2 Knead 2lb (1kg) fondant icing with ¼ cup (30g) sifted
cocoa powder. When evenly colored, roll out the icing
and use to cover the cake, gently pressing the sides to
emphasize the bear shape. Mark lines on the paws. Use a
little white and black icing, tinted with food coloring, to
make eyes, a nose, and a mouth.

Ladybug

1 Cut the cake into a dome-shaped body and use the
trimmings to make a small head. Brush the cake with
a little warmed, strained apricot jam.

2 Color 1lb (500g) of fondant icing red and 4oz (125g)
black, and roll both thinly. Use the red icing to cover
the body and the black icing to make spots. Use black
trimmings to make small antennae and let them set for
about 30 minutes before attaching them to the head.

Champagne Bottle

1 Trim the cake to a fat champagne bottle shape and
brush with a little warmed, strained apricot jam.

2 Roll 1¼lb (625g) white marzipan thinly. Use to cover
the cake. Set aside for at least 1 hour. Knead 1¼lb
(625g) fondant icing and color it dark green with food
coloring. When evenly colored, roll it out and use it to
cover the cake. Roll 2oz (60g) white icing and cut a label
shape. Pipe on the recipient's name or the occasion.

3 To make champagne truffles, stir together 4oz (125g)
melted white chocolate, 3 tablespoons heavy cream,
3 tablespoons champagne, and 2oz (60g) cake crumbs. Chill
until firm. Shape into 25 balls, dip in 6oz (175g) melted
white chocolate, and let set. Arrange around the cake.

Wedding Cake

1 Double the cake ingredients and divide the mixture
between two prepared cake pans, 6in (15cm) and 9in
(23cm) in diameter. Bake for 40 minutes before turning
the oven temperature down. Cook the small cake for
25 minutes longer, the larger one for 45 minutes. Cool.

2 Cover the cakes with 8 tablespoons orange-flavored
buttercream. Roll 1½lb (750g) fondant icing thinly and
use to cover the larger cake. Roll another ¾lb (375g)
fondant icing and use to cover the smaller cake.

3 Place the small cake on top of the large cake, then
pipe a fine trail of icing around the base of each.
Decorate the cake with a garland of fresh flowers.

Christening Cake

1 Make the cake batter as instructed and spoon into a
buttered and lined 9in (23cm) petal-shaped pan. Bake
for 40 minutes, then reduce the oven temperature and
bake for 55 minutes longer. Let cool.

2 Brush the cake with warmed, strained apricot jam.
Roll 1½lb (750g) of white marzipan and use to cover
the cake. Leave for 1 hour. Knead 2¾lb (1.25kg) of fondant
icing and color, if desired. Roll and use to cover the cake.

3 Pipe the child's name on the cake using a little
decorating icing. Pipe a little more icing around the
base of the cake, if desired. Decorate with flowers cut
from 2oz (60g) fondant icing, colored as desired.

LARGE PARTIES, BALLS, AND WEDDINGS CAN NEVER BE
PLANNED TOO SOON. THE SECRET OF SUCCESS IS TO TAKE A
YEAR TO ORGANIZE A TRADITIONAL WEDDING, AND UP TO SIX MONTHS
FOR A LARGE-SCALE PARTY. WRITE A TIME PLAN AND STICK TO IT.
BOOK A VENUE EARLY – IF YOU FIND A BETTER PLACE, YOU CAN USUALLY

PLANNING
A PARTY

CANCEL A TEMPORARY BOOKING. COLLECT PICTURES, MENUS, AND
PRICE LISTS, AND ASK FRIENDS FOR RECOMMENDATIONS ON MUSIC
AND FOOD. SAMPLE FOOD BEFORE A BOOKING. LISTEN TO THE MUSIC
OR ENTERTAINMENT, EITHER LIVE OR ON TAPE, AND GIVE A
SONG LIST WELL IN ADVANCE. ABOVE ALL, DELEGATE, ASKING
FRIENDS AND FAMILY TO HELP MAKE THE DAY UNFORGETTABLE.

ESSENTIALS

TO MAKE SURE YOUR PARTY IS A

GREAT SUCCESS, THINK ABOUT

THESE BASICS FIRST.

WHEN & WHERE

Make the timing and setting of the party your first decision. Exact dates and venues can be written in later, but decide now tentatively on the time of year and kind of venue you would prefer. To increase party space at home, consider renting a tent.

BUDGET

How much you want or can afford to spend should be set firmly at the outset, and the amount adhered to. For some, food may be more important than drinks. Others may want to spend more on entertainment or the venue. Whatever your choice, bear in mind that a cocktail party is usually less expensive than a sit-down meal for a large number of people, especially if the meal involves hiring equipment and paying professional staff to help. Borrowing tables, chairs, linens, and silverware rather than renting them is a big saving. Budget is a major factor in menu planning, since it dictates what you can or cannot serve (*see opposite*).

THEME & DECOR

See pages 8–73 for numerous party theme ideas. Decide on the size of your budget, then adapt the idea to suit the occasion. Pay special attention to lighting – it can transform a dingy venue. On a big budget, seek the help of florists and party planners to bring originality and drama to a party.

GUEST LIST & NUMBERS

The length of the guest list will be dictated by the type of event you are planning and the size of your budget. Plan the list early and be flexible, allowing for a few late invitations.

★ **Ideal numbers for parties:** small party, up to 30 guests; medium party, 30–100 guests; large party, over 100.

ENTERTAINMENT

Entertainment choices are listed on page 122. To avoid disappointment, watch the entertainment live prior to booking or listen to a sample tape. Give a band or dj a music list in advance to ensure guests enjoy the music. Remember that entertainers will need a private dressing room at the venue.

FOOD & DRINK

If you are planning to use a catering company, ask friends for recommendations and consider how you would like the food and drink to be served. Options include:

★ **Buffets** allow good interaction between guests, who can circulate freely. Generally less expensive than full sit-down meals, they allow for a greater choice of food, with lots of different dishes.

★ **Seated buffets** allow a cold appetizer to be set up at the table. Some guests prefer to sit while eating.

★ **Sit-down meals** are best for formal occasions. Table-planning ensures that like-minded guests can be seated next to each other. More expensive than buffets, a sit-down meal should include at least three courses.

★ **Cocktail parties** (*see pages 8–13*) are ideal for entertaining large numbers, when it is an advantage that not everyone arrives at once and that some guests only stay half an hour. Cocktail parties generally last 2½ hours.

★ **Drinks,** both alcoholic and nonalcoholic, should be plentiful. When assessing suppliers, which may include wine merchants and supermarkets, ask if they deliver or supply glasses.

VENUE IDEAS

There are exciting party venue ideas on page 49, and a list of wedding venues on page 34. Here are more ideas to inspire:

★ **Leisure and cultural:** theater, movies, museum, amusement park, fast-food restaurant, nightclub, health club.

★ **Indoor sports:** sports club, swimming pool, bowling alley, yacht, ice-skating rink.

★ **Outdoors:** theme park, cruise, public park.

★ **With a difference:** double-decker bus, train, pier, ferry, hot-air balloon, fairground, barn, ski resort.

PLANNING

THE BIG MATTERS DECIDED,

MORE DETAILED PLANNING

CAN NOW BEGIN.

INVITATIONS

Send out invitations at least two months before a large event to allow guests time to make travel plans and arrangements. A response card, with a respond-by-date, helps guests. Make sure you state the dress code for the party on the invitation.

MENU

When planning the menu, in addition to budget, consider who is coming; whether guests are young or old; any specific dietary requirements, such as vegetarian, vegan, kosher; whether a special occasion demands specific food. Sample a menu if you are using outside caterers before confirming the booking.

★ **Plan a range** of tastes and textures. Include a varied mix of ingredients, trying not to repeat them in different dishes, and think of color and presentation, course by course. Try not to overload a meal with calories and never be too sparing with portions.

★ **Food at cocktail parties** should be bite-sized for ease of eating. Always provide cocktail napkins. Allow 10 pieces per head for a cocktail party of approximately two hours; for longer durations, allow 15-20 pieces per head.

DRINKS & GLASSES

Drinks should be ready as guests arrive. It is disastrous for a party to run out of liquor, so be sure to have an ample supply.

★ **Allow 3–4 glasses per guest.** Guests served from trays will put a glass back on the tray and take another one.

★ **Provide plenty of chilled mineral water** and soft drinks, especially in hot weather. One bottle of mineral water is approximately 5 glasses.

★ **One bottle of wine** is 5-6 glasses. Allow two thirds of a bottle of white wine and one third of red wine per guest. If only wine or champagne is being served, allow half a bottle per guest.

BUFFETS

Set buffet tables at each end of the room so guests don't all have to line up in one place. Use tables large enough to allow space for plates, cutlery, napkins, and condiments as well as the food. Avoid bottlenecks by setting buffet tables well away from the bar. To prevent a long line, invite small groups, one at a time, up to the table to get their food.

SEATING PLAN

A seating plan should combine an alphabetical list of guests and their table numbers with a numbered table plan, both positioned at the entrance to the dining area. Give someone a copy of the list to help those who cannot find their table. At a sit-down meal, choose round tables for 8, 10, or 12 guests.

★ **Have a contingency plan** for "no shows," so that if a guest at the main table does not arrive, the place can be filled by another guest.

★ **Use place cards** at formal, sit-down occasions. It is useful to have the name on both sides of the card so that guests know who is sitting opposite them.

STAFF

While you may be able to cope well using volunteers at a party at home, at an outside venue, it is best to employ professional staff. Allow one waiter per 20 guests at a cocktail party, and one per 10 at a sit-down meal. Depending on the event and venue, you will need bar, reception, coatroom, and security staff, and parking valets. Djs and bands are responsible for bringing and setting up their own equipment. At home, the kitchen should be separate from the party room so that the sounds of cleaning up are not heard.

VENUE

Use the checklists on pages 122-23 to ensure that your chosen venue and the decorations are perfect.

SCHEDULE

A schedule helps everyone know who is doing what and at what time. At home, make sure neighbors know of your plans for a party well in advance.

CHECKLISTS 3

WORK YOUR WAY THROUGH THE
FOLLOWING LISTS, CHECKING OFF
ITEMS AS YOU DEAL WITH THEM.
THEY WILL HELP MAKE ANY
PARTY, LARGE OR SMALL, GO OFF
WITHOUT A HITCH AND BECOME
AN EVENT THAT GUESTS WILL
ALWAYS REMEMBER.

FOOD & DRINK

DEPENDING ON THE NATURE OF YOUR PARTY, USE THIS
LIST TO ENSURE THAT YOU HAVE THE ESSENTIALS FOR
SERVING THE FOOD AND DRINK YOU HAVE SELECTED.

★ Sufficient tables and chairs, including buffet table, gift table, cake table, occasional tables, babies' high chairs. ❏
★ Table linens, napkins. ❏
★ China, including for tea, coffee. ❏
★ Cutlery, for three-course meals, tea, coffee. ❏
★ Condiments for savory and sweet dishes, tea, coffee. ❏
★ Serving dishes, bowls, and utensils. ❏
★ Serving dishes/stands for special foods; e.g., cakes. ❏
★ Adequate cooking, food-warming facilities. ❏
★ Glasses for alcoholic and soft drinks. ❏
★ Ice, ice bucket, and tongs. ❏
★ Cocktail shaker, stirrers, and twizzle sticks. ❏
★ Bottle openers and corkscrews. ❏
★ Serving trays and napkins. ❏
★ Fruit for decorating drinks, with knife, board. ❏
★ Refrigerator within reach of bar/serving table. ❏
★ Seating plan at entrance, if necessary. ❏

VENUE

FOR A VENUE OTHER THAN YOUR OWN HOME, USE
THIS LIST IN ADVANCE TO CHECK THE SUITABILITY OF
THE SPACE FOR THE PARTY YOU ARE PLANNING.

★ Number of guests the rooms hold. ❏
★ Availability of coatrooms, rest rooms. ❏
★ Lighting, ventilation, heating of rooms. ❏
★ Availability of cutlery, china, table linens, etc. ❏
★ Standard of catering, menus, if available. ❏
★ Use of outside caterers, florists, entertainers. ❏
★ Adequate kitchen facilities for outside caterers. ❏
★ Presence of administrative staff for advice, liaison. ❏
★ PA system for speeches. ❏
★ Possibility of bringing one's own decorations. ❏
★ Easy to reach by car or public transportation. ❏
★ Closeness, ease of parking. ❏
★ Facilities for disabled, including entrance ramps. ❏
★ State of fire alarms, emergency exits, security. ❏
★ Any other events at the venue on your date. ❏

ENTERTAINMENT

CONSIDER THESE AS POSSIBILITIES FOR MAKING YOUR
PARTY MEMORABLE. CHOOSE ENTERTAINMENT TO
COMPLEMENT AND ENHANCE THE EVENT.

★ Disco and DJ. ❏
★ Dance floor: rent if the venue's is inadequate. ❏
★ Live band/orchestra/string quartet. ❏
★ Master of Ceremonies (MC). ❏
★ Entertainers for adult parties: singer, comedian. ❏
★ Entertainers for children's parties: magician, clown. ❏
★ Informal entertainers, such as stilt-walkers, fire-eaters, magicians, jugglers, etc., moving among guests. ❏
★ Fireworks display. ❏
★ Laser show. ❏
★ Casino. ❏
★ Quiz night. ❏
★ Square or line dance caller and musicians. ❏
★ Carnival attractions. ❏
★ Indoor sports competitions; e.g., ping pong. ❏

DECORATION

USE DECORATIONS TO SET THE MOOD FOR A PARTY, ENHANCING THE THEME OF THE OCCASION AND MAKING THE VENUE LOOK INVITING AND FUN.

- ★ Table arrangements, low table centerpieces. ❏
- ★ Decorative napkins, place settings for tables. ❏
- ★ Place cards. ❏
- ★ Flowers, large-scale floral decorations. ❏
- ★ Lighting: candles, scented candles, tapers, votive candles, incense, lamps, tiny white lights. ❏
- ★ Balloons (and means to inflate them), streamers, silly string, party poppers, disposable cameras, crackers. ❏
- ★ Entrance decoration. ❏
- ★ Chair decorations. ❏
- ★ Decorative party bags for children. ❏
- ★ Favors and gifts. ❏
- ★ Banners, paper lanterns. ❏
- ★ Weights to tie helium-filled balloons to. ❏

EQUIPMENT

RENTING EQUIPMENT FOR A PARTY MAY RELIEVE YOU OF ORGANIZATIONAL PROBLEMS AND EXPENSE, BUT MANY RESPONSIBILITIES REMAIN.

- ★ Equipment should be delivered in enough time before the event so it can be checked and wrong items returned and missing items replaced. ❏
- ★ Glassware, china, etc., should be checked as soon as received; suppliers told of any breakage. ❏
- ★ Djs/live bands have enough time to set up equipment and check sound – allow two hours before the party starts. ❏
- ★ Tent rental company has enough time to erect tent, assemble equipment, and remove it afterward (check with company). ❏
- ★ Dance floor should be assembled, if necessary. ❏
- ★ PA system for speeches is in place. ❏
- ★ Entertainers have all equipment/space needed. ❏
- ★ Entertainment such as fireworks or laser display, casino, carnival, or sports equipment should be installed and/or double-checked. ❏

STAFF/CLEANUP

WHETHER YOU USE PAID PROFESSIONALS OR VOLUNTEERS FROM THE FAMILY, KEEP IN MIND THESE KEY ITEMS TO CHECK ON THE DAY.

- ★ Staff is well turned out. ❏
- ★ Administrative and catering staff have schedule and timings for the day. ❏
- ★ Waiters are briefed on the food and drink served. ❏
- ★ Waiters know which guests need special attention or have special food requirements. ❏
- ★ Bar staff, reception, and coatroom staff, security staff, and parking attendants are in place. ❏
- ★ If at home, you have help to prepare food and clean up afterward. ❏
- ★ Every home helper has a specific task and is thoroughly briefed. ❏
- ★ Cleanup essentials are on hand: garbage bags, brushes, mop, vacuum cleaner, detergent, rubber gloves, dish towels, air freshener. ❏

EXTRAS

OUTSIDE IMMEDIATE PARTY CONCERNS, TO MAKE ANY OCCASION REALLY SPECIAL, A CARING HOST SHOULD PAY ATTENTION TO EXTRA DETAILS.

- ★ Maps, bus, and train timetables should be sent out with invitations. ❏
- ★ Availability of taxis to and from train stations, bus stations checked. ❏
- ★ Arrange private transportation, if necessary (tell guests if they are expected to pay for it). ❏
- ★ Accommodations for out-of-town guests should be checked. Price lists of local hotels, motels, etc., should be sent with invitations. ❏
- ★ Insurance should cover theft of gifts, loss of jewelry, damage to cars in parking lot, accidents to guests, etc. ❏
- ★ First-aid kit, with telephone numbers for doctor and ambulance, should be available. ❏
- ★ Soap, hand towels, and sewing kits should be in bathrooms. ❏
- ★ Give favors to guests, party bags to children. ❏

COUNT4DOWN

THIS PLAN ALLOWS SIX MONTHS
TO ARRANGE THE PERFECT PARTY. YOU
MAY NOT NEED THIS MUCH TIME, SO
ADAPT THE COUNTDOWN TO SUIT
YOUR REQUIREMENTS.

MONTH 6

★ Choose party theme. ❑
★ Decide on number of guests. ❑
★ Plan type of entertainment. ❑
★ Decide how much money to spend. ❑
★ Research and short-list suitable venues/caterers. ❑
★ Visit short-listed venues/caterers. ❑
★ Discuss with venues/caterers what is included in their charges, specifying any extras you may need and confirming that they can supply them. ❑
★ Research entertainment and ask for examples of work; e.g., video/tape recordings, or go see live. ❑
★ Check estimates off against budget. ❑

MONTH 5

★ Make final choice of venue/caterer, confirming the date and requesting detailed contract(s). ❑
★ Make final choice of entertainment. ❑
★ If you want a photographer, research suitable ones. ❑
★ Pay deposits. ❑

MONTH 4

★ Prepare wording for all printed material; e.g., invitations, menus, place cards, programs. Research and select a printer. ❑
★ Make final choice of photographer and confirm date. ❑
★ Organize and book transportation. ❑
★ Hold initial planning meeting with venue/caterer. ❑
★ Plan a complete program of the work needed between now and the party date. ❑

MONTH 3

★ Check proofs of all printed material and collect final copy from the printer. ❑
★ Mail invitations (plus map, hotel list, etc.), requesting replies and notes of dietary needs. Monitor replies. ❑
★ Select and buy gifts. ❑
★ Sample and confirm menu choice and other catering requirements with venue/caterers. ❑
★ Check estimates against budget; are you on track? ❑

MONTH 2

★ Draw up seating plan. ❑
★ Plan flowers and floral decorations; book florists. ❑
★ Hold update meetings with venue/caterer, entertainers, using the checklists on pages 122-23 as necessary . ❑

MONTH 1

★ Send final guest list to venue/caterer, with confirmation of menu and dietary requirements. ❑
★ Use a final meeting with venue/caterer to check all arrangements. ❑
★ Process invoices requiring payment before the party. ❑
★ Draw up a schedule and timing for the day. ❑

THE BIG DAY

★ On arrival, check that the venue is all set and that rest rooms and coatrooms are clean. ❑
★ Check the venue for damage before equipment arrives. ❑
★ Check that all rented equipment is on site, that printed matter has been delivered, and that gifts are present. ❑
★ Reconfirm catering numbers to venue/caterer, and provide final table/seating plan, plus place cards. ❑
★ Put up decorations and put out gifts. ❑
★ Make sure venue/caterer and entertainers have your final party timings and schedule. ❑
★ Maintain constant touch with venue/caterer and entertainers throughout the party. ❑

THE DAY AFTER

★ Return all equipment to suppliers, checking that no damage has been done to it or to the venue. ❑
★ Check all invoices in detail before payment. ❑
★ Write thank you letters to suppliers. ❑
★ Start planning your next party! ❑

HINTS 5 & TIPS

BOTH HOSTS AND GUESTS HAVE

LARGE PARTS TO PLAY IN A PARTY'S

SUCCESS. FOLLOW THESE TIPS

AND EVERYONE WILL HAVE

A GREAT TIME.

TIPS FOR HOSTS

★ Make sure that guests are given a drink on arrival, or have set up a bowl of punch and glasses for guests to help themselves to.

★ Be a vigilant host and make an effort to introduce guests to people with whom they have something in common.

★ Keep guests mingling. Ask male guests to move down two places at the end of each course at a dinner party; make the ladies ask the men to dance every fifth dance; keep the party confined to two or three rooms so guests can't go far.

★ Make sure that a professional photographer does not interrupt the flow of the party and uses the camera discreetly. Formally posed photographs, involving large numbers of guests, should be taken before the event or reception is well under way.

ETIQUETTE FOR GUESTS

★ When invited to a party, reply as soon as possible. If you cannot attend, thank your host for the invitation.

★ Be considerate: do not arrive at the party with more guests than the host has invited. If your children are not named on the invitation, they are probably not expected.

★ Be punctual: lateness is no longer as fashionable as it used to be.

★ Dress according to the time of day and the type of occasion, observing any dress code on the invitation.

★ If you bring a still or video camera to the party, use it discreetly to avoid bringing the party to a halt.

★ Be a good guest: wear the name tag or funny hat the host hands out, and take part enthusiastically in ice-breaking games or contests.

★ If you wish to smoke, be considerate of others. Ask your host or other guests at the table before lighting up, and never stub out cigarettes in the table china or glasses. If in doubt, smoke outside.

★ If, at the last minute, something happens to prevent you from attending the party, notify the host.

COPING WITH HANGOVERS

Having a hangover is often part and parcel of a party, but it does not have to be. There are a few good ways to avoid a hangover and several methods of getting rid of one.

★ Have a good meal before going to a party: food slows down alcohol absorption. If you have no time to eat, at least drink milk.

★ Avoid mixing grape and grain (wine and beer); stick to one type and brand of drink throughout a party.

★ Go easy on smoking: it makes you want to drink more.

★ Make every third or fourth drink a soft drink, top off wine with soda or sparkling mineral water to make spritzers, and drink liquor with mixers.

★ Know your limit and be ready to say "no thanks." Don't be egged on to "have one for the road."

Once the party is over, if you know you have had more than you should have, there are ways to minimize the effects:

★ Do not drive. Walk home, if possible. The exercise and fresh air will make you feel better.

★ Drink a pint of cold water and go to the bathroom before going to bed. The water helps rehydrate the body.

★ The next morning, drink fresh orange and citrus fruit juices and have a good breakfast.

★ Go for a walk, swim, or jog the next day, or enjoy a leisurely sauna and massage.

★ If all else fails, and drastic measures are called for the next day, mix yourself a Bloody Mary to help settle your stomach.

INDEX

Page numbers for party themes are in **bold**; those for recipes are in *italics*.

A ★ B

Anniversaries **53**
Antipasto Pasta Salad *105*
aphrodisiacs 58
Armchair Sports **60**
Arugula Salad *104*
Asian Banquet **52**
Asparagus & Fresh Pea Quiches *86*
Asparagus & Lime Pasta *94*
Associations (party game) 47
baby footprints 73
Baby Parties **73**
Baby Shower Party **73**
Back to School Party **51**
Backward Bash **60**
Baked Alaska, Mini *110*
Baked Bananas *24*
Ballroom Dancing **12**
Bananas, Baked *24*
Banquets & Balls **28–31**
Barbecues **18–19**
barbecue preparation &
    equipment 18
beach mats 80
Beach Parties **24–25**
Beaujolais Nouveau Party **54**
beef
    Beef in Beer *98*
    Boeuf en Croûte *102-3*
Beside the Ocean Celebration **25**
Birthdays **50–52**
Black Tie 21st Party **50**
blindman's bluff (party game) 19
Blini with Quail Eggs & Smoked
    Fish *89*
Blueberry Muffins *114*
Boeuf en Croûte *102-3*
Bombe, Mincemeat Christmas *110*
Boned Stuffed Turkey *103*
Bonfire Cakes *114*
bowls
    bread 78
    floating fruit 82
    flower & pebble bowl 35
    ice 66
boxes, shortbread 45
Brandy Butter *110*
Bring a Cocktail Party **12**
Bruschetta *89*
budgets 120
buffets 120, 121
Burgers, Lamb *101*

C

cake stands 65
Cakes **114-17**
Calamari *93*

candles & candleholders
    bamboo candles 52
    cake-pan candleholders 21
    candle table setting 46
    carved pumpkin lighting 38
    floating candle centerpiece 83
    floating fruit bowl 82
    flower & pebble bowl 35
    glass jar lanterns 41
    lacy candles 82
    lavender candle collars 82
    leaf-decorated candleholders 39
    luminaries 42
    orange candles 82
    petal flares 19
    summer lanterns 82
    tea party candleholders 65
    tin-can lights 39
    vegetable candles 82
canopies
    instant beach 24
    tented 17
Caramelized Onion Quiches *86*
cards, Valentine's day 58
Cassoulet, Quick *98*
catering companies 120
centerpieces
    cornucopia 40
    floating candle 83
    flower 66
    sandcastle 24
chains, paper 43
chairs
    child's stool 81
    golden 35
    midsummer ivy heart 29
    olde English throne 29
    personalized 60
    tulle 35
Champagne Bottle Cake *117*
checklists 122-4
cheese
    Cheese Twists *88*
    Cheesy Baked Potatoes *106*
    Festive Phyllo Pie *107*
    Rich Chocolate Cheesecake *109*
    Ricotta Tart with Seasonal Fruit *112*
    Savory Scones *88*
    Three-cheese Pizza *97*
chicken
    Chicken Tikka *99*
    Cock-a-leekie Soup *92*
    Grilled Chicken with Figs *99*
    Quick Cassoulet *98*
    Smoked Chicken *98*
    Thai Green Curry *103*
Chickpea Dal *106*
Children's Parties **68–73**
    Beside the Ocean Celebration **25**
    Fire & Ice Party **43**
    Midnight Mass **41**
    Summer Slumber Party **17**
    Summer Splash **23**
Chinese New Year **46**

chocolate
    Chocolate Cake *116*
    Chocolate Roulade *109*
    Chocolate Tart *108*
    Rich Chocolate Cheesecake *109*
    Triple Choc Cookies *116*
Christening Cake *117*
Christmas **41–4**
Christmas Bombe, Mincemeat *110*
cleanup checklist 123
coasters, play money 31
Cock-a-leekie Soup *92*
Cocktail Parties **8–13**
cocktails *see* drinks & cocktails
Coconut Ice Cream *113*
Come as a Cocktail **12**
confetti
    rose petal 34
    Valentine's Day treat 58
Cookie-baking Party **71**
Cookies, Triple Choc *116*
Cornbread *88*
cornucopia centerpiece 40
countdown plan & checklist 124
Country Wedding **33**
Couscous Salad, Pesto *105*
crackers, homemade 44
Creamy Pumpkin Soup *92*
Croquet Party **22**
Cupcakes, Simple *115*
Curry, Thai Green *103*
cushions, silk ring 34

D

Dal, Chickpea *106*
decoration checklist 123
decoupage, flower 83
Dessert Club, The **59**
doodling games 72
drinks & cocktails
    alcohol-free 91
    Apple Whizz *91*
    Apricot Fruit Cup *91*
    Banana Daiquiri *90*
    Beachcomber *10*
    Blue Lagoon *10*
    Boozy Pops *13*
    Champagne Cocktails *90*
    Cranberry Cocktail *91*
    Hot Buttered Rum *10*
    Hot Toddies *13*
    Iced Tea *64*
    Irish Coffee *13*
    Margarita *90*
    Martini *11*
    Mimosa *90*
    Mulled Wine *91*
    Passion Fruit Mix *91*
    Pimm's *90*
    Pink Gin *91*
    quantities required 121
    Sangria *91*

Sea Breeze *90*
serving suggestions 13
Sex on the Beach *10*
Swedish Glogg *43*
Tea Toddy *66*
Tequila Sour *10*
Tequila Sunrise *10*
Vodka Shots *12*

E ★ F

Easter **67**
    Easter eggs, stained 67
    Easter Tea **67**
Egyptian Extravaganza **30**
entertainment checklist 122
equipment checklist 123
etiquette 125
extras checklist 123
fancy dress ideas, children's parties
    70
Festive Phyllo Pie *107*
50s & 60s Coffeehouse Party **55**
Fire & Ice Party **43**
Fire! Fire! (party game) 72
Fireworks **39**
first-footing 45
flowers
    country wedding 33
    Easter 67
    floral napkins 78
    floral table swag 80
    flower & pebble bowl 35
    flower centerpiece 66
    flower decoupage 83
    flower platters 78
    lavender candle collars 82
    meanings of 33
    organza flower seed pouches 34
    place mat decorations 16
    rose petal confetti 34
    stained Easter eggs 67
    Summer Salad *17*
    winter lighted table 80
    winter wedding 32
food & drink
    catering companies 120
    checklist 122
    see also drinks & cocktails;
        individual recipes by name
footprints, baby 73
Fourth of July Picnic **21**
Fruit Cake, Luxury *116*
Fruit-picking Party **20**
Fruit Salad, Tropical *113*
fruit-stamped linen 82
furniture
    beautiful table legs 80
    painted garden 80
    see also chairs; tables

G

games 47
  beach 25
    children's 72
  blindman's bluff 19
  children's 72
  icebreaking 61
Games Evening **60**
Gangsters Party **54**
garden furniture, painted 80
Garden Parties **22**
Garlicky Mixed Olives 89
gift wrapping
  customized 76
  musical 77
gifts *see* presents
Gingerbread 114
  children's place settings 70
  tree decorations 41
Girls Afloat **23**
glasses
  choosing the right cocktail glass 9
  etched 79
  floating candle centerpiece 83
  frosting 13
  gold-swirled 28
  jeweled goblets 79
Greek Dancing Party **61**
Green Finger Party **22**
Grilled Chicken with Figs 99
guests
  etiquette 125
  guest lists & numbers 120

H ★ I

Halloween **38**
Ham & Mushroom Pizza 97
hangings, Moorish 28
hangovers 125
Hat Party **60**
Hazelnut Meringue Cake 108
Horror Party **38**
Hotpot, Venison & Sausage 98
House-hopping Christmas Dinner **37**
House Warming **61**
ice
  borage ice cubes 90
  crushed & cracked 13
  decorative ice cubes 13
  ice bowl 66
  ice tray 78
ice cream
  Coconut Ice Cream 113
  Mincemeat Christmas Bombe 110
  Mini Baked Alaska 110
ice pops
  Boozy Pops 13
  children's 71
icebreakers 60, 61
Impersonate a Friend **59**
invitations
  baby parties 73
  button 76
  cherub 77
  coordinated 76
  country wedding 33

Halloween 38
mirror 30
picture perfect 76
plate 76
ribbon 76
timing of 121
winter wedding 32

J ★ K ★ L

James Bond **11**
Jell-O®, sailboat 71
Kabobs, Monkfish & Bacon 101
Kedgeree 96
Kofta Meatballs 95
Ladies' Pampering Night **59**
Ladybug Cake 117
lamb
  Kofta Meatballs 95
  Lamb Burgers 101
  Meatballs with Red Sauce 93
lanterns
  glass jar 41
  oriental 46
  pumpkin 38
  summer 82
Lazy Summer Party **19**
leaves
  banana-leaf plates 78
  leaf-decorated candleholders 39
  leaf-decorated place settings 40
  leaf prints 76
  oak leaf table runners 42
Lemon Relay (party game) 72
Life Begins at 40, 50, or 60 **51**
lighting
  intimate parties 57
  outdoor 35
  winter lighted table 80
  see also candles & candleholders
luminaries 42
Luxury Egg & Kedgeree 96
Luxury Fruit Cake 116

M

Mad Hatter's Tea Party **65**
Madeira Cake 117
Making Hay Picnic **17**
masks, Venetian 28
meatballs
  Kofta Meatballs 95
  Meatballs with Red Sauce 93
menus
  Asian banquet 52
  barbecue 18
  Christmas 43
  cocktail food 12
  dinner party 61
  fireworks 39
  Halloween 38
  high tea 65
  informal party 55
  menu planning 121
  New Year's Eve 46
  summer party 17
  Thanksgiving 40

meringue
  Hazelnut Meringue Cake 108
  Mincemeat Christmas Bombe 110
  Mini Baked Alaska 110
  Mini Meringues 115
Mexican piñata 70
Midnight Dip **25**
Midnight Mass **41**
Midsummer Night's Ball **29**
Mincemeat Christmas Bombe 110
Mini Baked Alaska 110
Mini Meringues 115
Mini Picnic Pies 97
Minted Potato Salad 104
Mississippi Steamer **23**
Modern Wedding **35**
Molasses Glazed Ham 102
Mongolian Barbecue **18**
Monkfish & Bacon Kabobs 101
Moorish Feast **28**
Mousses, Prosciutto & Egg 95
Muffins, Blueberry 114
Murder-mystery Party **51**
Mushroom Bundles 86
Musical Cushions (party game) 47
Mythology Banquet **31**

N ★ O ★ P

name tags, decorated 76
napkins
  candycane 70
  children's 70
  daisy chain 78
  fabric-painted 21
  floral 78
  money napkin rings 31
  napkin roses 59
  orchid 52
  personalized 78
  sweetheart 79
  tartan-trimmed 45
  water lily 78
New Year's Day Dip **25**
New Year's Eve **45–6**
Night of Nostalgia **53**
1950s Hollywood **11**
1970s Nostalgia Party **55**
Olde English Banquet **29**
organza pouches 34
Orient Express Birthday **51**
oriental lanterns 46
origami table decorations 61
Oscar Night **50**
Oysters & Guinness **61**
Pampered Pooch Party **22**
Pancake Party **55**
paper chains 43
Parties Afloat **23**
Parties for Friends **59–61**
Party Games **54**
Party in the Park **16**
Pass the Bottle (party game) 47
Pasta, Asparagus & Lime 94
Pasta Salad, Antipasto 105
Peach Melba Trifle 111
Peaches, Poached 111
Pecan Pies 112
Pepper & Tomato Soup, Roasted 92

Pesto Couscous Salad 105
petal flares 19
Petits Fours 115
photographs
  paper photograph album 76
  photograph album anniversary present 53
  picture perfect invitations 76
  using professional photographers 125
  Wonderland Ball 30
picnic mats 24
  beach 80
Picnic on the Ski Trail **20**
Picnics **20–1**
pies
  Festive Phyllo Pie 107
  Mini Picnic Pies 97
  Pecan Pies 112
piñata, Mexican 70
pineapple shells 13
pinecone bundles 42
Pizzas 97
  Puff Pastry Pizzas 88
  Valentine's Day 58
place mats
  flower-decorated 16
  picnic 21
place settings
  children's 70
  leaf-decorated 40
  origami 61
  rose 34
  sugared almonds 44
plates
  banana-leaf 78
  olde English platter 29
  personalized anniversary 53
  plate invitations 76
  platters 78
  ribbon-threaded paper 78
  Valentine's day 58
Plum Pudding 110
Poached Peaches 111
Poached Salmon in Aspic 100
Pops
  Boozy Pops 13
  children's ice pops 71
potatoes
  Cheesy Baked Potatoes 106
  Minted Potato Salad 104
  Pommes Dauphinois 106
  Potato Bake **24**
  potato pebble-print stamps 80
  Potatoes with Chorizo & Aïoli 93
  Roasted Sweet Potatoes 107
pouches, organza 34
presents
  anniversary photograph album 53
  children's party-bag gifts 71
  children's table gifts 70
  money-no-object 52
  naming ceremony 73
  paper photograph album 76
  romantic surprises 58
Prohibition Party **54**
Prosciutto & Egg Mousses 95
Puff Pastry Pizzas 88
pumpkin lanterns 38
Pumpkin Soup, Creamy 92

Q ★ R

Quiches 86
Quick Cassoulet 98
Quiz Night **60**
Rain forest Safari **22**
Rich Chocolate Cheesecake 109
Ricotta Tart with Seasonal Fruit 112
ring cushion, silk 34
Roasted Sweet Potatoes 107
Roasted Pepper & Tomato Soup 92
Roulade, Chocolate 109

S

salmon
  Kedgeree 96
  Poached Salmon in Aspic 100
  Salmon Pinwheels 86
  Smoked Salmon Triangles 95
Sardines (party game) 47
Savory Scones 88
Scottish New Year's Eve **45**
Scrambled Eggs in Brioche 96
Seared Tuna 100
Secret Santa Party **43**
Sensory Party **73**
Shimmy Party **31**
Shrimp, Sweet & Sour 94
shortbread boxes 45
Silver & Gold Party **44**
Simple Cupcakes 115
Simple Kedgeree 96
Smoked Chicken 98
Smoked Salmon Triangles 95
snowflake scene 43
Soups 92
South Pacific Party **16**
Spaghetti Western **10**
Spanish New Year **46**
Sports Picnic **64**

Squeak, Piggy, Squeak (party game) 72
staff 121, 123
stamps
  daisy 81
  fruit 82
  potato pebble-prints 80
Stargazers' Party **39**
Stir-fried Green Vegetables 105
stool, child's 81
Summer Berry Tarts 112
Summer Parties **16–17**
Summer Salad 17
Summer Slumber Party **17**
Summer Splash **23**
Summer Tea Dance **64**
Sun-dried Tomato Quiches 86
swags
  Christmas 44
  floral table 80
  winter lighted table 80
Swedish Christmas **41**
Sweet & Sour Shrimp 94
Sweet Potatoes, Roasted 107

T

table runners 80
  oak leaf 42
tablecloths
  anchors for 80
  for beach parties 25
  for picnic cloths 21
  daisy-stamped 81
  fabric-painted 21
  fruit-stamped 82
  1950s table 55
  opulent 81
  paper mosaic 77
  tartan-trimmed 45
  Thanksgiving 40
  Venetian or harlequin 28
tables
  beautiful table legs 80

buffet 121
  wedding cake 34
Taboo (party game) 47
tags, decorated name 76
Tapas Selection 93
tarts
  Chocolate Tart 108
  Quiches 86
  Ricotta Tart with Seasonal Fruit 112
  Summer Berry Tarts 112
  Tarte au Citron 112
Tea Parties **62–67**
teas **62–65**
tea service, painted 65
Teddy Bear Cake 117
Teddy Bears' Picnic **20**
Telephone (party game) 72
Tennis Tea **22**
Thai Green Curry 103
Thanksgiving **40**
Theme Parties **54–55**
Three-cheese Pizza 97
tips
  beach parties 24
  cocktail party 12
  guest etiquette 125
  for hosts 125
  perfect picnics 21
Tiramisu 109
Treasure Island Party **24**
trees & tree decorations
  Christmas 43
  gilded 82
  gingerbread 41
  space-saving Christmas tree 41
  Tree-planting Party **73**
  twig fir tree 42
Trifles 111
Triple Choc Cookies 116
Tropical Fruit Salad 113
Tubing Party **23**
Tumeric Pilaf 106
Tuna, Seared 100

Turkey, Boned Stuffed 103
Tuscan Bean Salad 104
Tuscan Picnic **21**
Twilight Sailing **23**

V

Valentine's Day **58**
Valentine's Dinner **58**
vases, colored glass 66
Venetian Masquerade Ball **28**
Venison & Sausage Hotpot 98
venues 120
  children's parties 70
  special occasions 49
  unusual wedding 34
  venue checklist 122

W ★ Y ★ Z

Waterbaby Party **73**
wedding anniversary themes 53
Wedding Cake 117
Weddings **32–5**
What Were You Doing When the Ship Went Down? **10**
White Wedding **35**
Who am I? (party game) 72
windmills, beach party 25
Wine-tasting Party **61**
Winter Trifle 111
Winter Wedding **32**
Witches' Party **38**
Wonderland Ball **30**
wreaths
  chili 42
  dried apple 83
  winter wedding 32
Yahoo Party **19**
Yard Cleanup Party **22**
Yule log 42
Zucchini with Garlic 107

ACKNOWLEDGMENTS

Lauren Floodgate's Acknowledgments
I am indebted above all to my husband, Richard, thank you for your tireless support behind the scenes; to my mum, Hazel Floodgate, I couldn't have done it without you – enthusiastic, patient, and brimming with good ideas and, yes, you can type faster and more accurately than me! My sister, Bryony Hoad, who has such good taste and worked so hard designing and making all the beautiful projects; Simon Smith, the consummate professional and a very good friend, thank you for your recommendation, I hope I did you justice; Simon's assistant Alex MacDonald, who kept us going with intravenous coffee and tales of his exploits; Lucy and Sarah for the delicious recipes and wonderful food; Clare Hunt for her support and thoughtful styling; and to all my friends who so kindly shared their ideas.

A special thanks to my designer, Tracey Ward, and my editor, Monica Chakraverty, two more patient, hard-working, and agreeable colleagues I couldn't have wished for; and to Susannah Marriott and Carole Ash, who invited me to write the book.

Final thanks to Mary-Jane Vaughan at Fast Flowers, 609 Fulham Road, Fulham, London, SW6 5UA (0171 381 6422), for supplying the stunning flowers and arrangements, and to Penny Harrison at Homecrafts Direct (0116 251 3139), for supplying all the craft materials used in the projects.

Publisher's Acknowledgements
Dorling Kindersley would like to thank Janice Anderson for editorial help; Sue Bosanko for the index; Brightside; Emy Manby and Rachana Shah for design assistance; Dorothy Ward for help with props. Additional photography by: Peter Chadwick, Philip Dowell, Steve Gorton, Stephen Hayward, Dave King, Ian O'Leary, Stephen Oliver, Tim Ridley, and Stephen Schott.

DK Publishing, Inc., would like to thank Barbara Minton and Kathy MacKinnon for testing some of the recipes, and Joan Whitman.